*To my grandchildren*

CARLOTTA, GIL, GRAY, CATHERINE AND MICHAEL

Upon whose innocent
heads would descend
the fall-out of the
totalitarian wel-
fare state.

10 00
Cont

9-24-63    (62-10715)

*Anthology of*
# CONSERVATIVE WRITING

*Anthology of*

# Conservative Writing

*in the*

# United States
# 1932-1960

*Compiled and Edited with Commentary*

*by*

A. G. HEINSOHN, JR.

HENRY REGNERY COMPANY

Chicago 1962

# TABLE OF CONTENTS

PROLOGUE — xi

I. THE START OF HUMAN FREEDOM IN THE U.S.A. — 1

II. THE DEATH STRUGGLE BEGINS IN AMERICA — 5

Power Corrupts—*Admiral Ben Moreell* — 8
The Battle for Freedom—*Dan Smoot* — 10

III. HOW DID IT EVER HAPPEN? — 12

Growth of the Communist Conspiracy—
*Dr. Revilo P. Oliver* — 15

IV. EGGHEADS ADRIFT — 28

For a Moral Revolution—*Hon. Spruille Braden* — 30
√ Ten Mistakes of Marx—*W. H. Chamberlain* — 32
I've Had Enough Socialism—*Charles B. Shuman* — 41

V. YEARS OF RETROGRESSION — 44

When Retrogression Begins—*Crawford H. Greenewalt* — 45
Morality and the Bill of Rights—*Hon. Spruille Braden* — 46
Roots of the Liberal Complacency—*Richard M. Weaver* — 54

VI. DISHONEST DOLLARS AND INFLATION — 59

How You Have Been Victimized—*T. Coleman Andrews* — 60
Let's Face the Facts of Inflation—*Fred G. Clark* — 64
The Future of the Dollar—*Dr. Wilhelm Vocke* — 69
The National Debt Peril—*Thurman Sensing* — 77
How to Stop Big Spending—*Indianapolis Star* — 79
Inflation—The Handmaid of Socialist-Communism—
*Charles B. Shuman* — 82

VII. TVA—SOCIALISM'S PRIDE AND SHOWPLACE — 88

Socialism Makes Nobody Richer—*L. Robert Driver* — 90
TVA—*Dan Smoot* — 95

The Hidden Cost of Public Power—*Cobleigh and Gilbert*     104

A Reply to TVA Director Brooks Hays—*Tennessee Independents*     108

Communism American Style—*George Peck*     110

VIII. LABOR UNION POWER UNLIMITED     113

Economic and Political Tyranny—*Senator Barry Goldwater*     114

Senate Committee Testimony—*Admiral Ben Moreell*     120

Senate Committee Testimony—*William H. Colvin, Jr.*     125

Senate Committee Testimony—*Luke Sawyer*     126

How Would YOU Settle the Steel Strike?—*American Economic Foundation*     128

Personal Freedom and Labor Policy—*Sylvester Petro*     132

The Right to Work—*W. L. White*     138

Can a Free Economy Tolerate Union Violence?—*Herbert V. Kohler*     145

The Labor Racket Is America's Mafia—*Westbrook Pegler*     152

The Right to Work—*Rev. Irving E. Howard*     154

Growing Labor Union Monopolies—*Donald R. Richberg*     157

University of Michigan Press Release     160

The Voluntary Basis of Trade Unionism—*Samuel Gompers*     161

IX. THE SOCIAL SECURITY SWINDLE     164

Free Rides and Free People—*Leonard J. Calhoun*     167

Social Security Makes Nickel-shooter of Ponzi—*Hon. Noah M. Mason*     171

Social Security Is Bankrupt—*Dan Smoot*     174

Straight Talk—*Tom Anderson*     178

Social Security's Salvage Value—*Paul L. Poirot*     180

Legislated Security Is Bondage—*Samuel Gompers*     182

X. THE HIRED HANDS OF WASHINGTON     185

They Would Remake the United States—*George N. Peek*     185

Storing Insanity—*Wall Street Journal*     188

CONTENTS

Payments—Permits—Peasantry—*Charles B. Shuman*     189
Farmers Dislike Federal Farm Program—*D. B. Hendrix*     191
Stop Bureaucracy from Breaking Our Backs?—*Farm and
     Ranch*     192
The End of the Road—*Rev. Irving E. Howard*     196
I Think Freedom Is Everything—*Stanley Yankus*     198
A Farm Program That Will Work—*Charles B. Shuman*     200
Farm Subsidies Must Go—*Thurman Sensing*     203
Freedom and Dictation—*Hon. Barry Goldwater*     205
Nature's Laws and Man's Laws—*William H. Peterson*     210

XI. FOREIGN AID AND YOU     214

Foreign Aid and You—*Citizens Foreign Aid Committee*     216
Petition—Just a Minute, Mr. Congressman     232
Report on Foreign Aid—*Harding College Based on
     Scripps-Howard Survey*     235
The Great Giveaway—*Eugene W. Castle*     237
Foreign Aid and Economic Progress—*Elgin Groseclose*     247

XII. FOREIGN TRADE AND YOU     257

Low-cost Imports Imperil Us—*Lewis and Goodman*     258
An Economic Danger—*Robert T. Stevens*     260
The Export of Jobs—*Robert T. Stevens*     264
Foreign Trade in Our Changing World—*Leland I. Doan*     265
Giving Away America—*A. H. Vandenberg*     270

XIII. EDUCATION—FOUNDATIONS—GOVERNMENT—CHURCHES     275

They War on Our Schools—*John T. Flynn*     277
The Quicksands of the Mind—*E. Merrill Root*     283
Two Open Letters—*Ida Darden and A. G. Heinsohn, Jr.*     290
Foundations—*Dan Smoot*     294
Foundations and Radicalism in Education—*Rene A.
     Wormser*     298
The Sham of Federal Aid to Education—*C. R. Pettigrew*     324
Federal Control of Education—*Thurman Sensing*     328
No Federal Scholarships, Thank You—*V. Raymond
     Edman*     330
Federal Support for Education Is Unnecessary—
     *W. W. Hill, Jr.*     331
Unnecessary School Aid—*Raymond Moley*     334

Conservatives and Education—*Russell Kirk*     336
Conservatives and Religious Faith—*Russell Kirk*     342

XIV. SPARKS OF RESISTANCE     347

The Runaway Court—*Indianapolis Star*     347
Servitude Without Pay—*George Peck*     359
Repeal Income Taxes—*Willis E. Stone*     361
Letters of Protest     363
The Great Monopoly Myth—*Roger M. Blough*     369
Letter Published by *Knoxville News-Sentinel*     371
We Can't Have Freedom Without Capitalism—
    *Harold B. Wess*     374

XV. RAYS OF HOPE     378

The Urgency of More Economic Education—
    *L. R. Boulware*     379
The Master Blueprint—*American Economic Foundation*     386
The Penalty of Disregarding Natural Law—
    *Frank Chodorov*     392
What Can a Minister Do to Save Freedom?—
    *Rev. Irving E. Howard*     396
Ad Hoc Committee Report—*National Association of
    Manufacturers*     399
Toward a Point of No Return—*Robert C. Tyson*     405

EPILOGUE     409

Two Greatest Enemies of Freedom—*John Clark Ridpath*     409
Prayer Is Power—*Dr. Alexis Carrel*     411

# PROLOGUE

WHEN OUR GRANDCHILDREN of today are old enough to read these pages, the results of the steady chipping away of our precious human freedom by political promises of material betterment through the welfare state should be thoroughly known.

Suppose the welfare state works out as promised and succeeds in advancing the spiritual, moral, and material development of American citizens? Then the welfare state will be rated as "good," and this book will simply be ignored, as old-fashioned, behind-the-times.

Suppose, on the other hand, as I both firmly believe and fear, the welfare state does not work out as promised? That instead it results in destroying the spiritual, moral, and material well-being of American citizens and reducing them to a state of servitude? Perhaps even then it will not be impossible for our grandchildren to correct our mistakes, and this book may help them. As Grover Cleveland said in his Inaugural Address of May 4, 1893:

"The lessons of paternalism ought to be unlearned and the better lesson taught that while the people should patriotically and cheerfully support their Government, its functions do not include the support of the people. . . . The unwholesome progeny of paternalism . . . is the bane of republican institutions and the constant peril of our government by the people. It degrades to the purposes of wily craft the plan of rule our fathers established and bequeathed to us as an object of our love and veneration. It perverts the patriotic sentiments of our countrymen and tempts them to pitiful calculation of the sordid gain to be derived from their Government's maintenance. It undermines the self-reliance of our people and substitutes in its place dependence upon governmental favoritism. It stifles the spirit of true Americanism and stupefies every ennobling trait of American citizenship."

At about the same time, Yale's Professor of Political Economy, William Graham Sumner, said the same thing more succinctly:

"whenever we try to get paternalized we only succeed in getting policed."

Those in control of both political parties today, Democrats and Republicans alike, giving little heed to the lessons of history, compete with each other in the further extension of the welfare state. These pages reflect the opposite effort—the effort of those who so valiantly try to resist the growth of bureaucratic control in the welfare state with its resultant withering of religious, economic, and personal freedom.

This record may generate a spark of hope in those who have lost faith, and it may stir into action those who are now seemingly inclined to drift into destruction because of an apathy which stems from a false belief in the futility of resistance and counter-attack.

At the very least a factual account will be made available for posterity, so that they may know how precious human freedom in America was destroyed through varying degrees of political fraud, intellectual prostitution, religious heresy, and economic ignorance.

# I

# The Start of Human Freedom
# in the United States of America

*"That this Nation, under God . . ."*

REVERENTLY AND HUMBLY, the founders of our nation sought divine guidance in writing the creeds that became the guiding light of this new and independent country.

The first sentence of the Declaration of Independence speaks of "the Laws of Nature and of Nature's God"; and its final sentence expresses a "firm reliance on the protection of Divine Providence." The Articles of Confederation, which preceded the Constitution, declare, "It has pleased the Great Governor of the world to incline the hearts of the legislatures we respectfully represent in Congress to approve of, and to authorize us to ratify, the said Articles of Confederation and perpetual union."

Engraved on the hearts of these Americans who had just won freedom from big government in England was the belief that a force greater than man had created the universe and in so doing had imposed certain Natural Laws which would always prevail over man-made laws.

Here, for the first time in human history, man called upon God to aid him in forming a government dedicated to the principle that each individual citizen, answerable ultimately only to God, should be free to work out his own spiritual and material destiny—a government whose restricted powers came from the citizens themselves and which was prohibited from ever usurping tyrannous powers.

George Mason, of Virginia, gave clear expression to the principle that man's God-given natural rights should not be subject to governmental interference: "All acts of legislature contrary to natural right and justice . . . must be considered as void. The laws of nature are laws of God, whose authority can be superseded by no power on earth. All human constitutions which contradict His laws, we are in conscience bound to disobey."

The clergy, not only during pre-Revolutionary days but throughout many years following, wielded immense influence through their politico-theological preaching which stressed the basic religious origins of self-government and freedom. They really laid the cornerstone of the Republic and the foundation for our Constitution. The highest glory of the American Revolution, said John Quincy Adams, was that it connected in one indissoluble bond the principles of civil government and Christianity.

To make certain that the newly formed government would never usurp forbidden power and attempt to legislate against these Natural Laws, our forefathers spelled out in detail the power of the new federal government and its limitations. They sought thus to protect the citizens of the respective states against undue interference with their private lives.

The great concern of the founding fathers to restrict the powers of the new central government in Washington appears constantly in their many works:

"In question of power, then, let no more be heard of confidence in man, but bind him down from mischief by the chains of the Constitution."—Thomas Jefferson

"A just estimate of that love of power, and proneness to abuse it, which predominates in the human heart. . . ."—George Washington

". . . there is no danger I apprehend so much as the consolidation of our government by the noiseless, and therefore unalarming, instrumentality of the Supreme Court."—Thomas Jefferson

". . . the supervision of agriculture and of other concerns of a similar nature, all those things in short which are proper to be provided for by local legislation, can never be desirable cares of a general jurisdiction (Federal Government) ."—Alexander Hamilton

"The powers delegated by the proposed Constitution to the federal government are few and defined. Those which are to remain in the state governments are numerous and indefinite."—James Madison

"They that give up essential liberty to obtain a little temporary safety deserve neither liberty nor safety."—Benjamin Franklin

"Government is not eloquence—it is force! It is a dangerous servant and a fearful master."—George Washington

"Can the liberties of a nation be sure when we remove their only firm basis, a conviction in the minds of the people, that these liberties are the gift of God? That they are not to be violated but with His wrath?"—Thomas Jefferson

Scholarly Woodrow Wilson, 28th President of the United States (1913-1921), sounded the following warning:

> The history of liberty is a history of the limitation of governmental power, not the increase of it. When we resist, therefore, the concentration of power, we are resisting the processes of death, because a concentration of power is what always precedes the destruction of human liberties.

As late as March 3, 1930, this fear of centralized power in the hands of the federal government was stated by none other than Franklin D. Roosevelt, when he was the governor of New York:

> The doctrine of regulation and legislation by "master minds," in whose judgment and will all the people may gladly and quietly acquiesce, has been too glaringly apparent at Washington during these last ten years. Were it possible to find "master minds" so unselfish, so willing to decide unhesitatingly against their own personal interests or private prejudices, men almost god-like in their ability to hold the scales of Justice with an even hand, such a government might be to the interest of the country, but there are none such on our political horizon, and we cannot expect a complete reversal of all the teachings of history.

Concerning the threat of complete control being centralized in Washington, Roosevelt went on to say: "We are safe from any such danger so long as the individual home rule of the States is scrupulously preserved and fought for whenever it seems in danger."

How tragic it was for this nation of free men under God that the one who spoke those words should later attempt "a complete reversal of all the teachings of history"! This he did as a four-term President driven by an insatiable lust for power and glory.

So in our own time we were forced to witness the working out of a principle expressed by William Graham Sumner more than sixty years ago: "The thirst for glory is an epidemic which robs a people of their judgment, seduces their vanity, cheats them of their interests, and corrupts their consciences."

# II

# The Death Struggle Begins
# in America

SOME FIFTY-EIGHT YEARS after the Constitution of the United
States of America was ratified, another creed on human government
was written: the Communist Manifesto, by Karl Marx and Frederic
Engels. Their rule book is based on pure materialism, devoid of
all spirtual values. Denying the existence of God and the Laws of
Nature, they held that the individual citizen has no rights and is
incapable of living his own life; that the state is all-powerful and
the individual lives only to serve the state.

They outlined a plan for communist conquest of the world and
prescribed certain steps to accomplish this. Major planks in their
platform designed to destroy the nations who believed in God and
in individual freedom called for the imposition of a steeply graduated income tax and a confiscatory tax on inheritances. They
knew that such a system of taxation would not only provide the
central government with money, which is power, but also gradually
confiscate existing accumulations of private wealth and prevent
further accumulations.

On two separate occasions, in 1862 and again in 1894, abortive
attempts were made in America to tax individual earnings, but the
law was declared unconstitutional by a Supreme Court which still

held to the ideals and purposes of the authors of the Constitution. Therefore, to legalize the taxing system which the communists prescribed for our own self-destruction, it became necessary to amend our Constitution. This tragedy was brought about in 1913 when the 16th Amendment (sponsored by a Tennessee Congressman named Cordell Hull) was ratified by the unsuspecting legislatures of the various states.

The progressive expansion of the income tax is highlighted by some comments made at the time of its humble beginning, when the levy ran from one per cent on all net income above three thousand dollars, with further exemptions for married men, to a top limit of six per cent on incomes above half a million dollars.

In the Congressional debate on this tax bill there were charges to the effect that it was an attack on wealth and a penalty for success. To this, Senator Williams of Mississippi, with rare foresight, made a reply (August 27, 1913) that would transcend party lines today:

> No honest man can make war on great fortunes per se. The Democratic Party has never done it; and when the Democratic Party begins to do it, it will cease to be the Democratic Party and become the socialistic party of the United States; or, better expressed, the communistic party, or quasi-communistic party of the United States.

But it was Senator Weeks of Massachusetts who, on that same day of August 27, 1913, put his finger on the real issue:

> But I do think the country wants to know where there is to be a limit to this form of taxation that is to be imposed on incomes, and whether in the future we are to assume that when additional revenue is required it shall be raised in this way.

The reply from the other side of the Chamber to Senator Weeks was in substance that that bridge would be crossed when it was reached.

That bridge has not only been reached, but crossed. And who is there who does not know the meaning today of the crossing almost half a century ago?

Thus, with the power to tax without limit firmly lodged in Washington, the New Deal eventually seized full control in 1933 and proceeded to socialize America by passing laws which concentrated in Washington powers prohibited by the Constitution.

For four years the people were protected by the Supreme Court against this arrogant centralization of power. New Deal laws were declared unconstitutional, one after another. Enraged to the point of desperation, Roosevelt madly strove to pack the Supreme Court with justices favorable to socialistic controls. However, his brazen attempt to increase the number of justices on the Court was roundly rejected by an aroused Congress.

In the intervening years, as vacancies have occurred, men with little or no judicial experience have been appointed to the Court for political considerations, by Roosevelt, Truman, and Eisenhower.

So, today, instead of being a bulwark against socialism, the Supreme Court has cast down the barriers. Recent opinions completely reverse long-standing decisions of the Court and violate the clear meaning and intent of the 10th Amendment which specifies: "The powers not delegated to the United States in the Constitution, nor prohibited by it to the States, are reserved to the States respectively, or to the people."

An entire generation of Americans has grown up in a dream world, subjected to brainwashing that has been successful to an alarming degree. The lessons learned from antiquity, the proven facts of life learned the hard way, the wisdom of the ages, and the teachings of Christ are tossed aside as old-fashioned. A constant flow of propaganda over the air and on the printed page praises the power of the government in Washington to regiment us into a better world. Effort is made to deify the occupant of the White House and to clothe him with the mantle of infallibility. The people are made to feel helpless and unable to care for themselves in this modern, fast-moving world.

To trust in God and in individual effort is to revert to the horse and buggy days, say the brainwashers.

Years of political fraud have changed the function of the government in Washington from that of protecting the individual under God's laws to that of providing special privilege for pressure groups.

While we have slept in America, assuming that freedom inherited is freedom everlasting, our elected public officials have removed the constitutional limitations of power that they had sworn to uphold. We have been betrayed by the human "love of power" which Washington feared and which Jefferson wanted bound "down from mischief by the chains of the Constitution."

Why this "love of power" must be bound "down by the chains of the Constitution" is explained by Admiral Ben Moreell, former chairman of Jones & Laughlin Steel Corporation.

## *Power Corrupts*

### BEN MOREELL

When a person gains power over other persons—the political power to force other persons to do his bidding when they do not believe it right to do so—it seems inevitable that a moral weakness develops in the person who exercises that power. It may take time for this weakness to become visible. In fact, its full extent is frequently left to the historians to record, but we eventually learn of it. It was Lord Acton, the British historian, who said: "All power tends to corrupt; absolute power corrupts absolutely."

Please do not misunderstand me. These persons who are corrupted by the process of ruling over their fellow men are not innately evil. They begin as honest men. Their motives for wanting to direct the actions of others may be purely patriotic and altruistic. Indeed, they may wish only "to do good for the people." But, apparently, the only way they can think of to do this "good" is to impose more restrictive laws.

Now, obviously, there is no point in passing a law which requires people to do something they would do anyhow; or which prevents them from doing what they are not going to do anyhow. Therefore the possessor of the political power could very well decide to leave every person free to do as he pleases so long as he does not infringe upon the same right of every other person to do as he pleases. However, that concept appears to be utterly without reason to a person who wants to exercise political power over his fellow man, for he asks himself: "How can I 'do good' for the people if I just leave them alone?" Besides, he does not want to pass into history as a "do nothing" leader who ends up as a footnote somewhere. So he begins to pass laws that will force all other persons to conform to his ideas of what is good for them.

That is the danger point! The more restrictions and compulsions he imposes on other persons, the greater the strain on his own morality. As his appetite for using force against people increases, he tends increasingly to surround himself with advisers who also seem to derive a peculiar pleasure from forcing others to obey their decrees. He appoints friends and supporters to easy jobs of questionable necessity. If there are not enough jobs to go around, he creates new ones. In some instances, jobs are sold to the highest bidder. The hard-earned money of those over whom he rules is loaned for questionable private endeavors or spent on grandiose public projects at home and abroad. If there is opposition, an emergency is declared or created to justify these actions.

If the benevolent ruler stays in power long enough, he eventually concludes that power and wisdom are the same thing. And as he possesses power, he must also possess wisdom. He becomes converted to the seductive thesis that election to public office endows the official with both power and wisdom. At this point, he begins to lose his ability to distinguish between what is morally right and what is politically expedient.

—From an address in 1951.

---

Instead of being a nation of free men under God, we are being dragged back by today's power-hungry politicians and bureaucrats into the bondage of big government—to escape from which our ancestors shed their blood.

For many years, while pretending to resist the spread of communism abroad, the Executive, the Congress, and the Supreme Court (Democrats and Republicans alike) have led America step by step toward bureaucratic enslavement and bankruptcy. Nothing could suit the communists better, because their conquest of the world would be impossible if Christian America were to remain a solvent nation of free men.

Today in America is being waged the death struggle between Christian freedom and atheistic slavery, while neither of the existing political parties has the character to place truth and principle above political fraud.

The fundamental nature of this battle for freedom is brought into sharp and brilliant focus by the words of Dan Smoot, a distinguished former F.B.I. investigator and Administrative Assistant to J. Edgar Hoover. These words are taken from his address in April, 1959, before the Christian Freedom Foundation in New York.

# The Battle for Freedom

### DAN SMOOT

The beginnings of America were Christian—and I don't mean simply that Pilgrims were Christians, fleeing from persecution. The ideal of the American revolution was a product of Christian thought. Hence, the essence of Americanism is Christian.

Read the Declaration of Independence. There is the essence of Americanism; and the essence of the Declaration is a Christian assumption:

"We hold these truths to be self-evident, that all men are . . . endowed by their Creator with certain inalienable rights. . . ."

There were no arguments or committee meetings or panel discussions about it: Simply, we proclaim these things as truth because we know them to be truth.

What things?

God created man and endowed him with all his rights. Man is not beholden to government for anything, because government gave him nothing. Government can give man nothing except what it has first taken away from him. Government has nothing to give but power. This power is dangerous and always potentially evil; yet it is necessary for the maintenance of order and individual liberty in a civilized society. Therefore, we will form a government and give it the minimum of power necessary; but, to keep this arrangement in proper focus, we here go on record before all the world that the power we delegate to government is ours to take back, if government becomes tyrannical. We derive no rights or power from government.

It is vice versa.

Government derives its just powers from us, the governed. We want it clearly understood, moreover, that the grant of power which we make to government is very limited. Even though we must delegate to government enough power to protect all of us from one another, and from possible foreign enemies, we have certain rights which we are not willing to surrender or modify for any purpose whatever. We call these rights inalienable because God, our Creator, endowed us with them: we consider them sacred.

That is the meaning of the American Declaration of Independence.

After winning the independence they had declared, and after writing a Constitution to make the necessary grant of limited power to a central government, the Founding Fathers worried about that matter of their sacred rights. In the section of their Constitution, where they granted power to the new government, they started off by saying, "The powers herein granted."

They meant that the government should have no powers except those specifically listed in the Constitution. But was that sufficiently clear and emphatic? Perhaps not. The Founding Fathers decided to make certainty doubly certain. They wrote a Bill of Rights (the first ten amendments to their Constitution), not asking the government for any rights, but specifically listing certain God-given rights and telling government that it must not, could not, tamper with them.

Congress shall make no law abridging these specific, sacred rights of ours.

That is the meaning of the American Constitution and Bill of Rights.

The Christian concept of the equality of men (also written into the Declaration of Independence: All men are created equal) is not tainted with materialism.

The Christian concept of equality is spiritual. It has nothing to do with my income or my health or my environment. It simply gives me—a little, imperfect man, born in sin—an individual, personal relationship with God: a relationship equal to that of any other man on earth. In short, Christianity exalts individualism, stressing the importance and the exclusive dependence on God and self of the human individual.

Could the Founding Fathers have founded a nation on the assumption of God-given human rights, if they had left God out? Of course not. Neither can their heirs maintain that nation, if they leave God out.

The conflict of our time is the irreconcilable clash of these two opposite ideologies; individualism versus collectivism.

The great battle for freedom is primarily a battle for the minds and souls of men. It can be won only if free men are aflame with a faith greater than that of their enemies.

# III

# How Did It Ever Happen?

IT SEEMS INCREDIBLE that a nation of free men should ever vote themselves into any form of servitude.

But it happened, and to understand why we must first understand the difference between "government" and welfare state. Man's first instinct is to live, and while living he seeks to improve his lot with the least expenditure of physical effort. His appetite is insatiable, and his wants are unlimited.

There are only two ways to make a living—to work for a living or to "ride a gravy train." In working for a living, man must apply physical effort and mechanical power to raw materials in order to produce things for his use, convenience, and comfort. Those who ride the gravy train do not actually produce anything; they either seize by force or are voluntarily given a portion of what is produced by others who do work.

Since there are those who prefer to live by seizing instead of by working (robbers, confidence men, etc.), government is necessary to protect those who work from the predatory acts of those who prefer to live by stealing. The prime function of government is to protect each member of the community and to insure the safety of his life and possessions. In order to afford this protection government must have power to arrest and punish those found guilty of violating laws designed to protect life, liberty, and property.

In a small community, government is simple and is limited to this primary function. For example, in a frontier settlement one sheriff was probably the only full-time public servant, and his salary came from a modest tax-levy upon the inhabitants of the area receiving the protection.

As the frontier settlement grew, it needed more services (roads, sewers, courts, police, fire, schools) which called for a considerable increase in the number of full-time, non-producing, public servants whose salaries had to come from taxes levied upon those receiving the service.

Thus government on the local level was expanded to include services other than simple protection of life and property. But this expansion came by common consent of the local tax-payers, and they were always able to control by ballot the expansion or contraction of such services. At no point did the local government attempt to dictate, interfere with, or regiment the lives of the citizens. At no point did the local government have the power to seize the production of some citizens and confer it upon others in exchange for their votes. At all times the local government was the sum total of the services wanted by the citizens and voluntarily supported by them. It was always the servant; never the master.

The keen foresight of our founding fathers is evident when one reads and studies the records of their time. They knew that man's greatest enemy is, and always has been, power in the hands of the political demagogue. They used every means they could think of to prevent the unprincipled politician from using the government in Washington as a tool of exploitation; to prevent it from changing its role from servant to master; from becoming the welfare state. But the constitutional safeguards they devised were not sufficient to prevent the transition that has taken place.

The politician who advocates foolishness is rarely a fool. He understands human nature and knows of man's desire to better his lot with the least possible physical effort. He knows man is covetous, that man is perfectly willing to accept something-for-nothing as long as it appears to be just that and is dressed up as a noble, legal act and said to be for the common good. He knows that leading members of the church, leading members of the community, men who would not think of robbing at the point of a pistol, can nevertheless be counted upon to accept money seized by force from others as long as it is done with legal sanction and in a sancti-monious manner—and, of course, allegedly for the common good.

Therefore, the strategy of the unprincipled politician is to get control of the law-making branch of government and change it into a welfare state by removing the constitutional limitations on his political power. This is done by passing laws which give those in control the right to seize the possessions of some and redistribute them to others in exchange for their votes—professedly, of course, for the common good.

At this point, undreamed of "social services," such as never would be tolerated on the local level, are imposed by force upon the people. The more money that can be seized from the people through confiscatory taxes, the greater becomes the scope of the "social services," the greater is the army of non-producing bureau-crats needed to enforce the "social services," and the greater grows the number of camp-followers dependent upon the perpetuation of the welfare state.

Thus, by stealth and by fraud, the unprincipled politician has reduced this nation of free men, trusting in God and individual effort, to a bewildered, cynical, divided mass of humanity forced to pay in about one-third of their total production to the public feed-trough and then compelled to fight like hogs in an effort to get back as much as they can—all under rules and regulations laid down by the unprincipled politician and his bureaucratic hench-men.

From servant to complete master—from "government" to welfare state—all for the common good.

After twenty years of the welfare state the people of America voted out the party that originally visited this communist-tinted program upon America and voted in the opposition party which was pledged to return to sound American principles. Sad to relate, that pledge was not fulfilled. There has been no change of direc-tion, which means that a continuation of the welfare state has been our lot.

The will to resist has been badly worn down, because with both parties dedicated to the welfare state there is now no way to vote for a change. There is no third party in sight. Incredible as it is, no political party in America today is wholeheartedly dedicated to human freedom, states' rights, and constitutional government. And this once great country used to be fondly referred to as "the land of the free and the home of the brave"!

It is by no accident that this deplorable and dangerous condition exists in America today. Step by step, our descent into servitude has been carefully planned over a period of years by a group of fanatics dedicated to the downfall of America. It is all part of the communist conspiracy, thoroughly documented and proven by committees of Congress; by J. Edgar Hoover, Chief of the F.B.I.; and by scores of former communists whose testimony has built a sizeable record.

Perhaps the most concise statement tracing the growth of communism in America from its beginnings to the present is this one by Dr. Revilo P. Oliver of the Department of Classics, University of Illinois, at the Annual Congress of Freedom in Colorado Springs, April, 1959.

## Growth of the Communist Conspiracy

### DR. REVILO P. OLIVER

There is a large and ever-growing number of Americans who sense that something is seriously wrong, who are made uneasy or even afraid by a menace that they feel in the atmosphere about them but that they have not yet clearly identified, and who do not know what they can or should do.

There are thousands, perhaps millions, of people in this country, including a considerable portion of our conservatives, who, confronted by obvious and cogent evidence, are still wishing that they could be sure about the Communist conspiracy, how big it is, who belongs to it, and even what it proposes to do.

Most Americans . . . are not only woefully uninformed about the nature and extent of this international criminal conspiracy, but have had their minds so systematically conditioned and poisoned . . . that they have great difficulty in understanding even the nature of the problem. The enormous task before us is that of undoing within the next two or three years all that the Communists have accomplished by their incredibly patient, laborious, and cunning efforts since that black day in 1872 when the headquarters of their international conspiracy were openly and officially transferred to New York City.

On the 3rd of March, 1958, Congressman Francis E. Walter, Chairman of the House Committee on un-American Activities, published a report stating that "the Kremlin has succeeded in enlisting, at a conservative estimate, more than a million Americans. . . . There are at this moment the equivalent of some twenty combat divisions of enemy troops on American soil . . . troops that are loyal only to the Soviet."

In other words, you are now living in a country that has been partly occupied. Unless the American people now make a desperate effort to save themselves, they will find themselves in the position of the Hungarians when they made their frantic and hopeless effort to regain their freedom three years ago.

There are two basic facts that one must bear in mind when one tries to understand Communists:

First, all the talk about an "ideological struggle" is mostly nonsense. No Communist, except gullible college boys and other children, really believes in the doctrine of socialism. Marx's absurd theories are merely a propaganda device, a means to an end. The intellectual processes of the Communist mind have been well explained by Czeslaw Milosz in his *Captive Mind*, and by Gerhart Niemeyer in his *Inquiry Into the Soviet Mentality*.

It is quite incorrect to say of a Communist, unless you mean that he is a juvenile or a fool, that he believes in Communism. Communism is not a theory in which men may believe; it is a conspiracy in which men participate. So far as Communism has an intellectual basis, that basis may be found in the doctrine, not of Karl Marx, but of John Dewey. The Communist is the perfect pragmatist; he is a nihilist; he believes that there is no such thing as truth. He repudiates and hates all the traditions and culture of the past.

Perhaps the neatest illustration of the intellectual processes of a Communist and the jargon that he loves to use will be found in comments made to me by a university president some time ago. In a conference with him, I happened to mention the old ideal of scholarship and learning: disinterested pursuit of truth. I thought that he would at least pay lip-service to this ideal, but he interrupted me imperiously.

"There is no truth but social truth," he said.

"And what," I asked, "is social truth?"

He replied quite simply: "It is what it is expedient for a society to tell its members."

"And who," I asked, "determines what story it is expedient to tell the suckers?"

He smiled. "We do."

Now, to be sure, I cannot be certain that the university president was a member of the Communist underground, but the reasoning that he employed is that of the Communist mind. There is no truth; there is only expediency.

But intellectual nihilism, the repudiation of all concepts of truth, justice, humanity, is not sufficient to explain the terrible energy of the Communist conspiracy. That energy is emotional: it is a lust, a craving, a quasi-religious passion. I had my first glimpse of this passion early in my days in Washington.

I met a young man who had just come into the army. He looked like an amiable college boy, and as a matter of fact, he had been graduated from law school only two or three years before. He had been working for the Labor Relations Board, and he enthusiastically described to me the way in which he and his colleagues would raid small American corporations that were inclined to be recalcitrant, seize their books and cart them off, ostensibly for the purpose of photographing them, but actually to force the company, paralyzed by the loss of its records, to submit. I was a little shocked, and I asked, "Lieutenant, didn't it seem to you that you were violating the constitutional rights of American business men?" He was a young man, and he answered promptly, "Rights? Why, they're capitalists. When we stand them against a wall, we will shoot them in the belly: they die longer that way."

That was how I first came to suspect the basic orientation of Communist minds, but only after years of observation, and with help from the illuminating analysis by Denis de Rougemont, did I realize that the young man was exceptional only in the readiness with which he let slip the mask. That is the explanation of the fact that puzzles so many Americans who have not closely observed Communists—the seemingly strange fact that the so-called "liberal intellectuals" are not perturbed or shaken in their faith by the innumerable and indubitable reports of Communist atrocities, tortures, and massacres.

We all know that when the Bolsheviks took over Russia, they proceeded systematically to murder some 5,000,000 men, women, and children, including the best part of the population. We all know, for example, that when the White Russians in Odessa agreed to an armistice under the most solemn pledges that they and their families were to be transported unharmed to Constantinople, the Communists massacred part of the men as soon as they were disarmed, and reserved another part for tortures so scientifically administered that many of the victims took more than a week to die. The women were compelled to witness this amusement and then placed in brothels for sadistic sexual tortures; some lived as long as three months. This procedure has continued ever since.

Very many men do not adhere to Communism in spite of its indescribable atrocities, on the contrary, they become Communists because of those atrocities. The true hardcore Communist, whatever the disguise he may wear when he moves among you and however much he may think it expedient to snivel about "social good" or "brotherhood," is, in the literal and exact meaning of the English word, a thug, that is, a man who has made a religion of murder. He is driven by an overwhelming lust to destroy and uproot, to annihilate civilization, to kill—and even more than that, to make decent men and women suffer, to degrade them to the level of animals. That is his ideal, and for it he works constantly, tirelessly, and with infinite cunning.

The Communist conspiracy has a basically dual organization. From 1876 to 1907, it is true, the conspiracy was entirely secret and underground, but since 1907 there has been a public segment, first called the I.W.W. and reorganized in 1919 as the official Communist Party, headed in both instances by William Z. Foster. This official party has never been large. It probably has never had over 90,000 card-carrying members at any time. It has served on the one hand as a recruiting and testing agency to enlist talented conspirators who, after they have proven their worth and ability, could quietly be transferred to one or another division of the underground, and it has served on the other hand as a shield to mask and facilitate the work of the underground apparatus that consists of conspirators who pose as "liberal intellectuals," and who urge the American people to save themselves from Communism at home by reforming their legal and economic system along Communist lines, and to save the world from Communism by taxing themselves to finance Communist governments abroad.

The official party, which currently pretends to be even smaller than it is, has never been more than a small segment of the conspiracy. Louis Budenz recounts with wry humor that when he had worked his way up in the Communist Party to become managing editor of the *Daily Worker* and a member of the National Executive Council, he began to fancy himself a person of some importance, until one of his superiors remarked dryly, "Son, all that you have seen is the periscope of the submarine."

The Communist underground is our real danger, and no one can accurately measure its total strength. Its members all vociferously deny that they are Communists, and they are now so organized that when everything is working properly no one conspirator can positively identify more than five of his accomplices. Two members of the F.B.I. and an ex-Communist agree in assuring me that since the 1930's, at any rate, it has been the fixed policy of the Communists to find a young man and young woman, arrange for their marriage, help them through college, if necessary, and then send them into an American community, often a small town.

For fifteen years the Party provides them with such support as they may need to establish themselves firmly in the professional or even the business life of the community. During these fifteen years they are to keep themselves clear of all suspicion; the party asks of them no single overt act, not even a signature on a Communist-front petition. After fifteen years, they begin to receive orders— and carry them out.

The underground works under innumerable guises on innumerable projects, many of which seem irrelevant to their purpose. Mr. William Rusher, who was for some years a member of the legal staff of the Senate Internal Security Committee, estimates that there are now 10,000 separate organizations, each directed toward a single goal, and many of them apparently innocent. All of these fronts have one thing in common: they simulate a charitable or altruistic interest in human welfare, and pretend that they are working for some "social good." These fronts serve primarily as a means of establishing and maintaining control over a mass of dupes —well-meaning and sometimes intelligent people who never even guess who is doing their thinking for them. They unwittingly form the third and largest circle of Communist strength.

The international conspiracy has penetrated every segment of American life, and has attained effective control of many of the most strategic. That is, including the confessions of repentant Communists and the many reports issued by the Congressional committees. But let me remind you that all the investigations by the

House and Senate committees have been fragmentary and have involved only minor members of the conspiracy. Even the late Senator McCarthy operated for the most part on the periphery of the conspiracy, and you will remember that when he opened a line of investigation which was evidently leading to a nest of traitors in the Pentagon, the forces of international Communism, utilizing their control of the press, the radio, and television, struck down that great American patriot on what was perhaps the darkest day in American history since Valley Forge.

There has been no searching investigation of Communism in the United States. You will, perhaps, remember that Judge Robert Morris, who was Chief Counsel of the Internal Security Subcommittee of the Senate, stated in a radio broadcast last year that no Congressional investigation of Communism had ever gone very far in penetrating the structure of the conspiracy because whenever the committee seemed likely to follow the trail of major conspirators, its work was stopped by "irresistible pressures." And even Judge Morris did not dare to specify the nature or source of these pressures.

The Communist web of subversion now clearly extends from the humblest primary school to the highest court in our land. In many areas, of course, the Communists' work is done for them by puppets and stooges who do not realize that they are being manipulated, or by frauds, racketeers, and other social parasites, such as typical bureaucrats, whose minds can focus on just one thing: the fast and easy buck. But conspiracies, like armies, must first be measured by the number of troops they can put into the field, not by the number who know and approve the strategic plans of the High Command.

In the public schools, for instance, the techniques of what is called "progressive education," designed to stultify the minds and brutalize the character of adolescents, are essentially an elaborate fraud perpetrated by a gang of parasites who exploit the gullibility of taxpayers. But the inculcation of illiteracy and the incitation of sexual promiscuity serve the Communist purpose of degrading mankind, and have been largely accomplished under Communist direction. They are now reaping what they so diligently sowed. Last year one of my younger colleagues in the University thought to ask his class of freshmen—twenty boys and girls, probably from twenty different high schools all over the state—about Communism, and

90% of them—eighteen little parrots—replied: "Everyone knows that Communism is the ideal form of government. We learned all about that in high school."

In the universities the Communists have zealously promoted, and in turn profited by, the relaxation and now even the repudiation of the old standards of scholarship and intellectual integrity. The colleges and universities, indeed, were probably the first great Communist target. No one, so far as I know, has examined the recorded membership and activities of the Socialist Clubs which, under the leadership of John Dewey, were established in 1905-1910 in colleges and universities throughout the country; I cannot say, therefore, whether or not these clubs were a Communist-front activity. The first Communist cell of which I have heard is said to have been organized at Harvard in 1910.

One must take it for granted that every college and university of prominence has strong Communist cells in its faculty. Dr. J. B. Matthews, who has virtually devoted his life to study of this conspiracy, estimates that the Communists control, as members or as committed allies, more than three thousand teachers in colleges and universities. Louis Budenz, on the basis of information he acquired while he was a member of the party, estimates that there are 3500 members. Another ex-Communist informs me that there were cells of which Budenz evidently had no knowledge.

But if you wish to see how far the poison has gone, you must go beyond these figures to the now open repudiation of the basic conceptions of scholarship by the freebooters who insist that they are just sweet "liberal intellectuals." In the recent book, *The Academic Mind,* by Paul F. Lazarsfeld and Wagner Thielens, Jr., you will discover that back in the horse-and-buggy days it was the function of scholarship to preserve the cultural and scientific tradition, but that in the modern world the proper function of the university professor is (I quote) "to determine . . . custom and social authority." Now that, of course, is not a specific recommendation to join the Communist conspiracy, but lest some "intellectuals" might not be bright enough to get the point, the authors elsewhere in their book "prove" by sociological gobbledegook that the "scholarship prestige" of a university is directly proportional to the percentage of its faculty that welcomes Communist colleagues and is eager to see Communist cells set up in the student body.

In fairness to the academic world, however, one must remark that

American churches have proved themselves no more resistent to penetration by the conspirators. In fact, Herbert Philbrick, the agent of the F.B.I. who spent nine years in the Communist underground, believes that the conspirators have won more support among American ministers than in any other profession.

It is not my purpose to review one by one the segments of American society in which evidence of Communist penetration has been published and should be known to everyone. Instead I should like to indicate summarily a few areas in which, so far as I know, an investigation has not been made, but in which inquiry is urgently needed. In these areas, of course, I can suggest no conclusions—only terrifying possibilities.

To begin with, has anyone investigated the possible connections between the great criminals of the Communist conspiracy and their humbler counterparts, the robbers, rapists, and murderers of our ordinary underworld? Given the uniformity of Communist methods throughout the world, the question is worth asking. I note that when the pro-Communist government came to power in Latvia, the civil service was reorganized and new chiefs of police were appointed. The interesting thing is that every one of these new chiefs of police had a prison record of one or more convictions for burglary, armed robbery, rape, or homicide. The national director of police services was, of course, the most distinguished of the lot: he had, as I recall, served eleven prison sentences and was serving the twelfth when he was released to assume his duties in the new welfare state.

There are some indications that the same natural alliance may exist in this country. You may remember that in the 1920's two bank robbers and murderers named Sacco and Vanzetti, were arrested and finally executed for a crime of which their guilt was indubitable. But these men, like Stalin in his youth, were bank robbers and Communist agents, and accordingly a long and frenzied agitation, led by such exalted figures as professor Felix Frankfurter, of Harvard University, was begun to procure their release. And I note also that in the new Communist state recently set up in Cuba, one of the official executioners is, according to Robert Siegrist, a man from Milwaukee, Wisconsin, named Hermann Marks, who has a long police record of 32 arrests and was only recently released from the penitentiary to which he had been sentenced after being convicted of rape. I suppose the answer is that ordinary criminals with sadistic tendencies are naturally attracted to Communism, but an investigation might disclose some interesting details.

Second, I suggest that we need urgently to ascertain the Communist use of organized charities. We all know, of course, that public welfare agencies are as natural a habitat for Communists as sagebrush for rattlesnakes. Herbert Philbrick estimates that one-third of the top echelon of Communist conspirators is lodged in just one federal agency, the Department of Health, Education, and Welfare, and observers in Washington estimate that between seventy and eighty per cent of the responsible officers in that agency are members of the conspiracy—that, by the way, is a datum which will help you to understand why the Department of Health, Education, and Welfare was granted the largest increase of any governmental department in the President's so-called "economy budget" this year. But I am thinking now of private charity, of the agencies that solicit money from you every year.

The Communists have a strange sense of humor which makes them take pleasure in bamboozling the public. You may remember that the first and unsuccessful Communist revolution in China in the 1920's was partly financed by funds collected in this country for the "starving Chinese." You remember that the broadcasting station called Radio Free Europe, exposed last year by Fulton Lewis, Jr., is partly supported by funds collected from American suckers for the ostensible purpose of fighting Communism. You may have seen the American Legion's report on the weird organization called UNICEF, which revealed that three-quarters of the money collected by the children who each year beg from door to door was either sent to admittedly Communist countries, such as Red China, or completely unaccounted for.

But no charity is too small to escape the notice of the Communists, for it will at least serve to provide an income and scope of activity for some of their members. We Americans so automatically assume a noble purpose whenever we hear a plausible slogan that we must provide endless laughs for the comrades. Just four days ago I was shocked when I learned something of the activities in a small town of a charity to which I have regularly contributed. Since I do not know whether this one town is an exception or is typical of the organization throughout the country, I shall not name the charity other than to say that it claims to finance scientific research on a common disease.

In this one town volunteers go from door to door on one week-end in the year to solicit contributions. Most of these volunteers do not even know that the charity for some reason maintains a local office with a permanent Executive Secretary whose annual salary alone takes almost half of the money that is raised in that town each year. Office rent and secretarial expense must consume most of what is left, so that in this town, at least, virtually nothing or nothing at all is left over for the scientific research of which we hear so much. Why does this town need an Executive Secretary? I think I can tell you why. The Executive Secretary in the town in question is active in various Communist-front organizations, including the N.A.A.C.P. And a few days ago at a small party, according to a person who was present, the Executive Secretary told my informant quite bluntly: "Sure. I'm a Communist. By now, more than half the United States is Communist. What I can't understand is why people like you don't join up."

It is also of vital importance that we learn to what extent the Communist conspiracy has gained control in the profession which, for many Americans, replaces the clergy: psychology and psychiatry. We have all noticed the frenzied agitation on what is euphemistically called "mental health" throughout the nation. We all know that the agitation was begun by the World Health Organization, whose president was that ubiquitous traitor, Alger Hiss, and sponsored in this country by the National Association for Mental Health, whose director, Julius Schrieber, refused to tell a Congressional committee whether or not he was a Communist on the grounds that his answer might incriminate him. We know that the agitation is financed by funds taken from the pockets of the taxpayers by that great Communist department of our government, the Department of Health, Education, and Welfare.

Mr. Kenneth Goff, who was trained in "psycho-politics" while he was in the Communist party, in his booklet, *Brain-Washing*, reports that Beria, then Chief murderer in the Soviet State, in 1936 told the American Communists:

> With the institutions for the insane you have in your country prisons which can hold a million persons and can hold them without civil rights or any hope of freedom. And upon these people can be practiced shock and surgery so that never again will they draw a sane breath. . . .
>
> Therefore you must dominate as respected men the fields of psychiatry and psychology.

The ghastly question that we must ask ourselves is, How far have the conspirators advanced toward this goal in the past quarter century? It is imperative that the American people, including every man sincerely interested in the study of the human mind, have an answer to that question.

Equally agonizing, equally imperative is the question how far the conspiracy has penetrated our armed forces. Senator McCarthy was struck down for raising the question even in the most tentative form. That is, perhaps, the most significant fact of all. But through chinks in the iron curtain of "military secrecy" gleam occasional incidents that are profoundly alarming. Many of you have probably read the recent novel, *The Pentagon Case*, by Colonel Victor J. Fox. A friend of mine is a close friend of the author, and I am assured that all military episodes in that story are accounts of what actually happened, transposed only enough to protect the author from a charge of having disclosed "classified material."

In June, 1949, Senator McCarran sent to Admiral Hillenkoetter, who was then head of our Central Intelligence Agency, an inquiry concerning one hundred new appointees to the so-called United Nations. Admiral Hillenkoetter replied that a preliminary check of his records showed that 29 of these appointees were officers in the Communist Party, and that 32 others were known members of the Russian espionage system. Admiral Hillenkoetter was immediately transferred to a desolate outpost in the Pacific. We need urgently to know who transferred him—who has the power to terrorize the loyal officers of our army and navy.

Our foreign policy for the past two decades is an almost unbroken record of betrayal and shame. I trust, by the way, that you have not overlooked the latest triumph of what may fairly be called the Washington-Moscow Axis. The Batista government in Cuba was not, to be sure, a perfect government but it was probably as good a government as one could reasonably expect to find in an island largely populated by mongrels. Batista, however, had committed the one sin that is unforgivable in the eyes of the people who call themselves our "liberal intellectuals": he was an enemy of Communism. Not only was he a reliable ally of the United States, but he had even gone so far as to sever diplomatic relations with Russia, an act which greatly embarrassed our State Department. It was clear, therefore, that he must be eliminated. Accordingly the revolt led by Fidel Castro was organized. You will recall that some of the preparations for it were quite openly made in Florida.

Now, although Castro thought it worth while to say that he is not himself a member of the Communist Party, his principal assistants including his brother were notorious Communists, and no reasonable person, even slightly acquainted with Latin-American affairs could ever have doubted that the Castro revolt was a Communist operation intended primarily to secure bases for the many Russian submarines which are constantly cruising along our Atlantic Coast, and to permit the establishment of rocket bases within one hundred miles of American soil.

During the progress of his take-over in Cuba, Castro received supplies from Russian submarines, and large quantities from the United States. The shipments from Florida were, of course, technically smuggled to him but oddly enough our government was never able to intercept them.

But even with this help Castro would have failed but for the energetic intervention of our State Department. The technique used is a standard procedure and should be quite familar to all of us by now. You will recall that when General George Marshall was sent to China to arrange for the Communist occupation of that country, he was able to accomplish his mission by simply cutting off from General Chiang Kai-shek the supplies of ammunition that he needed for his soldiers' rifles, which were all, of course, of American manufacture. $150,000,000 worth of ammunition on ships that were about to land was simply dumped in the ocean, and, of course, no further shipments were made. Thus Chiang Kai-shek's men could not use even their rifles, to say nothing of machine guns and artillery, and he had to retreat before the Communist invaders, who had been equipped with the huge Japanese stores of weapons and munitions that we had turned over to them in Manchuria.

Following this established pattern, our State Department cut off all supplies of ammunition to the small army of Colonel Batista in Cuba which was equipped with weapons purchased in the United States. Even ammunition that Batista had bought and already paid for was confiscated on the docks. It seems quite clear that Batista's men did not desert: they simply had nothing to shoot.

You will also remember that while the great betrayal in China was under way under the direction of such eminent figures as General Marshall and Professor Owen Lattimore, the controlled press in this country was filled with propaganda to the effect that Chiang Kai-shek was a scoundrel, and that the Communists in China were just innocent "agrarian reformers."

The same technique is, of course, now being used. The press is once again filled with manufactured reports of the past iniquities of Batista, and with glowing accounts of Fidel Castro—an "agrarian reformer" and the "George Washington of Cuba."

Then you will witness another act in the farce. You will recall that when the Communists were firmly established in China, our "experts" blandly told us: "Ooops! We said they were agrarian reformers, but we were mistaken. They're Communists after all. Ha! ha! ha!"

As soon as the Russians have built their submarine bases and set up the launching fields for ballistic missiles in Cuba, our State Department will no doubt again tell us: "Ooops! We were mistaken. But now that launching sites for atomic missiles have been set up within one hundred miles of the United States, war is unthinkable, ain't it?"

I have said enough, I think, to suggest how desperate our situation is. Our ancestors were never confronted by a danger so terrible and immediate.

This is a fight to preserve our lives, and an open offensive against the whole Communist conspiracy is imperative, if we are to survive.

# IV

# Eggheads Adrift

THE GREATEST ALLY of the political demagogue is the "do-gooder," the person of self-proclaimed intellectual superiority who acts as if he believed that man-made laws should supersede the Laws of Nature which are the laws of God.

The term "egghead" is of recent coinage and is applied to these self-appointed saviors who are vain enough and shallow enough to think that they can remake the human race. Today, their presence is felt in the impact they exert over the air waves, in the press, from the pulpit, in the movies, in the classrooms of America, and in organizations too numerous to mention.

All the unprincipled politician needs to do to enlist the support of the eggheads is to play the side of the record that grinds out the tear-jerking "ill-fed, under-nourished, under-privileged, ill-housed, ill-clothed, down-trodden" tune of Karl Marx. He has only to promise to wave a magic wand and correct all these misfortunes by passing laws, and he finds himself the leader of an army of eggheads. Of course, the eggheads say they do not believe in a dictatorship, but they crusade for the passage of "up-lift" laws which give dictatorial powers to the political leadership of the country.

The public is bombarded with propaganda from the eggheads

pointing out existing faults and promising a simple, quick cure if the public will only bestow sufficient power upon those in authority.

At no time does the egghead stop to consider that no human being is perfect and that no human system of government is perfect. Not for one moment does the egghead weigh the good points against bad. His sole emphasis is upon the imperfect, which is in need of immediate correction; and his constant theme is that only the coercive power of the state can deliver salvation.

The egghead does not even stop to consider whether the proposed cure has ever been tried in the past. In fact, a derisive snort of impatience is the egghead's standard response when he is shown that throughout the long, long history of the human race all such past attempts to regiment the public into utopia have failed.

Before the egghead came into his own under the protective wing of the unprincipled politician, it was generally accepted in America that complete concentration of power was a thing to be avoided at all costs. It was generally agreed that enslavement was worse than freedom. To all the world the name America meant personal freedom with a form of government guaranteed to preserve it; a belief in God and in the Natural Laws; an aversion to tyranny of any kind, whether vested in one man or in a majority. To all the world America was the land of promise, a land that prospered and grew great because its basic idea was the protection of man's right to live as he chose and keep what was his, and not be pushed around by bureaucratic masters.

But suddenly there was a change, aided and abetted by the eggheads who jumped at the opportunity to remake America by forcefully imposing their pet theories upon the people. From freedom to bureaucratic enslavement; from trust in God to worship of the welfare state; from solvency to bankruptcy; from self-reliance to bewilderment—all of this in the name of uplift and progress!

Hasn't the time come for the eggheads to take another look? Couldn't they be wrong? Would it be amiss to ask the eggheads to look at the record, to look at themselves in the mirror, and to admit that no divine power to remake the world has been bestowed upon them?

Would it not be in order for the eggheads to turn the record over and to play the other side? The side that says the universe was made by God—not by politicians, bureaucrats, or eggheads? The side that denies bureaucratic enslavement is better than freedom? The side that says the best society is made up of the best men, and that individual effort with trust in God makes better men than hand-outs in exchange votes?

Isn't it time for university trustees to live up to their responsibility by ridding faculties of welfare-state eggheads and by flushing Communist poison out of the textbooks?

Isn't it time for a moral revolution?

Indeed it is, according to Hon. Spruille Braden, former Ambassador to Argentina and Cuba.

## For a Moral Revolution

### HON. SPRUILLE BRADEN

So consistent is the record of history, that I dare say it could be stated as a natural law of societal behavior that: "The measure of morality in public office will be in inverse ratio to the amount of state interventionism which may exist."

There is nothing new in state interventionism. It is as old and reactionary as societal organization itself. Always, when it permeates the body politic, it kills the nation.

This assertion repeatedly is confirmed by history. The Hammurabi Code, promulgated earlier than 2000 B.C., by imposing controls over wages, prices, production, consumption, and all the rest of the economy, wrecked Babylonia. Governmental extravagance and a bloated bureaucracy killed individual initiative and led to the fall of ancient Greece. A planned economy of state maintenance for the slothful—plus excessive taxation—brought the collapse of the later Roman Empire and the regression of a civilized society into the Dark Ages. The welfare state of the Incas became so debilitated as to become easy prey for Pizarro and his "Conquistadores." In its turn, the great Spanish Empire broke when the throne so regimented every activity that no one could earn a living except by being a public employee, a priest, or a sailor. For the same reasons the British Empire is now dissolving before our eyes.

You are all too sadly acquainted with how low the ethical standards of a few public servants have sunk. Equally bad and even worse occurrences have been uncovered in many of our state and municipal governments.

Almost everywhere politicians and "do-gooders," by camouflaging ill-considered or bad enactments as welfare or defense measures, are enticing their peoples down the path of dalliance into systems of state interventionism. They are leading them to eventual destruction. They are concentrating power in Washington under a bureaucracy already expanded beyond manageable dimensions and which increasingly resorts to uncontrolled extravagance and extravagant controls. They are murdering the nation. Can there be greater treason?

Too many laws create confusion, unwise laws corruption. Together they nurture absolutism and criminality.

There are, for example, many enterprises which could not operate profitably were they to obey, to the letter, a complexity of laws and regulations, which sometimes almost seem to have been enacted with malice of aforethought. As a result, these businessmen are easy prey for gangsters and crooked officials, both high and low, who exact tribute for what they call "protection." In these cases the quickest prophylactic would be to do away with the unwise laws and regulations.

Jefferson once remarked that a revolution every so often is a good thing. This country desperately needs a moral revolution right now. I pray that it comes soon, before it is too late. I pray that it will be brought on by an outraged public opinion, resulting from each individual reassuming his personal responsibilities and then lining with others to make their voices heard. I pray that it will reimplant the Decalogue and the Golden Rule as the ethical code of the American people. I pray that under its impact the love and old-fashioned discipline within the families of this nation will again be exercised against immorality and crime, corrupting and veniality.

Such a revolution will return the United States to morality and straight thinking, and thereby resolve the crisis which now confronts us.

Then, we may hope the rest of the world may emulate the salutary results obtained here.

---

The contention that today's swift pace makes it impossible to return to individual effort and trust in God is not borne out by the facts—nor does it follow the teachings of any religion. After all, how long does it take to make a baby in this modern, moon-shooting era? How long did it take nineteen hundred and sixty-one years ago? The Natural Laws are here to stay, and stupid is the nation that permits its politicians to evade them or try to repeal them—the long history of the human race shows it cannot be done.

What more positive proof could be needed than the miracle of modern West Germany? Here was a nation utterly destroyed by war, completely ravished by that monstrous Morgenthau plan which permitted the Russian Communists to dismantle and move entire factories to Russia. Today West Germany is the bright spot of the world because they have rebuilt on the early American pattern of minimum government interference and maximum individual freedom and responsibility.

To those well-meaning eggheads, who have tried in vain to bend life and human nature to their liking, there are available many inspiring examples of honest re-examination. One of the most lucid is that of William Henry Chamberlain whose *Evolution of a Conservative* explains his return to a reliance on individual freedom after years of living in Russia and other parts of Europe, where regimentation proved to be a dismal failure.

So completely does his chapter, "Ten Mistakes of Marx," refute the basic elements of socialism and communism that it is reprinted here.

## Ten Mistakes of Marx

### WILLIAM HENRY CHAMBERLAIN

"The evil that men do lives after them." This applies with singular force to the work of Karl Marx, a man infinitely more influential after his death than during his life. The existence of this apostle of socialism, communism (he used the two words interchangeably), and class war was spent, for the most part, in obscure and sometimes squalid poverty. Marx could not make even a humble living as a writer and journalist; he had no other profession or trade. He would probably have had to go on poor relief, less generous in England in his time than it is now, if it had not been for handouts from his disciple and collaborator, Friedrich Engels, who enjoyed the advantage of a successful capitalist father.

Marx's record of political achievement at the time of his death in 1883 was quite sterile. Because, in a moment of thoughtless bravado, he had renounced Prussian citizenship, he could not go to Germany or take any intimate part in the young German socialist movement. He played no role in British politics. To put it mildly, Marx was not a mellow or lovable character. His habit of excommunicating from the socialist movement all who disagreed with him and of launching torrents of personal abuse and slander against political opponents, like Lassalle, kept his circle of personal friends very limited. But even if there were few mourners, literally or figuratively, at the grave of Marx the man, the theory of Marxism, the vision of a world in which the workers, or proletariat, oppressed by capitalism, would break their chains and become the architects of a new millennial order, marched from success to success.

By the time of the first world war, Marx was revered as the founding father of their creed by the socialist parties which had sprung up in most European countries. Because a Russian genius of revolutionary action, Vladimir Ilich Ulyano, better known as Nikolai Lenin, swallowed Marx's ideas whole, without reservation, Marxism became the official doctrine of the new communist state in Russia. This state, whose rulers have never wavered in their conviction that their power will one day encompass the entire world, is the result of a successful revolt against all the values of Western civilization, against religion and moral law, against natural rights and civil and personal liberties. After the second world war, communism extended its dominion over China and the countries of eastern Europe so that today, it has been imposed as a dogmatic faith on more than one-third of the inhabitants of the globe.

The influence of Marx is by no means limited to nations under communist rule. The appeal of Marxist ideas to European socialists, to the often intellectually half-baked leaders of newly emancipated countries in Asia, has been considerable. And, although the number of persons who can honestly claim to have read through, with comprehension, Marx's supreme work, the immensely long, dry, and abstruse *Das Kapital,* must be small, the simplified outline of Marxist theory presented in the *Communist Manifesto* possesses considerable psychological appeal.

Marx professed to know all the answers, to offer a complete explanation of human activity on the basis of his theory of historical materialism. In the Marxist scheme, there is a hero, the proletariat, and a villain, the bourgeoisie, and the hero is represented as the certain winner in the struggle. There is a vision of revolutionary triumph that will transform the conditions of human existence and usher in a millennium, of the precise nature of which, to be sure, Marx offers few and vague hints. To the trusting minds that accept Marx's premises and assumptions without question, there comes an intoxicating sense of being in step with history, of professing a faith rooted not in fantasy but in infallible science.

Favorable winds followed the launching of the Marxist ship. Scientific discoveries and progress in so-called higher criticism of biblical theories had shaken the bases of traditional religious faith, especially among the educated classes. The harshness and social inequality of capitalism in its early stages, even though, in the opinion of Professor Hayek and other competent scholars, these traits have been overemphasized, had aroused many dreams of social reorganization along more equitable lines.

Marxism supplied a new secular faith to those who had lost their old religion and furnished a blueprint to those who were dreaming rather vaguely of altering the existing economic system. Although phrased in dry, materialistic terms, Marxism could appeal to a generous imaginative mind as a challenge to action, with the suggestion of a struggle between right and wrong and an assurance that right would triumph in the end. And the proposal to nationalize all means of production in the hands of the state, which would be under the control of the proletariat, furnished a target at which leaders of movements of discontent could aim.

The Achilles' heel of the Marxist secular religion is that it voiced statements and uttered prophecies which can be measured against the background of the actual course of human events. Marx has already been proved a singularly uninspired prophet, with an abnormally high proportion of bad guesses chalked up to his discredit. Other thinkers, especially Oswald Spengler and Jakob Burckhardt, were far more successful in divining the shape of the twentieth century, which, in Spengler's phrase, might produce another Caesar but not another Goethe.

Examination of the works of Marx and his colleague, Engels, reveals ten big mistakes, some so fundamental that they completely discredit, as a preview of the future, the whole superstructure of faith in capitalist ruin and doom and inevitable socialist triumph. Marx had laboriously erected this superstructure on a foundation of Hegelian metaphysics and minute research into the seamy sides of British capitalism, as revealed in British government reports. Here are these mistakes.

Mistake Number One. *The doom of capitalism is assured because under its operation the rich will become richer and fewer: the poor will become poorer and more numerous.* This is the prospect set forth in the *Communist Manifesto,* a far more rhetorical and colorful work than *Das Kapital:*

"While there is a progressive diminution in the number of the capitalist magnates, there occurs a corresponding increase in the mass of poverty, oppression, enslavement, degeneration and exploitation. But at the same time there is a steady intensification of the wrath of the working class—a class which grows ever more numerous and is disciplined, unified and organized by the very mechanism of the capitalist method of production. Capitalist monopoly becomes a fetter upon the method of production which has flourished with it and under it. The centralization of the means of production and the socialization of labor reach a point where they prove incompatible with their capitalist husk. This bursts asunder. The knell of capitalist private property sounds. The expropriators are expropriated."

These are resounding words, but their resonance is that of a dud shell because during the eleven decades that have passed since young Marx and Engels hurled their *Communist Manifesto* in the face of Europe, capitalist countries have developed along lines completely different from those foreseen in the *Manifesto.*

What was in Marx's time a social pyramid has become more like a cube, with the top enlarged, the bottom contracted, and the difference between top and bottom considerably diminished. The capitalist system has brought to the working class not increasing "oppression, enslavement, degeneration and exploitation" but an ever-growing increment of new inventions and comforts that did not exist, even for the wealthy, a century ago: automobiles, radios, washing machines, television sets, to say nothing of money in the bank, insurance policies, or stocks and bonds. The most eloquent soapboxer would have difficulty now in convincing the American or western European worker that, in the climactic words of the *Communist Manifesto,* he has nothing to lose but his chains.

Mistake Number Two. *Socialism can only come about when capitalism has exhausted its possibilities of development.* Or, to put it in Marx's own words, in his *Critique of Political Economy:* "No form of society declines before it has developed all the forces of production in accordance with its own stage of development."

But of the three countries which, according to Marx, were ripest for the transition to socialism (as most industrially developed), the United States is still, by and large, the freest from socialist experiments, as well as the most prosperous. The larger part of Germany, which developed under free political and economic institutions, achieved an amazing recovery after shedding Nazi and Allied occupation controls and resorting to old-fashioned individualist incentives. Great Britain has gone farther in collectivism, but its socialistic "New Deal," enacted without violence and outright uncompensated expropriation, falls far short of Marx's imagined "dictatorship of the proletariat."

On the other hand, the countries in which violent revolutions were carried out in the name of Marx, the Soviet Union and China, were, on Marx's own theory, altogether unripe for socialism. At the time of the Bolshevik Revolution, capitalism in Russia was in a fairly early stage of development. It was very far from having "developed all the forces of production." Capitalism had made still less impact on China, where most of the peasants lived in pre-capitalist conditions.

Experience has shown that in precise contradiction of Marxist dogma, capitalism is harder to overthrow as it strikes deeper roots and proves what it can do. There is strong probability that, although political and economic changes would have come to Russia in any event, there would have been no communist revolution if Prime Minister Stolypin's far-sighted agrarian policy had been given enough time to yield solid results. Although Alexander II abolished serfdom in Russia in 1861, the peasant remained severely curbed in economic initiative by the *Mir,* or village community, to which he was forced to belong.

All too late, Stolypin, after the disorders in the Russian countryside during the 1905 uprising, conceived the idea that one cause of revolutionary unrest was poverty and that the best way to attack poverty was to give the capable and energetic peasant the chance to get away from the restrictions of the *mir* and set himself up as an independent farmer. Legislation permitting the peasant to demand his share of land and leave the peasant community, where the periodic redistribution of land was one of a number of features which tended to keep all its members on a low level of production, was therefore enacted. Large numbers of peasants responded to the invitation, but this reform, which in a generation would have given Russia a solid class of politically and economically conservative land-owning peasants, was nipped in the bud by the outbreak of the first world war. The legislation was suspended for the duration of the hostilities, and the whole idea, one of the most promising in Russian economic history, perished irretrievably during the wild anarchy of 1917 and the communist despotism that followed.

Mistake Number Three. *The "dictatorship of the proletariat" is a just and feasible form of government.* Here are two assumptions: that the proletariat, or industrial working class, has some kind of inherent right to rule, in preference to other groups in the population, and that the working class can exercise governing power.

Both of these assumptions are false. Marx himself never clearly explained why the workers, for whom he foresaw increasing misery and degradation, would be qualified to rule. And Soviet and Red Chinese experience offers the clearest proof that dictatorships *of* the proletariat in theory become ruthless dictatorships *over* the proletariat in practice. It is not the workers in factories and mines who exercise absolute governmental power in communist states. The communist "elite," the real power in these states, is composed of bureaucrats, some of whom have never done any manual work, while the remainder ceased to do any after they became bureaucrats.

Mistake Number Four. *Under socialism the state will "wither away."* This is derived from Marx's belief that the state is an instrument for the suppression of one class by another. In the classless society of socialism, therefore, there will be no need for the state.

Events have played havoc with this theory. Nowhere is the state more powerful, more arbitrary, more of a universal policeman, snooper, and interventionist than in the Soviet Union. Yet the new regime there has certainly done a thorough job of abolishing private property in means of production, thereby, according to Marx, inaugurating a classless society. One is left to choose between two alternatives: either Marx's theory of the state as an instrument of class rule is humbug, or the kind of class rule that prevails in the Soviet Union must be uncommonly crude and ruthless. Actually, insecurity of private property has been historically associated with despotism and lawless dictatorship. Respect for private property has gone hand in hand with the maintenance of political, civil, and personal liberties.

Mistake Number Five. *All ideas, all forms of intellectual and artistic expression are merely a reflection of the material interests of the class in power.* This belief finds repeated expression in Marx's writings, notably in *German Ideology,* where he writes: "The class which has the dominant material power in society is at the same time the dominant spiritual power. . . . The dominant ideas are nothing but the ideal expression of material conditions."

One of the few wisecracks associated with the name of Marx is that the Church of England would give up all of its Thirty-Nine Articles of Faith rather than one thirty-ninth of its property. But the historical record shows that this interpretation of human conduct is inaccurate. Men die far more often for ideas than for material interests. Proof of this can be found in the course of the Bolshevik Revolution in Russia. The communist victory there was not due to any improvement in the material condition of the masses after the communist take-over of power. This definitely did not happen.

What did happen was that the organized, disciplined communist minority held the masses in an iron grip with its double weapon of propaganda and terror, kept passions of class hatred and envy at the boiling point, whipped laggards into line by ruthless regimentation, and thereby kept the communist regime in power during the years of civil war and famine. The qualities of human will and energy, apart from all materialist factors, are vastly more important than Marx was willing to recognize.

Sometimes the materialistic interpretation of culture becomes comical absurdity. I once heard a Moscow musical announcer, with a straight face although possibly with tongue in cheek, offer the following contribution to aesthetic theory: "Comrades, we will now hear Glinka's overture, *Russlan and Ludmilla.* This is a cheerful, buoyant piece of work because when it was written, Russian trade capitalism was expanding and conquering the markets of the Near East." To carry any semblance of plausibility, this would seem to require proof that Glinka owned stock in the expanding companies —a highly improbable contingency in view of the traditional improvidence of musicians in general and Russian musicians in particular.

Ironically enough, there are cases when this idea of culture as the direct reflection of the interests of the ruling class are true. But these cases are only in the Soviet Union and other communist countries, where the novelist or playwright who gives too unfavorable a picture of the ruling clique soon finds himself in trouble. The literature of free countries, on the other hand, is full of very unfavorable representations of the so-called pillars of society.

Mistake Number Six. *Capitalism in the nineteenth century had exhausted its productive possibilities.* This flat statement is made by Marx's alter ego, Friedrich Engels, in his *Anti-Duhring*, which was written before the appearance of the internal combustion engine, X-rays, aviation, synthetic chemistry, and a host of other enormously important additions to the productive process, all of which were brought into existence by the stimulus of capitalism.

Mistake Number Seven. *Production depends on class antagonism.* To quote Marx, in *The Poverty of Philosophy:* "From the very moment in which civilization begins, production begins to be based on the antagonism of orders, of states, of classes, and finally on the antagonism between capital and labor. No antagonism, no progress. This is the law which civilization has followed down to our own day."

Like many of Marx's "laws," this is a mere unsupported assertion of a pedantic dogma. No proof is adduced. The greatest human constructive achievements, from the cathedrals of the Middle Ages to the skyscrapers and dams of modern times, have been the fruit of co-operation, not of antagonism.

Mistake Number Eight. *Nationalism is a negligible force.* Marx and Engels lived in an age of rising national consciousness. Conflicting nationalism was the strongest of the forces that unleashed World War I. Yet in all the writings of these prophets of socialism, the attitude toward nationalism is one of contemptuous deprecation. As Isaiah Berlin, a fairly sympathetic biographer, writes: "He (Marx) consistently underestimated the force of rising nationalism; his hatred of all separatism, as of all institutions founded on some purely traditional or emotional basis, blinded him to their actual influence."

Mistake Number Nine. *War is a product of capitalism.* This idea has found some acceptance outside the ranks of the Marxist faithful. The temptation to seek an oversimplified scapegoat for war is strong. Although theoretically, such Marxist motives as the struggle for trade, colonies, and commercial spheres of influence might lead to international conflict, there is no serious historical evidence that any great war was touched off by such considerations. There were differences of interest between the industrializing North and the mainly agricultural South before the Civil War, but these could easily have been compromised without bloodshed. What made the fratricidal conflict "irrepressible," in Seward's phrase, were two big political and moral issues: secession and slavery.

World War I was entirely political in origin. The starting point was the clash between Slav nationalism and Austro-Hungarian determination to hold together an empire with a polyglot population. A system of tight and almost automatically functioning alliances turned what might have been an Austrian punitive expedition into Serbia into a general European war.

World War II was the handiwork not of any magnates of capitalism but of a plebeian dictator, Adolf Hitler. His motivation, conquest and military glory, antedate the modern capitalist system by centuries. The three governments that proved best prepared for war were the communist dictatorship in the Soviet Union, the Nazi dictatorship in Germany, and the authoritarian militarist regime in Japan. Capitalism makes for free trade, free markets, limited governmental power, and peace. The principal war threat now comes from the expansionist urge of Soviet communism.

Mistake Number Ten. *The worker is cheated because the employer, instead of paying him the full value of his work, holds out on him profit, interest and rent.* Or, as Marx himself states his theory of surplus value:

"All surplus value, whatever particular form (profit, interest or rent) it may subsequently crystallize into, is in substance the materialization of unpaid labor. The secret of the self-expansion of capital resolves itself into having the disposal of a definite quantity of other people's unpaid labor."

It requires little reflection or research to realize that surplus value, like other Marxist catch phrases, is a myth. How, under any economic system—capitalist, fascist, socialist, communist—could industry expand and provide more jobs for more people if part of the value of present production were not withheld from immediate consumption to finance future construction? Perhaps the best refutation of Marx's rabble-rousing myth of surplus value as a peculiarly dirty trick played by capitalists on workers is the extraction of what might fairly be called surplus value on a gigantic scale in the Soviet Union. One of the most striking examples is the imposition of a sales or turnover tax that exceeds 100 per cent on many articles. Another is the forced sale of state bonds to the population, followed by the repudiation of these bonds.

It is amazing that with such a demonstrable record of failure to understand either the world in which he was living or the direction in which that world was going, Marx should be hailed as an unerring prophet. Perhaps the explanation lies in his appeal to psychological and emotional factors, to Utopian idealism, to individual frustration, to class hatred and envy, to the need which some intellectuals felt for a secular religion to replace the other-worldly faith they had lost.

Actually, there is nothing remotely scientific about Marx's socialism. He started with a set of dogmatic, a priori assumptions and then scratched around in the British Museum for facts which would seem to bear out these assumptions. Like the emperor in the fairy tale, Marxism, for all its ponderous pretensions, has no clothes on when examined in the light of realities, in Marx's time or in our own. His supposedly infallible system of interpreting historical development is riddled with errors about the past and bad guesses about the future, of which the foregoing ten are only some of the most obvious and glaring.

In spite of these obvious fallacies in the socialist theories, we continue to move on toward the socialistic welfare state. It is significant to note that the distinguished farm leader, Charles B. Shuman, President of the American Farm Bureau Federation, has had enough of it.

## I've Had Enough Socialism

### CHARLES B. SHUMAN

Socialism is more than a nasty word. It is a system based on government ownership or control of property—especially land and capital investments. This limitation or denial of property rights is invariably accompanied by increased government restrictions on the freedom of individuals. The "superior" minds in the bureaucracy direct the planned economy through control of production and prices while the extremely high costs of government are reflected in tax rates that destroy incentives.

The extent to which we have unwittingly accepted socialism may be measured by the level of taxation. More than a third of our total national income is now taken to support government. Thus, we continue to move towards the welfare state.

Why should we resist this creeping disease?

Why do I say, "I've had enough socialism"?

First, socialism is a proven failure wherever and whenever it has been tried. It failed in ancient Rome; it brought starvation to the early American settlements of Jamestown and Plymouth Rock; it is failing miserably today in England and Russia.

Socialism fails because it costs so much to manage the economy that the high tax rates destroy the incentives to work and save. It fails because the decisions of a few political planners are more likely to be in error than the combined judgment of thousands of individuals bargaining in a free market for goods and services. It fails because political law cannot replace fundamental economic principles.

Second, socialism will inevitably lead to some type of communistic dictatorship. The proven failure of a socialistic scheme always brings proposals for further experiments in government management—never a return to free enterprise. Practically everyone recognizes that government farm crop price fixing is a costly failure, yet many members of Congress now propose to substitute a new panacea—conpensatory payments. When all is said and done, the only difference between socialism and communism is the degree of state control over the individual. They are blood brothers.

The third reason for my statement, "I've had enough socialism," is that under the Marxist system productivity declines and the standard of living is lower than in a free choice capitalistic system. State capitalism appropriates the individual's earnings for investment in government enterprises. Pride of ownership and the desire to save are destroyed.

The abundance of the better things of life which we enjoy in this country is a result of the stimulation of human energy and initiative that comes when folks can keep a substantial part of their income for their own use. Socialism dries up the wellspring of progress—human energy released in response to incentives.

Fourth, socialism is an atheistic philosophy. It depends upon force rather than freedom of choice by individuals—in fact, it is economic slavery. It offers security but eliminates opportunity. It encourages individuals to shift responsibility from themselves to the state. In all ways, it tends to destroy self reliance and promote moral deterioration. Christianity challenges individuals to give of their best—socialism minimizes the dignity and importance of the individual while it glorifies the all-powerful state.

Yes, I've had enough socialism.

—Reprinted by permission from *Christian Economics*.

# V

# Years of Retrogression

No OCCUPANT of the White House since 1933 has had the character to speak out against the socialistic-communist laws that are
leading America into self-destruction. Some have been the leaders
of disintegration.

All three of them (Roosevelt, Truman, and Eisenhower) have
placed the gaining of votes over and above the moral and spiritual
and economic welfare of the country. In doing this each has played
the part of the unprincipled or naive politician. It matters not
whether it has been done with a golf swing and a smile, or with a
curse and thump on the piano, or with deliberate disregard of the
truth because of an insatiable lust for power. The end result is the
same. Enslavement is enslavement, and loss of freedom is loss of
freedom, regardless of who occupies the White House.

As long as the laws which deprive us of freedom remain on the
books, enslavement will become more and more absolute. As long
as the control of both parties remains in the hands of power-
hungry political demagogues who have no regard for the economic
facts of life there is little prospect that either the Democrats or the
Republicans will repeal the laws that have created the welfare state.
However, the sordid record is clear, and it is available for those
who wish to see it.

The brave words of those trying to expose the fraud are also clear and available. Crawford H. Greenewalt, President of E. I. du Pont de Nemours & Company, stressing the historical significance and modern importance of industrial research, makes note of the point at which progress falters.

## When Retrogression Begins

### CRAWFORD H. GREENEWALT

Women were not freed from their 18th century servitude by feminist agitation, but by the invention of the sewing machine, the washing machine, the refrigerator, and the dishwasher, together with the revolutionary developments for handling and distributing foodstuffs.

Peasantry on the farm was not banished by reform or edict, but by the iron plow, the reaper, and the tractor.

The 12-hour shift and the six-day week could not have disappeared from the scene through laws or social upheaval. It was modern machinery, developed by research, that made it possible for the American workman of 1950 to produce many times as much goods as the workman of 1850.

The automobile, pre-eminently a product of research, has widened and enriched lives in a manner impossible to achieve through legislation. At every hand, it is plain that the improvements leading to advancement have their origin in invention and development. There is no alternative.

Ideas formed in a man's mind, after it has been trained and sharpened by education and experience, are the basis of successful research. Without the creative brain of the scientist, all investment in research is worthless. American scientific laboratories are the best equipped in the world. Yet continued progress will be insured only if the rights of the individual to exercise freely his initiative are re-established and jealously guarded.

American research prospered by providing rewards for success; the inventive genius of the nation was kept alive by adding to it what Lincoln called "the fuel of incentive." Further, the integrity of American research was kept inviolate; the research worker was spared the necessity of finding "political" conclusions as the goal of his investigations.

In this atmosphere of free inquiry and of freedom of the individual to enjoy the fruits of his labor, science here flourished. Elsewhere in the world, it has suffered serious setbacks.

The German scientist, once a leader, found under Hitler that he was falling behind. Specified results at a specified time could not be guaranteed, no matter how urgent or peremptory the orders. The Russian scientist under communism has learned that his findings must satisfy the official view, regardless of the facts. The British scientist under socialism has seen the rewards of his enterprise virtually confiscated by taxation.

Without freedom, scientific research and the progress in its wake will falter in the United States, as has happened elsewhere. The individual must be assured the freedom of incentive. The university scientist must have freedom of inquiry, of discussion, and of publication.

And sponsors of industrial research, such as Americans companies, must have the freedom and incentive to win as well as to lose—the freedom to grow and expand, as is necessary to fulfill their responsibilities. The means to carry on future research will be forthcoming only as long as it can pay its way.

When it can no longer do so, it will stop, and the retrogression process begins. In that event, a well-known principle would again be proved: A hoop rolling downhill moves faster than one going up.

—From an address in 1951.

---

The Honorable Spruille Braden, former Ambassador to Argentina and Cuba, appearing before the Society of the National Shrine of the Bill of Rights at St. Paul's Church, Mt. Vernon, N. Y., December 13, 1959, gave an address which highlights important aspects of the retrogression that has taken place during the past quarter of a century.

## Morality and the Bill of Rights

### HON. SPRUILLE BRADEN

For the honor of addressing the Society of the National Shrine of the Bill of Rights, I am grateful. Such an informed audience can appreciate how humble I feel, as I discuss the grand and only completely new idea to appear in political thinking through the many centuries of differing civilizations—the Bill of Rights. For the first time in history, a basic document specifically prohibited anyone ever to use the always dangerous powers of government against the people; it forbade government to infringe upon or violate their inalienable rights, liberties and responsibilities.

My theme for today, "Morality and the Bill of Rights" is, I believe, appropriate for this hallowed house—for St. Paul's Church —because both the moral principles which always should guide this nation, and the Bill of Rights are derived from our religion, without which this country's way of life and purposes would become meaningless. It behooves us always to remember and insist, at every turn, upon the fact that ours is a Christian nation, and must continue so to be if it is to survive. The United States of America was founded upon and is dedicated to the Faith that God is the Author and Dispenser of human dignity and freedom, with corresponding individual responsibility.

The declaratory and restrictive clauses of the Bill of Rights apply that holy concept to society and the conduct of government.

To defend the Bill of Rights in its pristine form and meaning, for each and every man and woman in this great Republic, is not only a patriotic responsibility, but even more, a profoundly religious and moral obligation.

To meet this solemn obligation and respond to that responsibility, has become more difficult than ever before, due to the breakdown in morality everywhere. This breakdown becomes most sinister when it occurs in government, because of its huge powers. Also, honor, integrity, reliability and all the other virtues—and, incidentally, the fear of punishment—are the attributes of individuals and never of Governments. Therefore, individual human rights increasingly are being invaded and scorned, infringed upon and violated, as Government grows and State interventionism expands.

The most obvious evidences of this universal crumbling in morality are Soviet aggression, Communism, and its treacherous infiltration and subversion of every field of endeavor in all countries, including our own.

Further evidence appears in the shocking increases in crime, narcotics and juvenile delinquency; gangsterism and labor racketeering; crooked athletes and college boys corrupted by gamblers;

deep freezers and mink or vicuña coats, and favor-seeking and granting politicians. These and other melodramatic evidences of the breakdown in morality are to be deplored, but they can be suppressed by an enraged public opinion and competent police. Of themselves, they do not, as a rule, so directly menace the Bill of Rights, as does the indoctrination of our people with collectivism and socialism. Big, centralized government and the spread of welfare-statism are among the most dangerous corrosives of individual dignity and freedom and personal responsibility.

Contributory to, and preparing the ground for the general breakdown in morality, especially as it erodes human rights, freedoms and responsibilities, are the many insidious myopias and naivetes, failings and evils, characteristic of our times. Among these are public complacency or apathy; laxity in marriage and home life; abandonment of spiritual for material values; inability to distinguish between right and wrong; indifference to principles; resort to expediency and compromise; adulation for success, irrespective of how it be attained; laziness, the "easy way" and phlegm as to whether or not a job be well done; looking to and depending on Washington for every economic aid and sustenance; the shady deal and getting something for nothing; anything goes, so long as one isn't caught; and so on, through a long variety of indiscretions, improprieties, and worse. The massive effect of these less spectacular, but nonetheless destructive immoralities materially undermines respect for and obedience to both the Ten Commandments and the Ten Amendments to the Constitution.

The recent TV quiz show exposures are a case in point. That an adult and cultured university instructor should sell his integrity for an offer of one thousand dollars is pathetic and even frightening. It is demoralizing, especially to young people, that by continuing this deliberate swindle, he ran his winnings up to $129,000 plus substantial extras. Nor is it to be taken lightly that our educational system, the very essence of which is to tell the truth, should produce this and other contestants, who were willing, in full public view, to deceive millions of people and to lie to everyone, including the Grand Jury. It is more disturbing that the young man's lacrimose and theatrical contrition, coming only when a perjury indictment hovered over him, should lead all but one member of the Congressional investigating committee, with maudlin sentimentalism, to acclaim his tardy and enforced "mea culpa." This showed a startling indifference to the principle involved and an inability by these law makers to choose between right and wrong.

Much of the editorial comment and public sentiment generally were equally insensitive to the moralities. Some kind of low was reached when the producer of "Twenty One," after his indictment for perjury, described quiz shows as a "breath of fresh air."

But this whole dirty business became ominous when the New York District Attorney told us that about 100 of the 150 quiz show witnesses (presumably an educated and intelligent group, with good backgrounds, and enjoying lucrative and responsible positions in their communities), perjured themselves before the Grand Jury. They were not being accused of any crime, but merely called upon as citizens to aid in curing a disgraceful and possibly illegal situation. Yet, they deliberately and cynically lied. They showed themselves to be either ignorant of, or ready to set at naught, one of the greatest safeguards for the public under our way of life—the Grand Jury system, as provided for in the Fifth Amendment of the Bill of Rights.

Another and better known perversion and violation of this vitally important Fifth Amendment has been the widespread "taking of the Fifth" by traitors and criminals. No lawyer is required to interpret the language of this Amendment. In clear and simple terms, it is a mandate to protect a defendant from being forced to be a witness against himself, and to insure him a just trial under due process of law. It was not conceived to become a sanctuary for traitors and criminals, or to aid the accused by sealing the lips of frightened and pressured witnesses. As Wigmore on Evidence * says:

> For three hundred years it has now been recognized as a fundamental maxim that the public . . . has a right to every man's evidence. . . . It is a duty not to be grudged or evaded. Whoever is impelled to evade or resent it should retire from the society of organized and civilized communities, and become a hermit. He is not a desirable member of society.

The misapplication of the Bill of Rights by "taking the Fifth," or for that matter, any other Amendment, might be cured, were we to adopt the Canadian Evidence Act, which reads:

> No witness shall be excused from answering any question upon the ground that the answer to such question may tend to incriminate

* 4 Wigmore Evidence Sec. 2192, 2nd Ed. 1923.

him. . . . The answer so given shall not be used or receivable in evidence against him in any criminal trial, or other criminal proceeding thereafter taking place.

Abuses and distorted interpretations of the Bill of Rights have been fortified in recent years by the Supreme Court's and other judicial findings or decrees usurping legislative powers, making policy and, in effect, amending the Bill of Rights and Constitution. This is immoral.

Jefferson foresaw some such development when he said: ". . . there is no danger I apprehend so much as the consolidation of our Government by the noiseless, and therefore unalarming, instrumentality of the Supreme Court."

But what deference for the first ten Amendments can we expect from a Supreme Court which based a most important decision, not on the Constitution or Bill of Rights, on law or precedent, but on the philosophical speculations in a book by Gunnar Myrdal and his sixteen collaborators, all of whom had communist front affiliations. This Swedish Socialist sneered at our Constitution as "impractical and unsuited to modern conditions," and said its adoption was "nearly a plot against the common people."

Recently the Presidents of several leading universities and the American Council on Education have shown that they had little, if any, conception of the real nature of patriotism—of loyalty to country. Nor do they know what constitutes morality in handling other peoples' money. In a spurious appeal to what they called academic freedom, they denounced the fact that recipients of Government paid-for scholarships, by law, must pledge their loyalty to the United States and sign an affidavit that they belong to no subversive organization. This Act of Congress does not encroach on the Bill of Rights in the slightest, and there is no justification for any resentment. On the contrary, every patriotic citizen should be proud to take such an oath.

The students are no more singled out by legal compulsion than are others who are compelled to swear allegiance, such as young men enlisting in the Armed Forces, including Annapolis and West Point, or manufacturers receiving classified contracts.

Surely, these educators would not advocate subsidies being given to make murderers and criminals more competent in their lines. Yet they want the taxpayers' money used to finance the education, and make more proficient, the traitors and others who either are indifferent to or dedicated to the destruction of the United States, the Constitution and the Bill of Rights.

My Alma Mater's most distinguished alumnus, Nathan Hale, regretted that he had but one life to lose for his country. In contrast with this noble attitude, President Griswold of Yale now thinks it odious to ask his students to take an oath of allegiance, when their education is paid for by their fellow citizens. He advocates their taking your and my money, but giving nothing in return. Such dishonesty, aggravated by tolerance of disloyalty, nullifies the intent and spirit of the Bill of Rights and vitiates its effectiveness.

But, permit me to go on to other repudiations of the Bill of Rights. While the 3rd and 7th Amendments cover certain property rights, the 4th and 5th specify that "The right of the people to be secure in their persons, houses, papers and effects against unreasonable searches and seizures shall not be violated. . . ." and "No person . . . shall be deprived of life, liberty, or property without due process of law; nor shall private property be taken for public use, without just compensation." These stipulations are in keeping with the Bible and Ten Commandments, which makes attack on these Amendments all the more immoral. They are being infringed and violated every day by government and pressure groups, by state interventionists, and a hodgepodge of selfish interests. Gradually but surely the effectiveness of the Bill of Rights is being destroyed in respect of private property.

Under the Income Tax, papers are searched. Unjust fines and penalties are assessed arbitrarily, but the cost and risk of fighting them often is so high, that the victim cannot or dare not try to protect himself. Our hard-earned dollars are seized by the tax collectors and then distributed through subsidies and grants to farmers and labor, business and transportation, to all manner of endeavor at home and abroad. Unquestionably, in all of this, there is much extravagance, waste and corruption. Parenthetically, it is pertinent to ask who can have any confidence in the validity of the Bill of Rights, when they see us disgorging billions of dollars to Yugoslavia, Poland and other Communist governments, who are dedicated to the destruction of the U.S.A. and of every moral principle, of liberty, dignity, and elemental decency?

Incidentally, hundreds of thousands of superfluous bureaucrats, as the money for these "giveaways" goes through their hands, take handsome cuts for themselves in salaries, expense accounts and other perquisites. Misuse of the taxing power is robbing Peter to pay Paul. We would not stand for the recipients of these huge benefactions sticking their hands in and taking cash out of our pockets, but it is just as much unadulterated stealing when Government is used as the intermediary, or cat's paw.

One of the many collateral immoralities and stultifying aspects of this tax procedure was described by T. Coleman Andrews, former U.S. Commissioner of Internal Revenue, when he said: ". . . this evil levy has made us a nation of liars and cheats. The fast buck artist is favored and the great American sport seems to be . . . finding a way around the income tax."

These billions of tax dollars are disbursed by a myriad of governmental agencies operating in practically all fields of activity. Drunk with power, they have lost all sense of moral values. They ignore the 4th, 5th, 6th, 7th, and 8th Amendments in all the particulars I have mentioned, but also in respect of Grand Jury indictments, the enjoyment of a speedy and public trial by an impartial jury, the ability of a defendant to obtain witnesses in his favor and Counsel for his defense, and the infliction of cruel and unusual punishment.

Let me give you an example: A farmer does not enjoy the protection of the 4th Amendment against illegal searches and seizures. Federal farm agents can and do enter properties without search warrants, or other legal instruments. If they think too much wheat is being grown, or other bureaucratic regulations—mind you, not laws, but regulations—are being broken, they pronounce the farmer guilty and fine him without even a formal hearing, let alone a trial by jury. If the fine is not paid, the Federal agents can and do seize the farmer's bank account and personal property, including automobiles, tractors, tools, and other instruments of his livelihood. All this happens even when the farmer never has accepted any payment or loan from or signed any kind of contract with the Government. Walter T. Carroll of Florida, for standing on his rights in this manner was thrown in jail for an indefinite period and has not had a jury trial yet. No tyrant more immorally seizes that which is not his. No dictator more ruthlessly could destroy the Bill of Rights.

Similar violations of personal and property rights are now appearing in connection with "urban renewal" programs.

We are not at war, yet a boy or young man may be drafted into the Armed Forces, sent to another country, and then for any alleged crime or misdemeanor, indiscretion, or even when innocent, be turned over to foreign police and officials for trial and punishment under a completely alien jurisprudence and penology. For him thus to be denied by our Government the protections guaranteed him under the 4th, 5th, and 6th Amendments, by what is known as the Status of Forces Act, is an immoral breach of faith, and a flagrant violation of the Bill of Rights.

Those young recruits no longer can trust their own government. Even if they have had the good fortune to have been taught something about the Bill of Rights, they now are likely to lose all confidence in it. Moreover, they come from a population which is letting the spirit which brought that glorious document, the Bill of Rights, into being seep away; a society which is becoming impotent and vacillating, abandoning self-reliance for dependence on governmental paternalism under an ever-expanding centralized government. Is it any wonder that so many of our boys taken prisoner in Korea were ripe for brainwashing? The breakdown in morality, especially in government, left them without ethical principles wherewith to fortify such confidence as they might have had in the Bill of Rights. Like so many people in this country, they forgot that individual dignity and freedom and personal responsibility are inseparable. And so they faltered, and became easy prey for the Communists. Never before has such a breakdown in morality occurred in this nation during war or peace.

Were it not for the limited time at my disposal, I should like to outline for you many other facets of my subject, together with fitting examples. Especially I should like to emphasize in detail the importance of those marvelous catch-all Amendments:

9th. "The enumeration in the Constitution of certain rights, shall not be construed to deny or disparage others retained by the people."

10th. "The powers not delegated to the United States by the Constitution, nor prohibited by it to the States, are reserved to the States respectively, or to the people."

If these two Amendments are destroyed by the breakdown in morality, now gradually enveloping this nation, the magnificent structure of our constitutional representative republic will crumble into the insecurity of welfare state democracy. The noble experiment of the founding fathers incorporated in the Bill of Rights will have failed, and our beloved country will follow the ancient cycle, repeated time after time through all history: democracy degenerates into chaos, order is restored by despotism or dictatorship, which evolves into monarchy, then into aristocracy or oligarchy, and finally back to democracy, thus completing the circle.

This will happen to these United States, unless each and every one of us assumes his personal responsibility to discipline himself and, in keeping with the moral precepts of our religion, to give a rebirth to the Bill of Rights. It is the duty of each citizen to make certain that, as originally intended, the Bill of Rights be a shield to protect the people from the excesses of government, and that it not be made a sword raised by government against the people. If it is not respected and adhered to by everyone in and out of government, this free Republic is doomed.

A limp and demoralized country inevitably invites aggression from abroad. In contrast, a physically and morally strong United States, holding fast as a representative republic and not as a welfare state democracy to the Constitution and Bill of Rights, would insure our victory if attacked, probably would prevent war, and in any case, would preserve our individual and collective liberty and dignity. This is our only hope for peace with freedom.

The time has come, on this issue of morality and the Bill of Rights, to ask ourselves the first question addressed by God to man: "Where art thou?" (Genesis 3:9)

---

The extent to which the current philosophy of Liberalism has contributed to national retrogression is brilliantly discussed in this article by Richard M. Weaver, Professor of English, University of Chicago.

## Roots of the Liberal Complacency

### RICHARD M. WEAVER

That today's Liberal is marked by complacency will appear to some a paradoxical charge. Most Liberals may shrug it off as something which, in the very nature of the case, cannot be imputed to them. Does not the Liberal creed make criticism of any and all matters a cardinal point? Does it not invite the free competition of ideas in the marketplace? Has not the Liberal set up a kind of eternal restlessness of the mind as the only enlightened condition?

Until fairly recently, one's answer to all of these might have been yes. But the question today is whether the Liberal has not succumbed to certain fallacies of unwarranted assumption, which is the father of all complacency. It is not an unknown thing to have the very vices one is denouncing slip up on one from the rear in some pleasing disguise. This the Liberal has done by not being truly circumspect, and by giving in to certain weaknesses which disqualify him for leadership.

The complacency of this new, and often financially well-to-do, Liberal is fed by a number of roots.

The Liberal has become, to all intents and purposes, a materialist. I mean by this that the Liberal is now inclined to accept wholly the objectives of an efficient material civilization and to judge policies by their relation to the "standard of living." To universalize this "standard of living," he seems ready to carry statism to any length whatever. Writing a few years ago in the *Atlantic Monthly*, Joseph S. Clark, Jr., graduate of Harvard *magna cum laude*, then mayor of Philadelphia, and now United States Senator, offered this curious definition of Liberalism.

> To lay a ghost at the outset and dismiss semantics, a Liberal is here defined as one who believes in utilizing the full force of government for the advancement of social, political and economic justice at the municipal, state, national, and international level.

This is a naked profession, which reveals how far the new Liberal has gone toward embracing the very thing to which the nineteenth century Liberal was, in the name of liberty, most opposed. The last phrase of the definition leads of course to Point Four thinking, to the materialist illusion that envy, hatred, and violence can be removed from the globe by handouts, by "economic assistance," and by making the "underprivileged" nations of the world urban, industrialized, motorized, and sanitized in an equal degree with Detroit and Los Angeles.

A national consequence of this is the Liberal's idealization of comfort. His philosophy now shows a definite antagonism toward all strenuous ideals of life. The code of the warrior, of the priest, and even the scholar, denying the self for transcendent ends, stands in the new lexicon as anti-liberal. "For they are moderate also in virtue—because they want comfort," says Nietzsche in *Thus Spake Zarathustra.* Today popularity is substituted for greatness and conformity for heroism. The Liberal preaches an altruism that is sentimental, and therefore he is hostile to all demands that the individual be something more than his natural, indolent, ease-loving and complacent self.

More damage has resulted from this attitude than from anything else which the Liberal has spread. But quite likely he has been betrayed into it by his scientism. Scientism is the belief that science is competent to deal with every level of reality. It even goes so far as to assume that the scientific method creates reality as it proceeds, this being a favorite tenet of the "instrumentalist" philosopher, John Dewey.

The effect of this theory of man's attitude toward the world in general can be disastrous. For what it does is rule out the given, the contingent, the inscrutable—in sum, all that is greater than or independent of man. The ground for that humility which all the great ethical systems have inculcated is thereby withdrawn. Man, with his Method, leaps into the seat of the Creator, which in the wisdom of poetry, and religion, is the ultimate act of pride.

Despite the tone of their expression, most Liberals today are not real intellectuals, and their lack of real intellectualism leaves them complacent where wiser men are alert and discerning. This may seem an audacious statement when one thinks how they preponderate on college faculties. Yet the fact is proved by the Liberals rejection of logical rigor and by his complacency in the face of contradiction.

One of the chief directives of Liberalism is to deny the existence of either-or choices. This is why the Liberal ends up "in the middle of the road." A desire to squeeze in between two contradictories leads to a breaking down of the very categories by which men think. There is a decisive difference between saying that there are no clear-cut principles of right and wrong and saying that principles cannot always be applied with rigor in a world that is concrete and various. The latter is the policy of all men of sense and experience, but it is prudence, or what the Greeks called *sophrosyne;* it is not "liberalism."

It is the sentimentality of the new Liberal which leaves him incapable of accepting rigid exclusion. And this propensity to moral and intellectual flabbiness leads to an inordinate fear of a certain type of man, of which Taft and MacArthur are good examples. Such men reveal, by the very logic of their expression, that they think in terms of inclusion and exclusion. Their mentality rejects cant, snivelling and double talk. There is, in fact, a great deal to be inferred from the almost hysterical reaction which any man of Plutarchan mold inspires in the Liberal. It accounts for the voluminous outpouring, from supercilious dismissal to vituperation, when an individual of clear mind and strong personality appears on the scene. On these occasions the Liberals' complacency is succeeded by, one may say, a fear for their complacency.

Despite these occasional disturbances to his peace, the Liberal feels most of the time that he is protected by an invincible dogma, which is that everyone today must be a Liberal. It is the hidden premise of numberless college textbooks; it predominates in political philosophy; and it shows up alarmingly in judicial decisions. The assumption is that Liberalism represents a new level of consciousness, which will never be given up.

One striking result of the dogma in our country today is the complacent idea that both political parties must be "Liberal." It used to be felt that one political party was enough to represent the point of view that is Liberalism; now some of our political leaders are saying by their acts if not by their very words that a party must be Liberal to deserve consideration at all by the electorate. Hence the amazing attempt to transform the Republican party into a second Liberal party in plain emulation of the Democratic. So the voter is left without a real choice and has only the opportunity of voting "ja" for Democratic Liberalism or "ja" for Republican Liberalism.

So successful have the Liberals been in establishing this dogma through education, publishing, and politics that many people today are literally unable to understand the conservative point of view. They can grasp neither the meaning of its terms nor the spirit of it. This means that they cannot even conceive the possibility of alternatives they may one day have to face. To be in this condition is to be uneducated.

If Liberalism stemmed out of some deeply anchored and coherent philosophy of life, if it expressed some compelling vision of existence, we might not apply the term complacency to its habit of mind. But with its non-committal attitude toward all the positive issues of life, it cannot rise to the dignity of a philosophy which

might unify an epoch and provide ground for constructive crea-
tions. With its lack of attachment to anything save its own relativism and tentative success, it cannot manage, with all its thousand
tongues, anything better than the superficial and often contradictory observations about its own chaotic world.

 —Republished in *Christian Economics* from the original
version in *The National Review,* June 8, 1957.

More than one hundred years ago, in 1859 to be exact, President
James Buchanan said:

> Should the time ever arrive when the state governments shall look
> to the Federal Treasury for the means of supporting themselves and
> maintaining their systems of education and internal policy, the char-
> acter of both governments will be greatly deteriorated.

You can take it from there. It will not be difficult, on the basis
of President Buchanan's yardstick of one hundred years ago, to
determine about how far along the road of retrogression and deterioration we have gone since he spoke those prophetic words.

# VI

# Dishonest Dollars and Inflation

HONEST MONEY perhaps comes second only to man's trust in God and in the Natural Laws as a prime requirement of human freedom. Dishonest money has inevitably led to bankruptcy, destruction, and enslavement.

An honest dollar is one that can be exchanged upon demand for precious metal, such as gold.

It was Lenin who advocated the debasement of currency as a means to cause the self-destruction of the free nations of the world.

Before the welfare state was imposed upon America, the United States' dollar was a very highly prized currency throughout the world. It was based on the gold standard and at anytime, at any bank in America, it could be exchanged for $20.67 per oz. gold. The American dollar was prized because of the long-standing record of fiscal honesty of the American government, up to the advent of Franklin Roosevelt and his welfare state.

Today the American dollar is slipping rapidly to the bottom of the totem pole. No American is permitted even to possess gold, let alone exchange his paper dollars for it, but foreigners, upon demand, can get one ounce of gold for thirty-five American paper dollars.

As a result of the dishonest, irresponsible fiscal policy of the American government since 1933, the dollar has dropped in value to an astounding degree.

This is clearly shown by Hon. T. Coleman Andrews, former U.S. Commissioner of Internal Revenue, in the following article.

## How You Have Been Victimized

### T. COLEMAN ANDREWS

The federal government is spending eight times what it was in 1939. The federal tax collector has raised his take to nearly 28 times the 1939 income tax and over ten times the Social Security tax. The cost of living has more than doubled and is still going up. The values of the dollar has been reduced to well below 50 cents and is still going down!

What have these years of wastefulness and extravagance—which are the roots of our high taxes and inflation—done to us as individuals? And what do these evils have in store for us in the future?

The following three exhibits tell the unpleasant story frankly.

Obviously, impoverishing taxes and inflation are deteriorating our buying power so fast that our pocketbooks will be empty, years before 1975 rolls around. If this is allowed to happen—and it can be prevented—no power on earth will be strong enough to prevent development of a depression that will make the dark days of the '30's seem like an era of boisterous prosperity.

Inflation must and can be stopped. It cannot be stopped by more inflation. It can be stopped only by removing the causes. There are several causes, but the primary one is wasteful spending. Reprehensible on moral grounds, it is equally bad because it gives the government too *much* choice, and leaves the people too little choice, as to how their own income shall be spent.

Tax reduction is urgently needed. But tax reduction without equivalent expenditure reduction would invite resumption of deficit spending and intensify the forces that are driving prices up and thus make the already bad situation worse.

Any individual who gets into the habit of overspending his income has no choice but to balance his budget or suffer the shame of bankruptcy. It is the same with nations because a nation is but organized people. Its finances come only from its people. It cannot afford anything its people can't, and it cannot violate the rules of thrift and provident living without suffering the consequences that people do for the same offense.

Our government now finds itself trapped by an inflationary spiral of its own making. The alternatives are clear. Washington must either cut out the waste, get down to essentials and balance the budget, or go back to deficit spending. It does not appear likely that the government will balance the budget unless there is a grass-roots demand that it do so. If, therefore, there ever was a time for the people back home to build a fire under their congress-men, senators and the administration, this seems to be it.

## Exhibit A

Here is what high taxes and inflation have done to your income since 1939. Burdensome as taxes have become, this shows that inflation has become even more so. Inflation's assault upon our incomes has become especially vicious for those in the low income brackets.

All tax references are to the federal income tax only for single persons. Determinations of the effect of inflation are based upon the government's consumer price index.

| In 1939 | | In 1957 | Why? | |
|---|---|---|---|---|
| The recipient of a taxable income of | had left after taxes | The same amount of income after tax was worth only | because taxes had increased by | and inflation had taken |
| $ 2,000 | $ 1,975 | $    863 | $    215 | $    897 |
| 3,000 | 2,943 | 1,265 | 365 | 1,313 |
| 4,000 | 3,910 | 1,658 | 530 | 1,722 |
| 5,000 | 4,878 | 2,051 | 696 | 2,131 |
| 6,000 | 5,830 | 2,429 | 878 | 2,523 |
| 7,500 | 7,227 | 2,990 | 1,132 | 3,105 |
| 10,000 | 9,536 | 3,877 | 1,632 | 4,027 |
| 12,500 | 11,818 | 4,715 | 2,205 | 4,898 |
| 15,000 | 14,074 | 5,500 | 2,861 | 5,713 |
| 20,000 | 18,486 | 6,916 | 4,386 | 7,184 |
| 25,000 | 22,711 | 8,180 | 6,035 | 8,496 |
| 30,000 | 26,776 | 9,325 | 7,764 | 9,687 |
| 40,000 | 34,646 | 11,443 | 11,316 | 11,887 |
| 50,000 | 42,216 | 13,347 | 15,004 | 13,865 |

## Exhibit B

Here's how much income you needed in 1957 just to keep even with the purchasing power of your 1939 income, and why.

| In 1957 | | Why? | |
|---|---|---|---|
| You have to have a taxable income of | to match a 1939 income of | Because the increase would have entailed additional taxes of | and inflation already had taken |
| $   4,806 | $ 2,000 | $     755 | $ 2,051 |
| 7,370 | 3,000 | 1,313 | 3,057 |
| 10,097 | 4,000 | 2,036 | 4,061 |
| 13,004 | 5,000 | 2,937 | 5,067 |
| 16,098 | 6,000 | 4,042 | 6,056 |
| 21,178 | 7,500 | 6,171 | 7,507 |
| 30,971 | 10,000 | 11,066 | 9,905 |
| 41,840 | 12,500 | 17,064 | 12,276 |
| 54,208 | 15,000 | 24,589 | 14,619 |
| 83,476 | 20,000 | 44,274 | 19,202 |
| 121,044 | 25,000 | 72,453 | 23,591 |
| 162,689 | 30,000 | 104,876 | 27,813 |
| 248,111 | 40,000 | 172,123 | 35,988 |
| 333,377 | 50,000 | 239,526 | 43,851 |

## Exhibit C

The way things are going now, here's what it's going to take 16 years from now (in 1975) to make buying power as great as it was in 1939.

| In 1975 | | | |
|---|---|---|---|
| It will take a taxable income of | to match a 1939 income of | It will take an income of | to match a 1939 income of |
| $10,538 | $ 2,000 | $137,246 | $12,500 |
| 16,867 | 3,000 | 185,584 | 15,000 |
| 24,415 | 4,000 | 285,880 | 20,000 |
| 33,240 | 5,000 | 383,748 | 24,000 |
| 44,800 | 6,000 | 477,823 | 30,000 |
| 58,945 | 7,509 | 660,039 | 40,000 |
| 92,141 | 10,000 | 835,393 | 50,000 |

To further illustrate the dishonest, irresponsible fiscal policy of the federal government, the following article is reprinted from the *Economic Trend Line Studies* of April 13, 1959:

## Deficit Financing as a Fiscal Policy

As a fiscal policy our Nation's program of deficit financing had its inception in 1931. In only five years since then has the Nation operated with a surplus of income over expenditures. In twenty-four of the years since 1931 the Nation has operated with an excess of expenditures over its income. Deficit financing does not just happen when it is practiced so persistently and over such a long period of time. Here is the record since fiscal 1931 (for 1959 and 1960 we have used estimates) :

| Fiscal Year Ending June 30 | Deficit (−) Surplus (+) | Fiscal Year Ending June 30 | Deficit (−) Surplus (+) |
|---|---|---|---|
| | (In billions of dollars) | | |
| 1931 | $−0.5 | 1946 T | $−20.7 |
| 1932 | −2.7 | 1947 T | +0.8 |
| 1933 | −2.6 R * | 1948 T | +8.4 |
| 1934 | −3.6 R | 1949 T | −1.8 |
| 1935 | −2.8 R | 1950 T | −3.1 |
| 1936 | −4.4 R | 1951 T | +3.5 |
| 1937 | −2.8 R | 1952 T | −4.0 |
| 1938 | −1.2 R | 1953 E * | −9.4 |
| 1939 | −3.9 R | 1954 E | −3.1 |
| 1940 | −3.9 R | 1955 E | −4.2 |
| 1941 | −6.2 R | 1956 E | +1.6 |
| 1942 | −21.5 R | 1957 E | +1.6 |
| 1943 | −57.4 R | 1958 E | −2.8 |
| 1944 | −51.4 R | 1959 E | −12.9 (E) |
| 1945 | −53.9 T * | 1960 E | $−1.5 to −4.5 (E) |

\* R-Roosevelt; T-Truman; E-Eisenhower.

"High wages," "high prices," "high profits," etc., are not the causes of our inflation, as claimed by so many members of the Congress, economists and others. They are the results of the Nation's deficit financing. They are not the causes of an eroded dollar, they are the effects of an eroded dollar. The dollar erosion is caused by the consistent deficit financing of the National Government. Deficit financing has always been coin clipping, whether practiced by ancient governments, medieval governments or modern governments. Persistent deficit financing always wears away the value of the monetary unit. As long as they who can balance the budget of our National Government, the Congress, are able to blame inflation "on businessmen who continually raise our prices," on "unions who demand high wages," just so long will we have unbalanced budgets.

---

Perhaps one of the simplest explanations of inflation and dishonest dollars is the following statement by Fred G. Clark, General Chairman of the American Economic Foundation.

## Let's Face the Facts of Inflation

### FRED G. CLARK

### I

If you are average citizens, you are, according to the polls, ignorant about the basic causes of inflation and high prices.

And you have every reason to be, because the average citizen does not go to college and the basic laws of economics are not taught in our high schools.

And if, after you finished your formal education, you tried to learn about these things on your own, your confusion has been compounded by the conflicting statements of our politicians (in labor and government) and the self-appointed authorities whose writings appear in our leading newspapers, the net result being that you have gotten the cause of high prices all mixed up with the effect and vice versa.

Now that America is in an economic race with Russia for survival, it is high time that the truth be known about inflation and about the handicaps which, in our ignorance, we are allowing the politicians to place on our path in this life or death race.

If the truth is not made plain, and if the policies that cause high prices are not understood, there is danger that the American people will start demanding anti-inflation miracles from the politicians; and, in the field of economics, there are no miracles.

If we stick to simple fundamentals we do not have to be political scientists to understand what has been going on; we merely need to discard the ten-dollar words and the technical phrases that are now hiding the truth from us.

The truth is that prices are high for a very definite and simple reason, and no political party will do very much about it until we average citizens get wise and demand it.

## II

We can figure this thing out together.

To get off on the right foot, we must think of inflation, not in terms of the results (increased prices), but in terms of the cause (increased supply of money).

The story of our inflation starts in the year 1933.

At that time the Federal government announced its policy of driving up sluggish prices. There are only two ways of doing that: creating a scarcity of goods or creating an abundance of money.

The method used, the latter, was imported from England, devised by Professor Maynard Keynes, and the idea was to increase prices by having the government spend more money than it had: that is, the idea was to create new, *unearned* money through the banking system, add it to the money already in circulation and thus raise prices by reducing the purchasing power of *all* the money.

If you or I created and circulated this worthless money, we would be arrested for counterfeiting, but the Federal government can do it legally by causing banks to create and turn over to the government new, extra money in exchange for its I.O.U.'s.

This method of adding to the money supply, when explained in simple words, is not difficult to understand.

For example, the commercial banks could easily create some new money for you or me: all we need to do is take to the bank something of value, and pledge it against a loan.

The bank would then give us what is called a deposit against which we can write checks.

When the bank does this, the money supply of the nation is increased by the amount of our deposit or, put another way, by the amount of our debt to the bank.

While most of this new money of ours circulates in the form of checks, it is just as real as if it were paper or metal money.

## III

This new extra inflationary money created for us, as individuals, for our private use is short lived: it disappears from the nation's money supply as soon as we pay our debt to the bank. But the extra money created for government stays and stays and stays in the economy.

There is now more than 100 billion dollars of it in our system, and the most for which we can reasonably hope in the near future is that it will not get any worse.

This year, however, it seems that another $13 billion will be added.

The point most often forgotten is that high prices do not cause the issuance of this money: it is the issuance of this money that causes high prices.

The reason that this extra money increases prices is that it does not represent the production of any extra goods or services for which the money can be exchanged; the people simply use more dollars to produce and exchange the same quantity of goods and services.

We hear demands from some quarters for some sort of political or economic magic that will bring back the purchasing power of the dollar without reducing the number of dollars in the pay envelope.

This wishful thinking ignores the fact that the flood of new unearned money has forced the worker into chasing his own tail in an endless effort to keep his wages abreast of living costs, and that a great part of every raise he got was almost immediately taken from him by still higher prices.

These higher wages are called "social gains for labor," and the higher costs are called "greediness of the selfish interests."

As it happens, neither of these definitions is true.

## IV

One of the most frequently asked questions is: What is the reason that prices rise every time wages and salaries rise?

The reason is that selling prices are practically the same as wages and salaries.

To prove this point, take an average manufactured product selling for $10.

About eight and one half dollars must go for wages and salaries; that is, between the time the raw material is produced and the finished product passes into the hands of a customer, about eight and one half dollars is paid out in payrolls.

About one dollar must go for taxes, depreciation, and other unavoidable expense.

Eight and one half dollars plus one dollar is nine and one half dollars, leaving about 50 cents for payment (profit) to the people who supplied the tools of production which, on the average, account for about 95 per cent of the work performed on the product.

To be realistic, we must face the fact that when any substantial increase is made in wages, without a corresponding increase in hourly productivity, prices will go up.

It follows just as surely as night follows day.

## V

The basic trouble is that we have over 100 billion dollars of stage money in our economy and are seeking desperately to avoid the inevitable penalties of its presence.

The government started out in 1933 to inflate prices, and gave organized pressure groups a rational foundation on which to base demands for increased income. These demands, which have accelerated the upward price spiral, are not limited to farmers and organized labor, but include pressures for bigger appropriations for bigger budgets from most government bureaus because they, too, must pay higher prices for what they buy.

The "forgotten ones" in this whole procedure are those on fixed or near-fixed incomes, owners of savings accounts, life insurance, Federal savings bonds, and some 20,000,000 people trying to live on pensions and annuities.

## VI

In addition to the high cost of living, inflation creates two other problems.

One of these is a government problem.

Government has to spend billions of dollars for many things such as airplanes, missiles, aircraft carriers, etc., that take a long time to build.

When inflation is going on the cost of these things goes up between the time the money is appropriated and the time the contract is completed.

The original budget, therefore, is not enough.

This extra money must come either from more taxes or from the creation of more unearned money through the banking system thus adding more inflationary fuel to the fire.

The other problem is a business problem.

Inflation has made it enormously difficult for corporations to replace their obsolete or worn out equipment.

The reason is that the law permits business to set aside for the replacement of assets only an amount equal to the original purchase price.

If you had a $10,000,000 plant that was 20 years old and had to be replaced you would have only ten million tax free dollars with which to do it.

Inasmuch as the new plant would cost at least $20 million, probably a lot more, you would have to get the rest of the money out of profits (if you could) after paying about 50% Federal tax.

In other words, the replacement of your $10 million plant would require that you collect at least $30 million from your customers instead of the $10 million that would have been the case if inflation had not increased prices.

Today it is estimated that American industry is about $100 billion "light" on the amount needed to replace existing tools.

The effect this might have in our production race with the Soviets (who boast that they are catching up) should be a matter of far greater concern to the powers-that-be in Washington than is indicated by their indifference to the problem.

## VII

There are still many ignorant but optimistic people who want to keep prices down by law; who want to control prices by freezing profits and wages and shackling us once again to the ration book.

What they really mean is that they want to control the price tag on the product, which is a very different thing from controlling the cost to the customer.

There is nothing unique about the situation in which we find ourselves.

Since the beginning of recorded history, governments have been inflating currencies and they have been trying to avoid the consequences by passing laws against high prices.

The modern punishments for black marketeering are nothing compared to the historical methods used by desperate governments in their efforts to keep prices from going up as the money supply went up.

The histories of Egypt, China, Turkey, Assyria, Rome, England and Colonial America all bear testimony to the impossibility of repealing the law of currency inflation.

It would seem that the earlier types of punishment would have been effective, because they included nailing the offender's ears to his own door, amputation of hands, skinning alive, tearing in two, boiling in oil, branding, and exile.

But the laws of human nature and the laws of economics change for no government.

It would be childish to pretend that we have not violated the law that controls prices, and it is more than childish to believe that we can avoid the penalty of high prices.

The basic cause of high prices is the whopping amount of new unearned money that has been pumped into the American economic system.

Until we stop this we will accomplish nothing.

---

A remarkably clear warning against continuing our present dishonest and irresponsible fiscal policy comes from Dr. Wilhelm Vocke of rejuvenated Germany.

Doctor Vocke has been active in German banking affairs since 1912. Hitler dismissed him as a Managing Director of the Reichsbank in 1939. He was returned by the British, in the Hamburg Zone, in 1945. As President of the Bundesbank (the central bank of the Federal Republic of West Germany) he was a staunch supporter of Professor Ludwig Erhard, the Federal Minister of Economics, and his policies. When Dr. Vocke speaks of a stable currency he speaks from experience, not assumption or theory. The following is a condensation of remarks made in this country by Dr. Vocke on April 13, 1959.

## The Future of the Dollar

### DR. WILHELM VOCKE

You have invited me to discuss with you the problem of the dollar, which is a task that I approach with some hesitation since it concerns, after all, your country. Yet the issues that are involved clearly reach beyond national frontiers and indeed affect the world as a whole. There would be little value in my joining this debate on monetary problems if I thought the world were headed toward another war. But I firmly believe in peace—many years of peace; and I am convinced that the United States can promote peace most effectively not only through the power of its armaments, but through the strength of its financial system as well.

The current debate over the future of the dollar and economic growth has advanced to the stage where the issues are now clearly drawn. The choice is between the path of creeping inflation and that of a strong and stable dollar. A clear decision as to which path is to be taken must be made now in the interest of the business community and the nation, which must know the direction in which the economy is moving and how much trust can be placed in the currency. Things cannot be permitted to drift, creating uncertainty and confusion among longterm investors who must plan ahead and on whose appraisal of the future the economic growth of the country depends.

### Lessons of the German Experience

Let me first make a few observations on the German monetary experience, from which some fundamental lessons can be drawn. When I assumed office as President of the Bank Deutscher Lander ten years ago, monetary conditions in Germany were in a desperate state. Several experts, both German and foreign, with world-wide reputation and extensive experience declared frankly that the Deutsche mark had virtually no prospects of ever becoming a hard currency. That these well-meant opinions proved wrong, as time has shown, is no doubt in part due to a good deal of luck and favorable circumstances. But I, for one, never wavered in my conviction that a monetary policy, consistently and energetically pursued in order to establish and maintain a stable currency, must succeed.

There are perhaps two principal lessons to be learned from the German experience. The first is that currency stability can be achieved and preserved even under the most adverse circumstances. The second, and even more significant, is that a monetary policy, firmly committed to currency stability, not only does not conflict with a high rate of economic growth but indeed is essential to its achievement. Germany's remarkable economic recovery and expansion over the past decade was closely linked to the restoration and preservation of a strong and stable monetary unit.

Obviously, these policies did not escape the test of public opinion. In 1955 the German economy was unmistakably headed toward a dangerous boom. All economic indicators—production, employment, income, exports, and above all wages and prices—were surging upward at a high pitch. Under these conditions prompt and energetic measures by the central bank were called for, in order to keep the economy from losing balance. The steps taken to bridle the inflationary forces proved highly unpopular and were severely criticized by industrialists, government officials, and the public on the grounds that they would undermine economic growth. As matters turned out, none of the somber predictions came true. On the contrary, as a result of the early effort to defend the Deutsche mark, the economy quickly regained both its equilibrium and the basis for continued expansion in an orderly manner. This experience proves that a central bank must be persistent and unruffled in its pursuit of a determined course of action, and must not shrink from occasionally taking unpopular measures if its obligations and responsibilities to the nation are to be properly fulfilled. In Germany, such monetary measures had to be taken on several occasions in the face of widespread criticism. But now that the economy is vigorously moving forward at a high level of prosperity and on the basis of a stable currency, what were once unpopular policies have now become the object of rather general praise.

The experience in the rest of Western Europe has been much the same. Comprehensive monetary and fiscal measures have helped restore financial stability and have revitalized the economies. The United States may regard the accumulation of gold by these countries with mixed feelings, but the fact remains that the gold had to be earned by productive effort. After years of bitter experience with inflation, Western Europe has now turned to monetary stability. The rejection of policies leading to continual depreciation of the currency was dramatized last December when thirteen European countries took steps to make their currencies fully convertible.

## The "Creeping Inflation" Thesis

To a foreigner it seems almost absurd that there should be certain quarters in the United States where inflation is tolerated or even recommended. Surely any price to be paid for inflation must be excessive, considering not only the adverse economic and social effects, but the irretrievable losses in national prestige it may entail. The path of inflation in the United States would not only mean the depreciation and ultimate devaluation of the dollar, but also an acute decline in the moral authority, power, and international stature of the United States. That there are close links binding a nation's prestige to its financial posture is evident from the manner in which the emergence of the Deutsche mark as a sound and stable monetary unit has enhanced the stature of the new western Germany in the family of nations.

The arguments advanced by the advocates of inflation must be earnestly and thoroughly considered. To begin with, the arguments set forth are, above all, political in character. The inflationists purport to show that inflation is an inevitable tide that can be stemmed only at the cost of economic progress. Consequently, they say, the attitude toward inflation must be rendered more flexible, and economic doctrine and policy must be adapted to a new institutional setting instead of plodding along the old rut of a stable currency.

Certainly, the proponents of this thesis by no means favor galloping inflation, but only the mild, creeping kind. In fact, they would for the most part readily admit that even a moderate inflation entails certain evils. Nevertheless, they would argue also that, whatever these evils may be, they are far less serious or significant than the grave political repercussions bound to result from a policy that tolerates an impairment of full employment, however temporary. To the advocates of creeping inflation full employment and monetary stability are incompatible. And, if there exists a choice, the decision would have to be in favor of full employment, for political reasons. Superficially, at least, these arguments may appear more or less plausible, particularly since they rest on political considerations. Yet on closer examination their contradictory nature becomes self-evident.

Let us turn first to full employment. What does it mean and to what degree can it benefit the nation and the economy? If full employment should mean that the labor force is occupied 100 per cent, the law of supply and demand cannot function normally in the labor market, and there exists, in effect, a state of over-employment. Under such conditions, employers can expand output only by outbidding each other for the available work force and by drawing workers away from one another. Labor, in turn, is enabled virtually to dictate its own wages. Such a state of affairs clearly cannot be regarded as a desirable optimum for the nation or the economy, either in its domestic or international aspect.

It is also evident that in a free economy the level of employment cannot be maintained constant to any greater degree than the level of production, consumption, investment, or trade. But, while it may not be possible to eliminate economic fluctuations entirely, the magnitude and duration of the cycles can be at least minimized. In this connection, one ought to bear in mind that, even at fairly high levels of prosperity, it is easier to influence or control the oscillations in employment and business activity than to bridle a cumulative inflation which must eventually lead to the proverbial bust. Nonetheless, the proponents of creeping inflation recommend yielding to overemployment, continually rising wages, and the price-wage spiral, while declaring at the same time that what they envisage is merely an inflation that crawls along at the leisurely rate of, say, 2 per cent per annum. Let us examine how this invention will work.

## The Cumulative Process of Inflation

The initial phase of inflation has a certain appeal. Rising money income activates the economy like a breath of spring that brings out the blossoms everywhere. Industry invests and production expands; credit volume rises, with borrowers planning to repay loans in depreciated money as inflation progresses. Employment climbs, and for a considerable part of the population the standard of living actually increases as consumption moves up, while the incentives to save wane. All economic indexes surge upward, mutually reinforcing each other, and setting the inflationary spiral in motion. At this stage, and at this stage only, inflation finds many adherents. But this happy state is usually short-lived and lasts only as long as some faith in the currency is still maintained. Even while this phase continues, an increasing segment of the population, dependent on fixed incomes, begins to feel the ruthless grip of the inflationary pressures.

The inflationists have a remedy at hand for the sectors that are squeezed between rising prices and lagging incomes: the escalator clause. This clause, which automatically links wages, salaries, and even some business transactions to the cost-of-living index or gold, was widely used in France, but with results that proved far from encouraging. In fact, the escalator clause is merely an illusion. As long as the depreciation of the currency is minor, the clause is not invoked. And when inflation progresses, it is satisfactory neither to income receivers nor to income payers; meanwhile the government is forced to inflate to an even greater extent, in order to compensate those groups that remain unsheltered by the index clause. More importantly, however, the escalator clause, in itself, officially discredits the currency and therefore intensifies inflation. Moreover, what it clearly reveals is that, once the currency no longer serves as a stable standard of value, a substitute must be found. Since stability is, after all, essential, the absurdity of abandoning a stable standard of value in the first place becomes patently obvious.

All the various adaptations, compensations, and adjustments to a rising price level may well be bearable as long as inflation remains within narrow limits. But the fact is that inflation is progressive and eventually becomes full-blown. That point is reached when the public begins to lose faith in the currency and the material-value psychosis spreads. The scramble for goods is matched only by the rush into equity investments, while the bond market sags. The damage that inflation inflicts on the market for fixed-interest securities eventually makes it virtually impossible for the government to consolidate its short-term debt. For no one will acquire bonds when the money invested continually shrinks. The inevitable consequence is that the central bank will be asked to absorb the unmarketable public debt, which adds further fuel to the inflationary surge.

The reluctance to hold money or fixed-interest securities finds expression also in the rapid decline in savings. Wasteful consumption and misdirected investments suddenly become rational economic actions, compared with the foolishness of saving money that is rapidly becoming worthless. At this point the reckless spendthrifts and speculators are proved right and amass fortunes, while the honest, conscientious, and weak lose the little they have. As the process continues, customary standards of behaviour are swept away and accepted moral attitudes are shattered. Soon everyone flees from the currency and joins in the furious dance of inflation, while the nation is rapidly moving to the brink of disaster.

The succession of events that I have just outlined would probably be considered a gross exaggeration by the proponents of creeping inflation. They would assert that the idea is not to let the inflation get out of hand, but to confine it to a delightful 2 per cent per annum. How is this feat to be accomplished? Obviously, inflation cannot be kept automatically within prescribed limits. There is no stable coefficient of inflation. Once begun, inflation spreads like fire and feeds on itself. Moreover, even if a limited depreciation of the dollar is envisaged, the public will try to protect itself, and by doing so will inevitably accelerate the pace of the price rise. Stability of the rate of inflation is an illusion, for if the public knows there will be a creeping inflation of 2 per cent per annum then the 2 per cent will be reached not at the end of the year, but at the beginning, and the pressure for inflation will mount.

Since inflation is not self-regulating, by what method would the advocates of creeping inflation confine it to the predetermined limits? One answer is by credit policy, including restrictions on the volume of borrowing and increases in the rediscount rate. But the applications of such measures would be precisely those which the inflationists had sought to avoid in the first place. This means in effect that, while the inflationist would not be prepared to sacrifice full employment to monetary stability, he would nevertheless be disposed to sacrifice it for the sake of keeping the rate of inflation within arbitrary limits. The contradictory nature of the creeping inflation thesis now becomes self-evident.

We may even go one step further. What is really meant by a 2 per cent rate of inflation? If it refers to the average price level, and not to the prices of individual commodities, say, straw hats or the wages of particular workmen on the bench, then the statisticians may well find that, after they have assembled and averaged the prices of all the separate commodities, the actual rate of inflation has surpassed the stipulated maximum. The consequence might then be the application of an elaborate network of physical controls over individual prices and wages. Adoption of a policy that is defined in terms of hitting a rigid target for average prices greatly increases the chances of detailed regulation to assure its fulfillment. Such economic regimentation would severely shatter the foundations upon which this nation was built and radically alter its way of life. Inflation inevitably breeds economic controls, regimentation, and moral corruption.

## The International Aspect of Inflation

Let me now touch briefly on the international aspect of the creeping inflation thesis. During my years as President of the Bank Deutscher Lander, that institution accumulated and kept a considerable amount of dollar assets in this country as backing for the Deutsche mark. Other central banks did likewise. And today, foreign central banks alone hold almost $10 billion here as part of their international reserves. These substantial holdings reflect the confidence of the world in the strength and stability of the United States dollar. One should hasten to note, however, that this faith in the dollar is by no means unshakable, and developments affecting its future are closely watched abroad.

There can be little doubt that a green light for creeping inflation would entail grave international repercussions. Acceptances of the doctrine—which to me is virtually unthinkable—would severely undermine the position of the United States dollar and would set in motion forces leading to its rapid replacement by gold as an international standard and store of value. The inevitable result would be a massive withdrawal of foreign dollar balances and heavy gold losses for the United States. Under these circumstances the question of raising the price of gold and hence the devaluation of the dollar would again arise. I have not discussed this issue here; suffice it to say, however, that there are few things that I would regard as more detrimental to the United States and to the world than an increase in the dollar price of gold.

For all reasons stated, nothing must be permitted to give the world the impression that the stability of the dollar is in doubt. For any action that might signify yielding to the inflation thesis would involve irretrievable losses to the United States and would inflict immeasurable damage to the international monetary mechanism.

## Concluding Comments

As a final word I may ask what there is to be gained by setting free the forces of inflation, except a postponement of the unavoidable adjustments that every economy must make sooner or later. It is certainly easier and less painful to curb incipient inflation or moderate the magnitude and duration of economic fluctuations than to tame an inflation that has reached the stage where only drastic deflationary remedies can be administered to restore balance. The measures taken in the United States last year illustrate that recession need not turn into depression and can be short-lived even without turning on the engines of inflation. Inflation essentially means weakness and thus cannot furnish a sound or lasting basis for economic progress. It is the line of least resistance, and not the road to an effective solution of economic problems or to the realization of economic aspirations.

We are living in a critical period in which courageous decisions must be made in order to win the struggle for freedom. This struggle, however, cannot be successfully waged by yielding to the disease of inflation, whether creeping, crawling, or any other kind.

The United States need not fall victim to the grip of inflation if that be the nation's firm will. But any wavering in the determination to preserve the strength and stability of the dollar may lose the battle before it is even begun. I am confident that the underlying beliefs and traditions of this country are strong enough to give unhesitating expression to the will to preserve monetary stability on which much of the power and moral authority of the nation rest.

The words of President Eisenhower and the firm attitude of the Federal Reserve System leave no doubt that the right choice is being made. This should be recognized throughout the world. And, as the spectre of inflation is dispelled, the future of the dollar as the world's best monetary unit continues to be assured. One of the qualities that has rendered this country strong and powerful has been common sense. If common sense is to continue to guide American policies, the stability of the dollar cannot be in doubt.

---

But will reason and common sense prevail? It is a moot question. The first thing is that the spenders have to be checked and honest attempts made promptly to reduce the national debt which has become a peril to the nation's life.

This is sharply pointed up by Thurman Sensing of the Southern States Industrial Council.

## The National Debt Peril

### THURMAN SENSING

President Eisenhower's assurance that his next budget will show a $4.2 billion surplus came as a pleasant surprise to the American people. Equally pleasant was the President's stated desire that the surplus be applied to the retirement of the national debt.

But whether this surplus will materialize is yet to be seen. The end of the next fiscal year is still eighteen months away. We have seen many such optimistic budget surplus predictions melt away in recent years like snowflakes on a Spring day. Moreover, the estimate of a surplus is based entirely on increased income. The best way to assure a surplus is to reduce expenses. This was not advocated.

Senator Harry F. Byrd (D–Va.), the watchdog of the U.S. Treasury, is reported as being baffled as to where the money for the surplus is coming from. And no doubt he has in mind that Congressional spenders—in both political parties—will view any surplus as a melon ripe for cutting. The Foreign-Aiders, the Welfare-Statists, and the Share-America advocates undoubtedly will do their utmost to spend more instead of lowering the national debt.

The need for debt retirement is very pressing. Senator Byrd, in a recent speech before the American Farm Bureau Federation, addressed himself to this subject. Federal deficit financing, he pointed out, has been the rule for more than a quarter of a century. "But," he noted, "the fiscal situation in the United States government deteriorated faster in fiscal years 1958-59 than in any comparable peacetime period during my 26 years in the Senate." In this two-year period the nation twice was forced to raise the statutory limit on federal debt. "Today," said the Senator, "the federal debt is at its all-time peak in the history of this republic. The debt is now $292.5 billion."

This terrible burden of debt is the result of 24 deficits in the past 29 years. Half of these deficits were incurred during the years when the United States was fighting neither war nor economic depression. Senator Byrd cited the appalling fact that there have been "four deficits totaling $23 billion since the Korean War was stopped."

The grave meaning of this debt has yet to be made clear to the American people. For if they understood what it meant, they surely would demand that their representatives in Congress hew the line of fiscal responsibility. They would call for drastic cuts in federal spending on such boondoggles as foreign aid and farm subsidies, which account for more than $10 billion a year!

Senator Byrd is no scaremonger. A sound, unemotional man, he does not say that the United States is doomed. What he does say is this: "When individuals become insolvent they take bankruptcy and dispose of their obligations. When governments become insolvent their money becomes worthless and they go through a revolution wringer. The nature of the revolutions may vary, but change in the form of government is inevitable."

We need look no farther than France, where bankruptcy was imminent not many months ago, for a good illustration. They solved the problem by accepting a virtual dictatorship. Is that what we want?

This, then, is the danger the nation faces when its representatives don't take steps to live within a budget and reduce astronomical debt. Tragically, American complacency about such fundamental issues is amazing. The national weakness of character in this respect is ominous. Unless Congress can reform and hold expenditures to a reasonable level, cut down some of the mountain of debt being piled up for future generations, the prospect of this republic enjoying personal liberty and a free economy is bleak indeed. The task of curbing the unreason of the spenders is one that must be pursued.

---

The key to the whole problem of financial irresponsibility on the part of government is well summed up in the following editorial taken from the *Indianapolis* (Ind.) *Star*.

## How to Stop Big Spending

How can the American people stop the ever-growing government spending in Washington? Only by demanding that Congress reduce the taxes it imposes on them. The Congresses of the last 20 years have rarely reduced spending except by reducing taxes.

In 1960 the Federal government will spend over $100,000,000,000 including the $20,000,000,000 for trust funds for highways, social security and the like. Together with state and local taxes, government will take 30 per cent of the nation's income in 1960. The administration has been spending $8,000,000,000 in foreign aid and support programs every year. There is a Federal payroll of over $20,000,000,000. And very little has been done to save the $7,500,-000,000 Congress is wasting each year by not putting the saving recommendations of the Hoover Commission into effect.

These tremendous sums of money come from nowhere else but your pocket. By 30 per cent your freedom to spend what you earn has already been taken away from you. The beginning of this fast growing expansion of Federal spending was in 1913, with the imposition of the income tax. The income tax has become since then a vast engine of burgeoning bureaucracy and an engine of government stimulated inflation. It has made possible the government establishment of tax-free businesses and industries that now comprise over 20 per cent of the nation's industrial capacity.

Every American citizen is in debt to the government by $5,700. The average tax load on every American family is $2,400 a year in all forms of taxation. The national debt is $292,000,000,000. IOUs for future payment of veterans and government employes and other retirement programs are another $350,000,000,000. The Federal government is obligated to spend an additional $98,000,000,000, on roads, public works and housing. The real total debt of your government is thus around $750,000,000,000—more than the entire national gross product and almost double the total wages and income of our people.

There is only one way to stop this growing debt, this heavier tax burden, this erosion of the people's right to spend what they earn and to be free from the prying eyes and heavy hand of the tax collector. That is to demand major surgery on the nation's tax structure, not just minor changes that might well be soon changed right back. The income tax is a dangerous tax—as can be seen by its history. It has been made even worse by adding the withholding provision, which not only forces employers to do the government's tax collecting for it—without compensation—but also seizes part of every worker's pay check before he even sees it.

Even another small cut in income taxes is not likely to stop the big flow of our tax dollars to Washington. In 1954 taxes were cut 10 per cent. Yet in 1960 government will collect almost $20,000,-000,000 more in taxes than in 1954! The cost of the Federal government has increased by $16,000,000,000 since the Korean War. The national debt has increased by $13,000,000,000.

Government spending is virtually out of control. No real efforts have been made by Congress to cut either spending or taxes. A constant inflation has accompanied this massive Federal spending, cutting the value of our dollars, but not cutting the cost of our taxes. According to the Tax Foundation, a married man with $3,000 in income paid $269 Federal taxes in 1942 when the rates were about the same as today. In 1959 a man with the same income would pay the equivalent of $716 in taxes, when they are adjusted to the rise in consumer prices. Consumer prices have increased by 77 per cent. But this man's taxes have increased by 166 per cent! Inflation, caused by government spending, has in fact become an additional tax on our incomes.

Not only does the income tax seize large chunks of our incomes. It also causes us all extra expenses and extra effort just to figure out our taxes and try to avoid paying more than we owe. This is especially true of corporation income taxes. As Dr. Emerson P. Schmidt has written in "The Annals" of the American Academy of Political and Social Science, "The taxpayer, whether individual or corporate, is increasingly making his business and economic decisions in terms of minimizing his tax burden. This drains energy and ingenuity from constructive economic activity to the negative activities of tax avoidance. . . . Vast armies of high salaried attorneys as well as business executives devote a prodigious amount of time, energy and resources to minimize the tax burden. A significant reduction or elimination of the corporate income tax would not only reduce this misallocation of resources, but would encourage industrial modernization and new investment which, in turn, would lead to lower real prices." Elimination of the personal income tax would, as we have pointed out, have the same effect.

"The cost of living today is three and one-half times as high as it was just after the turn of the century," says the Institute of Life Insurance. "By a striking coincidence, total government spending has risen three and three-quarters times as fast as economic activity during this period (which coincided with the life of the income tax)." Not only has inflation resulted, but "considering today's tax burden and its impact on savings, capital formation and incentive, excessive growth of government spending tends to become a drag on the growth of the economy rather than a stimulus."

Every attempt to make a major reduction in spending and taxing has failed—except in 1946 when the "do nothing Congress" reduced both substantially. It is obvious that merely to try to change the income tax structure will neither stop government spending nor reduce taxes. Only a bold and all-out attack on the income tax aiming at its abolition can do this. This is the key to the whole problem.

———

Charles B. Shuman, President of the American Farm Bureau Federation, the largest and most influential farm organization in the country, was guest speaker, April 19, 1959, on the radio forum conducted by Clarence Manion, former Dean of Notre Dame Law School.

In this address Mr. Shuman discussed the problem of inflation, as related to all phases of our national economy. His powerful voice needs to be heard by all.

## Inflation—The Handmaid of Socialist-Communism

### CHARLES B. SHUMAN

The big question today is: What is inflation? It is simply a constantly rising price level with the resulting decline in the purchasing power of money.

We are in the midst of a long sustained period of inflation. During the last 18 years, the prices of goods and services have doubled in the United States. In other words, the dollar of 18 years ago is now worth 50 cents. The price of a pair of shoes up from $5 to $12, gasoline from 14¢ to 31¢ per gallon, the carpenter's wages from $1.50 to $3.00 per hour.

The $750 that you invested in a Government bond ten years ago was the cash difference between your old tractor or your old car and a new one. Today you would need to add more money to the $1,000 from the bond to make the same trade.

Higher wages cause higher prices which bring on demands for another wage hike and so on until the bitter end. This is inflation!

Inflation—what does it do to you?

Constantly rising prices destroy much of the value of insurance policies, annuities, social security, pension and other savings plans for old age. The incentive to save is reduced. Capital for business, industry and agriculture becomes scarce. Unemployment increases because of reduced investments in factories and tools.

With either gradual or rapid inflation, savers become spenders as they lose confidence in the value of tomorrow's dollar. Young people find their savings for the education of their children or the business they hope to own is destroyed by inflation more rapidly than it accumulates.

Yes, inflation hurts us all. Inflation is short-changing today's citizens and threatening to bankrupt the next generation. Inflation is the Nation's number one economic problem.

This short-changing, or failure to receive full value of income dollars, has reached a serious stage when the purchasing power of the United States dollar has been cut in half in 18 years.

Worse yet, if the inflationary trend continues at the present rate, it appears that the dollar's purchasing power will be cut in half again in the next 18 years.

If allowed to continue unchecked, inflation could well destroy the value of our dollar, bringing economic ruin to the Nation. And I need not tell you how the men in the Kremlin would feel about that.

The recent collapse of the French Government was largely due to long continued inflation by failure of government to live within its means.

As the value of the dollar is robbed, so is the value of savings, insurance policies, social security payments, and pensions. By causing a continual depreciation of the dollar's value, inflation hurts more and more people—hitting hardest those least able to afford it.

Inflation—What are its causes?

After the Civil War, it was printing press money issued to avoid tax increases to pay Government debts. Today, there are two major causes—the continuous round of wage-price increases and excessive spending of the Federal Government.

During World War II, there was a logical excuse for huge Federal budget deficits—but why should they continue for 13 years?

It is easy to spend money, especially when it does not seem to belong to anyone. Demands by citizens for Federal aid for highways, schools, river dams, slum clearance, airports and hundreds of other desirable projects, plus additional billions for foreign aid, veterans' benefits, and farmer ACP payments add up to deficit financing and great inflationary pressure.

When Government spends more than it takes from the taxpayers, it competes for goods and services and drives prices up with money that has not been earned.

Excessive Government spending long has been recognized as an important cause of inflation. Government creates inflationary pressures whenever it spends beyond its income.

Why don't we do something about it?

All new demands for Federal money in the form of such things as aid to schools and highway construction in addition to the old demands, such as funds for payment to farmers and subsidized housing for cities, are based on the assumption that the Federal Government is in a better position to deal with such matters than are the states. Such an assumption is not based in fact, however.

With the exception of a few states, which are in financial trouble, most states are not as heavily in debt in proportion to their population as is the Federal Government.

With the present Federal debt level, the only ways the Federal Government can distribute aid to states are to (1) increase taxes or (2) further depreciate the value of the dollar through deficit spending.

Farmers as well as manufacturers and other businessmen will suffer from the continued effects of inflation. The farming business today is similar to other businesses in that it has high cash inputs, such as fuel and equipment used in production.

The cost of these supplies is going up very rapidly as a result of inflation. With agriculture today plagued by surpluses and yet having the ability to produce even more commodities, it is clear that inflation intensifies the cost squeeze on farmers by causing farm costs to rise more rapidly than farm prices.

I repeat, there are two major inflationary pressures at work and both are, in a sense, either Government induced or sanctioned. One is the wage-price spiral, where strongly organized labor asks for and gets wage increases not necessarily based on increased productivity.

Many times, industry's resistance to unjustified wage demands is not as great as it should be. Too often, big business and big labor sit across the bargaining table to establish wage rates and selling prices of manufactured products with little regard for the consumer's interests. In my opinion, this happened three years ago in the steel wage settlement. Let us hope that it is not repeated this year.

The second pressure at work to cause inflation is that created by Government when it spends more than it takes in, thus competing for goods and services, driving prices up with money that has not been earned.

We in agriculture recognize that present excessive costs of the Federal farm program are contributing to the huge Federal deficit.

Changes in farm legislation advocated by the Farm Bureau, if adopted by Congress, would result in a gradual return to a market price system for farm products and the elimination of controls.

Government pricing and attempts to control farm production are proven failures. Sufficient evidence of the fact is the current $8 billion worth of Government-held surplus farm commodities.

There is no easy panacea for agriculture's troubles, but there has never been a greater need to make a start toward allowing the market rather than the Government to be the determining pricing factor in agriculture.

We believe every means should be used to eliminate the excessive accumulation of surplus agricultural production, to restore the farmer's freedom to grow crops he chooses, to allow prices to respond to supply and demand, and to reduce costs of farm programs to taxpayers.

The Farm Bureau's proposal for Federal farm price supports is based on setting supports at a percentage of the average market price of a commodity for the immediately preceding three years.

In contrast to the present system of using a percentage of parity, an outmoded system based on arbitrary formulas and administrative decisions, the Farm Bureau program would take account of competitive conditions, supply and demand, and market trends of farm products.

Unfortunately, serious consideration is being given by some members of Congress to a variety of proposals which have a common denominator—that of making direct payments from the Federal Treasury to farmers. Generally, these schemes envision payments large enough to bridge the gap between the market price of a commodity and a support goal based on a high percentage of parity.

Regardless of the form in which it is presented, the production or income payment scheme would stimulate production, depress market prices, and make farmers dependent on Congressional appropriations for their net farm income and probably a part of their costs as well. I might add that this, of course, would increase the inflationary pressures that are already running rampant.

I think you would agree that there are enough demands made on the Federal Treasury now without adding more than four million farmers to Uncle Sam's pay-roll. In effect, that would be tripling the present number of civilians employed by the Federal Government.

Since the size of the check to the individual farmers would have to be based on production, it follows that payments would stimulate production into a vicious chain reaction of more crops, more Government payment, more crops, more Government payment, and so forth.

Under such a system, it would not be long until farming would become a political privilege, to be divided among as many voters as possible regardless of efficiency—one share, one vote.

Inflation—who wants it?

A rabid speculator—a bureaucrat working on Government programs—a Congressman who likes to dispense favors to the folks back home—a United States Senator who advocates deficit spending and inflation to assure a "healthy, expanding economy which can produce the goods and services we need."

It is called "putting the Nation's needs ahead of a balanced budget." This is not the way we became the strongest nation on earth with the highest standard of living ever known—this is the road France followed to her ruin.

The competitive enterprise economy in the United States, which has brought us these things (the highest standard of living of any country in the world) depends in large part on capital from invested savings.

Inflation, especially in its later stages, strikes at capitalism by discouraging savings. If long continued, it results in capital shortages which will reduce productivity and reduce the number of jobs available to labor.

In fact, one of the present troubles with unemployment is undoubtedly a result of two things—the fixing of wages and prices by the monopoly power of big business and big labor, which has priced products of industry out of the market, and the inflationary spiral which has discouraged savings which have been needed to expand plants and to buy more tools to put more people to work.

There are three needs to combat inflation:

1. Monopoly and price fixing powers which big labor and big business have today must be curbed.

2. Spending by the Federal Government should be reduced to the level of its income—in short, balance the budget.

3. Citizens must take a greater interest in local and state governmental affairs and improve their ability to perform necessary government functions at the local level.

A lot of talk has been going around about Socialism and the dangers of Socialism. What is Socialism? It is simply big government and its domination of the decisions on the affairs of individuals. Communism is Socialism with the whip. Communists say that the failure of Socialism is because it doesn't use force.

If we in this Nation look around us, we will see that the record discloses that both Communism and Socialism fail. They fail because they disregard the great moral and ethical principles and the incentives that have made the people in this Nation work for the things they want.

If we do not discontinue the continued pressure of inflation, if we don't set our financial house in order, we strike a serious blow at the structure that has made for success in this Nation.

# VII

# TVA

*Socialism's Pride and Showplace*

THE TENNESSEE VALLEY AUTHORITY is a government corporation created in 1933 by Act of Congress for the primary purpose of harnessing the Tennessee River and its main tributaries to promote navigation and control floods.

Toward this end, TVA was authorized to construct dams and reservoirs, and "so far as may be consistent with such purposes" and "to avoid the waste of water power," TVA could "provide and operate facilities for the generation of electric energy."

The Act further authorized TVA to transmit and sell any of this energy over and above its own operating requirements and the needs of other federal agencies. But in disposing of the surplus, TVA was directed to "give preference to States, counties, municipalities and cooperative organizations of citizens or farmers, not organized or doing business for profit, but primarily for the purpose of supplying electricity to its own citizens or members."

But only about fifteen years later, TVA seemed to have forgotten what the law said, and came forward to ask for funds to construct a steam-powered electric generating plant. This would have nothing to do with flood control or navigation. It would remove, too, the limitation that the power TVA has for sale is surplus power.

It would, in fact, mean the out-and-out establishment of the government in the power business.

And this is what has happened. TVA has fashioned a vast empire for itself. It has its steam plants. It has extended its operations far outside the actual watershed area. It produces power for all but a small bit of the State of Tennessee and for portions of six neighboring States, an overall area of 80,000 square miles.

In the hearings held on the question of steam-powered plants for TVA, the House Committee on Appropriations noted that the approval of such action "will justify unlimited future expansion of the electric generating facilities by TVA by means of steam plants or other methods having nothing to do with navigation or flood control."

In fact, the Committee found that "there is presented a serious question of whether the TVA has a constitutional right to engage commercially in the development and sale of power."

The report on the investigation of Federal power projects by the House Appropriations Committee, dated December 20, 1948, further stated:

> In general, federal power is not cheap but can be made to appear so by allocating substantial portions of the investment and expense to other than power. Also, our studies indicate that if the federal project paid taxes at the level paid by privately-owned utilities, the federal rates would be higher than the rates of privately-owned utilities in the contiguous areas.

But TVA marches on—the pride of the socialists and a threat to freedom. Federalization of the power business in one area of the country clearly establishes a precedent for federalization in other parts of the country. Nationalization of one business also establishes a precedent for nationalization of other businesses. These things are happening in countries abroad; the danger is imminent that they can happen here on even a vastly larger scale than they have already happened.

These facts are exactly stated, even though in slightly different words, by one Dwight D. Eisenhower, not as President of the United States, but in 1945 when he was installed as President of Columbia University:

> Government ownership or control of property is not to be decried principally because of the historic inefficiency of governmental management of productive enterprises; its real threat rests in the fact that,

if carried to the logical extreme, the final concentration of ownership in the hands of government gives to it, in all practical effects, absolute power over our lives.

With these various points firmly nailed down by official statements, we can now turn with a clearer understanding to other authorities.

## Socialism Makes Nobody Richer

### How Public Power Has Failed in Two "Showplaces"

#### L. ROBERT DRIVER

To read the outpourings by politicians from what you might call the "Take-Away States"—like those in the TVA area or the Pacific Northwest, where millions have been spent on vast dams and public power plants—one might reasonably conclude that everybody in those regions was richer than Americans in other places. New industries are supposed to flock in to profit from cheap electricity and the other advantages offered by these great socialistic enterprises. Thousands of visitors from all over the world put TVA high on their list of the American sights worth seeing.

Similarly, a few decades ago, Americans flocked to Sweden to observe the operation of the "Middle Way," touted by Marquis Childs as the perfect "mixed economy." American tourists rode in buses to watch workers in a socialist sausage plant turn out bologna, probably less efficiently than it was done in the local packing plant in their home towns. Even in the United States, people who accept as a matter of course the functioning of a private power plant become awe-struck when they see the same thing done by a Government "authority"—at the taxpayer's expense.

As with all grandiose socialist projects, TVA has received frenzied salvos of praise from a variety of sources. *The Washington Post* called TVA "one of the greatest of American successes" and rebuked President Eisenhower for referring to it "sneeringly" as "creeping socialism." If the President's remark is open to criticism, it is for the use of "creeping," because the TVA brand of socialism is really on the gallop. John Gunther, the inside-everywhere man, thinks that "quite possibly the TVA is the greatest single American invention of the century, the biggest contribution the United States has yet made to society in the modern world." (Ah there, Thomas Jefferson!)

Senator Lister Hill reported in a speech how the symbol of TVA is revealed: "when the lights go on at nightfall they shine out at dusk from barns, from kitchens, and from parlors deep in the coves and high on the hillsides." Why can't Consolidated Edison or Duquesne Power and Light be the beneficiaries of oratory like that?

Tennessee is one of the most widely advertised states in the country and it is known in most foreign countries by reason of the TVA. The annual report of TVA for the fiscal year ended June 30, 1957, is a 300-page affair with many beautiful pictures and maps. It would lead one to believe that it is the most prosperous part of the country. Then, too, Tennessee gets much free advertising in the *Congressional Record*. Its Governor and two Senators are very vocal.

It would be ridiculous to disparage Tennessee or its people. Tennessee has a great history and a vigorous present. All this article is intended to do is raise these questions: "Has socialism as exemplified in TVA done Tennessee any good, beyond providing artificially cheap electric power at the expense of the rest of the Nation? If TVA is such an epochal step upward from the Capitalistic morass, does it show in the figures?" And the answer to both these questions is "NO."

This is remarkable, since the taxpayers of the country have poured into Tennessee as much as $4.6 billion, of which about $1.2 billion is invested in TVA. The Atomic Energy Commission has spent another $1.7 billion in the state for plants alone. Then Tennessee got another $1.7 billion as grants-in-aid and for direct relief—not including social security or flood-control work furnished by the Army Engineers. Well-paid technicians and bureaucrats have come to the state to operate the installations set up by the Federal Government. According to Senator Estes Kefauver, TVA "has altered the face of the earth and certainly has altered the nature of our economy and our way of living." Only "a relatively unfriendly Administration and an extremely unfriendly Bureau of the Budget" have prevented the miracle from being even more miraculous.

All this pump priming ought to show up in the prosperity figures, but it doesn't, as can be shown by the Government's own statistics. The U.S. Department of Commerce has published figures showing the per capita income of persons from 1929 to the present time-by states. The last year available is 1957. The people of Tennessee are, of course, far better off than they were in 1934, as it is true of the rest of the Nation. But relative to the gains made by other states, Tennessee has slipped back.

In 1934, 40 states could show at least as much per capita income as Tennessee; by 1957, 42 states were ahead of her. Although 57 per cent of the investments in plant and property of TVA are in Tennessee, and although the increase in per capita income of Tennessee residents in 1957 was 476 per cent greater than in 1934, in Georgia, with less than one per cent of the TVA investment, the increase was 497 per cent.

The per capita income in the farm states, which are supposed to be poorer than church mice, increased far more than in Tennessee—North Dakota, 711 per cent; South Dakota, 756 per cent; Iowa, 574 per cent; and Nebraska, 613 per cent.

Tennessee's failure to keep up with the pace in national economic progress is also indicated by the fact that, while in 1934 she paid .74 per cent of all corporation income taxes collected in the Nation, by 1956 her percentage had dropped to .59 per cent.

As evidence of the fact that the billions of dollars poured into Tennessee by the taxpayers of the other 47 states have not helped much, I quote Senator Albert Gore of Tennessee, one of TVA's major prophets. Early in the present recession, he cried out that they had "bread lines" in Tennessee and should have more Federal relief.

The bankruptcies in Tennessee were 2.43 times as many per thousand of population as those in the United States as a whole. The ratio for Oregon was 3.13 times as many as for the Nation as a whole. As against individual states which have had little Federal aid, the two showplaces for socialist experimentation showed up even worse. Thus the Tennessee bankruptcy record was 89.09 times that of "backward" South Carolina, while Oregon's bankruptcies were 115 times those of the Palmetto State. Tennessee's bankruptcies were 2.4 times those in Idaho, a state served by privately owned utility companies.

Even horse for horse, the contrast is extra-ordinary. Thus Tennessee, with its population of 3,400,000 had 3,699 bankruptcies, as against 595 in Pennsylvania, whose population is about 11,000,000. Incidentally, Arkansas, which has a population of a little more than half that of Tennessee, has only 216 bankruptcies. Arkansas is not included in the TVA area. Oregon, where public power flourishes, has 2,170 bankruptcies against 281 in Idaho whose population is slightly more than a third that of Oregon. Adjusted according to population, Oregon's bankruptcies were 3.1 times those of Idaho.

Here again, for whatever it is worth, the people of Idaho are served by the Idaho Power Company, whose readiness and competence to build dams to add to its already good service has been fought tooth and nail by the public power bloc in the Senate—Gore, Morse, Neuberger, Kefauver, *et al.*

Perhaps this means that in the vibrantly stimulating atmosphere created by TVA and the Grand Coulee Dam, small businessmen are inspired to take risks they would not take in the stagnant environments of less progressive areas, and consequently fall on their faces. But whatever the interpretation, the figures are there, suggesting that Federal spending however lavish does not tend to trickle down to the ordinary businessman or worker.

None of this is taken into account by public power propagandists who are tirelessly promoting their case through speeches in Congress, later distributed under Government frank, as well as by institutional advertising of the kind frowned upon by the Internal Revenue Service when sponsored by private utility companies.

Undoubtedly the improvement of the lot of the people in the Middle South was in the minds of the founders of TVA. In his book, *The Democratic Roosevelt,* Rexford Tugwell declares that it was Roosevelt's purpose that TVA should improve the lot of all the people in the area "by improving the soil, preventing floods and erosion, and assisting them economically." Doubtless TVA technicians have had a hand in improving the soil. They have prevented floods by flooding more land than the disastrous floods of the past used to cover.

The Army Engineers spend some $22 million a year, in Tennessee alone, for these purposes but get little credit from TVA. The new lakes are being widely advertised as recreation areas. Accomplishment in "assisting them economically" is hardly provable, since the improvement in Tennessee's economic condition is less than that recorded in other Southern States unblessed by TVA. What appears not to concern Tugwell any more than it bothered his New Deal associates is the fact that the cost of improving the lot of one area had to be borne by the people of the whole U.S.A. More than 99 per cent of the TVA costs in Tennessee were borne by taxpayers from other states. Tennessee has never paid as much as one per cent of the Federal taxes.

This means that members of labor unions, in Detroit, for example, must contribute some part of their income to Tennessee. Not only is this true, but the users of electric energy in communities served by privately owned electric companies have to furnish the money to cover all taxes paid by private companies. The TVA pays none, and its exemption from major taxes is even more beneficial than the free capital contributed.

Whatever the condition of their logical processes, the TVA bloc, and public power propagandists all over, are very much in earnest. Last session they managed to get through the Senate a "self-financing bill"—a device to bypass Congress and the stingy Budget Bureau and expand TVA's steam-plant construction into areas far beyond the confines of TVA's present domain. Senator Kefauver was frank about it. The bill, he said, "would allow the TVA to support its own expansion without having to obtain appropriations from Congress, with all its attendant difficulty."

In the debate on this subject last year, Senator Barry Goldwater declared: "I can assure the people of the TVA area that the people of Arizona are not interested one whit in supplying the hundreds of millions of dollars necessary for the expansion of TVA area through electricity made cheap by the absence of the costs which are absorbed by established private enterprise."

Senator Goldwater represents a phase of what Senator Lister Hill of Alabama described as "the never-ending struggle between special privilege and democracy." According to Senator Hill, the private utilities hate TVA "because TVA is a yardstick against which the people in all states can measure excessive rates and monopolistic practices." More importantly, TVA is a yardstick to measure how nice it would be to do business without having to pay taxes, interest or other return on the investment. What even the enemies of public power have failed to point out is that TVA is also a yardstick to measure the achievements of socialistic schemes in the general economy of an area. When the record is properly and widely understood, we can expect to hear less and less about that TVA yardstick.

One can imagine what Presidents Jackson, Polk and Johnson, Tennesseeans who did so much to expand and preserve the Union, would have thought about spending billions for the benefit of their state—or any other state—at the expense of the Nation.

———

In his weekly *Report* for May 25, 1959, Dan Smoot devotes his always stimulating pages to some revealing and astounding information about TVA and its hidden background.

# TVA

### DAN SMOOT

The TVA Act of 1933 took the place of the TVA Fertilizer Program of Muscle Shoals, Tennessee, which had become so notorious that it had to be abolished. It was abolished on May 18, 1933, by simply changing its name and greatly increasing its authority . . . When a program falls into disrepute, just change the name and go on to bigger things; and by the time the public catches up with what's cooking, a new name and a new agency will take over. This can be repeated ad infinitum.

Over $2 billion of your money has already been appropriated to this project. Over $159 million has been charged off as an aid to navigation. If all of the freight carried on the Tennessee River, since the beginning of TVA, had been carried by rail and the taxpayers had paid all of the freight, the total amount of this freight would be less than 30 per cent of the amount charged off to navigation.

Another $184 million has been charged off for flood control on the Tennessee River, even though the project has permanently flooded more farm land than was ever damaged by all the floods from that river.

While the sale of falling water for the generating of electrical power was to be a by-product of this project, more than 80 per cent of this $2 billion appropriation has been used for power development and distribution, and about 80 per cent of the power produced comes from steam plants and not from falling water. The yearly growth in that area requires an annual expansion costing at least $150 million . . . The TVA still owes the taxpayers of the United States $1.2 billion, and H.R. 3460 authorizes the issuing of $750 million in revenue bonds . . . This legislation makes TVA's obligation of $1.2 billion to the taxpayers a second mortgage. It removes all control of this Federally-owned corporation from the Congress, from the Treasury, and from the Budget Bureau. The complete management would be in the hands of three directors appointed by the President to serve for terms of eleven years.

TVA constantly refuses to raise its service rates sufficient to meet its obligations, and remains the . . . biggest socialized project in America, and . . . a constant threat to our free enterprise system.

TVA should be sold to the people in the area which it serves, so that it could be operated as any other free enterprise public utility, pay its taxes; meet its expansion requirements; and return dividends to the investors. That would be the American way.

On May 4, 1959, U.S. Congress Ben F. Jensen (Republican, Iowa) spoke in the House about the Tennessee Valley Authority. Here are abbreviated excerpts from his remarks:

Socialization of power was the first step toward the goal of eliminating the American free enterprise or profit system. Socialists knew that control of electric power means ultimate control of all industry.

Carl D. Thompson (a leading official of the socialist party) was the guiding spirit of the Public Ownership League of America—a socialist organization which, in the 1920's, became a major front for promoting socialization of American industries.

The Socialist Party, parent organization for various socialist fronts, made intense political efforts in the 1920's to capture control of state legislatures and the United States Congress by offering candidates who openly supported government confiscation of all basic industries.

But the American people would not vote for socialism when it was called by its right name. The socialists had to resort to the technique of infiltration—worming their way into positions of power and influence and starting a gradual process of socialization which could be sold to the people as something for "the general welfare," and which would have our free-economy fatally enmeshed before the public realized what was happening.

In 1927, H. Stephen Raushenbush, a leading socialist, outlined this plan of attack against America.

Explaining that the electric power industry should be used as a bell-wether to lead other basic industries into socialism, Raushenbush said:

We cannot hope to take over the whole $8 billion industry successfully, even if it were desirable to do so at the moment.

But a scattered series of great generating plants selling their power within 300-mile radii might be expected to have a very considerable influence upon the extension of public ownership to the transmission lines and the whole industry. . . .

The students coming from colleges today . . . can be of enormous use to the movement, as government officials, starting in small, definitely working on the reasonable hope that in the course of another ten years we shall have government control of a much more definite kind over trusts, banks, and general industries. . . .

One good man with his eyes, ears, and wits about him, inside the Department—whether it is the Interior . . . or the Treasury—can do more to perfect the technique of control over an industry than can a hundred men outside.

Raushenbush himself got a job in the Department of the Interior, and, like all other energetic socialists and communists in government, rose rapidly during the New and Fair Deals. Raushenbush became Chief of Economics and Statistics of the Interior Department's Division of Power (and he stayed in that key position until 1947, when Congressional investigation forced him to resign).

Carl D. Thompson (leader of the Public Ownership League of the 1920's) also entered government and rose to power under the New Deal. By 1936, Thompson was a member of the Power Policy Committee in the Department of Interior. From 1938 to 1948, Thompson was employed by the government as a consultant to the Bonneville Power Administration, fostering public power in the Pacific Northwest.

The first major victory for socialists and communists who had infiltrated the New Deal was the Tennessee Valley Authority Act of 1933.

The preamble to the TVA Act avoided any mention of electric power. Even the mesmerized Congress and public of 1933 would not have approved TVA if they had known that it was the fruit of socialist-communist efforts to start the socialization of American industries. Moreover, the Act would have been held unconstitutional in those days if its real intent had been honestly spelled out.

TVA was not sold to the people as a means of putting government in competition with its own citizens in order to socialize a major private industry. It was sold as a flood-control and river-navigation project.

The idea was to build one dam at Muscle Shoals, Alabama, to help control floods in the Tennessee River Valley and to improve water navigation on the river. All of this was going to cost about $150,000,000. As soon as the Authority was formed, however, developing electrical power became the major objective. The "$150,000,000 project" has grown into a two billion dollars plus colossus.

Today, the TVA system includes not one but thirty major dams—plus more than a dozen steam-operated generating-plants, and 9,000 miles of transmission lines, distributing electrical power through a marketing area of 80,000 square miles.

But TVA planners intended TVA to become a government business. They used the "yardstick" argument, saying that private power companies were greedy monopolies, grinding the faces of the poor and overcharging on electrical rates; government ought to set up one power business of its own, to have some means of measuring the true cost of producing electrical power.

The government yardstick became a club. Ever since the first hydroelectric dam was built in the Tennessee Valley, the government has been selling electrical power in the region at rates lower than the average of power rates anywhere else in the nation. The socialist planners have used this fact to prove that only the government can provide cheap, abundant electrical power for the people.

But TVA accomplishments are a bookkeeping, rather than a production, miracle.

A privately-owned power company has to charge enough for its power to pay all costs of operation, plus local, state, and federal taxes, plus interest on its capital investment, plus whatever is reinvested for expansion and improvement. TVA doesn't have to bear all these burdens. TVA gets what it needs from American taxpayers—some of whom are the private power companies that TVA is underselling.

A private business must pay interest on its capital investment. When a private power company is formed to build a plant and produce power, it borrows, let's say, $50,000,000. It has to pay that $50,000,000 back—with interest. No comparable burden is placed on a government agency. TVA gets what it needs from the Treasury of the United States. If it shows any paper entry for interest on indebtedness, the bookkeeping is always joggled in such a way that this legitimate cost is never passed on to the people who actually use the power from the TVA facilities.

A great deal of the operating cost of TVA, moreover, is borne by other agencies of government, and therefore never shows up on TVA balance sheets. For example, pensions and retirement funds for TVA employees—personnel expenses which any private company would have to pass on in the price of its services to customers in order to stay in business—never show up as a part of the operating cost of the Tennessee Valley Authority.

In research and public relations—activities which if conducted by private firms would be carried as a business expense under the general head of advertising—TVA and scores of other governmental agencies have spent millions of dollars spreading the TVA idea; but none of this cost is ever included in TVA cost-of-operation.

Another maneuver which enables TVA to sell electrical power at below the national average cost and still show a "profit" every year is the allocation of funds for flood control and navigation.

Before TVA was ever started army engineers had estimated a probable annual flood damage in the Tennessee Valley of approximately a million and a half dollars. In the name of flood control, TVA has allocated some $200,000,000. The annual interest on this investment in flood control, even at low government rates, costs the American taxpayers approximately $7,000,000. In other words, we are paying out each year in interest alone almost $7,000,000 to prevent a million and a half dollars' worth of flood damage in the Tennessee River Valley.

Before TVA, the army engineers had estimated that a flood which would cover 666,000 acres of land in the Tennessee Valley would occur only once in 500 years. That, in effect, was considered the maximum flood that could occur in the Tennessee Valley. In order to protect these 666,000 acres from being flooded once every 500 years, the Tennessee Valley Authority has permanently submerged almost a million acres under TVA manmade lakes or emergency reservoirs. In other words, every 500 years the Tennessee River might have flooded two-thirds as much land in the Tennessee Valley as the TVA has permanently flooded or set aside in its flood control program.

And the land which TVA has thus destroyed was among the most fertile in the world.

Before TVA, floods in the Tennessee Valley did a million and a half dollars' damage annually. Now-a-days, the crop loss alone—due to TVA flooding of rich bottom lands—is well over $27,000,000 a year.

TVA has created a 650-mile-long "free" waterway in the Tennessee Valley. It is free to shippers who use it, but it costs the American taxpayers over $8,000,000 a year in maintenance. If people who ship freight on the government's "free" waterway in the Tennessee Valley were charged freight rates just high enough to pay for the cost of operating that waterway, the rates would be considerably higher than those which railroads charge in the same neighborhood.

As Congressman James B. Utt points out, if all the freight carried on the Tennessee River since the beginning of TVA had been shipped by rail, and paid for at prevailing railroad rates, it would have cost less than 30% of what taxpayers have paid out in taxes for navigation on the "free" waterway which the government has built.

The same, of course, can be said for electrical power produced in the Tennessee Valley. If the people who use that power had to pay rates high enough to meet the cost of production and distribution, power rates in the Tennessee Valley would be the highest instead of the lowest in the nation, for the simple reason that government, not being controlled by the stern law of profit and loss, cannot operate a business as efficiently as private individuals can. The necessity of paying bills and showing a profit tends to correct errors which private businesses make. When a government agency makes mistakes, it gets more money from the Treasury in order to make more mistakes; and for political reasons, it must continue to make the same mistakes in order to justify its past errors.

There has been economic improvement in the Tennessee Valley since 1933; but hasn't there been everywhere?

One of the shallowest arguments of governmental planners today is that government should be given credit for all technological, scientific, and economic improvements in this country since 1933. The fact is that advances have occurred in spite of government. God only knows how much material progress the American people would have made in the past 25 years if government had not embroiled them in wars and shackled them with taxes and regulations that are gradually reaching the degree of strangulation.

Congressman Jensen presents some interesting information on this point.

He remarks that the TVA Act established in the Tennessee Valley area a dictatorship empire, ruled by three appointed board members who run the Authority. The board members have dictatorial powers over their empire. And they have more tax money to spend—for forcing local political decisions and influencing the people—than all seven of the state governments in the Valley.

Surely, if government ownership and control and spending will produce real prosperity, the Tennessee Valley should be a paradise, because here the tax billions that have been spent were not even raised in the region that "benefitted." It is an eternal truth that government can give the people nothing that it has not first taken away from them—and that the amount which government gives back is always much less than what it takes. But in the Tennessee Valley, the government has spent billions that it took away from taxpayers in other regions—from bookkeepers in California, from elevator operators in Pennsylvania, from lumberjacks in Oregon, from businessmen in Chicago, from schoolteachers in New York.

Despite all this governmental management and spending, the TVA area has not kept up with the economic progress of the rest of the nation. Despite the "free" waterway transportation and the "low-cost" electrical power and the millions of tax dollars spent on advertising and the building of governmental industrial plants in the TVA area—the area has had a slower industrial growth than neighboring regions.

Congressman Jensen quotes an editorial from the *Journal* of Tupelo, Mississippi—one of the first towns to distribute TVA power:

"The time has come for TVA to back up and admit that the fastest growth in the south actually has taken place outside the TVA area; and we who live within its borders are still as a whole just about the poorest people in America. . . .

"With the exception of giant projects like the Oak Ridge atomic energy plant that Uncle Sam has plunked down in Tennessee, the TVA area has shown less rapid industrial growth than several other portions of the south.

"And in income, the TVA area is still dollar for dollar *further* behind the national average than it was in 1933 when the Tennessee Valley Authority was first established."

The great power plants, the mammoth dams and the manmade lakes in the Tennessee Valley, have become a government showcase, a favorite place of pilgrimage for school teachers, economists, and visiting dignitaries from abroad. It all makes a magnificent spectacle. You can ride around the Tennessee Valley and see what two billion dollars have built. But you cannot see what the same two billion dollars might have built elsewhere in all parts of the nation if it had been left in the hands of the people who earned it and had not been seized from them in taxes to be spent on government's grandiose projects in this one valley.

And the tourists never see the sinister purpose beneath it all.

Congressman Ben Jensen relates a personal experience of one of his old friends, who is now a United States Senator. In the 1930's the man who is now a Senator attended a communist cell meeting in a large city.

The communist speaker hung on the wall a map of the United States. The map was divided into nine sections—each section centering around a major river valley.

The communist said:

"Since river valleys are no respecters of state lines, and since America can never be communized so long as there are 48 sovereign states, we must create 9 river valley authorities, like the Tennessee Valley Authority, where 3 men who are not elected by the people, but who are simply appointed by the President, are in full control.

"When this is accomplished, then 27 all-powerful men will be in complete control of the United States—then all city, county, and state governments will be forced to surrender their sovereign powers; and we will be in complete control, because we communists will see to it that the right 27 men are appointed."

By 1952, it was widely recognized that the "TVA idea" was a Soviet idea. Opposition to the spread of this experiment in Soviet-type socialism became quite powerful. Even General Eisenhower referred to TVA as creeping socialism.

All of this resulted in a noisy and complicated political crisis in 1954.

In its budget request of 1954, the Tennessee Valley Authority asked for an additional one hundred million dollars for a steam generating plant to supply power needs of an Atomic Energy Commission installation at Paducah, Kentucky.

President Eisenhower disapproved the request and instructed the AEC to purchase its power needs from private industry.

The additional electrical power which the Atomic Energy Commission needed was approximately the amount of power that the city of Memphis, Tennessee, uses, and Memphis got its power from TVA.

The AEC reasoned that if a private power company would build a plant to supply Memphis, then the AEC could get the TVA power that Memphis was using.

Hence, the Atomic Energy Commission made a contract with a group of private companies headed by E. H. Dixon and E. A. Yates. Dixon and Yates were going to build, at West Memphis, Arkansas, a power plant to supply the city of Memphis, Tennessee.

Congress approved the Dixon-Yates contract in the summer of 1954—after a filibuster by Senators Wayne Morse, Albert Gore, Hubert Humphrey, Estes Kefauver, and others, who do not want private companies operating electrical power plants anywhere in the Tennessee Valley.

The Eisenhower administration insisted that TVA must not be authorized to build another steam generating plant in the Tennessee Valley—insisted that additional power needs in that region be supplied by private industry.

In the summer of 1955, a curious thing happened.

Rather than see a private power company get a foothold in the Tennessee Valley of socialized power, the City of Memphis decided to build its own power plant so that there would be no need for the Dixon-Yates installation at West Memphis, Arkansas.

President Eisenhower promptly cancelled the Dixon-Yates contract.

Estes Kefauver and others of his ilk are still pretending that the Dixon-Yates contract was some kind of crime—still calling it an evil scheme to "take away from the people something that should belong to all the people."

This "belonging to all the people" pitch in connection with socializing the power industry is a clever deception.

If you own something, you have a right to dispose of it if you don't want it. If you really think that you, as a taxpayer, are a part owner of the big power plants in the Tennessee Valley, try to sell your share of those plants some day. If you find a buyer, you'll probably wind up in jail, because you don't own any part of those plants. Your money helped build them, but the government owns them.

The only great industries in the world which are actually publicly owned are American private corporations—the big utility companies, United States Steel, and so on—whose stocks are owned by hundreds of thousands of individuals.

When an appointed official, with only vague responsibility to Congress and none to the people, has the latent power of economic life or death over individuals, businesses and local governments in seven states—as the TVA administrator does have—our constitutional safeguards against tyranny are in grave danger.

Congressman Utt suggests the way out of this dangerous mess: eliminate the TVA, and sell its facilities to people who will have to run them as private enterprises, paying taxes, instead of consuming them.

## The Hidden Cost of Public Power

### IRA U. COBLEIGH AND ROBERT A. GILBERT

The City of Memphis, Tennessee, is building a municipal power plant. It is also, incidentally, providing its taxpayers with an object lesson in the comparative cost of public and private power. The plant will not be finished and in operation until 1959, but already its collective owners are beginning to realize that it is going to mean higher rates for Memphis consumers and higher taxes for the citizens of Tennessee and other states.

For some years Memphis has been getting its electricity from the federally subsidized Tennessee Valley Authority, which supplies virtually all of Tennessee and parts of six other states with power, generally at less than the cost of production (with the federal taxpayers of course paying the difference). As everyone knows, TVA was formed primarily to improve navigation, assure better flood control and provide irrigation in the Tennessee Valley. The sale of electricity generated by the water power developed through this gigantic enterprise was secondary to its main purpose. But the TVA also supplies power to the Tennessee installations of the Atomic Energy Commission. And the Commission's needs have expanded, as have those of Memphis. The power generated by

TVA's hydroelectric plants became insufficient. Therefore TVA some time ago began to invest in coal-fueled steam generating plants; and in the past five years it has expanded investment in such plants from $18 million to $800 million.

But Congress took a dim view of the expansion. TVA, a majority of the members felt, was outgrowing its intended bounds; further power needs in the Tennessee area should be supplied by privately owned companies.

Therefore, in November 1954 the AEC entered into a contract with the Mississippi Valley Generating Company (MVGC), 79 per cent of whose common stock is owned by Middle South Utilities and 21 per cent by the Southern Company. This agreement became known as the Dixon-Yates contract, and was bitterly (and successfully) fought by the "public power" lobby. By its terms MVGC was obligated to build a 650,000-kilowatt generating plant at a cost of $107,250,000, and to have it in operation sometime this year. This plant would have removed the AEC power load from TVA, which thus could have continued to service the City of Memphis. The arrangement was inexpensive and offered an ideal solution to the problems of all involved. But the public power lobby shouted that it was an attempt to destroy TVA; that a "conflict of interest" was involved; and that the contract should be cancelled.

Then suddenly, as the result of skillful political maneuvering, the City of Memphis on July 11, 1955, decided to build its own power plant, and informed TVA that it would not renew its power contract, due to expire in June 1958. President Eisenhower thereupon cancelled the Dixon-Yates contract.

Memphis went ahead with its building plans. Even if its plant opens at the scheduled time it will not start generating electricity until February 1959, and then at only 62 per cent of capacity, as compared with 98 per cent anticipated for this year by the cancelled MVGC plant.

It was not until the City of Memphis began to look for the funds to finance its new plant that its taxpayers began to glimpse the shape of things to come. Last December Memphis floated a bond issue in New York. It sold $163,245,000 worth of bonds, and the cost was high. The bulk of these bonds bear a coupon rate of 4.40 per cent. The net cost of the money to the City of Memphis was 4.47 per cent, as compared with the 3.5 per cent MVGC would have had to pay for the money, to build the Dixon-Yates plant at the time it was ready to begin construction.

Experts report that the cost, installed, of the privately built plant, including some transmission facilities, would have been $165 per kilowatt, whereas that of the Memphis plant, which will have an 812,000 kilowatt capacity, will be $200 per kilowatt.

And power rates? Memphis would have obtained power delivery from MVGC at 3.98 mills per kilowatt hour. Deliveries from its own plant, on the other hand, will start at 4.48 mills per kilowatt hour. Rates may have to be raised later if additions to the plant become necessary. MVGC, on the other hand, was willing to guarantee level rates for twenty-five years, except for adjustments made necessary by increases in the cost of fuel.

So the citizens of Memphis will inaugurate their new plant by paying more, not less, for their electricity. Moreover, they will bear a load of $169,523,280 in interest payments on their $163,245,000 of electric revenue bonds before these are all retired in 1992. Nor is that all. The MVGC plant would have paid regular federal and state taxes, but the municipally owned plant will not. The taxpayers of Memphis and all Tennessee, as well as the other states, will, in effect, be subsidizing the Memphis power plant in the amount of those unpaid taxes.

One expert reports that over a period of thirty-five and a half years—the life of the Memphis bonded debt—the following concealed costs must be reckoned with in determining just what society is paying for this municipal power plant:

| | |
|---|---|
| 1. Extra capital costs per kilowatt, compared with what the same plant would have cost if built by the investor-owned Mississippi Valley Generating plant. . . . . . . . . . . . . . . . . . . . . . . . . . | $ 28,360,000 |
| 2. Higher electric rates at $1,700,000 per annum. . . . . . . . . . . . . . . . . . . . . . . . . | 60,350,000 |
| 3. Taxes lost (State and Federal) . . . . . . . | 104,725,000 |
| 4. Power production lost, due to delays. . . . . . . . . . . . . . . . . . . . . . . . . | 40,950,000 |
| 5. Interest saving lost due to delays in financing. . . . . . . . . . . . . . . . . . . . . . . | 57,934,580 |
| Total concealed cost. . . . . . . . . . . . . | $292,319,580 |
| Stated municipal power plant costs plus some transmission lines. . . . . . . . . . . . . . . . . . . . . . . | 163,555,000 |
| Total real cost. . . . . . . . . . . . . . . . . . . . . | $455,874,580 |

A bill for $455,874,580 for a $163,245,000 municipal power plant is really something! These figures may seem like fantastic exaggerations, but the loss to society is indeed stupendous.

Such is the plight of the people of Memphis as they embrace public power.

This current example of the difference between private and public power costs is another object lesson in the wastefulness of socialism in this field. Time and again public power, said to be cheaper, has turned out to be far more expensive. It is characteristic of the loose planning of socialists that they start low in their estimates, and end up far on the high side of the ledger. The Clark Hill project in Georgia–South Carolina was estimated in 1939 to cost $28 million; by 1955, for about the same installed capacity, $78.6 million had been spent. The Kerr Project in Virginia was to have cost $31.7 million in 1944; by 1955, the cost was $87.2 million. The Garrison Dam in North Dakota was estimated at $130 million in 1943, now the figure is $294 million. Hungry Horse, in Montana, in 1951 was estimated at $39.5 million; by 1954 it had cost $101.6 million. McNary Dam in Washington–Oregon was to cost $49.5 million in 1938; by 1956 the cost was $286 million.

Prices of equipment change, of course, and sometimes more capacity is added during construction, but the socialist planners never seem able to estimate accurately in the first place, even on the visible costs. In addition, there are the invisible costs such as lost taxes. These can be huge. On the projects cited above it is estimated that the taxes lost by federal and state governments would exceed $610 million over the forty-year average life of plant and machinery.

Many other socialized public projects will be proposed in this Congress. For example there will be a renewed attempt to socialize Niagara power.

It now seems likely that Congress may approve a compromise agreement under which the right to develop the Niagara project will be awarded to the New York State Power Authority instead of the five stockholder-owned taxpaying electric companies which have stood able and willing to undertake the project for the last five years.

As a "compromise," the Power Authority would eliminate the so-called "preferential clause" which would give municipalities and cooperatives first claim on all power produced. But preference clause or no, the Power Authority development would still be another costly experiment in socialism. Tax-exempt bonds would be sold to obtain the necessary funds. Millions in taxes would thus be lost to the state and federal governments; and just as in the case of the Memphis plant, every American taxpayer would have to help make up the loss by paying higher taxes.

If the full costs of every such project were to be analyzed as the Memphis figures are analyzed above, if the *real* cost of socialized power were to be explained, our politicians might care to take another long, hard look at what they are planning to do with the taxpayers' money. And they might also begin to question whether the federal government should continue to grant individual income-tax exemption on interest received from revenue bonds issued by states and municipalities for projects which needlessly compete with taxpaying private enterprise.

—Reprinted with permission from *National Review*, March 16, 1957.

## A Reply to TVA Director Brooks Hays

### by
#### TENNESSEE INDEPENDENTS *

The new director of the TVA in recent speeches has called for Federal control of the educational system, as well as further involvement by our Government in the affairs of foreign nations.

Since the opinion of the new TVA Director runs contrary to that of many, many Americans, the undersigned cannot permit such statements to go unchallenged.

To start with, Mr. Hays is not an elected public servant of this area. He is an appointed bureaucrat.

Arkansas citizens were so displeased with Mr. Hays' supine acceptance of questionable commands issued by the Federal Government that they removed him from Congress by the unusual means of a write-in vote. This record apparently, but unexplainably, qualified Mr. Hays for appointment to the TVA Board of Directors, but it did not endow him with the wisdom nor the power to determine how much more regimentation should be foisted upon us by Washington nor how much more of the world we should attempt to wet-nurse.

Just because socialized, cut-rate electricity is produced in this

* P.O. Box 152, Sevierville, Tennessee.

area, it does not follow that men like Washington, Jefferson, Hamilton, Madison, Adams, Franklin, Burke and de Tocqueville were wrong in their contention that government is best when it governs the least. The present crop of bureaucrats has not disproved the belief that man will fare best when he places his trust in God and depends upon his own personal efforts to get along.

Just because socialized, cut-rate electricity is generated here, it does not mean that we are to be forever silenced for fear of offending that false god, the TVA.

Where is the voice of the patriot demanding freedom again? The voice of the philosopher seeking eternal truth? The voice of the theologian decrying the belittlement of the individual for the glorification of the crowd? In short, where is the voice of America?

Are we to abandon the Christian belief upon which this country was founded? Are we to forsake the lessons of history to accept, blindly and silently, insidious bureaucratic pronouncements just because TVA cut-rate, socialized electricity is dispensed in this area?

In regard to Mr. Hays' arbitrary rejection of the philosophy of our founding fathers on the theory that our daily lives in this Atomic Age are too complicated for us to lead as individuals, and that someone (?) must lead them for us, let us consider the experienced opinion of Dr. Wilhelm Roepke. A world-renowned scholar, philosopher, economist and author, he is the architect of the economic policy of today's West German Government.

> I think I have demonstrated how I came to see that socialism did not have the cure for our social ills, that indeed socialism was a heresy which aggravated these ills the more men acted on it. . . . I look upon collectivism with the utmost distrust. And following from these convictions, along the lines of reason, experience and the testimony of history, I arrive at the conclusion that only a free economy is in accordance with man's freedom. . . . The welfare state, in its rage for egalitarianism, gives its citizens the status and opportunities of slaves, but calls on them to act like heroes. . . . The point is one of religious conviction; I will say in all candor: the nidus of the malady from which our civilization suffers lies in the individual soul and is only to be overcome within the individual soul. For more than a century we have made the hopeless effort . . . to get along without God and vaingloriously to put man, his science, his art, his political contrivances in God's place. It is as though we had wanted to add to the already existing proofs of God's existence, a new and finally convincing one: the universal destruction that follows on assuming God's non-existence.

The miracle of West Germany, rising from the ashes of destruction, should be sufficient proof that the shallow braying of our arrogant bureaucrats is like a discordant overture to our own funeral march.

Surely we do not have to have TVA, if having it means: exchanging our trust in God for the worship of human mediocrities in elective and appointive office; abandoning the wisdom of our nation's founders for the folly of Karl Marx; trading the limitless expanse of human freedom for the chains of bureaucratic enslavement. For to do this would bring to fulfillment the evil prophecy of the wily Lenin, who predicted that Russia would never need to fire a shot to conquer America, because we would spend ourselves into destruction and would drop like over-ripe fruit into waiting Soviet hands.

We do not have to have the TVA in order to exist any more than we need to have the personal income tax. The elimination of both would restore our freedom, our self respect, and would save us a fabulous amount of money annually. The Federal Government seizes in personal income taxes many, many, many times what the cut-rate price of TVA electricity amounts to.

The repeal of the personal income tax would not interfere with the constitutional functions of the Federal Government, including the maintenance of our military forces. We can prove this statement with the same documentary evidence that, last year, induced the legislature of Texas and Wyoming to pass a resolution calling for the repeal of this vicious tax. It is a communistic booby trap, devised by Karl Marx and prescribed by him in the Communist Manifesto for the self-destruction of America.

In further regard to Mr. Hays' prescription for increased regimentation of our daily lives, we would submit that the strongest society is composed of the strongest men; that men who trust in God and solve their own personal problems are stronger than men who worship bureaucrats and crawl on their knees begging for something for nothing.

## Communism American Style

### GEORGE PECK

Things have been going on in Cuba that have aroused the ire of most of the American people. The bearded Castro has confiscated private property, much of it owned by Americans, and in doing so has demonstrated his rank ingratitude to a country that liberated Cuba from Spanish oppression and which has contributed much since that liberation to the general welfare of the Cuban people.

Reprisals against Castro have been urged upon the U.S.A. Congress ranging from cutting off our sugar purchases to sending a squad of marines to Cuba to teach this revolutionary upstart a lesson. Fortunately, cooler heads have prevailed and no drastic action has been taken. Those cooler heads are convinced that Mr. Castro is digging his own political grave and that it won't be too long until the Cuban people bury him in that grave.

But while we have been castigating Mr. Castro for the socialist program he has launched in Cuba, perhaps we should take a closer look at some of the socialist programs we ourselves have launched right here in Free Enterprise America. It is high time that we take a gander at the beam in our own eyes before we so sharply criticize the mote in Castro's.

Now let it be clearly understood that we hold no brief for Castro. As previously stated we consider him to be an ingrate and a stupid one at that. But, at least the properties Castro has seized have for the most part been those of foreigners. He could even sincerely mistakenly believe that in so doing he is a patriot serving the best interests of the Cuban people. But what about confiscation of private American property by Americans right here in America? That seems to us to be a much greater crime than Castro's.

Let us give you the story of one confiscation of private property. To do so we pass on an editorial which appeared in the February, 1960, issue of *Employes' News*, published by the Kentucky Utilities Company. From here to end we quote this editorial:

"Recently, there has been a big 'stir' in this country over confiscation of private property by the Castro regime in Cuba. Already losses by conservative estimates exceed a billion dollars. Heated protests have been voiced on the floors of the Congress of the United States labeling these acts as a shame and disgrace.

"Yet this same Congress last year enacted into law an amendment to the TVA Act, together with Tennessee law already in existence, which permitted municipal agency to destroy our properties at South Fulton, Tennessee. Weakley County Municipal System is now overbuilding our system having refused to pay a fair price for the property.

"If it is Socialism–Communism in Cuba, what do you call the same thing in the United States?

"Is such a philosophy in line with the principles of our Constitution and its Bill of Rights?

"Is this the American Way bought and defended by the spill of blood and the loss of hundreds of thousands of our boys on battlefields almost all over the world?

"Is it fair and honorable to grab off a successful business after 43 years of costly development? Well, that is what is taking place at South Fulton.

"Our company started developing the uses and efficiency of electric service there back in 1917 with about two dozen customers. Over the years we have developed the business to the point where we had nearly 1,000 customers—but our days there are numbered. We will be there no longer than the time necessary for the Weakley County System to overbuild and take over the last one of our customers.

"If confiscation or destruction of business or personal property is permitted to continue by 'so-called' legal or any other process, can we continue as a Nation of free people for another 200 years, or even half or one-tenth that long?

"The fact that wholesale confiscation of private property is taking place in South Fulton, Tennessee, makes a mockery of our pious indignation at Castro's lack of regard for the rights of property in Cuba."

—Reprinted with permission of *The American Way.*

# VIII

# Labor Union Power Unlimited

AMONG THE EARLY SUPPORTERS of the New Deal were the heads of the various labor unions. These men were quick to see how the power of the labor bosses could be swelled if the government in Washington could be used as a tool to drive workers into labor unions. To elect men to office, who would later obey their commands, the labor bosses assessed their members extra dues and poured millions of dollars into the election campaigns.

They then forced through Congress two laws that accomplished just that, the Wagner Act in 1935 and the Fair Labor Standards Act in 1938.

So unfair was the Wagner Act, which denied freedom of speech to employers, that Congress repealed it over the veto of President Truman. In its place was passed the Taft-Hartley Act which tried to curb some of the flagrant injustices visited upon union members, employers, and the public by the arrogant, power-drunk union bosses.

Since then several books have been written by impartial authors showing in detail how today's labor bosses are establishing a dictatorial power over all America by forcing through Congress laws that lead straight to communism.

Donald R. Richberg, an early fighter for the legitimate rights of labor, has clearly exposed this dangerous trend in his book, *Labor Union Monopoly*. Professor Sylvester Petro, of the New York University School of Law, in his book *Power Unlimited—The Corruption of Union Leadership,* goes so far as to say: "Unions are destroying the competitive enterprise system by imposing upon it a rigid monopolistic structure, to the infinite abuse of the public, and to the great national peril."

Various committees of Congress have compiled a documented record that leaves no doubt that the labor bosses have just about seized control of the country, by having enough members of Congress beholden to them to pass laws as demanded.

From a fearless member of Congress, Senator Barry Goldwater, of Arizona, comes this warning which he delivered over the Manion Forum network on June 28, 1959.

## Economic and Political Tyranny

### SENATOR BARRY GOLDWATER

We hear a great deal these days of the dangers facing our country. Not a day passes without someone pointing to the perils that await at every turn in foreign affairs, in missile production or lack of it, in the race to space or to the poles, in every imaginable activity our Nation is engaged in.

And we could not have come this far as a prosperous republic if in the past we had not faced and met similar dangers. But to me the greatest danger we face as a nation is not aggressive force from without, but irresponsible power from within.

Power that we as a nation legally grant. Power that is unrestrained, irresponsible, unrelenting, and, most important, sanctioned by law!

This power is vested in three areas, government, business and labor, and is growing greater each day.

Let us examine the strongholds of this power. First there is government. Government has become so large today that nearly every move we make is met with Federal regulation.

Government after government in the history of this world has fallen because of the concentration of power in centralized government, and today, we are witnessing this growth in our own nation's capitol.

It can be successfully argued, in my own opinion, that big government spawns both big business and big labor, and that the three together constitute a real danger to our freedoms.

The second area of bigness is business. The usual explanation of the size of today's corporations is that through competitive struggle for survival, they have merged for technological reasons into massive combines.

But, can the immense size be explained alone in this way? Not at all. There are two factors causing it, but the underlying reason for both is governmental policy.

The wealth produced by capital is divided for supplemental wages, to pay the double tax of the state and Federal Government, and to provide a major portion of new capital formation. The Federal Government and most states levy such taxes on corporations doing business within their borders. Under these tax regulations, corporations and businesses which should be allowed to put back money produced by their efforts are restrained from doing so by the effect of corporate taxes.

As the size of the business grows, so grows the size of the unions with which management must deal in the determination of wage rates and benefits to be received by employees. As the unions grow, the trend snowballs for industry-wide bargaining, and this is followed by a greater body of Federal regulations prescribing such bargaining between employers and union representatives.

Government regulations on employee relations impose compliance burdens on today's businessmen such that only the largest can afford the staffs of accountants, lawyers, and researchers required to keep abreast of procedures imposed on them by bureaucratic proclamation.

If the businessman attempts to follow the normal course of free enterprise, ignoring Government channels, criminal sanctions are soon imposed on him and his business is terminated. Thus, Government practice in the employee-relations field encourages large corporations to grow.

Now, for the third area—the one with which we are now intimately concerned. In contrast to business regulation, our Government has created in the trade union movement the power and privilege to compel union membership and to regiment employers by economic measures which are irresistible.

This power today has a far-reaching effect. Oddly enough, in this age of vast government and proliferation of laws, we have, in the labor relations field, little government and less law. We have, instead, a series of special privileges for abusive and destructive trade union conduct.

In the labor relations field, freedom has become a fugitive trapped, held by a superstate, while giant unions slug it out. They are slugging it out with big business in the most fearful struggle of our time.

The outcome of this struggle is in the hands of Congress and, more essentially, in the hands of every citizen. This conflict of raw power left unchecked in its present direction can only result in government alone emerging as the sole survivor.

America is in danger. Not alone from the material or military threat of our enemies abroad, but from the complacency from within our boundaries.

This is a weakness which is reflected in the acceptance of the abuses of power and it is a weakness further demonstrated by our inability to face up to the real danger. The foreign threat is one which need not panic us so long as we avoid abandonment of our fundamental strength—the principle of freedom under law.

The danger lies in the excessive power of special privileges. All big unions, as they wield the club of economic pressures exploiting to the limit their privileges, have formed industry-wide monopolies fraught with abuses and corruption so rampant that it portends certain destruction of the trade union movement, with the attendant handmaiden of disaster for our country. What has brought this about? The answer lies in the failure of our Government to control power and corruption.

During the course of debate on S. 1555, the Kennedy labor bill, I pointed out that, unless strengthened, the bill would make it perfectly permissible for a union to deny a member his right to freedom of speech by means of "reasonable rules and regulations."

Just four days after the bill passed the Senate this hypothetical example became a reality. Citing the section of their constitution which permits expulsion for "conduct unbecoming a member," the International Association of Machinists denied the appeal of three members who had exercised their Constitutional right of free speech to support Right-to-Work laws.

Let me read from that decision the astounding reason the union gives in support of its position.

While it is agreed that the right to freely express one's views is a privilege guaranteed by the United States Constitution, this does not mean that a member of our association is entitled to openly denounce the considered position of the labor movement and particularly his own organization, without the possibility of losing his rights to retain his standing as an I.A.M. union member.

I draw your attention to this phenomenon because it is exactly here that I believe the bridge is being constructed between economic tyranny and political tyranny in this country. We are observing the transformation of economic compulsion into political compulsion.

We are probably strong enough to survive even the widespread corruption in union affairs which the McClellan Committee hearings have disclosed. It is an evil thing and weaves threads through our social fabric of which none of us can be proud and which we ought to remove. But it is not, by itself, necessarily fatal to the country, damaging as it may be.

We can probably survive entrenched hoodlums, but can free political institutions survive the clever men whom we hear talk piously of their high ideals and lofty purposes at the same time that they go steadily and stealthily about the job of transforming compulsory unionism into compulsory political activity? I suggest these latter may be the truly evil, the truly dangerous men.

On this point there has been a strange and inexplicable silence on the part of the usually loquacious men who call themselves "liberals." There has been a curious unwillingness on the part of some to concern themselves with civil rights of union members with the same relentless energy and determination they are accustomed to expend upon threats to the civil rights of other segments of the population.

Why is the union member the forgotten man? Why is this second-class citizenship for the union member held by "liberals" to be a negligible matter when applied to any other segment of the population it is held to be intolerable?

Where are the "liberals" who speak with such deep feeling and who are willing to undertake unlimited and immediate action to cure any diminution of that franchise in one part of the country but who are so strangely blind and deaf to this outrageous impairment of the franchise of union members which is especially conspicuous in another part of the country? This I have called the civil rights problem of the North and I invite the earnest attention of the Nation to this problem.

The basic evil infesting the union movement is compulsory membership. Not one other segment of our society has the coercive power of compulsory unionism, transformed as it has been into a massive and irresponsible political power.

What we witnessed only recently in Congress during the development of the Kennedy labor bill ought to demonstrate to everyone how far-reaching this ruthless power does now reach.

How humiliating it is for the Congress of the United States to have to conduct a sort of treaty-negotiation with a great internal political power almost as with a foreign power to find out what these union grandees would be willing to tolerate in the way of mild corrections! What level has this Congress reached when even a mild and inoffensive reform bill must be loaded with "sweeteners" to make it sufficiently attractive to the labor politicians so that they may be persuaded to permit its passage?

This overwhelming power, as I have said, is based on the transformation of compulsory unionism into compulsory political activity.

It is an appalling situation when Democrat union members can be required, as a condition of employment, to finance Republican candidates; when Republican union members can be required to finance Democrat candidates; or when any union member can be required to finance issues which he finds deeply repugnant.

When, for example, a profoundly religious Roman Catholic workman can be required by a Communist-dominated union leadership to finance the political designs of the Communist party, on pain of losing his job!

I say this is the kind of issue that ought not to separate liberals and conservatives. On this issue we must all be Americans or there may soon be no America as we have known it. What we in Congress must awaken to is the fact that freedom is the target of concentrated power. There is no question but that trade unions have been scoring bulls eyes for 30 years taking away freedom which belongs to you and me and our children.

How much more is there available for sacrificial offering? I submit that it may be too late. There is no question, however, that if we have any hope of retaining what little is left, we must deny the special privileges which allow the violence and monopolistic compusion against union members.

We have reached a point again in our history where we once stood, when the question was asked of men, "Where do you stand, sir?"

Do we want a republic whose Constitution recognizes that freedom is ours because we are individuals and that freedom comes from God? Do we want a government unfettered by power? Do we want an economic system unfettered by abusive power? Do we want a labor movement with special privileges denied to the rest of our society, the use of which has produced the raw power disclosed before the McClellan Committee?

The answer I say to my colleagues rests in the question: "Where do you stand, sir?" If we remain true to our oath of office, if we believe in the proclamations of freedom and liberty which we make from rostrums across the land, if we believe that power invested in any segment of our population is bad, then I suggest to those who hear my voice or who read my words that we can demonstrate this by recognizing the needed approach to labor reform, which is, attack the disease, not the symptoms.

If we fail at this crucial point in our history to measure up to our responsibilities, then history will judge us for what history will surely record us as—men who were timid when strength and courage were needed.

If, on the other hand, we want our freedom, we must work and sacrifice for it. There can be no compromise. Our Constitution is quite clear and we either stick by our basic principles or we don't have them.

There can be no compromise with those who would destroy us because time is on their side. There can be no compromise with courage, the courage to stand for principle with strength.

———

On the heels of these words spoken by Senator Goldwater in 1959, it is of unique interest and relevancy to turn back ten years to the words of three officials of three of the smaller steel companies.

On August 24, 1949, these three officials appeared, by invitation, before the Senate Committee on Banking and Currency to give testimony on the extent of the economic power of unions.

The three men were Admiral Ben Moreell, Chairman of Jones and Laughlin Steel Corporation, William H. Colvin, Jr., President of Crucible Steel Company of America, and Luke Sawyer, Executive Vice President of the Babcock and Wilcox Tube Company. Here are some excerpts from their testimony.

## Senate Committee Testimony

### ADMIRAL BEN MOREELL

The labor movement is progressing rapidly. We should determine where it is going and the probable consequences so that in choosing our future path as a nation we will do so with our eyes open. If we are to make changes in the current trends, we must act intelligently and soon, or we may have to resort to hasty and ill-considered measures in order to prevent our free economy from deteriorating by default.

The problem which faces us is an old one; it is to prevent the concentration of power in the hands of one man or of a few men, which power could be used to cause significant harm to the dominant public interest.

Our forefathers faced the same problem when they were drafting the Constitution. In that case, their task was to establish checks and balances on the use of governmental power.

Later, we faced the problem in the form of great concentrations of financial and industrial power. Restraints were established by antitrust and other legislation.

Now we have the problem of concentration of power in the hands of labor leaders. . . .

The concentration of economic power in the hands of labor leaders who are not responsible to the public and who are subject to little restraint by law is an extremely important development in our industrial life. I believe that we cannot safely accept this modification of our free economy in the hope that with the passage of time, the accumulation of experience, and the sobering effect of responsibility, this power will be tempered by benevolence and wisdom. All human experience discourages such belief. It teaches us that power is corrosive. Union organizations seem to pass through three stages— (1) the chaotic period of organization; (2) the period of stabilization and cooperation with management; and (3) the period of entrenchment and self-perpetuation by a powerful leadership. It is in this last stage that the corrosive effect of power makes itself felt. If this country is to have a controlled economy in spite of the many disastrous examples which steer us away from that course, let our economy be controlled at least by leaders who are responsible to all of us, and not by those who represent special interests and who are responsible only to a small segment of the people.

As a result of their ability to shut down strategic industries and to impose uniform conditions upon an entire competitive field, labor leaders can exert compelling economic pressure on all of the public, as well as on individual employers. The pressure brought to bear on the public is often more effective in gaining labor's objectives than would be the case if it were applied only to specific employers. The force of public opinion here comes into play. Alert labor leaders are thoroughly aware of this and they play the game accordingly. If the effects of a threatened steel strike could be confined only to the steel industry, many persons—workers and stockholders—would be injured; but their percentage of the whole public would not be great. But the effects of a steel strike cannot be so confined and, in fact, the effects will be felt by practically everyone. Individually, and collectively as a nation, such results cannot be ignored.

It follows, therefore, that most labor demands and the frequent result of unsatisfied demands—strikes—are, in effect, imposed on the public. The demands of organized labor, which have been mounting each year, are buttressed by so much economic power that employers have seldom refused some concessions. Each year, wages, costs and prices have gone up. A depression might curb this progression, but a depression is an exorbitant price to pay for something which intelligence and courage should enable us to avert. Furthermore, the power of organized labor will be exerted to maintain monetary wage rates even when prices are falling and, as a result, real wages are rising. This will accentuate unemployment and retard recovery from the depression.

In the process described above, smaller enterprises have usually been injured competitively more than the large companies because the demands of labor have been geared to the paying abilities of the large mass producers who operate with greater efficiency and at lower cost. It would be difficult for industry-wide unions to proceed in any other manner. Industrial competition is thus restrained to the detriment of the public interest, and more especially of those localities where smaller industries may be located. . . .

Through the period of increasing labor power, organized labor has obtained short-range benefits. Monetary wages are at a new high, as are real wages. It is important to note that industry-wide unions operating over large areas of the country are generally more concerned with monetary wages than with real wages. In the many instances where price rises have absorbed much of the labor gains, the bill has largely been paid by unorganized labor and the general public. Whether there has been a fair division of benefits and burdens could only be determined by a more comprehensive study than any I have seen.

Certainly it is true that since industry-wide wages and working conditions have changed uniformly, this element of competition among industrial concerns has been eliminated. That is an apparent benefit to the larger industries and to the labor unions concerned. Its contribution to the public welfare is doubtful. In some cases, small groups of workmen in small plants by alliance with employes in other plants, have undoubtedly been strengthened in their bargaining power with strongly financed and ruthless managements.

We must bear in mind, however, that "labor's gains" can be properly appraised only when we consider their long term effects. In the ultimate analysis, permanent gains for labor depend entirely on the stability of industry. Labor can be paid only out of the proceeds of production. I believe that while production per man-hour has increased, by far the larger part of this increase is due to improved equipment, rather than to increases in effort or skill of the workers. We then face the question—can industry continue to devise new tools, machinery and processes and find the capital necessary to finance them in order to offset the rising costs of labor by increasing production? If not, labor will have been shortsighted—and we will all suffer. . . .

As I see it, there are three courses open to us—first, we could so define the legitimate objectives of labor unions as to prohibit them from controlling production, preventing improvements, imposing any form of feather-bedding (including "made work"), fixing prices, excluding prefabricated articles and items manufactured in other cities or by other groups of labor, limiting the use of labor-saving machines and similar unjustifiable practices which still exist and for which we pay dearly; second, we could restrict the power of unions by limiting the size of unions, subjecting them generally to the antitrust laws, and forbidding industry-wide bargaining; or, third, we could proceed along a combination of both lines of legislative restrictions.

The first step can and should be taken immediately. I can see no justification for restrictive labor practices which seek to control prices or production. I have a strong feeling of resentment when I learn that my clothes cost more because a union leader has limited the use of the most efficient cutting machines, fixed the cost of labor to be included (irrespective of actual cost) in the price of each grade of suits, and prevented the introduction of new and cheaper methods of manufacture. No American should be permitted to exact that tribute from another American. Economically, it is unwise for all. I can see disaster ahead if we permit one man to restrict by personal edict the coal production of the nation. I know that building costs could be reduced in many sections if restrictive building trade practices were stopped. These evils are violations of our social and economic codes. They are seriously detrimental to the public interest. They should be eliminated forthwith. . . .

The second measure, the curbing of labor's power by restricting that power itself, is a more difficult problem. The principal suggestions for such legislation have been along the lines of strengthening and expanding our antitrust laws to treat labor unions and industry alike. There is, I think, a solid historical basis for trying to solve the problem along antitrust lines. I have been told by my counsel that the common law antitrust principles which really sired the English Statute of Monopolies and our Antitrust Laws were directed primarily at craft organizations. These common law and statutory principles broke up the ancient craftsmen guilds which in the fifteenth century dominated and restricted trade and competition. At that time, however, the artisan was an individual enterpriser and the restrictive regulations of the guilds had the color of labor and enterprise combinations in restraint of trade. I am told also that the inclusion of labor within the scope of our antitrust laws has been a subject of legislative discussion in the United States since the passage of the Sherman Antitrust Act in 1890. . . .

Industry-wide unions and industry-wide bargaining will inevitably lead to compulsory arbitration. We may struggle against that undesired result. We may delay its coming, but if we cling to industry-wide bargaining, compulsory arbitration will come. Labor's compelling force in industry-wide bargaining is an industry-wide strike. . . .

Labor, management and the public should all resist compulsory arbitration because all will suffer from its effects. It substitutes the judgment of outsiders—so-called experts—for the free play of economic forces. One reason for our adherence to the theory of a free economy is that no expert or group of experts is capable of planning and controlling our complex economy. Decisions by experts on the fair reward for the efforts of labor will not only ignore the capacities of individuals and diminish freedom, but also will impede the development of the individual. The principle of advancement of the individual in accordance with his ability will be superseded by rigid criteria applicable only to workers in the mass. Mistakes will be made with grievous consequences. Corrections will be difficult, if not impossible. Compulsory arbitration of wages will lead to control of prices—then of production—and then to the controlled—and weak-economy. As the system progresses, it is inevitable that the political power of labor will be displaced by an accumulation of precedents leading to rigid and uniform rules. . . .

To summarize briefly, the national economy is now subject, without any effective restraints, to the undue concentration of power in the hands of a comparatively few labor leaders. If our free economy is to be preserved, such labor power must be curbed. Power tends to corrupt and subjecting labor power to proper restraints is just as desirable as was the curbing of governmental, financial and industrial power.

Two necessary steps are clear. Labor leaders must be shorn immediately of their power to impose undesirable restrictions on industry—restrictions which directly control production, materials, prices and quality. Industrial unions should forthwith be confined to single industries and not allowed to cover several different industries. We must start on the elimination of industry-wide bargaining. Whether we should accomplish that by restricting the size of unions or by including unions within the scope of the antitrust laws or by some other means requires further study. Such study should be started promptly on a comprehensive and thorough basis if the basic structure of our incentive system of free enterprise is to be preserved.

## Senate Committee Testimony

### WILLIAM H. COLVIN, JR.

The magnitude and complexity of an organization such as the Steelworkers' Union leads its executives to conduct their affairs in much the same way as would business management under similar circumstances. That is to say, labor executives attack the large problems first. They meet with, bargain with and reach an agreement with a few companies which together represent perhaps 80% of the capactiy of the whole industry. In no case have we been included in this bargaining and actually in practice, the serious bargaining is more often confined to one company. The agreement reached is one which presumably is acceptable to the Union and livable for these companies—at least both parties do agree to it. The agreement establishes a pattern not only as to wages but as to other important phases of the labor contract, such as seniority, union security, grievance procedure, vacations, holidays, termination dates, etc. An analysis of the contracts of a number of the large steel companies recently completed shows almost complete uniformity on the subjects mentioned as well as on many minor subjects. The rub comes when the Union finishes with this 80% of the Industry and turns to the other 20% made up of smaller companies such as ourselves and requires them to make a tie-in deal and buy the entire package. In effect, the Union says to its 20% customers—if you wish to do business with us at all—buy all of our package regardless of consequences to your individual companies.

The fact that it is easier for the Union to require all companies to buy the entire package or be struck, would not cause serious results or concern if there were competing sources of labor supply. But when, as here, no alternative sources exist, and the Union is the sole representative of steel works employes, its power and its ability to exercise that power are monopolistic and beyond appeal. . . .

The tool and specialty steel producers thus find themselves in a serious situation, due not to obsolescence, or inefficiency, but to the failure of the Union to recognize the nature of the business which must be carried on if the thousands of small buyers are to be served. But neither this nor any other business can indefinitely survive these uniform applications of economic demands, renewed year after year by the Union and urged again this year on a scale which is not only alarming but catastrophic. If there were no manufacturers of tool and specialty steels equipped to serve this type of business, it would be necessary to create one to serve these small businesses and enable them to maintain their own productive enterprises.

It is apparent in any event that the trends . . . point toward diminishing competition in our segment of the industry and a probable concentration of production under semi-monopolistic conditions. In other words, the power of a labor monopoly thus applied, may, in due course, result in a monopoly of productive facilities. The serious disadvantages of such a result need no emphasis and it may be they can be avoided only by recognizing and prohibiting monopolistic practices wherever they exist, on the part of labor as well as on the part of business.

## Senate Committee Testimony

### LUKE SAWYER

We have industry-wide labor negotiations in several fields today: in railroads, the coal industry, and the glass manufacturing business, to list only a few. Whatever may be the advantages or disadvantages of the industry-wide system in such segments of industry, it can perhaps be said in its favor that the parties to the bagaining process have the same problems and the same interests and in general the same business and financial characteristics.

In our case, we do not merely have industry-wide bargaining—we have union wide bargaining which cuts across several industries.

The Steelworkers' Union claims and exercises jurisdiction over at least three industrial groups, viz.: (a) the fully and partially integrated steel producers, (b) the non-integrated producers of specialty steel products, and (c) the fabricators of steel. . . .

Our Company falls in a field somewhere between the non-integrated group and the fabricators. We do make a little steel by the electric furnace method but we buy more than 75% of our raw steel requirements from the large companies. Needless to say, we do not own ore or coal mines or other sources of raw material.

All of this is important background for the point I made at the start of my statement, that the system of collective bargaining has broken down as far as we are concerned. We no longer negotiate labor agreements except on insignificant local items. Labor agreements are imposed upon us, on the non-integrated companies, and on a host of fabricators, simply because the Union which deals with us dominates the integrated field. For almost eight years we have been required to follow the wage and labor conditions pattern of the United States Steel Corporation and not once have we had the opportunity of pointing out that there are substantial differences between Big Steel and ourselves.

The Government began this pattern of coercive collective bargaining in 1942, when the National War Labor Board arbitrarily applied the so-called "Little Steel" decision to almost a hundred companies, without regard to economic, geographical and other differences. Again in 1944, the same Board indiscriminately applied to these companies the same wage and other standards which it found appropriate for the United States Steel Corporation.

After the war, the Union continued the tactics it had learned from the National War Labor Board. In 1946, 1947 and 1948, we were required to accept the United States Steel Corporation wage agreements almost to the last comma. The Union was polite about it but both parties recognized that the Union demands were an ultimatum. The local negotiators simply told us they had no authority to accept anything less than the "Big Steel" contract.

We had hoped that this year we could get back to genuine collective bargaining on a local basis because the difference between Big Steel and our Company has become so obvious that we felt the Union could hardly ignore it. Once again, however, the Government has intervened and we have been thrown willy-nilly into Big Steel's labor dispute and about a week ago I found myself before the Presidential Fact Finding Board for the Steel Industry. It is most significant that in the Steel hearing practically all of the Union's statistical and economic information concerns nineteen, more or less, integrated companies. Yet this same financial and profit data, with which we are not concerned, is supposed to be used to develop a wage formula which might eventually be forced on us.

In that same hearing, Mr. Murray, the chief of the Steelworkers' Union, stated, in effect, that we deserved to be tied to Big Steel because we have always waited to see what Big Steel was going to do. In a sense, Mr. Murray's statement was true but he omitted to add that we have waited because we had no alternative. The

Union has in effect told us that if we wanted to close with them ahead of Big Steel, we could do so only by accepting all of their demands against Big Steel. The Union would never settle for less, because such a settlement would prove a costly precedent in their negotiations with United States Steel Corporation.

We have been made a party to the Fact-Finding case on the ground that negotiations between the Union and our Company have reached an impasse and the Government has intervened to prevent a strike. The truth of the matter is that though we may be at an impasse, we have not had any negotiations in any real sense of the term. We have had a perfunctory meeting but we were not even advised of the Union's demands until Messrs. Murray and Nathan enlightened us at the Fact-Finding hearing. We have not bargained because both parties have accepted the fact that The Babcock & Wilcox Tube Company no longer has the power to make its own wage agreements.

I have no doubt, gentlemen, that there has been lodged in the Steelworkers' Union a greater concentration of economic power than any business monopoly or cartel has ever enjoyed. Moreover, it may be serving to create a similar concentration on the employer side, because we are moving toward the point where the weaker companies on the fringes of the steel industry cannot be expected to follow the Steel Pattern at all costs and at all times.

I have been told that some labor experts now enunciate the doctrine that labor should not underwrite the losses of the smaller employers and that if there is to be a choice between going into liquidation and failure to meet the highest labor standards of the largest and most prosperous companies, the former alternative is to be preferred. Such a theory may or may not be sound; that is not for me to determine. I can only observe that it is a certain road to monopoly.

———

At the time of the great steel strike of 1959, the American Economic Foundation ran a full-page advertisement in the New York papers which struck at the heart of the problem.

## How Would YOU Settle the Steel Strike?

(1) The key issue of the steel strike is simple: *who should get how much for doing what in the production of steel?*

Everybody who can read can understand the argument when it is simply presented, and can form his own opinion as to how it should be settled.

Moreover, everybody has a right to an opinion in this strike because everybody is affected by it.

But the simple truth needed to form an opinion has, thus far, not been publicly presented.

Here it is:

(2) The incorrect assumption that has confused collective bargaining in the steel strike (and many others) is that wages should go up just as fast as production-per-man-hour goes up.

This theory has been accepted in the United States by most industries ever since World War II.

Obviously, as long as this theory prevails the consuming public will never again have the advantage of the lower prices that used to follow improved hourly productivity.

This error is based on the faulty conclusion that the human energy of the worker is responsible for the increased production.

As a matter of fact, less than 5% of the energy used up in steel production is supplied by the worker—the remaining 95% comes from the tools supplied for the worker's use.

To say that the steel workers supply the energy that makes steel is like saying that the locomotive engineer supplies the energy that hauls the train.

(3) So, in steel, as in all manufacturing, credit for the production belongs to two groups of people: those who *supply* the tools and those who *use* them.

A "set of tools" for a steel worker, that is, the production facilities per employee, amounts to $20,000.

In 1958 the reward to the stockholder for supplying this $20,000 set of tools was about $900, made up of about $600 in cash dividends plus the future benefit of about $300 of profit reinvested in the business.

Last year the reward per employee for using this $20,000 set of tools was $6,456, made up of $5,846 in cash plus $610 in future benefits.

The hard core of the argument is that the negotiators for the steel workers want increases which would require that the companies take away part of the payment for supplying the tools and add it to the payment for using them.

The companies have offered increases providing that the union will agree to certain changes in work practices that would lower the production cost of steel.

This the unions have not agreed to do.

Both sides claim to be firmly opposed to providing higher wages through higher selling prices.

There you have the heart of the issue—the facts on which public opinion should be based.

Both sides have talked themselves out, and it is now just an old-fashioned "tug of war."

(4) No one in his right mind would suggest that the worker receive only the share of production that his energy accounted for.

Such a policy would give the tool owners a fabulous reward, far out of line with the amount needed to stimulate saving and investment.

But no one in his right mind would suggest that the reward to the tool owners should be so small as to make them unwilling to continue to provide the tools on which the progress and welfare of the tool users depend.

In America, during times of peace, we have never had laws controlling wages and profits—we have always worked them out through free bargaining, which depends upon common sense and the spirit of fair play.

In this longest of all steel strikes, bargaining has broken down.

There are only two forces that can break the deadlock, government action which could sign the death warrant of free bargaining, and the force of public opinion which is the true supreme court in any free nation.

(5) Another angle from which to view this matter is the overall distribution of the steel dollars received from the customer in 1958. Here it is:

| | |
|---|---|
| Cost of Outside Goods and Services....... | 42.3 cents |
| Cost of Human Energy (Payroll, Benefits, etc.)............................... | 38.2 cents |
| Cost of Payments to Government (Taxes).. | 7.8 cents |
| Cost of Tools Wearing Out (Depreciation, etc.)............................... | 5.4 cents |
| Cost of Using Tools (Dividends and Reinvestments).......................... | 6.3 cents |
| Total.............................. | 100.0 cents |

These figures were derived from the consolidated certified reports of the companies whose combined output represents 95.2% of the steel ingot production in the United States.

(6) If *you*, personally, were the final judge in this settlement what would *you* do?

If *you* had $20,000 of your savings in steel stocks, would you think that your reward for supplying more than 95% of the productive energy was too much, too little, or about right?

If *you* were making your living using the $20,000 set of tools, would you think that your reward for supplying less than 5% of the productive energy was too much, too little, or about right?

It is high time that the general public, which is *you*, and *you*, and *you*, stopped being a disinterested, indifferent audience and started to make its opinion felt.

Whatever that opinion is, make it felt in your circle of influence whether that circle be great or small.

Talk about it, write about it, lay down your reasons for your judgment as to who should get how much for doing what in the steel industry.

If this strike is not settled with regard for the public interest it can turn into an American tragedy because the pattern of this settlement will become the pattern for many other industries.

—The American Economic Foundation, 51 East 42nd Street, New York 17, N. Y.*

---

Now a distinguished student of the law looks at this question of compulsory unionism in relation to personal freedom.

Sylvester Petro, author of several books on labor policy, is Professor of Law at New York University Law School, specializing in the law of labor relations. He is a graduate of the University of Chicago and from the same institution received his Doctor of Law (J.D.) in 1945.

Prior to his attendance at the University of Chicago, Professor Petro worked in steel mills for several years and was active in promoting unionization in the CIO.

Consequently his ideas are backed by both wide practical experience and legal authority. A brief study prepared for publication

* A non-profit research organization founded in 1939 "to locate the causes of, and find remedies for, the friction between economic groups."

by the Institute of Public Affairs of New York University merits wide attention and consideration. Some excerpts from this study follow.

## Personal Freedom and Labor Policy

### SYLVESTER PETRO

Almost a century ago, Sir Henry Maine set the whole matter straight in giving as his definition of primitive society, "It has for its units, not individuals, but groups of men." And he drove home the point with one of the most fruitful generalizations which social science has yet produced: "The movement in the progressive societies has hitherto been a movement from status to contract." In reality there are only persons, only individuals; only persons have hopes and dreams, fears and loves, aims and desires. The success of a society can therefore be measured only in terms of the freedom of choice of individual persons. This means that the person, not the group, must be the unit of calculation in good society; and that freedom of contract, the formal term for the personal freedom which Whitehead called a necessity to mankind, must be a basic social institution.

Of all aspects of contemporary life, none serves better than labor relations to demonstrate the vicious, antisocial consequences of the holistic view, with its subordination of the individual to the group, its sacrifice of personal freedom to group power and authority. Here the individual, undifferentiated person, he whose dignity poets and political philosophers have sung and extolled, has been thrust rudely out of sight and out of consideration. Labor relations law, policy and practice have for the past generation been a continuing, large-scale experiment in suppressing the individual and glorifying the group.

The fruit has been bitter. But it all could have been, in fact it was, predicted. Protection of personal rights and personal freedom was necessary not only if real persons were to achieve their personal goals. The primacy of the individual as against the group was necessary also if the greatest group—society—was not to be exploited and abused by the leadership of subordinate collectivities. For the expression "glorification of the group and subordination of the individual" is merely a rough and imprecise way of saying that the most aggressive and often the most unscrupulous persons—those who become leaders of groups through coercive practices—are to have their way as against the desires of all others, that is, society.

Anyone with moderate awareness must realize that trade union leaders in the United States today are generally guilty of antisocial conduct, that the habits and tendencies of some threaten the foundations of society, and that a good many are cheap crooks and embezzling scoundrels. As a matter of fact, today almost everyone thinks that there is something wrong in labor relations and that something needs to be done about it. This is all to the good. Yet we must be sure that we know what we are doing before we act. If we wish to accomplish an enduring result, we must identify and attack the basic cause of the evil. Another law against stealing will do no good. We already have such laws. They deal with only the most superficial symptoms of the things that have gone wrong in labor relations.

The basic cause of almost every antisocial aspect in labor relations today lies in the fact that, owing to legal and political errors of omission and commission, individual workingmen are daily denied and deprived of the rights which our longest traditions and most carefully wrought principles designate as the rights of free men.

The labor relations process begins with the organizing stage and continues through the stages of collective bargaining and administration of the collective agreement. At no point in this complex process do law and government adequately protect the rights which men must have if they are to be free. At some points, indeed, law and government themselves deny those rights.

Under the law, workingmen are declared to have the right to join or not to join a union, free of either physical or economic coercion by trade unions or employers. It will be shown presently that this law is substantially unenforced as regards trade-union coercion; but first it must be noted that the law itself lacks inherent integrity. For after thus declaring the right of workingmen to join or not to join unions, the law goes on to permit unions to impose arrangements (sometimes called "compulsory-unionism agreements," sometimes called "union security contract") which require union membership as a condition of employment. All such arrangements are forbidden by law in 19 states, but federal law permits some, and the laws of almost all industrialized states allow all forms of compulsory unionism, including the most drastic form

—the full closed shop, which means that a man must belong to the union before he is hired.

Compulsory unionism and personal freedom are incompatible. Employment in a free society is a volitional contractual arrangement between a person seeking work and a person seeking someone to work for him. But compulsory unionism is a device by means of which an outsider to the employment relationship imposes a toll upon both real parties involved. It is, therefore, indistinguishable in principle—sometimes indistinguishable in fact—from the tolls imposed by brigands and the "protection money" demanded by extortionists. If corruption prevails among the leaders of unions which practice compulsory unionism, no one should be surprised.

Compulsory unionism is, as the name accurately discloses, coerced unionism. But the basic principle of current national labor policy is the principle of free employee choice—free of physical or economic coercion by either unions or employers. We cannot have it both ways. Either we are in favor of permitting unions and employers to use economically coercive devices in order to impose or to prevent union membership, or we are not. Integrity demands that if unions be allowed to impose compulsory unionism agreements, employers must be allowed similarly to impose non-union agreements. As things stand at present, the acceptance of compulsory unionism must mean in the long run that every worker will have to join a union, or shortly become a member, if he wishes to work. To speak of personal freedom in such circumstances would be a cheap fake. Legal acceptance of compulsory unionism arrangements amounts to an anomaly in any legal system having as its basic principle the idea of personal freedom and free employee choice.

The law lacks integrity too in that, while declaring a right of employees to join or not to join unions, it also provides that a union selected by a majority of employees in any "appropriate bargaining unit" is the exclusive representative of all employees in that unit. Suppose that there are 1,000 men employed in an "appropriate bargaining unit." An election is held in which 600 cast ballots. Of the 600, say that 301 vote in favor of the union and 299 against. In every such case the union will be hailed as the "free choice" of the employees and will be "certified" as the exclusive bargaining representative of every employee in the unit—

including the 299 who voted against it and the 400 who did not vote at all.

Merely to understand the exclusive bargaining principle, let alone experiencing how it works out in practice, is to realize that it is irreconcilable with personal freedom. The exclusive bargaining (or "majority" rule) principle means that every intimate detail of the workingman's employment life is a matter for decision by the trade union. The workingman and his employer are barred by the full force of law and government from dealing directly together on any matter subject to collective bargaining. It is one thing for a workingman voluntarily to delegate such authority to a union or to any other person or entity. But for the law to decree that despite his own wishes to the contrary, a worker must accept the working conditions bargained for by a trade union is something entirely different. It amounts to nothing less than an absolute negation of that freedom of contract which is basic to a free society and which, Maine thought, distinguished the progressive societies. . . .

Current conditions in labor relations pose a clear threat to the things which Americans hold most dear. The power of trade union leaders, built as it is upon compulsion and coercion, holds the individual workingman tightly bound in a web of fear. His well-being, his hopes and dreams, must be worked out, if at all, within the interstices of the plans and ambitions of union leaders. The same power holds society in thrall as well. Inflation, monopolistic abuse, unemployment, uneconomic use of the most precious resource of all—manpower—these and some others, almost equally bitter, are the fruit of the way in which we have allowed trade unionism to develop. The causes, I have tried to show, are two:

First, the abandonment of personal freedom as the primary and exclusive goal of policy. Embodied for us in the principles of private property and freedom of contract, personal freedom is much more in our tradition than a mere philosophical abstraction or a romantic dream. It is the sturdy product of a heritage rich in experience of other systems and other methods of operating a community. Our civilization developed respect and reverence for personal freedom because it made complete sense; it worked; it brought to pass the things which real, living people wished to have brought to pass. Abandoning it has meant what it had to mean—the frustration of the goals of men. If we wish to resecure our liberties and our well-being, we shall have to make personal freedom—perhaps under the name "free employee choice"—the central, unqualified principle of labor policy.

Second, the neglect and distortion of law. This has come about largely as a consequence of the wrong ideas which have prevailed now for almost 50 years concerning legal and judicial administration. I shall enlarge upon this point, and suggest remedies, before dealing with the problem of restoring personal freedom in Labor relations.

For a generation, more or less, the administration of justice in labor relations has been taken away from the courts. Although our federal and state constitutions uniformly establish the constitutional courts as the appropriate agencies for the administration of justice, crippling legislation has left them in labor law not much more than figureheads. Their power to deal vigorously and straightforwardly with vicious and unlawful conduct by trade unions has been greatly reduced by anti-injunction legislation. These are federal and state laws which prevent the courts from ordering unions to end unlawful conduct.

While the anti-injunction legislation did not purport to prevent the courts from continuing to define the meaning of law and thus to direct the devolpment and growth of substantive law, this result was achieved in another way. Congress and a number of state legislatures set up administrative tribunals, usually called labor relations boards, and delegated to them the law-defining and law-developing functions which our constitutions give exclusively to the courts. I have but recently completed an exhaustive study of the way in which the federal labor board (the NLRB) has interpreted and applied the National Labor Relations (Taft-Hartley) Act. The conclusion of the study is that, although the constitutional courts worked manfully to correct the misinterpretations and distortions of the NLRB, the functional primacy of the board proved too much for them. A purely political agency, the board used political rather than legal criteria in interpreting and applying the Taft-Hartley Act. The results were, first, extreme distortion of the fundamental provisions of the Act; and second, the destruction of the free employee choice policy of the Act.

Proper administration of the law is at least as important as good law. The first thing necessary in order to correct the evils in labor relations, I therefore submit, is the restoration to the constitutional courts of the country the full responsibility for interpreting and applying our labor relations laws. Concretely, this means repealing all anti-injunction legislation and abolishing all labor relations boards.

As to the reforms needed in the substantive law itself, these may all be subsumed under a single heading: Unqualified supremacy of the principle of free employee choice. Put generally, this means the total outlawing of every form of physical and economic coercion used by either employers or trade unions to dictate to employees concerning their choice as regards joining or not joining unions, or participating or not participating in concerted union activities. In detail, full implementation of the principle of free employee choice will require:

(1) A broad prohibition of restraint and coercion by employers and unions of the right of employees to make up their own minds on the question of union membership or participation in strikes.

(2) A specific provision of law to the effect that picketing, even when peaceable, is subject to that ban when it has or is intended to have coercive effects, either physical or economic.

(3) A specific declaration that the ban on restraint or coercion applies to the economic coercion implicit in all "agreements" proposed by unions or employers which make union membership or non-membership a condition of employment.

(4) A general prohibition against inducing any work stoppage by the employees of one employer when a union has a dispute with any other employer. (This is designed to outlaw all secondary boycotts and other monopolistic pressures.)

(5) Emphatic repeal of the exclusive-bargaining, majority-rule principle, including a positive statement that unions shall be the exclusive bargaining representatives of only those workers who expressly delegate such authority to them. The present statutory and doctrinal requirement, imposing a legally enforceable duty upon employers to bargain only with majority unions, would need to be deleted.

In arguing the case finally for the principle of free employee choice, I shall say again what I and many others have already said. This sound and workable principle, commended by both theoretical considerations and the felt needs of a people, is being frustrated presently by conceptual and administrative deficiencies. The consequence has been the perversion and distortion of trade-unionism, to the general harm of society. Internal corruption in some trade unions and the external dangers to society posed by almost all industry-wide trade unions can all be traced directly to their compulsory, coercive practices. Besides presenting the gravest kind of social threat, these practices drain the vitality of the principles and policies generally. More is involved than the deprivations of human freedom which characterize our labor relations, more even than the corrupt and uneconomic practices which compulsion and coercion in labor relations are breeding. At stake, too, are the simple honesty, humanity, good sense and integrity of the United States, and its ideals as an intelligently conducted, enduring free society.

   —Reprinted by permission of the Institute of Economic Affairs,
   New York University.

The so-called Right to Work is one of the most bitter and controversial phases of the struggle for economic freedom for all men. W. L. White discusses this in his article published in the *Reader's Digest,* August 1958.

## *The Right to Work:*
## *Our Hottest Labor Issue*

### W. L. WHITE

Should a man be forced to join or pay dues to a union in order to hold his job? Compulsory union membership is permitted under the Taft-Hartley Act, provided union leaders can persuade or force the employer to sign a union shop contract. But the same federal act provides that employes may not be compelled to join a union in those states which have "right-to-work" laws. Such laws are now in effect in 18 states. Labor's top leaders bitterly denounce them, and they have become a hot political issue.

The basic arguments of the two sides may be simply stated. Those who support voluntary unionism—and hence the right-to-work laws —feel that nobody should be forced to join any organization against his will. They point out that many workers who do not wish to join a union are coerced by contracts requiring them to do so or lose their jobs.

Those opposed to right-to-work laws argue that, under the Taft-

Hartley law, unions represent both members and non-members; any benefits won by the union accrue to all, and therefore all should pay. Laws banning union shop contracts, they say, encourage free riders.

There are many other issues involved. For example, the AFL-CIO, in its policy statement opposing right-to-work laws, argues that compulsory union membership is "clearly in line with our great American democratic tradition" because "union policies reflect the views of the majority of the workers. If the individual member objects to any policy, he can vote to change the union officials who have recommended that policy."

What Union Members Say. Hear now the voice of Mary L. Crabtree, who testified last year before the Indiana Legislature when it was considering a right-to-work measure. She was a member of Local 1048, International Brotherhood of Electrical Workers, she said, "because I have to be. I don't agree with the union's political views. I have been a member for 9 years, and have not yet found any effective way to protest any policy."

Cecil C. Roeder, of Anderson, Ind., told the lawmakers about union democracy within Walter Reuther's United Auto Workers. A member of its Local 622, he said: "For seven years I was denied the right to belong to my local union because I came before the Indiana Senate Committee in 1948 and testified in favor of a bill to outlaw the union shop. I favor this right-to-work bill because it will give the union back to its membership."

Milo Graber, who has worked 12 years in the International Harvester plant at Fort Wayne, reported that its employes, in a National Labor Relations Board election, voted down compulsory unionism. "But in less than a year," he reported, "union and company officials negotiated a compulsory membership clause. If Indiana had had a right-to-work law in 1951, the company and union officials could not have forced the employes into union membership against their will."

Organizing Methods. In organizing members, unions sometimes use methods which leave little freedom of choice either to the employer or the workers. In California, which has no right-to-work law, an organizer for Teamster Local 912 approached the small firm of H. A. Rider & Son (it processes apple juice), asking that it sign a contract including a compulsory membership clause. When the Rider firm said it would sign only if the union got the consent of a majority of the employes, the organizer said this was "too much trouble." Instead, withdrawing his union shop demands, the organizer threw a picket line around the Rider plant in September 1956.

In theory the Taft-Hartley law provides a remedy, so Rider asked the NLRB for an election. It took six weary months to arrange one. Then, in a secret ballot, Rider's workers got their chance to speak. One voted for the Teamsters; 16 voted against.

The union, which said it "would not challenge the vote," nevertheless continued picketing. It took the NLRB four more tedious months—costly both to Rider and the workers—to decide that this post-election picket line also was unjustified.

Under a state right-to-work law, a judge can, in a few hours and by court injunction, stop illegal blockades established by unions to coerce compulsory membership clauses from employers. Many Californians want their local courts to have this power. William F. Knowland, leader of the U.S. Senate Republicans and also a candidate for Governor of California, urges such a measure. For this reason he has been marked for defeat by the AFL-CIO policy committee. [He was.]

On the Democratic side in the Senate, Frank Lausche of Ohio also favors the right-to-work principle. It should be, he says, "just as sacred as any constitutional right."

Case History: The Railroads. The AFL-CIO charges that right-to-work laws "have the effect of keeping unions from growing." But from 1934 until 1951, workers on American railroads were protected from compulsory unionism by a provision of the Railway Labor Act, and during those years most railway unions trebled in voluntary membership.

Nevertheless, in 1951, union leaders urged and got from Congress legislation permitting compulsory membership contracts with the railway companies. In this they were reversing the policies of the late Warren S. Stone, head of the Brotherhood of Locomotive Engineers.

"I do not believe," said Stone, "in forcing a man to join a union. It is contrary to the principles of free government. We work willingly side by side with other engineers who do not belong to our union, though they enjoy the advantages we have obtained.

But other union leaders carried the day. Since then, through coaxing and strike threats, they have obtained compulsory union membership contracts with all the nation's major railroads except the Louisville & Nashville. Latest to give in was the Santa Fe, which, during its long court battle, received hundreds of letters from employes imploring the company to stand firm.

A Santa Fe worker in La Jolla, Calif., asked why, if there really were "so many bleeding hearts" in favor of compulsory membership, "has it never been submitted to the rank and file for a vote?"

It never was. Instead, union leaders asked their Santa Fe members to authorize a strike on the issue.

An employe in Escondido, Calif., then wrote: "How can the union ask us to go on strike without first allowing us to vote on whether or not we want a union shop?"

On some roads the unions held a vote on compulsory membership. A California employe of another railroad (who wrote the Santa Fe that "I have been a union member all my railroad life, but compulsory unionism must go if we are to remain a free people") described two such elections:

"Of approximately 4500 switchmen, only 1700 were allowed to vote; 1000 voted for the union shop, and it was put in. In my class of yardmaster, only 200 out of approximately 350 were allowed to vote; (compulsory membership) was placed in effect with only 125 men voting for it. The union counted the ballots in both of these phony elections, so there was never any doubt of the outcome."

A Santa Fe union member wrote to the company from Riverside, Calif., "You probably understand that many employes fear to express their views, on account of possible union reprisals." Because of such fears, the names of the above-quoted railroad workers are not used here.

Are the fears justified? Consider the case of William T. Harrison, a veteran of 30 years' service with the Louisville & Nashville Railroad, 20 years a member of the Brotherhood of Railway Clerks, and for seven a District Chairman. Because his local opposed compulsory union membership by a vote of 208 to 1, Harrison dared to write his Congressman when, in 1951, the matter was coming up in Washington for a vote. For this offense, he was expelled by the Grand Lodge of his union.

Union Punishments. The two federal laws which now legalize compulsory union membership (Taft-Hartley and the Railway Labor Act) attempt to give protection to union members, willing and unwilling, who work for companies whose businesses affect interstate commerce. Both stipulate that the union cannot drop a member, and thereby cause him to lose his job if he pays initiation fees and dues. The Railway statute makes union "assessments" compulsory, while exempting the worker from union fines and penalties. But millions of Americans not working for companies whose businesses affect interstate commerce are unable to get any federal protection. They may be punished, fined or expelled for as great a variety of reasons as there are union constitutions, unless state laws protect them.

The American Federation of Musicians has expelled members for criticizing its president, James C. Petrillo, now retired. A Cleveland carpenter was expelled for revealing "union business in public" when he protested that he should have been a delegate to a union meeting. A wireless telegrapher with a family to support was expelled from his union (and lost his job) only because he spoke up in a meeting against Communist leadership. Unions have expelled men for "defaming" a politician supported by union officers, and for opposing a bonus to be paid to union officials.

Union Dues. George Meany, head of the AFL-CIO, says: "We have got to wipe off the statute books the so-called 'right-to-work' laws. They are destructive of the rights of union workers."

Often these "rights" seem illusory. For example, there is no legal ceiling on dues. In theory they cover the costs of collective bargaining. But, according to the testimony of witnesses appearing before the McClellan investigating committee, the International Union of Operating Engineers had, out of its collective-bargaining dues money, paid union president William E. Maloney (now retired) $13,387 in expenses for a trip to a labor conference in Europe—after Maloney's transportation and maintenance costs, totaling $1001, had already been paid out of federal tax money. Also charged to the collective-bargaining costs of this union were $120,535 to maintain a yacht which, for the convenience of President Maloney and other union officials, shuttled between Long Island and Miami.

The AFL-CIO, defending compulsory membership, insists that "union policies reflect the views of the majority of the workers." Yet Hunter Wharton, supervisor of the Philadelphia local of the Operating Engineers acknowledged to the McClellan Committee that although it has 4500 members, only 1250 are eligible to vote on local affairs. Senator McClellan said this made it "disgustingly clear" that the union was "holding men in servitude to a dictatorship."

Answering this type of charge, the AFL-CIO argues that a college fraternity has a right to suggest that unwilling members get out. "By the same token, union members say, 'If you don't like our arrangements, you can go elsewhere.' "

In the case of a crane operator who does not like the arrangement under which his dues money maintains a yacht for Maloney, "elsewhere" would have to be one of the 18 states whose laws now guarantee him the right to operate a crane without joining this union.

NLRB Delays. Nonunion workers, even when they can appeal to the NLRB, feel that it often moves too slowly to give them real help. Example: The Cisco Construction Co. was low bidder on an Army contract to build guided-missile installations in the state of Washington. Trouble developed because Cisco had never forced its employes to join a union. The carpenters' union put a picket line on the job site, which driver-members of Teamster Local 174 were ordered not to cross.

Few nonunion workers or small employers have the money to hire lawyers and then wait for the time (almost a year) it took the NLRB to rule that the union's real aim was "to secure the unionization from Cisco's unwilling employes." Washington lacks a right-to-work law, under which the guilty union officials would have been liable to fines or imprisonment.

In Lebanon, Ore., in 1956, the small sub-contracting firm of Morse Brothers was supplying concrete for a new high school. Because Morse employes paid no union dues, Teamster Local 324 picketed the school site. All other unions put down their tools. When the Teamsters then asked Morse for a compulsory membership contract, Morse said the firm was willing if the Teamsters could persuade a majority of the men "to sign for the union." The Teamster representative said that couldn't be done, but that he would talk to the men after Morse had signed the contract.

So that the job could go on, Morse signed. But the Morse workers found that Teamster membership would cost them a $40 initiation fee, quarterly dues of $15 and December dues of $5, with $10.50 per month paid on their behalf by the employer into the Salem, Ore., Teamsters' Security Fund, plus another ten cents per hour into the Teamsters' Pension Fund. Not surprisingly, the workers balked.

When the Teamster representative arrived, they asked what benefits they would get under his pension plan. The representative didn't know, "because it is still being worked out." He went on to say that they had to join now anyway, because their boss had already signed the contract—"or we can send men down to replace you."

It took the NLRB almost a year to rule that Teamster Local 324 "seems to have been interested in the acquisition of money for various funds, without regard to the rights or desires of employes."

Opinion—Here and Abroad. In legalized compulsory unionism, the United States stands in splendid isolation, with few allies outside the Iron Curtain. It is prohibited by the constitutions, laws or judicial decisions of Austria, Belgium, Denmark, France, Holland, Norway, Sweden, Switzerland and Western Germany, all of which have strong voluntary unions.

The Australian Labor Party, which once favored compulsory unionism, last year decided that "it does not assist in building up a virile union organization in which people become unionists because they believe in it."

The AFL-CIO contends that right-to-work laws are intended to "bust unions." Yet a *Fortune* survey made last year shows that in the states which have such laws union membership is as high as ever—in some cases higher. It would seem, therefore, that these laws, rather than driving members out of a union, simply give them some measure of control over their leadership.

An Opinion Research Corp. survey taken early in 1957, after the first disclosures by the McClellan Committee, gave right-to-work support a majority of 55 per cent. A Gallup poll, taken in August, after further hearings, gave right-to-work a 63 per cent majority. However, union members, faithful to their leaders' urging, were 61 per cent against it.

A political ferment over the right to work is brewing. In six of the states which now have right-to-work laws, the decision was reached by referendum of the voters. Initiative or referendum elections are in prospect this November in California, Colorado, Idaho, Kansas, Montana, Ohio and Washington. Have you thought through this vital issue for yourself?

—Reprinted with permission of the *Reader's Digest.*

---

In the whole history of strike violence, which in recent years has grown to appalling proportions, there is probably none more vicious in the pages of industrial history than the goon-led reign of terror let loose by the UAW-CIO in Wisconsin against the Kohler Company.

We will let Mr. Herbert V. Kohler tell the story as he presented it in an address before the Economic Club of Detroit, February 25, 1957.

## Can a Free Economy Tolerate Union Violence?

### HERBERT V. KOHLER

The right to strike is a legal right. I would not wish that right denied.

But—does the right to strike override all other legal rights in this country? To what extent are unions to be especially privileged and above the law? And if they have special privileges and immunities, what will be the effect upon our economy?

The union shop was one of the demands we refused the UAW-CIO in bargaining for a second contract. We have strong convictions on that subject. They are continuing to grow stronger as some unions use funds from membership dues to finance political programs and propaganda with which a large part of their members do not agree.

The "Monthly Labor Review" of the Bureau of Labor Statistics for June 1955 showed that over eighty per cent of union members were captives of the union shop, or some other form of compulsory unionism.

In our correspondence regarding labor relations, we have received a great many letters from union members, including UAW members, complaining of the outrage of compulsory unionism.

Other union demands included:

No shop rules without the union's agreement;

No increase or reduction of hours without the union's agreement;

No sub-contracting of work without the union's permission;

Automatic wage progression with no merit increases;

Promotions on a strict seniority basis without regard to fitness.

These are examples, and I am sure many of you have had similar experiences, of what are called "non-economic" demands. They represent union attempts to take over functions of management. If those attempts were successful, they would have far more economic significance than so-called "economic" demands for wages and fringes.

The UAW made "economic" demands upon us, too, but they said repeatedly that wages was not the principal issue. I think they told more truth than they realized or intended. Wage demands were bait for members. But the UAW really was after more and more power for the union leaders. If they could have got the union shop, the wage bait would have become still less important.

In April of 1954—nearly three years ago—the UAW-CIO started a strike against Kohler Co. The strike has been marked by mass picketing and violence.

Marching in lock step, a mob, led by professional goons, blocked the gates.

Men were enticed to go through the line to their jobs. When they tried, the strikers closed in and trapped them.

Non-strikers were beaten—kicked in the groin—manhandled—and thrown back.

"Nobody gets through," the pickets chanted.

And for 54 days, mass picketing kept the plant closed.

Here is a case of organized violence interfering with normal economic activity.

People who wanted to work—to earn a livelihood for their families—could not do so.

Interstate and foreign commerce was halted for a time, affecting carriers, the trade, and consumers.

I shall talk about our experiences only as they may shed light upon some of your problems, problems which face and menace our entire economy.

Mass picketing is prohibited under Wisconsin law, and also under Federal law.

The conduct of the pickets constituted unlawful assembly, and at times riot.

This unlawful conduct was deliberate and planned. It was in full effect and at full intensity from the first hour of the strike.

We were warned that this would happen and that we had better give in before it did happen. Among those who uttered the warning was Emil Mazey, Secretary-Treasurer of the UAW-CIO, who proclaimed himself "the Patton of the picket line."

Kohler is a village of less than 1800. The police force was too small to cope with the horde of pickets. The sheriff did not try.

Day after day his deputies were fed from the union soup kitchen, and they fraternized with the pickets. The payoff was his re-election, with union backing, in the fall of '54.

Hope for law enforcement came when the Wisconsin Employment Relations Board ordered a hearing. The board limited the number of pickets, and disbanded the blockade at the factory entrances. But it was not until the Attorney General moved for enforcement that the union agreed to obey the order.

Once the lines were open, men and women came streaming back to work—all of them unsolicited.

And everyone who has been hired since then has come to us unsolicited.

The union carried on a propaganda campaign that the jobs were temporary—that these people would later be displaced by strikers. We assured the new employees that their jobs were permanent.

With the ending of mass picketing at the plant, there followed a reign of terror away from the plant—sneak attacks—under cover of darkness. Non-strikers' cars were dynamited. Shotgun blasts were fired into their homes. They were assaulted. In all there have been more than 800 acts of violence and vandalism calculated to terrorize anyone who dared to work.

Of all the strike indecencies, the picketing of homes was the most outrageous. Men returning from work found mobs of two to five hundred besieging their homes, yelling obscenities, terrorizing their wives and children. They were subject to intimidation which would cause even a man of great courage to pause and weigh the danger to his family.

Such men were subjected to this terror because they had the audacity to hold an opinion different from that of the UAW-CIO.

The union disclaimed responsibility; but on the air and in printed publicity they were gleeful about these "reception committees," as they called them.

When a circuit court issued an injunction against the union and its officers, the home picketing stopped.

Since the first hour of the strike, there has not been a day when a man could work without fear of injury to himself and to his family.

Every time a vandal was caught the union came to his defense, providing bail bonds and lawyers.

In one case, four vandals received jail sentences, and then received salaries from the union while they were serving time.

One union goon imported from Detroit was sentenced to state prison for a felonious assault. The union asked its members to send him Christmas cards while he was in the "pen."

Another goon—John Gunaca—is a fugitive from justice. The Governor of Michigan has refused, for nearly three years, to extradite him. Gunaca is charged with assaulting and breaking the neck of William Bersch, who died some months later.

Bill Bersch, a screw machine operator in our brass division, was a high school classmate of mine.

I want to digress for a moment to say this. Another function of the goons was to keep strikers on the picket lines.

The UAW called these goons "morale builders." A striker, warned in the presence of his wife and family that he had been missed on the picket line, was quite apt to have his "morale" lifted and be back on the picket line the next day.

On July 5, 1955, a Norwegian ship with a cargo of English clay for our pottery docked at Sheboygan.

As preparations were made to unload and truck the clay to Kohler, a riotous mob descended on the dock area.

The trucking contractor's men were beaten and manhandled, and fled for their lives. The trucks and unloading equipment left behind were sabotaged.

Our plant manager and some associates were trapped. A squad car finally made its way through the milling, howling mob to rescue them. Strikers rocked the police car, and threatened our men and their police escort.

Law enforcement officials made no attempt to restore order.

As the day wore on the mob prowled the city, overturning cars, beating non-strikers.

The Mayor of Sheboygan ordered the police to keep Kohler unloading equipment away from the dock. Not one individual has ever been arrested, despite the fact that the rioting occurred in full view of the authorities.

One newspaper described the 24-hour siege as "a state of anarchy."

The ship was eventually unloaded at Montreal, where the police gave an abortive picket line five minutes to disperse.

But in Sheboygan, the UAW-CIO had shamefully demonstrated its power over its captive politicians, sworn to maintain law and order.

In a booklet directed against our company, the UAW complained: "The law prevents the men and women on strike from keeping the scabs out of the plant."

If they can get the law changed to legalize their violence, you can be sure they will.

By calling a strike the UAW held that it revoked our right to operate our plant and our employees' right to work—therefore, violence was justified by our refusal to shut down the plant and lock out employees who wanted to work.

That specious reasoning may reflect some of the current practices in strike situations. Shutting down a plant only postpones trouble and sacrifices principle. Employees who want to work are left at the mercy of ruthless union leaders.

One of the union attorneys uttered this gem: "When they (meaning the strikers) think they're in the right, they can't be held to this strict, straightline behavior of ordinary, common, normal relationship." And I ask, why not?

And let me repeat, the strike was violent from the first hour—deliberately so.

The UAW-CIO took the injunction against its unlawful strike activities to the Wisconsin Supreme Court. Finally they carried the case to the United States Supreme Court in their effort to strip Wisconsin of the right to prevent strike violence within its borders.

Had they won, the precedent would have had force the country over.

Don't think, however, that their having lost this case will end the matter. They will continue their efforts to whittle away the law.

The issue is basic. The question presented by our situation is this: Should one party to a labor dispute be immune from the law because it is a labor union engaged in a strike?

In the past the excuse offered for violence was that labor organizations were at a disadvantage in bargaining with employers.

The current union position is exemplified by the UAW, which boasts that its power is sufficient to bring to heel the largest corporations in the country. When does collective bargaining become collective coercion?

And now I want to tell you of the most important contribution, at least in our view, that Kohler Co. has made to combat the use of strike violence. We would not carry on contract negotiations while the union was engaging in mass picketing and open lawlessness. We refused to bargain with a gun at our head.

Our right under the law to take this position has been sustained.

Further, we discharged strikers who were guilty of the most flagrant illegal conduct—including union officers who fomented, directed and controlled the illegal conduct.

Why seek a remedy for union coercion in more laws, when the laws we have now are not enforced? Perhaps industry is at fault. Can we expect law enforcement if employers themselves close their eyes to illegal strike conduct to buy temporary peace?

Coercive and illegal conduct will cease only when employers make it clear that they will not buy peace by rewarding lawlessness. Employers must be ready and willing to assert two basic rights:

(1) to refuse to bargain under illegal duress;

(2) to discharge those who foment, direct, and control illegal conduct.

Unsuccessful with its violence and vandalism directed at Kohler Co. and its employees, the UAW turned to the boycott weapon.

Since September 1954, the union has been trying to destroy Kohler Co. by injuring those who do business with us.

What the UAW could not achieve directly, it has attempted by the intimidation and threats which underlie the secondary boycott.

They would use us as an example to convince other employers that anyone who dares resist their demands is under sentence of economic death.

But they will learn—if they have not already done so—that they have taken up a two-edged sword.

The boycott has not hurt us.

It has been a graphic demonstration to the public of the utter ruthlessness of the UAW-CIO. It shows the public clearly that their philosophy is one of rule or ruin.

*U.S. News & World Report* recently quoted one of our competitors as stating that the boycott often backfires. Many people resent the boycott, he said, and insist on Kohler products.

That is our experience. The sales we have lost because of the boycott have been more than offset by the sales we have gained.

There is coming to us more and more evidence that the leaders of other unions are becoming alarmed at the public reaction to this arrogant grasp for power.

And they fear that this public demonstration of irresponsibility will hurt the entire union movement—the responsible as well as the irresponsible.

I have not presented this résumé of the lawless tactics which the UAW has employed against us to elicit sympathy. Despite the union's threat to destroy us we look forward with confidence.

We finished 1954 in the black although the mass picketing closed the plant for 54 days. We had a good year in 1955 and again in 1956.

The men and women now working in our plant are friendly and cooperative. Production per man hour is better than before the strike, and the quality of our products has never been better than it is today.

To meet the demand for our vitreous china fixtures we are building a new plant at Spartanburg, South Carolina.

We expect to be in business for a long time.

It seems to me, that if the philosophy of force and coercion is supinely accepted, industry is speeding the time when it will be unable to operate with any regard for sound economics.

Collective bargaining was endorsed as a national policy on the theory that the economic bargaining power of the employer and his employees should be equalized. Labor unions were accorded many privileges and immunities, which they secured by pleading their weakness.

Today labor unions boast of their power and influence. And in our case the UAW deliberately elected to employ that power unlawfully, to force us to capitulate to their demands.

With unions now in a position to exert substantial force, it is imperative that they recognize their responsibility and refrain from abusing the privileges accorded them.

Collective bargaining cannot minimize industrial disputes or settle disputes upon rational principles, if labor unions are left free to use force and violence to accomplish their objectives.

Resistance to such tactics must be at the plant level if it is to impress upon irresponsible union leadership the fact that force and violence cannot succeed. An employer who succumbs to unlawful coercion, or the threats of illegal tactics, surrenders any real chance of keeping his management within the bounds of sound principles.

No plant can operate on the doctrine that bargaining on wages and conditions of employment can be geared to the threats of union leaders to destroy where they cannot control.

To compromise with lawlessness—whether it be direct force and violence or the more insidious secondary boycott—is to accede to a dictatorship diametrically opposed to a sound employer-employee relationship.

We have little confidence in any pious hope that the lawlessness of a union, if rewarded, will not be repeated.

We are convinced that the future operation of our plant upon sound principles demands that we oppose the coercion to which we have been subjected by the UAW-CIO with every lawful means at our disposal.

Too much power, unrestrained by the law, and much of it contrary to and in defiance of the law, gravely imperils our economy, our society. We need to be vigilant. We must be courageous.

---

Here Westbrook Pegler pin-points a few scenes in the drama of terroristic criminal power exercised by union bosses.

## The Labor Racket Is America's Mafia

### WESTBROOK PEGLER

The only Mafia in the United States are unions, a cabal of privileged henchmen of both political parties with terroristic criminal power extending from the White House and Congress down into the very neighborhoods of our cities and towns.

The recent murder in Chicago, by stabbing, of Herman Posner, 73, a brave but reckless rebel against licensed extortion under the charter of a certified notorious union Mafia, was a crime so familiar that it went practically unnoticed outside the city. It was a repetition of the murder of Dennis Bruce Ziegler, under almost identical conditions, 27 years ago.

Posner was stabbed in the yard of his modest home. Ziegler was shot dead on his own doorstep two nights after he had begged the intelligence office of the Internal Revenue to protect him because he was marked for death for giving information regarding the income of William E. Maloney, the president of the Union of Operating Engineers.

Maloney is a despicable thug on the order of Dave Beck, former boss of the Teamsters. He got rich exploiting workers in collusion with contractors against the interests of his subjects and government agencies which were forced to hire union workers on public undertakings. He finally was kicked out but he still is immune to even the routine examination that would be imposed on a suspect in a stolen car case.

Posner's union is the Stage and Moving Picture Employees' Union, the old, notorious AFL racket which was exposed beyond question in the newspaper coup which sent to Federal prisons Willie Bioff and George Browne, and two of Roosevelt's political accomplices in the Hollywood political corruption.

Bioff and Browne were ordinary Chicago guttersnipes but they became social lions in Hollywood by reason of their power to tax the actors and technical people and to sabotage the whole industry. There were about 20 famous "columnists" of New York papers and national syndicates peddling pap out of Hollywood in those days. Most of them are still at it. Not one of them ever published an exposé of Bugsy Siegel, the dictator of the Hollywood underworld, who finally was murdered by a rifle bullet in his girl's home. Stupidity, payola and fear protected this Mafia from injurious publicity.

Browne and Bioff got light sentences because they ratted on one of the magnates of the producing business. But he also got a light prison term, because the "industry" mightily plugged Roosevelt's "birthday balls," his Warm Springs realty promotion and the March of Dimes.

Ultimately six of the old Capone mob were sentenced to prison but were released before they were eligible for parole. They had paid tribute in the guise of legal fees to Harry Truman's machine in St. Louis.

Members of the Roosevelt family got many valuable favors from the movie industry, including insurance business and a job at $35,000 a year for Jimmy as technical advisor to Sam Goldwyn. Jimmy did not know enough about movies to chop tickets at a nickelodeon.

The Sicilian Mafia is an ancient organization of extortionists.

In proportion to the age of the United States, the unions are equally ancient. But the Italian Mafia never had the same relative power that the unions have held in this country.

During Roosevelt's term, the Department of Justice made many phony, noisy passes at rackets conducted by unions. This was plausible propaganda, but I began to notice that the Department of

Justice lost most of its convictions on the appeals. The government was committing errors to protect rackets which were pouring hundreds of millions of dollars into Roosevelt's political efforts.

In one case against Joe Fay, of the Maloney union empire, I went to Washington and urged Tom Clark, the Attorney General, to look into the record of a judge who was an open associate of the Fay mob in Hudson County, N. J.

Clark frankly said he had no worries about the judge but that he had doubts about the U.S. Attorney. The trial was such a raw fake that the day after Fay's acquittal I phoned Clark to ask what he thought of it. He replied "I think it is a damned outrage."

The U.S. Attorney died unchallenged and Clark went to the Supreme Court.

There has been no change. The American union Mafia still is all-powerful and the protegé of both parties and all phases and degrees of government.

—Reprinted with permission of King Features Syndicate, Inc.

---

Now, it is left to a minister-editor (Assistant Editor of *Christian Economics*) to state succinctly and unanswerably the religious and economic implications in and basis for the Right to Work.

## The Right to Work

### REV. IRVING E. HOWARD

Edward Chevlin of Kansas City complained that the Secretary-Treasurer of his Teamsters Union local collected dues and pocketed them. He also complained about doctored books and graft generally. Of course, he was beaten up and almost killed. Then, for trying to defend himself, he was convicted of felonious assault. The case made the newspapers across the country, but it was an old story. Similar tales could be told of workers beaten and driven from their jobs by the goons of labor unions in any industrial city of America.

To work should be a man's right. According to the Bible, work has been commanded as a duty, but it is also a privilege by which man cooperates with his Creator. The New Testament is full of injunctions such as: ". . . let him labour, working with his hands the things which is good, that he may have to give to him that needeth" (Eph. 4:28) .

By what strange twist of history has organized labor, born to protect the laborer in his work, become an instrument to prevent him from working? We used to hear of the "yellow dog" contract which described the employer-employee relationship in which the employer forced the worker to promise *not* to join a labor union as a condition of employment. "Yellow dog" contracts are illegal today, but—in most states—not their inversion, the union shop. In this latter situation, the labor union forces the worker to join its organization as a condition of continued employment. Right-to-work laws outlaw, on the state level, their *compulsory* membership in a labor union.

Right-to-work laws are not a threat to the working man, but are a benefit to him and to the whole community. The National Right to Work Committee, 1025 Connecticut Avenue, N.W., Washington, D.C., has carefully compiled statistics showing that the states which have adopted right-to-work laws have outgained the rest of the country in weekly and hourly wage rates, personal income, retail sales, value added by manufacture, bank deposits, motor vehicle registration, population growth and employment. With the recent addition of Kansas, right-to-work states now number nineteen.

The door was opened for right-to-work laws by the Taft-Hartley Act which in Section 14b permits states to make compulsory unionism illegal. The Taft-Hartley Act was the first legislative indication that the pendulum of public opinion was beginning to swing against labor after twenty years in which labor had been bullying the American public.

Nevertheless, at present a campaign is in the making to repeal Section 14b of Taft-Hartley. Perhaps it was part of this campaign when the General Board of the National Council of Churches meeting in Detroit last December adopted a resolution condemning the right-to-work laws. The resolution states: "Union membership as a basis for continuing employment should neither be required nor forbidden by law. . . . The decision should be left to agreement by management and labor through the process of collective bargaining." This reasoning would be valid if we could repeal the Railway Labor Act, the Norris LaGuardia Act and the Wagner Act as well as some features of the Taft-Hartley Act. With the labor legislation now in force, which grants labor unions immunities from laws which apply to everyone else and gives a labor union winning a N.L.R.B. election the exclusive right to represent labor in that bargaining district (which "right" obliterates the minority), the argument of the National Council of Churches is about as realistic as a garden hose against a raging forest fire. A back-fire is sometimes necessary to halt such a conflagration!

As it is now, the labor union is about the only legal private organization that can force people to join its ranks and then use force and violence to further intimidate them after they are in. The record of most labor unions in the last twenty years stands in direct contrast to every ideal for which America stands—to say nothing of the ideals of the National Council of Churches!

Charles Geddes, a labor leader and chairman of the British Trade Union Congress, made the following statement which appeared in the February 1956 issue of *Challenge*.

"I do not believe the trade union movement in Great Britain can live for very much longer on the basis of compulsion. . . . Must people belong to us or starve, whether they like our policies or not? . . . I believe the trade union card is an honor to be conferred, not a badge which signifies that you have got to do something whether you like it or not."

There may be a better answer to compulsory unionism than the right-to-work laws, but no better alternative is at hand at present. Right-to-work laws on the state level offer some hope of preserving the working man's freedom and dignity and of bringing some justice into an underworld of violence, exploitation and deceit.

—Reprinted by permission from *Christian Economics,* February 9, 1960.

---

Donald R. Richberg was a vital figure in the turbulent era which, reaching a mightly climax in the New Deal, has fed so abundantly on the preposterous idea that men can be made good by legislating or shooting righteousness into them, or both.

In 1943 Richberg wrote his autobiography not because of any "pessimistic desire to explain my disillusionment with the achievements of the political and social leadership of my times. It is a desire to provide an explanation for the apparent failure of social leadership to keep pace with the terrific material progress of mankind."

And the reason for that failure of our social leadership he makes clear and incisive. It is because this leadership has in general relied on "compulsory collective action to improve society," and such action he makes equally clear "will never elevate but always degrade the individual."

Few, if any, can speak with greater authority on the labor movement; great weight is carried by his following words, taken from an address in San Francisco, July 27, 1956.

## Growing Labor Union Monopolies

### DONALD R. RICHBERG

The monopolistic powers of American labor unions are not revealed by statistics of total membership. Otherwise it might be assumed that 17,000,000 unionists could not monopolize employments filled by over 50,000,000 industrial workers.

But a different picture is presented when key industries are viewed. Over 1,400,000 unionized automobile workers can paralyze not only a major industry but scores of other industries dependent on automobile manufacturing. Over 1,300,000 union teamsters cannot only stop vital transportation to advance their own interests, but can, and do, aid scores of smaller unions to force their demands on employers dependent on teamster hauling. Over 1,250,-000 steel workers have proved their ability to halt production of products most essential to continued economic health. Six hundred thousand mine workers can, and have, shut down the coal industry even in a time of war. Even smaller unions of longshoremen, building workers, electrical, textile and garment workers, printing and telephone employees and others too numerous to mention have demonstrated a capacity to exercise monopoly controls over local, sectional or national industries.

The simple fact is that all unions seek monopoly powers so they may transform collective bargaining into collective coercion and compel the acceptance of demands for wages and working conditions which would never be agreed to voluntarily. This is not the demonstration of a special wickedness among union officials. It is a natural ambition common to all human beings to relieve themselves of the uncertainties and losses of fair competition, by acquiring a power to make others yield to force when persuasion fails to achieve one's selfish aims.

From the time of President Wilson, and the passing of the Clayton Act exempting labor unions from anti-trust prosecutions, there has persisted the illusion that labor union monopolies were desirable and not, like business monopolies, destructive of a free economy. This illusion has been so prevalent that the A.F. of L. and C.I.O. even had the audacity to argue in the Supreme Court that monopoly power was the proper and ideal objective of all labor organizations although obviously a sinful objective for any business organization.

In pressing their compulsory legislation in Congress in 1951 and later before a Presidential Emergency Board the unions assumed to themselves a right to exercise Governmental powers over a society of workers exactly in accord with their arguments in the Supreme Court in 1949.

George M. Harrison, President of the Clerks and chief labor witness, told Congress frankly that he wanted compulsory membership, not only to bring in new members and their dues, but also to increase his power of discipline over old members. In the same vein he later complained to the Emergency Board that he had to police an organization of 300,000 persons without the police powers which the government of such a large city could exercise. Now think of the police power given by compelling all workers to join a union and pay it tribute and submit to its discipline or else lose their livelihood!

The same arrogant desire for governmental power was boldly explained to the Supreme Court a few years previously when the A.F. of L. brief opposing state right-to-work laws made these assertions:

"The worker becomes a member of an economic society when he takes employment. . . . The union is the organization for government of this society formed by the right of association. . . . It has in a sense the powers and responsibilities of a government."

This concept of labor unions as the government of an economic state, within and dominating a political state, is one which has grown and blossomed with the growth of monopolistic powers which are not only tolerated but actually fostered by our political governments. It is most surprising, however, that the socialistic, totalitarian-minded labor leaders of the present day still regard themselves as devoted to a democratic form of government supported by and supporting a competitive system of free enterprise. They will in one breath denounce all competition between workers, proclaiming and exercising monopoly powers, and in the next breath denounce business monopolies. In the same A.F. of L. brief from which I have quoted, the argument was made in one paragraph that "workers cannot thrive but can only die under competition between themselves," and they must have "the right to eliminate wage competition," but business men must not have "the right to eliminate price competition."

Today we are faced with a recent merger of the two great labor federations, the A.F. of L. and the C.I.O., for the declared purpose of limiting competition between them. Today we are faced with sweeping demands that the right of labor unions to impose compulsory unionism be accepted and that all state and federal laws sustaining the constitutional right of a worker to refuse to join a labor union be repealed. Today we hear loud threats that unless politicians become more subservient to labor demands they will be defeated and replaced by more labor puppets than now disgrace our public offices. Today we find big labor supporting every program for bigger and bigger government with only one qualification: That big labor remain the one dominant element in our society which by legal and illegal exemption from the criminal laws can exert a coercive power over us greater than that of government.

The fragmentary and inadequate newspaper reports of recent strike violence against the Louisville and Nashville, the Southern Telephone Company, the Perfect Circle plant and the Kohler Company should have at least made it plain that that foul shape of terrorism lurks behind every strike threat, even by the most respectable and comparatively law-abiding unions. It should be doubly plain why such organizations with extensive open records of law-defying violence, seldom need to actually begin a terroristic program. The strike call itself is enough to warn any opposition of the wrath and ruin that will follow any attempt to break the strike.

There is no mystery about the source or existence of labor union monopolies. They are born out of legalized power of lawless violence.

It isn't the difficulty of this problem—of analyzing and solving it that prevents a solution. It is simply the political, financial and corrupting powers of the labor union oligarchies that stifle every effort to end or even to check their monopolistic controls over industry. There are a comparatively few closely allied labor bosses in control of 17,000,000 harshly disciplined unionists. Their organizations are financed by an annual minimum of half a billion dollars regular dues. They are able in emergencies to raise millions more for propaganda and political contributions that too closely resemble plain bribery. These lawless aggregations are supported by thousands of well-meaning, deluded people, as well as by hundreds of thousands of half-socialists, who regard labor unions as a great democratic opposition to what might otherwise become a tyrannical conspiracy of big business operators to exploit the people.

Contrary to this delusion, the American people are actually being exploited today as never before by labor union monopolies exercising arbitrary and often very foolish controls over a free enterprise system to which they profess devotion, but which they are actually fast destroying.

This seems to be like crying in the wilderness. But to one who grew up with the labor movement and did all he could to aid in the development of strong, responsible, democratic labor unions, there is such a tragedy in this super-growth of labor bossism into menacing national monopolies that the least I can do is cry aloud, even in a wilderness of confused miseducated public opinion.

## Press Release

### UNIVERSITY OF MICHIGAN NEWS SERVICE

GRAND RAPIDS—During the 1960's, unions may come under increasing attack from their old friends, the "eggheads," Director George Odiorne (Ph.D.), of the University of Michigan Bureau of Industrial Relations, said Tuesday, February 2, 1960.

Addressing a U-M industrial relations conference here, Odiorne said unions have suffered heavy losses in their intellectual support during the post-war period. This has accompanied the general decline of liberalism as a philosophy since the end of World War II, he added.

During the Thirties the unions as the advocates of "more" for the underdog could attract the support of independent opinion-makers in pulpit and college classroom. This independent thinker today finds himself far less challenged by the plight of the simple workman who is often much better paid than he is for teaching college English.

Accordingly, the literature professor in the small liberal arts college today is more apt to become aroused about conformity and the wretched man in the gray flannel suit than he is about the horny handed son of toil who lives in a better house and drives a fancier car than the professor.

The pressing economic problems facing individuals today are not especially pressing on union members. Rather they are most excruciatingly apparent for the large unorganized work force, the farm laborer, the service employee, the lower level of white-collar worker, and the retired annuitant.

Without such intellectual respectability as was provided by active and important liberalism in this country, the union movement becomes a grand association of experts in propaganda and in lobbying for a special interest group.

The commodity theory of labor which they have denied so vehemently over the years begins to emerge as the dominant guiding principle. From such a climate the dedicated intellectuals who formerly inhabited union headquarters have fled to the universities, taking their Ph.D.'s with them. Here they write rueful exercises about the nature and role of unionism, no longer personally involved in the movement which once stirred them from deliberations into action.

Without a reconstituted philosophy of unionism which expresses the underlying sentiments of distressed and exploited people, this alienation of the intellectuals will continue. Within the decade we may well expect that many of these will turn on unionism and attack the very body which they once worked to support.

---

Finally and climactically we turn back to the "grand old man" of labor who left a challenging message for today when he gave his final presidential address to the A.F. of L. convention, El Paso, Texas, in 1924.

## The Voluntary Basis of Trade Unionism

### SAMUEL GOMPERS

Forty-four years ago in the city of Pittsburgh a group of labor men met to bring to fruition an effort extending over a period of years—to organize a national labor movement. We were a group of labor men with little experience in a national labor movement. We had to find our problems and devise ways of meeting them. There was little to guide us.

Again in 1886 a national labor conference was called. This time it was designated a trade union conference to be composed of representatives of trade unions and to consider trade union problems. The deliberations of that conference resulted in the formation of our present American Federation of Labor with which the old Federation of Trades and Labor Unions was merged. This new Federation recognized only the trade union card as a credential and proposed to deal primarily with economic problems. It was an organization that had no power or authority except of a voluntary character. It was a voluntary coming together of unions with common needs and common aims. That feeling of mutuality has been a stronger bond of union than could be welded by an autocratic authority. Guided by voluntary principles, our Federation has grown from a weakling into the strongest, best organized labor movement of all the world.

So long as we have held fast to voluntary principles and have been actuated and inspired by the spirit of service, we have sustained our forward progress and we have made our labor movement something to be respected and accorded a place in the councils of our Republic. Where we have blundered into trying to force a policy or a decision, even though wise and right, we have impeded, if not interrupted, the realization of our aims.

Men and women of our American trade union movement, I feel that I have earned the right to talk plainly with you. As the only delegate to that first Pittsburgh convention who has stayed with the problems of our movement through to the present hour, as one who with clean hands and with singleness of purpose has tried to serve the labor movement honorably and in a spirit of consecration to the cause of humanity, I want to urge devotion to the fundamentals of human liberty—the principles of voluntarism. No lasting gain has ever come from compulsion. If we seek to force, we but tear apart that which, united, is invincible. There is no way whereby our labor movement may be assured sustained progress in determining its policies and its plans other than sincere democratic deliberation until a unanimous decision is reached. This may seem a cumbrous, slow method to the impatient, but the impatient are more concerned for immediate triumph than for the education of constructive development.

Understanding, patience, high-minded service, the compelling power of voluntarism have in America made what was but a rope of sand, a united, purposeful integrated organization, potent for human welfare, material and spiritual. I have been with this movement since the beginning, for I have been given the privilege of service that has been accorded but few. Nor would that privilege have continued open to me had not service to the cause been my guiding purpose.

Events of recent months made me keenly aware that the time is not far distant when I must lay down my trust for others to carry forward. When one comes to close grips with the eternal things, there comes a new sense of relative values and the less worthy things lose significance. As I review the events of my sixty years of contact with the labor movement and as I survey the problems of today and study the opportunities of the future, I want to say to you, men and women of the American Labor movement, do not reject the cornerstone upon which labor's structure has been builded—but base your all upon voluntary principles and illumine your every problem by consecrated devotion to that highest of all purposes—human well-being in the fullest, widest, deepest sense.

# IX

# The Social Security Swindle

BACK ABOUT 1790, during the French Revolution, one M. Con-
dorcet introduced into the General Assembly what he termed a
"social security and old age pension plan." It was to be financed
by government taxes on payrolls and income and thus provide old
age security for all. The revolutionary Frenchmen of the times
were not quite revolutionary enough to stomach the scheme. They
turned it down flatly.

Thereafter, the scheme lay dormant until somebody turned it
up for Bismarck's use in Germany. The "Iron Chancellor" seized
upon it as a heaven-sent means of quieting the social unrest following the inflationary price rise of the Franco-Prussian war and its
inevitable concomitant of unemployment in that exporting country.

Sometime about 1904 the English picked up the scheme; by 1909
they were going all-out with it. The Australians and New Zeal-
anders followed suit. Since 1937 this same scheme has been imposed
upon Americans under the same old "confidence" and "gold-brick"
talk of old age security.

So America is off on the same fatal road, not only in regard to the
current "deducts" from pay envelopes, but the amounts that must

be taken out in the future to meet the staggering costs of the mounting number of social benefits the bureaucrats would provide "free" for a mounting number of people.

There is nothing free in these services. They are actually paid for by the people at an appalling price. It is this very program of confiscating the earnings and savings of the people under the pretext of guaranteeing them social security that the seeds of the gravest kind of social insecurity lie.

In this process of arbitrarily draining off the savings and earnings of the people, government is taking away from them what they could voluntarily save and invest for their own future security. They might do this through their own direct investment in any one or more of the many kinds of income-producing property, or by making deposits in savings banks, or through the purchase of their own security policies in private insurance companies.

Furthermore, and most importantly, these private investments either directly or indirectly end up in tools of production which make possible the jobs which are the only basic source of security now or in the future. The thoroughly documented fact is that since the launching of the grand "tax and spend" policy of government here there has been, for the first time in the history of this country, a decline in the per capita supply of tools of production which has been coincidental with the increase in government "take."

In brief, the story is that corporate and private savings are invested in tools of production which create the jobs which are the basis of all security. So it is that government, in draining the country of funds that should be left available for capital investment, is fostering a so-called social security program of a kind which all down through history has ended up in the creation of insecurity.

Such economic pitfalls in the path of a government social security program would be sobering enough even if the operation of the program were honest. Herein lies a thought for those who pay the freight in good faith and in the belief that their "deducts" are set aside by the government to be available for their use in later years, just as their premium payments are handled by a private insurance company. For government operates its so-called insurance business on principles and practices very different from those it demands of a private insurance company.

All Social Security payroll taxes taken by the government are loaned to the Treasury, which keeps the money and puts interest-bearing government obligations (I.O.U.s) in a Trust Fund. The Social Security Trust Fund now has the bond (I.O.U.s), and the Treasury has the money which it uses for the payment of current government operating expenses or for any of its financial commitments, which may vary from farm subsidies in the United States to subsidies for the socialist governments of Europe.

At any rate, the government takes the Social Security payroll taxes, puts some I.O.U.s in hock and immediately spends the money. When the Trust Fund is then called on to pay off on social security benefits, it has to cash some bonds, and this is done by taking cash out of current tax receipts.

In other words, the social security program as operated now is a political mechanism for providing an endless source of funds for government spending, an added tax which the bureaucrats would not dare call an income tax. It is a political scheme which guarantees its beneficiaries a certain consumption level out of future production to which the beneficiaries no longer contribute. The guarantee has little validity because no one knows what the production or productive facilities will or can be twenty or fifty years hence under bureaucratic control, or whether the relatively narrowing base of younger people can produce enough to pay the necessary taxes to care for the increasing older group.

Nothing could be more fraudulent than such a system, yet if any private insurance company, following its government's example, used all premium payments to pay for company operating expenses and thus had to call for additional premium payments from its policy-holders to pay off on its policy promises, the United States Department of Justice would haul all the company executives into court and put them in jail, and rightly so.

The fraud involved, the current economic pitfalls and those to be faced in the future, and the utter insecurity ultimately resulting from such a program are now perfectly obvious.

From whatever approach one considers this question of tomorrow's security, the individual must face the inexorable fact that it can be a gift from neither man nor government. Whether he buys real security or illusory security, it must be paid for, and paid for by him.

Over and above this economic cost stands the eternal issue of human freedom, the basic freedom of all freedoms—the freedom of choice which is the only alternative to human slavery. It was

Benjamin Franklin who said in effect that they who would sacrifice freedom for security are deserving of neither; and neither is exactly what we get under the coercive policies of the welfare state.

Before the advent of the New Deal it was considered the responsibility of every citizen to take care of himself, in good times and bad, in his prime and in his old age. American citizens were proud of their freedom and their right to keep all that they earned. It was established custom to save a part of one's earnings and to prepare for rainy days and for old age. There was no such thing in America as the compulsory socialistic seizure of part of a man's earnings under the pretext of government sponsored "security."

The increasing millions who are completely or partially living off the government makes an appalling picture as presented by Leonard J. Calhoun, one of the nation's authorities on Social Security.

## Free Rides and Free People

### LEONARD J. CALHOUN

If all of us depended entirely or principally on government pay or benefit checks for our daily bread, could we call ourselves free or distinguish our economic peonage from that of the Russians? That over 50 million of us—more than our entire 1880 population —are thus dependent, and that, under our benefit laws, this number will rapidly increase, is cause for concern. Here is the story in brief.

Prior to the depression of the 1930's, government by and large engaged only in essential government functions and required relatively few employees. Federal pensions were paid only to veterans and retired military and civilian employees. State and local governments alone had relief programs and these had the checks and balances of being financed solely by state and local taxes. But as the depression worsened with gold devaluation and other frenzied experiments, the Federal government adopted and financed a series of relief measures—PWA, WPA, CCC and NYA work programs, and also direct "emergency relief." Large numbers thus came to look to government for support, as program beneficiaries or administrative personnel.

In 1935 the Federal Social Security Act was adopted as a permanent program, intended largely to supplant the emergency programs. It provided grants to states for public assistance to the needy aged, to dependent children and to the blind. To gradually supplant such assistance, the bill established payroll-tax-financed Federal Social Security benefits. Also, with federal tax offsets and grants, it induced states to establish unemployment insurance systems. Repeated expansions, particularly since World War II, of these programs, of the companion railroad employee benefit programs and of veteran, farmer and civil service benefit programs, have resulted in mounting millions of benefit check recipients—and large increases in administrative employees.

While partly due to the cold war which we can hope will be temporary, much government employment expansion is attributed to these benefit programs and "Public Enterprise" programs such as TVA and to Public Housing, Health and Welfare programs. In aggregate, as of a few months ago, besides the 2.6 million in the armed forces there were over 8 million civilian employees of government at all levels. Even assuming that only one in five in the armed forces had a dependent, and that the average for civilian employees was only 1.2 dependents, the total who look to government pay checks is well over 20 million.

Though government payroll expansion has been large, it has been far outspaced by benefit roll expansion. Since 1943, when under one billion dollars was spent for public assistance—these benefits have expanded to a current annual rate of around three and a half billion, supporting or largely supporting, over six and one-half million persons.

This 350 per cent increase in relief benefit expenditures has occurred despite the even larger increase in the same period in social security, unemployment compensation, civil service and veterans' benefits. Costs of these benefits increased from a total of around nine-tenths of a billion dollars for 1943 to a current annual rate of some sixteen and one-half billion dollars—over 1,800 per cent. Also agricultural program checks are presently paid some million farm families. The total of the direct benefit recipients of these various programs and their dependents, including the six and a half million looking to public assistance, is currently well over thirty million.

The number of beneficiaries will increase rapidly. Actuaries estimate, for example, that benefit expenditures for Federal Social

Security, the principal program, which rose from under $159 million in 1943 to a current annual rate of over $8.3 billion, will exceed $11 billion in 1961, $16 billion in 1970 and $19 billion in 1975. This assumes no more pre-election liberalizations of the law.

Besides the over 50 million currently looking to pay checks or benefit checks, additional millions receive government subsidies. Some of these are (1) low rent subsidies to families living in the 436,000 Federally-managed and the many locally-owned public housing units, (2) electricity users subsidy to the millions enjoying public power from TVA, Bonneville, Grand Coulee and Bull Shoals, etc., (3) low-premium subsidy to the 6 million veterans with government insurance policies, (4) indirect subsidies to millions of members of cooperatives, credit unions, etc., through tax exemption and other favors extended to these business organizations. If these beneficiaries be added to the 50 million above, probably over a third of our population is receiving some degree of government subsidy at the expense of others—and worse, the number is growing each day.

These indirect subsidies violate the principle of equitable treatment of all competitive business enterprises, essential to maintaining free enterprise. The special bargains given "Public Enterprise" beneficiaries mean added burdens to other taxpayers.

The increasing millions who enjoy monthly and weekly benefit checks or other direct or indirect subsidies at the expense of other taxpayers mean added pressure for expansion and against reduction. Many in Congress feel that disagreement would threaten their political future. The frightening fact about public enterprise subsidy and welfare programs is this politically recognized and consequently effective pressure for, as compared with general public interest and pressure against, unwarranted expansion. As beneficiaries or prospective beneficiaries of public power, agricultural conservation and soil bank programs, special tax concessions, low rent public housing, government lending, social security, unemployment and other benefit programs, we may tend both to overestimate what is necessary, and to vote for candidates who favor unwise expansion, and also may be less likely to vote against them despite their unjustifiable and dangerous actions in other matters. However selfish or generous the politician's motives in advocating unwarranted welfare expansion, he can count on the advantage of claiming to speak for "the underprivileged," for "Social Justice" and for "Common Humanity."

Totalitarian states invariably claim to be welfare states. The basic unworkability of the socialist slogan, "from each according to his ability, to each according to his needs," has been slyly recognized even by Soviet Russia, who now says, "to each according to his value to the state." Russia has tightened up on its social security in the interest of increased production, but still capitalizes on the welfare concept. Its current propaganda frontispiece at the Brussels Fair is a craftily worded and illustrated social security pamphlet.

That the upward spiral of our benefit rolls will continue without further election year liberalizations by Congress, is clear from the actuarial estimates previously mentioned. That this requires constantly greater taxes is manifest. Official estimates are that the social security "contribution" burden of $7.7 billion for 1957 will be almost double this amount in 1963—$14.2 billion, and almost three times as large in 1970—$20.4 billion. Whether younger people will be willing later on to shoulder our ever mounting benefit costs is a critically important question.

Of necessity, the current aged ride "Piggy Back" on younger taxpayers. The total tax contributions made by the present retired social security beneficiaries do not pay even a tenth of the cost of their benefits.

Each government benefit check, each "Public Enterprise" run on a subsidy basis, each tax exempt business, means added tax burdens on others. That unwisely liberal benefits may destroy incentive to work, that subsidized "Public Enterprises" and that tax-favored businesses may destroy tax-burdened competition are considerations which must guide us, and through us our legislators, if a sound economy which makes our economic security possible is to be preserved.

—Reprinted with permission from *Christian Economics.*

The following speech by Congressman Noah M. Mason, of Illinois, over the Manion Forum Network on April 12, 1957, shows how the Social Security program is immoral and dishonest, one of the greatest swindles ever perpetrated upon a decent, unsuspecting people by their government.

## Social Security Makes Nickel-shooter of Ponzi

### HON. NOAH M. MASON

Our present Social Security set-up is unsound, inequitable and dishonest. The Brookings Institute, one of the best research organizations in the United States today, after a careful and exhaustive study, recommended that our Social Security set-up be scrapped, abandoned, and that a pay-as-you-go Social Security program be established in its place.

I agree with that recommendation. If it were adopted and carried out, it would mean, as the Brookings Institute expresses it: "Our generation would care for its own old people and trust future generations to do likewise."

In 1950, after 3½ months of exhaustive hearings before the Ways and Means Committee, I was one of the three members of that committee who voted "NO" on a bill that proposed to expand the coverage of Social Security and to increase the benefits. I was also one of 14 House members to vote "NO" on the final passage of that bill in the House.

Since then, I have opposed every attempt to expand our Social Security program, to increase its benefits, or to increase the Social Security tax rates. Yet, I am heartily in favor of a sound, liberal Social Security program to take care of our needy old people.

The overwhelming weight of the evidence gathered during the 3½ months of public hearings in 1950 was to the effect that our present Social Security set-up was unsound, dishonest and inequitable, that it was "a Ponzi-type shell game," sold to the American people by F.D.R. and his New Deal associates, as a plan to provide security in their old age.

It is an insurance program which if practiced by an insurance company today would land every director and every official of that company in the penitentiary for misuse or misappropriation of trust funds.

The present Social Security program is characterized in a report of the Brookings Institute as a plan whereby "WE (the present generation) do the promising; YOU (all future generations) do the paying." That is an accurate picture of our present Social Security program.

The following Social Security facts bear out these contentions; they cannot be ignored:

First: When the Social Security law was adopted in 1934, it provided that all money collected in Social Security taxes should be dumped into the Federal treasury and that such cash could be used for the general expenditures of the Government, placing Government I.O.U.s or Bonds in the Social Security Fund in lieu of the cash as a bookkeeping arrangement. That provision is still in the law.

Second: Under the law, some $50 billion has been collected in Social Security taxes, but less than half that amount has been paid out in benefits. The balance—all spent for the general expenditures of the Government—is debt that has been placed upon the backs of future generations.

Third: Our Social Security program, since its inception, has been used for political purposes by both parties. In election years, benefits have been increased to attract votes for the party in power, thereby making the Social Security fund actuarially unsound.

Then, in the off-election years, the Social Security tax rates have been increased to try to get the fund back on an actuarially sound basis. If that is not playing politics with the welfare of our retired old people, I do not know what is.

Fourth: The original purpose of the Social Security program was to establish a floor of security under the low-income worker for support in his old age. He was then expected to build upon that floor added security by buying insurance, by establishing a savings account, or by making investments with his extra cash.

To make this possible, a tax was levied only upon the first $2,000 of the worker's income. Today, we levy a tax upon the first $4,800 of the worker's income, leaving little if any cash for the taxpayer to invest for himself.

We have entirely forgotten the original purpose of Social Security. Today, Uncle Sam acts as though the worker is not capable of spending his own money wisely for security in his old age; therefore, the Government must do it for him.

These facts—and they are facts—added to the evidence given in the public hearings in 1950, convince me that we should, without further delay, adopt the Social Security recommendations of the Brookings Institute and place the Social Security program upon a cash basis—a pay-as-you-go basis.

If we did that, it would eliminate the present yearly $500 million interest charge upon our fictitious Social Security Fund—which will soon become a one billion dollar interest charge.

It also would do away with all need for reserves, all need for level premiums, all need for costly and elaborate bookkeeping systems, all need for the present heavy administrative costs of Social Security, and it would make possible the payment of more liberal Social Security benefits to our retired old people in the lower income brackets. That in itself would be well worth-while.

To demonstrate how unsound and dishonest our present Social Security program is, I offer the following hypothetical case:

John Smith decides to establish his own social security program, so he deducts a certain per cent of each pay check he receives and places the cash regularly in his safe deposit box. After doing this for several years and having thus set aside, say, $5,000, to insure security in his old age, John Smith starts to spend each month more than he earns—as Uncle Sam does now.

Then, John Smith hits upon the plan of taking a certain amount of cash out of his lock-box each month to spend, placing in the box, in lieu of the cash extracted, promissory notes to himself. If John Smith keeps this up, when he retires he will have only promissory notes to himself to live on—which he has no way of changing into cash for groceries.

That is exactly what Uncle Sam is doing with the social security tax receipts—the only difference being that Uncle Sam has the general taxing power to invoke in order to change his I.O.U.'s into cash to meet his future Social Security obligations.

But, that means of course new taxes, additional taxes, to meet obligations that are supposed to have been paid for already by the beneficiaries.

I wonder if that scheme of taxing the children and grandchildren of the Social Security beneficiary for something he and his employer are supposed to have paid for can be called anything but dishonest and immoral, a Ponzi-type shell game that has been sold to the American taxpayer as a plan to provide security in his old age.

For years I have been working in Congress, not to abolish Social Security, as some people would have you believe, but rather to place our Social Security program upon a sound basis, a cash basis, a pay-as-you-go basis, collecting each year just the amount of Social Security taxes needed to pay the benefits due that year for the support of our retired old people.

In that way—paraphrasing the words of the Brookings Institute Report—WE (the present generation) would take care of our own old people, and YOU (all future generations) would be expected to do likewise. To my mind, that would be the sensible thing to do in connection with our Social Security problem.

---

The following condensation of a Dan Smoot *Report* (July 1958) sheds further light on the current bankruptcy of the Social Security system.

## Social Security Is Bankrupt

### DAN SMOOT

Last year I asserted that the social security system is bankrupt, and reported a conversation with a Congressman friend of mine who refused to let me use his name.

The Congressman said: "The social security system is already bankrupt. . . . The whole idea was bankrupt from the beginning. But up until two years ago, social security was at least taking in more money every year than it was paying out—because there were 10 or 15 times more people paying than receiving.

"But about two years ago, after the 1954 Amendments to the Social Security Act went into effect, social security crossed the line into actual bankruptcy and started running a deficit."

I said: "This is serious. If the thing is in that shape now, it'll be horrible 15 or 20 years from now when another 30 or 40 million people are added to the beneficiary rolls."

The Congressman replied: "You're right. It would wreck our entire economy."

This report brought me quantities of mail—much of it from subscribers who had written Congressmen or Senators, or the Secretary of Health, Education and Welfare, asking for comment on my allegations. In most cases, my subscribers sent me the replies they received from Washington officials. In most cases, those replies indicated that Smoot was an irresponsible liar—indicated that the social security system is still in good shape: it is still taking in more than it pays out and has a "trust fund" of 22 billion dollars to meet future obligations.

It is significant that one year later (July, 1958) social security advocates are still saying that we have 22 billion dollars in the social security trust fund.

Meanwhile, the number of people who draw Federal Old-Age, Survivors or Disability payments under social security has been growing at the rate of 100,000 a month.

In a letter to me, dated June 4, 1957, the Department of Health, Education and Welfare said:

"As of June, 1957, slightly over 10 million people are getting old-age, survivors, or disability payments under social security, at the rate of $540 million a month."

On June 16, 1958, Marion B. Folsom, Secretary of Health, Education and Welfare, in a statement before the Ways and Means Committee, said that in May, 1958, the Federal Old-Age, Survivors, and Disability insurance system paid benefits to 11.8 million persons at the rate of $7.8 billion a year (650 million dollars a month).

In 11 months, the rolls of those who receive FOASDI payments increased by more than 1 million persons. The money value of the benefit payments increased 110 million dollars a month. But not a penny has been added to the trust fund to meet future obligations to the new millions being added to the social security rolls.

In fact, the social security trust fund, which, if the system were sound, would be increasing each year, is actually decreasing.

In his June 16, 1958, statement to the House Ways and Means Committee, Secretary Folsom admitted that the social security system operated in the red during the fiscal year ending June 30, 1958, and that an even bigger deficit (1.1 billion dollars) is now expected for the year ending June 30, 1959.

In other words, the social security system is, as I characterized it more than a year ago, bankrupt, and it is no longer possible for Washington officialdom to hide that fact.

Secretary Folsom claimed that the current deficits resulted from a "temporary decline" in our economy, but prophesied that everything would be rosy in the future.

He knows better, however. That's why the Eisenhower administration was opposed this year to increasing social security benefits.

Compulsory social security always has been the keystone of dictatorship. It puts government in control of the lives of people, and it enables politicians to buy votes with the voters' own money.

Every election year since the Social Security Act was passed in the United States, "liberal" politicians buy votes by promising to increase social security benefits—to take care of our "senior citizens." Every extension of the social security system has been made during an election year.

In 1956, Congress itself became alarmed at the biennial election-year orgy of buying votes by extending social security benefits. Congress extended the social security system in 1956, but tried to put some brake on future election-year vote-buying by setting up an advisory council which was supposed to review and report on the condition of the social security system prior to any increase in tax rates or extension of benefits. The first such report of this council is due January 1, 1959.

Apparently, Congress thought this would prohibit political expansion of social security during the 1958 election year.

Within a month after Congress convened in January, 1958, Congressmen and Senators had introduced more than 400 bills to expand and increase the social security system.

On July 17, 1958, the American Enterprise Association, Inc. (1012 Fourteenth Street, N.W., Washington, D.C.) published a scholarly, carefully documented study of the then pending proposals to amend the Social Security Act.

On page 3 of this study are statistics on the number of people already receiving some kind of social security benefits:

"As of April, 1958, 11.6 million persons were receiving benefits under FOASDI (Federal Old-Age, Survivors, and Disability Insurance), 5.6 million under public assistance, and 3.2 million under unemployment insurance. Although this totals (about) 20.5 million beneficiaries, correction must be made for those individuals receiving more than one type of payment.

"In December, 1956, the Department of Health, Education and Welfare estimated that 560,000 persons received both FOASDI and old-age assistance payments. Even in the light of this fact, however, it would appear that 19-20 million persons are receiving some form of social insurance benefits."

To be quite precise about it, these official figures (which the American Enterprise Association took from Secretary Folsom's statement to the House Ways and Means Committee) say that in April, 1958, nineteen million, eight hundred and forty thousand persons were drawing some kind of relief or pension benefits from the federal treasury under the social security program alone.

In March, 1958, there were 2,323,947 civilian employees on the federal payrolls. There were approximately 2,500,000 persons on the military payrolls of the federal government.

I have been unable to obtain exact figures on the number of persons drawing federal pensions under programs that are apart and distinct from the vast and complicated social security program: that is, retired civil service employees, retired military personnel, veterans, and so on. A safe estimate is that the federal treasury is paying pensions to at least 4 million persons, in addition to the 19,840,000 persons getting federal money under the broad social security program.

Total employment in the United States in July, 1958 (exclusive of federal civilian and military employees) was 62,600,000.

What do all these figures mean when you analyze them?

Number of persons living on payments from the federal treasury:

| | |
|---|---|
| Various kinds of "social insurance" | 19,840,000 |
| Other federal pensions | 4,000,000 |
| Federal civilian employees | 2,323,947 |
| Federal military employees | 2,500,000 |
| Total | 28,663,947 |

Even though the federal employees and pensioners do themselves pay taxes; even though a good many of them are certainly entitled (legally and morally) to everything they are getting—the fact remains that there are 62,600,000 people working outside the federal government and paying money into the federal treasury, while there are 28,663,947 people living on payments from the federal treasury.

How many of the "gainfully employed" 62,600,000 people outside of the federal government are local and state government employees? How many millions of them get direct subsidies from the federal treasury, for their businesses, or for banking the soil, or for not growing crops? How many millions of them have children who get free school lunches under the federal government's agricultural surplus disposal program? How many of them make their livings (either as businessmen or as laborers) from government contracts for producing goods to be given away to foreign governments?

How long can such a society endure before the total population is totally enslaved in a system of total socialism?

----

Tom Anderson, editor and publisher of *Farm and Ranch*, ably points out that government promises of "security" inevitably lead to loss of freedom with insecurity and slavery under a dictatorship.

## Straight Talk

### TOM ANDERSON

Once upon a time a hunter and his dog got lost in the forest and could find no game. Out of food, the starving hunter sat by his fire one night with his faithful dog by his side. Finally he could stand it no longer. He whisked out his knife, whacked off his dog's tail and put it on the fire to boil. When he was finished, only the clean bones were left. The kind hunter gave these to the whimpering dog who devoured them and then licked his master's hand in gratitude.

This is the story of "Federal Aid." The hunter is Uncle Sam. The grateful dog is us. Dogs can live without tails. But the hunter is still hungry.

Our Welfare State feeds off Federal Aid. What is a "Welfare State?" In the U.S.A., more than 41 million people are now getting checks from federal, state, and local governments. One-fourth of the people are living on the other three-fourths, completely or partially. That is a Welfare State. The subsidy-happy American people, with the enthusiastic cooperation of the Communists and socialists within and without, are destroying the land of the free. We are becoming slaves to a handout rather than masters of our own destinies.

Spending for welfare programs—federal, state and local—accounts for the greatest non-defense spending increases during the past 30 years.

One of the greatest Americans liked to tell this "welfare" story: "I used to know an old codge," Abe Lincoln said, "whose cabin burned down to the ground. The folks in those parts felt sorry because he'd lost all his earthly possessions. So they began bringing him presents to set him back on his feet.

"Well, they made such a good job of it that, when they were through, he was far better off than he ever had been before. One day the old man was sitting on the stoop of the new cabin his neighbors had built for him and along came a friend from down the road with a bag of oats on his shoulder. 'I want you to have these here oats, pardner,' said the kind neighbor, setting the bag down on the front step.

" 'I ain't takin' no oats," said the old boy. 'I ain't taking nothing but money.' "

Several years ago an eighteen-year-old country boy left home to try out for a minor league ball club. He wrote his dad shortly thereafter, saying he was being fired. The old man had probably never been on a psychiatrist's couch and learned how important a feeling of "security" is. He sent his son just a five word telegram. It said: "Don't come home a failure." The boy stuck it out—stuck it out to become the greatest ball player of all time. His name is Ty Cobb. I think his old man is due part credit for those records.

There are very few born geniuses. Genius is usually the power of making continuous effort. As Isadora Duncan said: "Great art is 75% perspiration." You have to want something very much—and then work for it. Ty Cobb was great not because he had the most native ability, nor the best coaching, nor lucky breaks. He was the greatest because he had a burning desire to be great, and worked at it unceasingly.

Practically every child today—farm and non-farm—has a greater opportunity than Ty Cobb—or than Abraham Lincoln. I can't help but wonder, sometimes, what Lincoln would have done if he'd had the opportunities our children have. Hardship builds character, like forging makes steel. Character is neither married nor inherited. It's a victory over one's environment and one's self.

Money and security are not synonymous. He who had 100% monetary security in 1939, now has 48%, and in 25 more years will probably have only 20% or less. No money in all the world's history has ever survived for more than 42 years after being transferred from a physical to a political basis. In matters of money all powerful central governments are crooked. Ours is no exception. So the man who seeks security in money usually finds added insecurity.

Next to money, we look to government welfare for security. We cannot achieve security by voting for it. For in the end, all welfare states become dictatorships. The road to socialism, like the road to Hell, is paved with promises. Satan promised Jesus the whole world for his soul. When a politician promises you security, don't forget the price: dictatorship.

There is only one place security can be found: inside ourselves. In character, not dollars; in principles, not pensions; in what we do, not what we intend to do.

How can we make our own security? By giving, not receiving; by giving the best we can, where we are, with what we have. By reassuming our local rights, responsibilities, and taxing powers; by re-taking our individual liberties the government usurped.

———————

One great value which might be salvaged from the Social Security program would be for American youth to learn the truth about it is the thought left with us by Paul L. Poirot, member of the staff of the Foundation for Economic Education.

## Social Security's Salvage Value

### PAUL L. POIROT

The 20 per cent jump in Social Security taxes, effective January 1 of this year, brought the total to 6 per cent on the first $4,800 of an employee's annual earnings. That's $288 a year. Technically, half is paid by the employee; half by the employer. But actually, the full amount is part of the employer's cost of hiring help—and the full amount is missing from the employee's take-home pay. In other words, it's $288 a year, all paid in effect by the employee. Incidentally, he's liable for the regular income tax on his half of that $288—at not over 20 per cent ($28.80) if he's lucky. However, that's double taxation, which is another story.

The next point of the present story is that the current Social Security tax of 6 per cent, or $288, is scheduled for three more jumps between now and 1969, when it will be 9 per cent on the first $4,800, or $432 per employee. Any reliable insurance agent can tell you that would buy a sizable chunk of old-age insurance from his company—particularly if you happen to be a young person.

But that's the third point of the story. If you're buying Social Security, it's not a good deal to be a young person. In fact, it's an exceedingly raw deal, as indicated in Actuarial Study No. 48 of the Social Security Administration:

"The sum of the present value of the contributions to be paid under the present schedule (1956) by present members and the existing fund is $269 billion less than the present value of the benefits to be paid to them and their dependents and survivors. . . . On the other hand, there is a 'surplus' of $228 billion for new entrants."

In layman's language, what that says is that the good old days of something-for-nothing from Social Security are drawing to a close, and that a "new entrant" (a young fellow at his first "covered" job) is going to help pay at least $228 billion more than he can ever expect to get back from his Social Security taxes. In other words, under the 1956 amendments (aggravated in 1958, and likely to get worse with each subsequent amendment), the new entrant can expect to pay a tax averaging about 8.3 per cent of payroll until he retires, as against benefits valued at 4.93 per cent of that same payroll. That is, the new entrant is scheduled to pay $1.69 for every $1.00 promised in benefits. At least, that's how the actuaries of the Social Security Administration figure it—and it's not their business to paint the picture any worse than it is.

The lead editorial in *Barron's* of January 4, 1960, carried this brief review of the program:

"Since Social Security was launched in 1935, benefit payments have increased sharply. Group after group has been added to the rolls, age limits have been lowered, and eligibility broadened. In 1956, Congress extended coverage to a whole new class of recipients, the disabled. Today, 13.4 million Americans are receiving monthly checks, which for the year just ended, totaled $10 billion. Nor will the process stop here, since the number of beneficiaries is mounting steadily. What's more, Congress is toying with dozens of ways to broaden the program. Some legislators would reduce the age of eligibility from 65 for men and 62 for women to 60 (or less) for everyone. Others would lower or eliminate the minimum age of 50 for payments for disability. Still others would boost all benefits by 10 per cent. Finally, Rep. Aime Forand (D., R. I.) proposes to add 'free' medical, hospital, and nursing-home care. This modest proposal, by government estimate, would cost over a billion dollars in the first year, and far more thereafter."

The bitter truth, which any conscientious parent should want his children—as well as his congressman—to understand here and now, is that Social Security has been tried and found wanting. The facts developed in these first 25 years under the program make abundantly clear what could have been known from the beginning: the only way the government can provide a windfall for the oldsters is to fleece the youngsters. With perhaps a few rare exceptions, the point already has been passed for entering the program with the chance of getting back as much as one puts into it. Nor is there the slightest political possibility of a soundly funded government insurance program that could give any other result.

As long as it afforded a chance of something-for-nothing, Social Security had its inducements for "practical" persons with no guide other than that of crass materialism. But, with that powerful inducement now wiped out by the soaring schedule of taxes, it should be easier for everyone to understand why the program was doomed from the beginning by its compulsory and immoral features. The immorality arises, not in freely giving of one's own to assist the needy or the aged, but in the coercion employed to make others contribute.

The lesson Social Security offers is that a morally defective procedure eventually must prove to be both economically and politically unsound. If the youth of America will learn that lesson, it could be a vital salvage—their most important benefit—from the Social Security burden thrust upon them.

—Reprinted with permission from *The Freeman*, March, 1960.

## Legislated Security Is Bondage

### SAMUEL GOMPERS

There has never yet come down from any government any substantial improvement in the conditions of the masses of the people, unless it found its own initiative in the mind, the heart, and the courage of the people. Take from the people of our country the source of initiative and the opportunity to aspire and to struggle in order that that aspiration may become a reality, and though you couch your action in any sympathetic terms, it will fail of its purpose and be the undoing of the vital forces that go to make up a virile people. Look over all the world where you will, and see those governments where the features of compulsory benevolence have been established, and you will find the initiative taken from the hearts of the people.

Social insurance cannot even undertake to remove or prevent poverty. It is not fundamental and does not get at the causes of social injustice.

The first step in establishing compulsory social insurance is to divide people into groups, those eligible for benefits and those considered capable of caring for themselves. The division is based upon earning capacity. This governmental regulation must tend to fix the citizens of the country into classes, and a long-established insurance system would tend to make those classes rigid.

Governmental power grows upon that on which it feeds. Give an agency power, and it at once tries to reach out after more. Its effectiveness depends upon increasing power.

Recently a gentleman of the highest standing stated to me that during the time he was in Germany, and in a position to know, German workmen came to him seeking aid to get out of that country to the United States. They told him that by reason of the taxes which they were compelled to pay into compulsory social insurance schemes, they had no money left except for absolute necessities of life, and were unable to secure sufficient funds to come to the United States even in the steerage. He said to me further that in Germany, where compulsory social insurance has been more extensively worked out than in any other country, the workmen of that country, by reason of their property interests in compulsory social insurance, have been compelled to remain in Germany and work under circumstances, wages, hours, and conditions of employment which forced them to endure conditions below standards of a living wage.

Is it not discernible that the payments required of workmen for this compulsory social insurance interfere very materially with mobility of labor, and constitute a very effectual barrier to the workers determining their whole lives?

Industrial freedom exists only when and where wage earners have complete control over their labor power. To delegate control over their labor power to an outside agency takes away from the economic power of those wage earners and creates another agency for power. Whoever has control of this new agency acquires some degree of control over the worker. There is nothing to guarantee control over that agency to employees. It may also be controlled by employers. In other words, giving the government control over industrial relations creates a fulcrum which means great power for an unknown user.

The introduction of compulsory social insurance in cases of sickness, or compulsory social insurance in cases of unemployment, means that the workers must be subject to examinations, investigations, regulations, and limitations. Their activities must be regulated in accordance with the standards set by governmental agencies. To that we shall not stand idly by and give our assent.

Men and women, I trust I may not be sounding my warnings upon the empty air. I hope that they may find a lodgment in the minds and the hearts of my countrymen. I bid you have a care in all these attempts to regulate the personal relations and the normal personal activities of the citizenship of our country ere it be too late.

There is in the minds of many an absence of understanding of the fundamental essentials of freedom. They talk freedom, and yet would have bound upon their wrists the gyves that would tie them to everlasting bondage. And no matter how sympathetic or humanitarian is the gloss over the plan and the scheme, I again bid you beware. We know not when or how this great struggle going on in Europe will terminate, or what it shall mean for the future of those countries; but at least let the people of the United States hold their liberties in their own hands, for it may come to pass that our America, the America whose institutions and ideals we so much revere, may be the one nation to hold the beacon light of freedom aloft, and thus aid in relighting the torch, rekindling the heart flame of the world's liberty.

For a mess of pottage, under the pretense of compulsory social insurance, let us not voluntarily surrender the fundamental principles of liberty and freedom, the hope of the Republic of the United States, the leader and teacher to the world of the significance of this great anthem chorus of humanity—liberty!

# X

# The Hired Hands of Washington

THE ENSLAVEMENT of American farmers was assured when the Agricultural Adjustment Act of 1933 was forced through Congress by the New Deal. Our historic free and independent farmers have become the hired hands of Washington.

These are strong words, but the truth of them is corroborated by none other than the first Administrator of the A.A.A.

George N. Peek, a highly successful mid-west manufacturer and a long-time student of the farm problem, accepted the call to Washington. Soon came disillusionment. Ultimately he resigned, and wrote a book entitled *Why Quit Our Own,* a phrase taken from George Washington's Farewell Address. In the following selection is the substance of his story about the plans for the socialization of the farmers—and then the whole country.

## *They Would Remake the United States*

### GEORGE N. PEEK

I went into the Roosevelt Administration because I saw a chance to do something for agriculture and, through agriculture, for the nation. I got out when I saw that I had no chance there to do anything either for agriculture or for the nation. I am in politics for agriculture—not in agriculture for politics.

The Administration has committed itself, by a distortion of the lately deceased Agricultural Adjustment Act, to a policy of socialized farming. It has committed itself, by a distortion of the Reciprocal Trade Agreements Act, to a low tariff policy which has all the worst features of that free trade which the nation has always turned down at the polls.

Both these policies are utterly destructive. They can add nothing at all to the wealth and prosperity of the United States. They can only subtract from what we have, shift jobs from American to foreign workers and transfer to foreign nations the control of what we have left. Exactly that has been happening. The facts are very clear.

The facts as exhibited by the official records mean little to many in this Administration. The major policies of agriculture and foreign trade are in charge of men who have never earned their livings in industry, commerce, finance or farming and who have little comprehension as to how such livings are earned. Presenting facts to them is a sheer waste of time. They are long on theories but short on simple arithmetic. They are full of very big thoughts. These thoughts are so big that the United States is not a large enough field for them to operate in.

They would remake the United States as an incident to remaking the world. . . . No one will ever know how many fantastic schemes were in the air. Many of them crossed the border line of sanity, but anyone who attempted to apply elementary common sense was denounced as an obstructionist. It was heresy to assert that two plus two had to equal four. . . .

I entered what I thought was a Democratic Administration, not because it was Democratic but because it was pledged to a certain course of action. I eventually found that I was not in a Democratic Administration but in a curious collection of socialists and internationalists who were neither Republicans nor Democrats.

They, fanatic-like, believed that their objectives transcended the objectives of ordinary human beings and therefore they could not allow themselves to be hampered by the codes of ordinary mental honesty, by platform pledges, by the Constitution, or by any other of the ordinary rules of human conduct. . . .

The Agricultural Adjustment Act was a hodgepodge of conflicting notions compromised into a bill which had to be passed in order to get action. In supporting the Act, I thought that it would be used for constructive purposes and I did not have the slightest idea that in its administration it would become principally an instrument to regiment the farmer through acreage control. . . .

A plague of young lawyers settled on Washington. . . . They floated airily into offices, took desks, asked for papers and found no end of things to be busy about. I never found out why they came, what they did or why they left. Perhaps all of them expected to be hired, and some of them were hired. I only know that in the legal division were formed the plans which eventually turned the A.A.A. from a device to aid the farmers into a device to introduce the collectivist system of agriculture into this country. . . .

Practically all the young lawyers who swarmed into Washington dangling Phi Beta Kappa keys were enveloped in the delusion that they carried with them the tablets containing a new dispensation. They were going to inform the established lawyers and the Supreme Court what the law really was. . . .

I resigned as Administrator of the A.A.A. . . . I felt that the A.A.A. was headed for trouble, for it was developing into an agency for permanent and wholesale acreage control from a central point and without due regard to local conditions.

Such a program is wrong in theory and is difficult, if not impossible, to adminster in a democracy. I could not then or now willingly be a party to seeing control of the land of the farmers taken from them and put at the disposal of a Washington bureaucracy. As the A.A.A. began to expand as a social reform instead of as a farm aid, it became inevitable that in time the farmers would own their farms in name only and that in fact they would be the hired hands of Washington. . . .

The objective of the Collectivist group was to use the Act to bring about a planned agriculture and to keep the farmers from finding out what was going on by deluging them with money. The plan, which seems to show up in the amendments to the Act, was first to undermine the independence of the farmer through putting him on a dole and, when that had been done, to regulate agriculture exactly as the Departmental bureaucrats saw fit. If the Government holds his mortgage and can decide his income by saying how much he may plant and what he will get for his crops, a farmer can assert his independence only by giving up all that he has worked for through the years.

This is the sort of thing which the A.A.A. eventually was diverted into. There is no use in mincing words. The A.A.A. became a means of buying the farmer's birthright as a preliminary to breaking down the whole individualistic system of the country.

---

Tax money, seized by force from the citizens of America, has been used for every conceivable purpose to reduce the nation's farmers to the status of slaves obedient to the commands of their bureaucratic masters in Washington.

From the plowing under of crops and the killing of little pigs, so ridiculous has the debacle become, that farmers are now paid not to farm. There is now piled up in public warehouses over nine billion dollars worth of government owned agricultural surpluses, on which the storage charges run over a million and a half dollars a day.

The *Wall Street Journal* (March 9, 1960) refers to this as "Storing Insanity." Here is the editorial.

## Storing Insanity

Would you care to know how much it costs the taxpayers every day for storage of commodities Uncle Sam has on hand because of the farm program's high price supports?

Let's ease into this with two low ones, honey and tobacco. Uncle Sam pays out only $131 a day for honey and only $238 a day for tobacco, which, if it indicates anything at all, suggests that people smoke nearly all the tobacco that's grown here and that the bees aren't nearly as busy as the peanut farmers.

The peanut storage costs come to $6,000 a day; flaxseed and rye costs come to $7,000 each a day. Oats cost the taxpayer $15,000 a day for storage; rice, $17,000 a day; soybeans, $23,000; milk and butter fat, $29,000; barley, $64,000 a day and cotton $76,000 a day.

But even these are peanuts compared to the big boys. Have a good look:

Grain sorghums cost $262,000 a day for storage.

Corn costs $444,000 a day for storage.

And wheat costs $579,000 a day for storage.

That's every day. None of these costs include what was paid by the taxpayers, through their agent, Uncle Sam, for the stuff. It's just storage costs.

Total cost of storage for all these commodities comes to $1,547,-000 a day or better than $555,000,000 a year—and that, in anybody's book, is a lot to pay for storing up our harvest of insanity.

---

Farmers themselves are alarmed and fearful for the future as is evidenced by the following from Charles B. Shuman, President of the American Farm Bureau Federation.

## Payments—Permits—Peasantry

### CHARLES B. SHUMAN

It is natural for many politicians to favor programs which put them in the position of dispensing favors to farmers. Years ago it was free garden seeds—today it is ACP payments—tomorrow it may be monthly checks from the U.S. Treasury. Sounds good, but let us take a good look.

Production or income payment schemes similar to the old Brannan plan are being revived by members of Congress who finally recognize the failure of the price fixing and control programs of the past. However, these congressmen refuse to face the fact that there is no way to legislate prosperity into agriculture or they wish to keep farmers dependent on political action for a large portion of their income.

What are the facts about payments? Subsidy payments to increase the individual farmer's income have been tried both here and abroad with little success—and then they have only been used for crops which are produced on a deficit basis. Payments stimulate increased production since the size of the check to the individual farmer must be based on his production—the larger the crop the more government money. This is the start of a vicious chain reaction. Income payments to offset low farm prices actually cause farmers to produce more and this increased output forces prices even lower, thus bringing on the demand for greater payments per unit of production. Each year the proportion of the individual farm family's income coming from payments would increase while market prices are forced to extremely low levels. Drastic production controls would undoubtedly be imposed as well as progressively lower limits on the size of individual payments. If farming becomes a political privilege it will be divided among as many voters as possible regardless of their efficiency—one share, one vote!

What would be the effect upon consumers while these discouraging trends are forcing net farm income to ever lower levels? The consumer would notice little or no reduction in price at retail levels—increased costs of labor and other handling costs would offset price drops just as has happened during recent years. Consumers would find that the inefficient production that is inevitable under a payment system plus increased taxes means high, not low, food prices.

Payments would inevitably increase to the point where farmers would, for all practical purposes, be on the federal payroll. The right to farm would need to be determined in some manner. Once farming becomes a payroll job, it is impossible to let all who wish engage in the profession. Civil service examinations plus political party endorsements are required of those who want to become postal employees—could we expect any better plan for determining who shall farm?

Fantastic? Improbable? I think not! Income subsidy payments to farmers will tend to make food a public utility by destroying the market price system. They will result in the use of political influence and license examinations to determine who shall farm. They will place the net income of each individual farm family in the hands of the Congress, most of whose members are elected by urban voters who are more interested in "cheap food" than in high per family net farm income.

A sorry picture—consumers expecting cheap food, farmers waiting for Congress to pass an annual appropriation to determine their salary payments, strict production controls and low maximum limits on individual farm family income to spread the government money among as many voters as possible. Yes, payments mean licensed peasantry on the farms of America.

—Reprinted with permission from *Nation's Agriculture,* April, 1959.

## Farmers Dislike Federal Farm Program

D. B. HENDRIX

*County Farm Agent*

How do the thinking farmers of the United States feel about Federal Farm Programs? The *Farm Journal,* with more than three million readers located in every state in the union, has just finished tabulating the results of a fair and impartial questionnaire. They found that 55 per cent of all farmers who returned ballots were opposed to any government program of any kind. This poll was approved by statisticians as being sound and fair. Tennessee farmers voted 65 per cent in favor of kicking out all government payments and control. This doesn't jibe with claims made by ASC votes on controls. However, the farmers voting in the *Farm Journal* poll were not selected nor dominated. They had a chance to express their honest opinions without fear or favor. Moreover, they were people who think for themselves.

It certainly is a comforting thing to see that farm people have returned to sanity. It is an indication that they have had a chance to really observe and think for themselves. In view of these facts, it would appear that an honest government group would be willing and anxious to allow the people to determine whether or not they want a government farm program. What would be wrong with the government asking the farmers to vote on it? Do you think they will do it? Do you think they are going to allow farmers to do what they want to do? It would save the farmers and taxpayers billions of dollars, but it would wipe out thousands of seat warmers, parasites and political job holders and prevent government domination of the whole farm population of this country.

What can you do about it? Write your Congressman and Senator about it. Tell your farm organization officials. Demand the opportunity of freeing yourself from the shackles of government domination. Only then will you be a free man. Free to operate your business as you see fit; free to build your own program and free from the taint of government doles.

---

A representative of the magazine *Farm and Ranch* went to Washington for an interview with Secretary Benson. Here is his story.

## Stop Bureaucracy from Breaking Our Backs?
## "Not from Here. . . . I Tried," Says Benson

BILL KENNEDY

If Ezra Taft Benson, Secretary of Agriculture, is as much against big, centralized government and high cost as he says he is; and if he has failed to cut the expense in a single bureaucrat's office in his department after two terms—as the record clearly shows—then what sort of a pickle have we got ourselves into?

From a political standpoint, Mr. Benson would like to slough off the responsibility for USDA spending—shove it onto Congress. But it can't be done. Some of it lies scattered in the rambling corridors of his own department. It's a terrible and frightening thing when a cabinet member admits that he simply cannot control high-flying costs of operations under his direct supervision . . . if he can't, who can?

Well, that's just about what the Secretary admitted to me in a special *Farm and Ranch* interview a few days ago.

The latest attack on expenses of USDA (by Rep. Jamie Whitten, D-Miss. on the floor of the House) was as biased and unfair as the usual political speech. It dumped all the blame at the doors of the Secretary. But it was no more "political" than the answer offered the following day by Benson's friends, who blamed it all on the laws passed by Congress. Neither argument holds water.

Truth is, all spending has increased—that dictated by Congress as well as that supervised by the Department. And when confronted with figures to prove it, Benson told me, in essence, "I have tried . . . "

He first told how billions—that giant portion of the budget caused by price supports and surplus handling—truly are the result of laws which he had to follow, and which he has tried to have changed. But this by no means explained how every one of the 17 offices and agencies in his department will spend more in 1960 (his last year) than they did in 1953 (his first).

During his terms USDA has added 30,000 people to its payrolls and increased employees' salaries and expenses by $233.5 million (includes only the cost of maintaining workers themselves). While eight of the offices actually reduced the number of workers, the department as a whole increased employment by 63.9%. Personal service expense, with all offices contributing, went up 114%.

In our exclusive interview the Secretary was asked to explain this to *Farm and Ranch* readers. We asked for two answers:

1. "Could you have prevented it?"
2. "If so, why didn't you?" Or. . . . "If not, why not?"

He took us 'round the barn. We talked about the growing population to serve (but also about the shrinking number of farmers). We agreed that we have inflation and higher costs of living. We granted that there are new functions—like the Soil Bank, PL 480 and stepped up Bangs' control (also that there are some we could do without). We talked about many things—none of which answered all the questions raised by the figures on the chart.

We stuck to the question . . . "Why, Mr. Secretary?"

He defended the expansion of Research and Extension Services said he will continue to. He said he was in favor of the stepped-up timber harvest of the Forest Service; also the transfer of foreign agricultural workers from the State Department to Agriculture. And he said he has greatly "intensified" USDA's Office of Information, for which he has no apologies.

We persisted . . . "Mr. Secretary, why has the cost gone up in every single bureaucrat's office? Has the monster called Bureaucracy so run away with us that a courageous Conservative like Ezra Benson can't stop it in his office? Because—if it has—we think it is high time somebody in the know had the guts to admit it. We think it has. And we hoped you'd say so to our readers.

In fairness to the Secretary's political future, he did not admit it in a word—or in so many words. But he did say . . .

"I think it (Bureaucracy) is a real threat to this country. There is no doubt about it; entirely too many people are on the federal payrolls."

Benson went on to say that when he took office he was determined to stop the drift toward centralized government in Agriculture. He cited instances where he had tried. But things happened . . .

He did abolish the regional offices of SCS (after a howl and a struggle). But now there are 3,500 more SCS workers than before—and the budget is 70% bigger.

He reminded me that every time he tried to get ACP funds reduced, he got increases instead.

"Did you have to spend it, Mr. Secretary?"

And the answer came back, "Yes, if I wanted to get other items in my budget which I thought were essential."

(This has been proved in Agriculture and other departments. Appropriations committees hold the purse strings; in order for executive offices to get what they need, they have to carry out "pet" programs of the committee members. Only the President and the Defense Department have succeeded in defying them, and they on very few occasions.)

Benson could have talked about the powerful REA, which has shown even the President to be helpless in trying to have cooperatives pay a fair rate of interest. He did say it is almost impossible for anybody to dissolve a federal agency—or even reduce it, although he hesitated to talk about all the reasons.

Benson knows, even as you and I, that representatives of some agencies put on unlawful campaigns all the way to the branch heads to get more money. (He remembers well the howl from "home"—due in no small way to the workers themselves—when those SCS regional offices were abolished.)

Now and then there are investigations of political activity by bureaucrats (some are under way now). But it's hard to get enough "goods" on a smooth "career" man—to fire him. The Civil Service sees to that; once a worker gets a career appointment, he has a contract for life—and if his job peters out, you find him another one. And you give him an automatic raise from time to time.

Over 90% of USDA workers here are on career status Civil Service —will be around until death or retirement "do us part." What's more, any time a department head can finagle enough additional workers under his wing . . . his own "Grade" goes up automatically. So does his pay. While seldom is one "sorry" enough to fire, thousands of big and little department heads are scrambling and scheming for new employees.

This is Bureaucracy at work. And it can end but one place. With continuous growth—with more and more influence of the workers reaching into the voting districts—how long before the federal workers can out-vote the rest of the country? As a matter of fact, their influence already reaches a vast majority now (via Social Security if no other way) .

Ezra Benson is either a very poor administrator—or the situation is even worse than he admits. Only defense left is that this is happening throughout government—not just in Agriculture.

Agriculture is merely an example. While five administrative offices in the cabinet (one of which is Benson's) have slightly reduced the number of people working (with five others showing increases), every single one shows increased expenses for the workers.

Does this excuse the Agriculture Department? No! It just means the sins are compounded. Instead of Agriculture being a rotten apple in a barrel—the whole barrelful is rotten.

Benson is frank to admit that the decay caused by Bureaucracy has not been halted. He still believes it can be—"but not from here."

"We made a little progress," he believes, "but it merely retarded the drift (toward centralized government). It by no means reversed it.

"The drift can be halted and reversed, but only by the states (people in the states) insisting upon their share of responsibility for problems within the states," he says.

Does keeping some of the responsibility and authority at home mean more local expense? He says, yes, but that this is good over the long pull . . . "because a dollar can't make the round trip to Washington without a bureaucratic bite being taken out of it."

These are the answers we got. More excuses? Political fence building? Or just the scary facts? Either way, it adds up on the way—Socialism, here we come!

Who can stop it? You can.

Where? In the voting booth.

How? By demanding that all candidates dedicate themselves to returning responsibility and taxing powers to local government.

Why? Because if you don't act now—too soon it'll be too late. Your children and theirs will live in a socialistic country—never knowing the freedom that was once your priceless inheritance.

---

In the course of human events future Americans may read the story of Stanley Yankus and the almost countless number of persecuted farmers as we read today of our Embattled Farmers of long ago.

# The End of the Road

### REV. IRVING E. HOWARD

Most living Americans have never known the merciless rule of tyranny. Their forefathers came to these shores to escape despotism, but the exact nature of that despotism has long since been forgotten. However, more recent immigrants still have a vivid memory of a different kind of life than we used to enjoy in America.

Stanley Yankus is like that. He had heard the tale from his father, who migrated from Lithuania to America for freedom. Stanley Yankus, Jr. is a 39-year-old poultry farmer in Dowagiac, Michigan who has been so devoted to freedom that he has steadfastly refused to accept any government subsidies. He saw that government control would follow hard and fast after any government give-away. Moreover, he scornfully rejected the implicit "something for nothing" philosophy.

However, the freedom that Stanley Yankus' father came to America to find is dwindling. Something is happening to us. At least, Stanley Yankus has found it that way. He wished to plant wheat, feed it to his chickens and sell the eggs in market. He could see no reason why it was the concern of anyone how much wheat he was planting since he had never accepted a government hand-out. Nevertheless, since 1954 the Agricultural Stabilization and Conservation Board has been fining Stanley Yankus for raising too much wheat for his chickens. Yankus has refused to pay the fines until they have accumulated to over $4,000.

After five years of contending against the "wheat police," Stanley Yankus has been forced to give up saying: "I can't fight all the people who want something for nothing. I am no longer fighting bureaucrats. I am fighting those people who think the world owes them a living."

It is not easy, after you have spent years of long hours and hard work to acquire your own farm and you have succeeded so well that you have the largest poultry farm in your county, to sell it and bow out for no other reason than you insist upon being self-supporting. That is Stanley Yankus' situation and he has admitted sadly: "It looks as if the end of the road is near." The end of the road for Farmer Yankus may also mean the beginning of the end for American freedom!

The tattered army of George Washington fought the hired soldiers of King George III, but that was easy compared to Yankus's struggle. Given a generation that has been trained to look to government for salvation; whose High School textbooks have been carefully censored to delete the idealism of early America and to substitute the idealism of the United Nations; a generation whose very moral sense has been corrupted until they call stealing a virtue and self-reliance an evil; a generation with no inspiring memory of its heritage and no sure hope for the future; a generation of blind leading the blind, then who can tell them of the virtue of independence and self-help? How can they understand when Stanley Yankus warns: "There is nothing to be gained in losing the right to control one's own destiny"?

Mr. Yankus has preached his gospel of self-reliance again and again, but his neighbors have only wondered: why fight a government that is giving you something for nothing? Why? John Stuart Mill issued a warning to such governments many years ago: "A state which dwarfs its men, in order that they may be more docile instruments in its hands, even for beneficial purposes, will find that with small men no great thing can be accomplished."

Small men! Is that what Americans are becoming? When Mr. Yankus said: "I find my friends and neighbors are afraid of the Federal government" was he getting at the very root of our modern malaise?

This farmer is of the stuff that liberty is made of. Woe to the nation that breaks the spirit of such a citizenry! Once a government has pauperized its citizens, it will find no heroes to fight its battles.

Stanley Yankus had his well-wishers. They wrote letters full of heat and insisted: "They can't get away with it in America!" but it had already happened before the letters were written! Do you remember Garet Garrett's essay "The Revolution Was"?

American farmers are the last group one would expect to be demoralized by "something for nothing." However, they have received special attention since the New Deal.

A farm leader once pointed out that if one wished to collectivize a nation, it would be of prime importance to break down the individualism of the farmers and, if one wished to control a nation, it would be necessary to control the producers of food and fibre of that nation. To suggest such a Machiavellian plot is to endanger one's reputation for sanity, but the confessions of former plotters have lifted the "conspiracy theme" above the level of paranoia to the level of grim reality.

Who has ears to hear what Stanley Yankus is saying?

—Reprinted by permission from *Christian Economics*.

What *did* Stanley Yankus say?

"I think freedom is everything," were his ringing words before a Committee of Congress.

## I Think Freedom Is Everything

### STANLEY YANKUS

Mr. Chairman and Members of the Subcommittee. Permit me to express my deep appreciation for the opportunity given me to very briefly call attention to one of the inevitable results which follow the enforcement of the Agricultural Adjustment Act of 1938, as amended.

The following is a very brief statement of what I would like to say and I hope that after it is read, I may be permitted to enlarge upon the present situation.

What will happen if the present trend in government continues, in my opinion, based upon my experience, is that the people of the United States of America will no longer be free and independent, nor will this be a "free" nation.

My name is Stanley Yankus. I have lived on my 100 acre farm since April 1943. I raise wheat and barley and feed it all to my chickens. I have never signed an agreement with the A.S.C. (Agriculture Stabilization and Conservation Board). I have never accepted any subsidies. In the Fall of 1953, an A.S.C. agent said I could not raise wheat and feed it to my chickens. I thought this was contrary to everything American. I asked the A.S.C. man how I would be able to make a living if I couldn't use my land. In 1954, my wheat fines equalled my entire net income. That particular year 1100 chickens died in 10 days from a bad disease. Eggs were cheap and feed was high due to support prices. My wife and I made only $1,000 that year.

In the year 1955 I was fined about $1,034.00. The March issue of *Reader's Digest* magazine has an article entitled "The Strange

Crime of Stanley Yankus." What is my crime? A man does have to commit an offense to get fined or punished. I did not sell any wheat so my offense is not selling wheat. Then my offense had to be using land for producing crops.

Now, Congressmen, I would like to put the shoe on the other foot. You have passed laws permitting the Bureau of Reclamation to put new land into production. In the year 1955 alone, the Bureau of Reclamation added 136,000 acres of land into production. So who is more guilty of the strange crime of producing crops? The Bureau of Census also states that 6 million bushels of wheat were imported in 1955. I did not add to the surplus of wheat, but you did since you have the power to regulate imports.

During the years 1954 to 1958 inclusive, I was fined $4,562 plus interest and costs. Because many of the farmers in my situation had been through courts and received adverse decisions, I decided to appeal through the Press to the American people. The Detroit Times was the first large newspaper in the Nation to champion my cause.

The division of power—legislative, executive and judicial—has been a fundamental concept of English and American law.

The A.S.C. has nullified this concept because a bureaucrat in the Department of Agriculture can write a regulation through the Federal Register which has the effect of law. The A.S.C. can and does execute and administer these laws, and the A.S.C. acts as judge and jury in determining a farmer's guilt. I am not fighting for the right to grow wheat. I am fighting for the right to own property. If I am forbidden the use of my land, then I do not own it. My rights do not extend much beyond the right to pay taxes. This is tyranny.

The Fifth Amendment of the Constitution says "no person shall be deprived of life, liberty or property without due process of law." The right to trial by jury is one of the due processes of law which has been denied to me.

My right to liberty should certainly be my right to earn my own living on my own farm.

Federal law should apply equally to all citizens. Yet in 36 states there are wheat restrictions, and in 12 states there are none. Thus, I am a second-class citizen because I live in a state where restrictions are imposed.

For five years my wheat allotment has been about 10 acres per year. Since I began to seek publicity, the A.S.C. gave me an allotment of 28 acres for 1959. This is ample proof that allotments are established arbitrarily.

Not only have I fed all the grain I have raised but I have purchased $12,000 worth of commercial chicken feed each year. This feed contains wheat and so I have been reducing the surplus of wheat.

I have not harmed any other farmers. I have earned my own living. I have paid my taxes. How can you Congressmen justify the laws which have destroyed my means of making a living?

Many people have told me that I would lose everything by opposing these wheat laws. What is everything? Money is of no value to a slave. I think freedom is everything.

———

Stanley Yankus moved himself and family to Australia. What can we who stay in America do? Charles B. Shuman, President of the Farm Bureau Federation, suggests a plan which he believes will bring freedom back to the farmer.

## A Farm Program That Will Work

### CHARLES B. SHUMAN

If the family farm is to remain strong and competitive we need to make sure that family farm operators are permitted to adjust to meet changing conditions. The Government acreage control and price-fixing programs of the past 25 years have discouraged needed adjustments and stimulated the production of large quantities of crops that consumers did not want. The result of these unwise political decisions is that thousands of family farm operators have not made adjustments to changes which are inevitable. Their future is jeopardized by the very programs which were supposedly intended to help them.

In comparing the experience of farmers who produce commodities that have been under the production control and political pricing schemes with those who have produced for consumer markets without government programs, it is now apparent that government programs have not improved farmers' income. The billions of dollars spent on price support purchases and subsidy payments have not added to farm income—they have only been an offset against the losses that farmers have suffered as a result of restricted production, increased costs of operation and surplus-depressed prices under the programs.

Many panaceas will be proposed to the new Congress. Bushel and poundage quotas, income subsidy payments, strict marketing orders for all crops, multi-price schemes and many others. Those who believe in government direction of individuals and those who do not recognize that our successful system in this country depends upon freedom of individuals to choose always advocate more government controls over the economy when faced with the failure of current programs. Some are even so foolish as to advocate that the cost of these unworkable schemes be levied on farmers.

Most of the so-called new proposals being offered have the same built-in weaknesses that brought failure to past programs and would, if adopted, accelerate the trends toward socialized agriculture. Excessive production is encouraged as certainly by income payments as by price guarantees. In fact, the income insurance feature of these various schemes assures uneconomic stimulation of production. Present excessive wheat and cotton production has been in part caused by the insurance feature—the price and market being guaranteed by government before planting—as well as by the level at which prices were fixed.

In fact, I believe that milling quality wheat and good quality cotton would have brought higher average prices on a free consumer market during the last 10 years than they have had with government as the market. If we place all farm production under a control and pricing scheme or add farmers to the public payroll under some income payment plan, we will have moved a long way toward peasantry in American agriculture. The way to a healthy, prosperous agriculture is not to make farm income dependent upon Congressional appropriations. 175 million people must eat and wear clothing—they will pay prices that will return a good income to farmers if we produce what they want and keep farmers free to make the changes that are indicated by changing demand.

The question is often asked—why is there so much opposition to every attempt to take a small step toward a return to a market price system for agriculture?

There are three groups who like things as they now are with large surplus stocks and farmers dependent upon political action by Congress.

The first group consists of a few devoted Marxists who wish to see our free competitive capitalistic system replaced by a system of state ownership and control of property and individuals.

The second group is the increasing number of warehousemen and handlers of farm products who are profiting from the government storage programs. Included in this group are a few farmer cooperatives.

The third group is the relatively small, but powerful, group of politicians who like to be in the position of dispensing favors to farmers. They like government farm programs because they can take credit for all improvements in farm income or make extravagant promises when conditions are not so good.

The adoption of three simple proposals would help return farming to a sound and prosperous basis.

First, discontinue all acreage and production controls and use the soil bank to ease the adjustments for a short time.

Second, use a percentage of the previous three-year market price as a basis for price support for those products that have been price-fixed. The free market should operate most of the time. All other price fixing or payment schemes would be discontinued.

Third, freeze existing stocks of the Commodity Credit Corporation so that they can not be sold in competition with new crops on domestic or foreign markets. Disposal of existing stocks should be accomplished over a ten year period by discount sales or gifts to those nations which are in distress or which could not normally purchase the commodities. Public Law 480 sales should be restricted and eliminated completely within a short time.

This program will work.

—From Mr. Shuman's Annual Address before the 40th Annual
Convention of the Federation, Boston, December 9, 1958.

———

A demand to repeal all the farm laws written since New Deal days and restore free enterprise to the farmer is voiced by Thurman Sensing, Executive Vice President of the Southern States Industrial Council.

He, like Mr. Shuman, one of the great farm leaders of the day, calls for a free market for the farmer.

## Farm Subsidies Must Go

THURMAN SENSING

In calling for a farm program that is "sensible and economically sound and not a political poultice," President Eisenhower raised the hopes of Americans who know something must be done to end the shameful annual waste of $6 billion on farm subsidies. But the President dashed these hopes with the detailed suggestions he offered to Congress—suggestions that embodied the old disproved answers to the farm problem.

Certainly, the President understands the dimensions of the farm problem. He sees the danger to the nation in costly waste, for he cited examples of colossal waste. "The government," said Mr. Eisenhower, "sustains a net cost of more than $1,000.00 a minute—$1.5 million every day—the year round, to stabilize wheat prices and income." He also revealed that the nation has $3.5 billion tied up in stored wheat. "Although this means that well over 30 per cent of the total funds invested in inventories and loans of the Commodity Credit Corporation goes for wheat," he said, "this crop provides only 6 per cent of the case receipts of farm products."

These costs are for wheat alone. All farm surplus storage and handling costs the government $3 million per day. The government has a total of $9.5 billion tied up in surplus crops. The budget for next year includes an additional $5.6 billion for agricultural price supports, second in size only to interest among non-defense budget items.

Anyway, recognizing the existing farm plans only further distort the wheat market and lead to new and higher costs, the President should have outlined new remedies. Unfortunately, the President's own farm program, like that of the Democrats, seems more concerned with the vote of the farm states than with the farm problem.

Instead of repudiating the idea of farm subsidies, Mr. Eisenhower actually suggested that they should be expanded! He proposed that the Soil Bank raise its conservation reserve to 60 million acres. The result of this would be to tremendously enlarge the group of agriculturists who are engaged in what Southerners call "piazza farming." By that, I mean the practice of sitting in a rocking chair on the front porch and farming the U.S. Treasury instead of fields. More and more so-called farmers will cease planting and depend on the postman to deliver a monthly check for not planting.

The hard truth is that no progress can be made on solving the nation's farm program until the subsidy idea is firmly and permanently rejected. To get farming back on a sane basis means that farmers must learn to do without federal aid.

And why shouldn't farmers do without federal aid? Or, if farmers should have it, why shouldn't everybody have it? Take the automobile industry, for instance; why not pay the manufacturers for not making automobiles? Why not pay a manufacturer for placing one of his plants in the Automobile Plant Bank? Or, if they make more automobiles than they can sell, why doesn't the government purchase and store the surplus? It would be just as sensible.

The massive federal aid received by the farmers amounts for many of them to a guaranteed annual wage. Of course, the farm programs of the last quarter-century are, in themselves, grossly unfair to some farmers. Only growers of certain crops receive this federal aid. Farmers who grow collards, sweet potatoes or lettuce, raisers of cattle—who actually declined price supports and have been better off ever since—receive not a cent from the federal treasury. Instead they pay taxes to help the growers of wheat, cotton, tobacco and other favored crops.

What the nation's farm communities need is free enterprise. By that, I mean the free operation of economic forces so that marginal, inefficient producers are weeded out. "You can't do that to us," says the farm bloc. But the nation can, if it has the courage of its convictions. The nation must do it if it wants efficient farms, instead of large numbers of farmers on what amounts to a dole. The existence of this dole is grossly unfair to the taxpayers, who must contribute to it; it costs them double—in higher taxes and higher prices in the grocery stores.

And so the need is to repeal all the farm laws written since New Deal Days, and start over from scratch. That may be politically difficult, but it's not impractical. Unless the idea of subsidy payments is directly challenged and defeated, billions will continue to be spent annually to feed the rats in government storage warehouses, and the farm problem never will be solved.

———

Cattlemen have valiantly resisted all regimentation, controls, supports and subsidies.

They have prospered.

On January 29, 1960, the Senator from Arizona, Barry Goldwater, addressed the American National Cattlemen's Association. His message has a ringing challenge for all Americans.

## We Cannot Have Economic Freedom and Political Dictation Nor Can We Have Political Freedom and Economic Dictation

### HON. BARRY GOLDWATER

It is a real privilege to appear before a group of Americans who have steadfastly maintained their independence and who have resolutely refused to barter away their economic freedom.

In this age of subsidy and supports and special privilege it is a refreshing and encouraging experience to visit with men and women who have never been taken in by that beguiling promise of something for nothing—which is the universal bait employed to secure citizen consent for federal intervention.

For 30 years we have experimented with farm programs. Supports and controls and subsidies now extend to 30 per cent of our farm product and after 30 years of failure we are still experimenting.

And what have we accomplished by this 30 years of failure?

We have succeeded in making the farmer the whipping boy of our economy.

We have assessed direct and indirect penalties against the people of America—cattlemen who buy grain are forced to pay an artificial price, cotton mills must buy their raw material in an administrated market, and we have deprived the general public from the benefits which should be theirs—of our improving farm technology.

Oh, and one more thing, we have compelled the taxpayer to foot the bill for political folly.

Perhaps more damaging than all of these—we have, in some measure, created a dependent society.

We are maintaining a herd of boarder cows at public expense.

And let me emphasize here and now that the farmers are the victims and not the creators of our disastrous farm policy.

I've got a bale of figures in my briefcase covering the cost of our folly. I guess six CPAs and three Philadelphia lawyers could make real good sense out of these reports. But I can read the total, and the total "realized cost"—that's Washington language—from '32 to '59 has been 17,753,000,000 dollars.

Since 1953, the government has disposed of some 16 million dollars in surplus commodities overseas, below cost. And we still have 9 million dollars worth left. Farm surpluses today are three-and-a-half times as large as they were at the beginning of 1953. Carrying charges, transportation, interest and the cost of storage amount to more than one billion dollars a year—or 2,739,726 dollars per day.

Well, I am sure that you are familiar with all these figures. But please let me point out that, generally speaking, producers of agricultural products—under the price support and acreage limitation program—are finding rough sledding. While producers outside the program—operating on market place values in response to the law of supply and demand—are faring much better than their subsidized brothers.

Even though this program has been a monumental failure, one thing is obvious—we can't end it overnight.

Out in Arizona, my friends in the cattle business tell me that when you suddenly take a calf away from its mother both the cow and the calf do a lot of bawling.

I suspect that if we were to end subsidies, the mother cow—in this case, the big government interventionists who administer the subsidy program—would out-bawl the recipients.

You remember back in the days of the depression when Henry Wallace wanted to plow up every fourth row we had planted—creating an artificial scarcity so prices would rise—most Americans were shocked, and a lot of unkind things were said about Henry Wallace. We are more enlightened than he was—we don't plow the crops under—we just put it all in storage and call it surplus and keep on wondering what to do with it.

Democrats say the Republicans are responsible for the farm mess and the Republicans say it's the Democrats who got us into this fix. The truth is, neither one of these statements is correct. We got ourselves into this mess.

Our trouble commenced when we first accepted the notion that governmental intervention—subsidies, controls, concessions, etc.—could be substituted for the creative strength of a free people.

We forgot momentarily that liberty is indivisible.

We cannot have liberty in any realm of our personal activities unless we are willing to accept liberty in all areas. We cannot have economic freedom and political dictation, nor can we have political freedom and economic dictation.

Radical liberals in our century behave as if they believe liberty could be divided.

Economic freedom is rapidly disappearing as the result of a radical liberal attempt to create a society in which one segment of the economy is subsidized while another segment is controlled and a third segment asks to operate on the market place values.

The tragic thing about all of these programs of big government intervention is that they invariably produce waste and create a dependent society. What is more destructive is the creation of a soft and weak people—conditioned to look to big government for the solution of every problem. This was the pattern which preceded the downfall of Egypt, and Rome, and Greece. Are we to sit idly by and witness the destruction of this Republic?

Sophisticated modern know-it-alls have almost succeeded in selling us the destructive marxisms of the welfare state. And I would suggest now is the time to recall the truth of those copybook admonitions we cherished as children.

I would suggest that you and I remember, and probably still respect, that common sense, colloquial admonition "Waste not, want not."

If we are to be victorious in this cold war struggle against the alien doctrine of communism, we cannot afford to continue wasting human resources; nor can we continue to proceed on the assumption that man's creative ability can be blueprinted and pigeonholed.

Each year in Washington the statisticians with their slide rules have estimates of cotton production.

The cotton farmers in Arizona, when they found their planting limited to a certain number of acres, improved their technology. They used more fertilizer, they were more careful in their cultivation, and they succeeded in producing a greater total yield of cotton on a substantially decreased number of acres.

When you tell a free American that he can't do something, or try to fence him in, the chances are his inventive genius and tenacity of purpose will find a way to get around the fences and accomplish the thing he was told he couldn't do.

I am reliably informed, for example, that wheat farmers in the semi-arid lands of eastern Washington have developed a strain of wheat which resulted in a doubling of the yield per acre.

Does it make sense that this increase of yield and improved technology should become a storage headache for all the people when it should be a blessing for all people?

We are not going to answer the problems created by our unsuccessful approach to them by imposing more limitations.

No one has yet suggested we should set up a governmental agency and put price supports under automobiles or telephones, televisions or refrigerators or any of the products of manufacturing.

I did read once the humorous suggestion of a professional writer who proposed that the government establish a word bank in Washington—in order that he might have a market for his total output. He suggested the government buy the words he couldn't sell in the open market and put them in a surplus bank. Or how about the buggy whip manufacturer who had no more markets for his product and suggested that the government buy them at $1.25 and sell them to Europe at $1.00.

We accepted governmental intervention in the field of agriculture on the assurance of its sponsors that we would achieve these objectives: 1. Assure the farmer an income commensurate with that enjoyed by men in other occupations; 2. Produce better food at lower costs; 3. Conserve, rather than waste, our natural resources.

The difficult problem of farm surpluses was created by the radical liberal group who mistakenly believed they could apply controls and central planning to only one segment of the nation's economic life.

Not long ago, one of the Democrat presidential hopefuls made a speech on the west coast in which he deplored the fact that Americans had gone soft.

I don't think Americans have gone soft, but if we have, I would suggest it is the direct result of the spoon-fed, administered society which the radical liberals have attempted to create here—it is the result of our failure to deal bluntly and openly with unpleasant problems and difficult situations.

You and I, as citizens of this republic, must accept a portion of the responsibility for the present dilemma in which the farmer finds himself.

Common sense tells us the only way to rescue the farmer and re-establish his dignity in our economy is to get farm products back on the open market and free the farmer of governmental controls and intervention.

Mr. Henry Hazlitt has suggested the way to do this was to end all farm subsidies and payments on crops not already planted. And then to sell back to the farmers—at prices lower than the cost of production—all the surpluses now being held in government storage.

Mr. Hazlitt pointed out that no farmer would grow crops when he could buy the crops from government for less than the cost of' production. He suggested that most farmers would take advantage of the situation to build up the soil and adopt practices which would assure less expensive production when it became necessary to produce crops once more.

Mr. Hazlitt also pointed out the farmers would conform to market demands in the resale of the surplus commodities bought back from the government.

Since the beginning of the Eisenhower administration, the Republican Secretary Benson has tried desperately to end the present wasteful practices and restore market place values in the agricultural industry.

Political pressures and the farming of the farmer for votes, rather than voting for the farmers' good, has prevented this. I would suggest the farm program is only one symptom of the distressing malady of big government intervention which threatens the economy and the future of this nation.

You and I must decide whether we intend to continue down the road of federal aid and federal subsidy. Last year the federal Congress passed the so-called "Defense Education Act." This year they are being urged to pass a federal subsidy for the construction of schools. We have federal aid for highways. These programs always start small, and end big, and the bureaus administrating these programs multiply like rabbits—and are just as hard to kill off.

If we continue down this road, we will become a people who will be leaning on Uncle Sam—and the more we lean, the greater the habit becomes. And no people dependent upon the subsidies of central government can claim to be free.

The preservation of the Republic is not a partisan political issue. We are not divided as Republicans or Democrats. Indeed, had it not been for the valiant efforts of many effective and dedicated Democrats, we might be much closer to complete socializing than we now are.

Growing cattle isn't all beer and skittles. Merchants and manufacturers and doctors and dentists have their problems. But 170 years of progress should certainly convince us that free men, free from governmental interference, produce more, distribute more and contribute more to man's ultimate destiny than a race of dependent, controlled creatures.

I would suggest this nation still has the strength and courage to face the truth—to reverse the course we have been following the past 30 years—to turn our backs on the errors we have made without indulging in the luxury of name calling and recriminations.

Washington won't do this, and no remote governmental corporation can do this. But you and I can—and must. By apathy and greed we created this situation—with courage and sacrifice we can correct it.

We can reject self-indulgence and demand self-sufficiency.

We can return to those principles of thrift, industry and person-to-person charity which conquered this hostile continent and made America the goal and the beacon light for all men, everywhere.

---

Dr. William H. Peterson, Associate Professor of Economics at New York University, has written a book, *The Great Farm Problem,* and from it emerges a conviction not unlike those which have been expressed here by farmers, industrialists, and politicians. The closing part of the Epilogue to his book is fitting at this point.

## Nature's Laws and Man's Laws

### WILLIAM H. PETERSON

The tragedy of modern farm intervention is twofold. One tragedy stems from man's efforts, in a sense heroic, to repeal Nature's laws, to substitute bureaucratic rule for the market place, to set prices below the market price and decree, vainly, that there shall be no shortages, and to set prices above the market price and assert, again vainly, that there shall be no surpluses. So under the banner of farm policy, and armed with legislative authority, court order, administrative directives, and no little courage and smugness, the interventionists commandeer the market place and "adjust" farm prices and, ultimately, the farm itself. Politics enters (e.g., the farm bloc). Pressure groups pull this way and that. One intervention fails, and a new one is tacked on. The jerry-built edifice wobbles anew. So still more intervention.

A generation of "farm policy" adds up to hopeless tinkering, fantastic losses, planned chaos, a lost war against Nature's laws. The battles have been man's laws: the Fordney-McCumber Tariff, the McNary-Haugen bills, the Farm Marketing Board, the Smoot-Hawley Tariff, the A.A.A., soil conservation, the ever normal granary, the Food-Stamp Plan, 90 per cent of parity, the Brannan Plan, flexible parity, the Soil Bank, overseas surplus disposal. These man-made laws have snares. Tens of thousands of American farmers run afoul of the farm laws every year. In 1954, for example, fourteen thousand wheat violations and more than twenty-three thousand tobacco violations were prosecuted. Although the government collects millions of dollars in fines, so wide a disrespect for the law suggests that the fault lies in the legislation—legislation that is clearly in conflict with human nature, much as was Prohibition, which converted the nation to bathtub gin, speak-easies, and mass lawbreaking. An Indian mission school in Montana raised wheat enough to take care of its children's needs. Its allotment was twenty-eight acres; it raised sixty-five acres. A monastery in Georgia, given too small a wheat allotment to provide for its members, defied controls and planted what it needed.

The irony is that the farmer to be saved wasn't; since the New Deal, one of every three farmers has quit. The exodus from farming, in a sense a triumph of efficiency over intervention, continues to the present day.

The second phase of the tragedy of modern farm intervention is that it is but a chapter in a much longer but unfinished story; it is a part of a philosophy, a way of life, a return to mercantilism, a recall to the planned society of Imperial Rome. How will the story end?

Many farmers bemoan the loss of their economic liberty, but do they bemoan the censorship of a movie in Philadelphia or a play in Boston, the lifting of mailing privileges for a radical weekly? Does the interest of a Jehovah's Witness in freedom of religion extend to an interest in the publisher's concern for the freedom of the press? Does the publisher worry over the worker's loss of civil liberty in having to join a union against his will? Does the worker lose any sleep over the scientist who is denied a passport and hence is not free to travel abroad? Does the atomic scientist complain when the Japanese-American is put into a federal concentration camp or the Nazi is judged under ex post facto laws?

Freedom is all. As long as man exercises neither force nor the threat of force against his fellow man, freedom exists. The duty of government, then, is to preserve freedom, to use its force only to repel force; the spirit of free enterprise and liberalism will do the rest. The modern dilemma is that competition, the law of supply and demand, however worshiped in the abstract, is nowadays shot through with privileges extended by government and eagerly sought by its citizens.

The farmer is not alone. Government, as Voltaire noted, has become the art of taking from some and giving to others. The business man looks for a tariff, the veteran for a pension, the shipper for a subsidy, the worker for a minimum wage, the periodical publisher for an artificial mailing cost, the industrialist for a defense contract, the silver producer for the monetization of silver, the labor official for immunity from the anti-trust laws, the elderly for social security, the bureaucrat for power, the debtor for inflation, and so on and on, the state ever swelling, the individual ever shrinking.

It is an age of amorality, an age of seeking something for nothing, of shedding private responsibility and becoming wards of the state—the welfare state. It happened before. Rome, for instance, had its "bread and circuses." It tried to repeal Nature's laws—for example, the law of self-reliance and law of supply and demand. Nature was not denied then. Will she be denied now?

These are the words of Ralph Waldo Emerson, written more than a century ago:

> The harvest will be better preserved and go farther, laid up in private bins, in each farmer's corn-barn, and each woman's basket, than if it were kept in national granaries.
>
> In like manner, an amount of money will go farther if expended by each man and woman for their own wants, and in the feeling that this is their all, than if expended by a Great Steward, or National Commissioners of the Treasury.
>
> Take away from me the feeling that I must depend upon myself, give me the least hint that I have good friends and backers there in reserve who will gladly help me and instantly I relax my diligence.

Give no bounties, make equal laws, secure life and property, and you will not need to give alms. Open the doors of opportunity to talent and virtue, and they will do themselves justice and property will not be in bad hands. In a free and just commonwealth, property rushes from the idle and imbecile to the industrious, brave, and persevering. The level of the sea is not more surely kept than is the equilibrium of value in society by demand and supply; and artifice and legislation punish themselves by reactions, gluts, and bankruptcies.

Said President Grover Cleveland, in vetoing federal aid to the Texas drought farmers of his day: "It is the business of citizens to support the Government, not the Government to support the citizens."

In the words of Michigan chicken farmer Stanley Yankus, who sold out his farm to meet a fine for overplanting wheat which he fed to his chickens, and now an American expatriate: "I'm a Paul Revere trying to alert the country about the dangers to freedom."

Which will triumph, Nature's laws or man's laws?

# XI

# Foreign Aid and You

IT CANNOT BE SAID that there was some specific date when the American people put their heads together and decided that it was in their interest to put most of the rest of the world on our charity list. There was no such date; and no such decision was ever made by the American people. By gradual stages and steps, it was decided for us.

In the hectic days of emotional mass delusion following World War I was blown the "bubble that broke the world." Loans (?) and gifts of billions were poured into Europe. There were the outpourings under the Dawes Plan; and, when that failed, there were more outpourings under the Young Plan; and when that failed, the Hoover Moratorium was launched in a desperate effort to save Europe.

Some years later in a resurgence of mass delusion we poured out billions under the guise of "Lend-Lease;" and when that phrase had served its purpose with the ending of World War II, new schemes in the mounting giveaway phobia had to be devised. The Truman Plan was born. Under it we poured out billions to our "friends" across the seas for the purpose of stopping the advance of that self-same communism which our billions had been nurturing so heartily during preceding years.

Then came the launching of the Marshall Plan at the Harvard Commencement in 1947. This umpteenth plan for saving the world by giving away our wealth was sold to Congress by its high-ranking supporters as the last and final one—only a "temporary" measure to restore economic recovery everywhere. Congress was assured that the job would be done completely and finally in only four years and with only seventeen billion dollars. Congress passed the necessary legislation with the limitations specified.

Now, more than a decade and many billions of dollars later, there is still no sign of discontinuance. In fact, the official attitude now seems to be that this whole foreign aid program should be put on a permanent basis. What kind of a basis has it been on for the past forty years? As we look upon the past and current "temporary" government aid programs, it is to muse sadly that the most permanent thing in the world is a temporary plan of government aid.

The decade after the launching of the Marshall Plan, instead of producing solutions, recovery, and stability as promised, has brought forth only a nightmare of crises and explosions around the world, and the consequent creation of more and more agencies for dispensing more and more billions.

In March of 1959 a group of thirty-eight citizens formed the Citizens Foreign Aid Committee. The purpose was to make available to all who wished to read it, a factual report on the foreign aid program. The Committee consisted of former government officials, former generals, former members of Congress, distinguished lawyers, jurists, educators, writers and a few industrialists:

Chairman, Mr. Walter Harnischfeger, Milwaukee, Wisconsin
Hon. T. Coleman Andrews, Richmond, Virginia
Hon. Spruille Braden, New York, New York
Mr. Frank C. Brophy, Phoenix, Arizona
Hon. Howard Buffet, Omaha, Nebraska
Mr. F. Gano Chance, Centralia, Missouri
Mr. Robert B. Dresser, Providence, Rhode Island
Mr. E. M. Elkin, Pittsburgh, Pennsylvania
Hon. Guy George Gabrielson, Bernardsville, New Jersey
Mr. Luther O. Griffith, Huntington, West Virginia
Mr. Robert M. Harris, Forest Hills, New York
Mr. A. G. Heinsohn, Jr., Knoxville, Tennessee

Mr. R. A. Hummel, New York, New York
Mr. Clarence Budington Kelland, Scottsdale, Arizona
Hon. James S. Kemper, Chicago, Illinois
Hon. J. Bracken Lee, Salt Lake City, Utah
Mr. William Loeb, Reno, Nevada
Mr. R. Chesley McCormick, Wichita, Kansas
Mr. William L. McGrath, Cincinnati, Ohio
Mr. Sterling Morton, Chicago, Illinois
Mrs. Ruth Murray, Oshkosh, Wisconsin
Hon. Gerald P. Nye, Cooperstown, North Dakota
Hon. Samuel B. Pettengill, Grafton, Vermont
Mr. J. Howard Pew, Philadelphia, Pennsylvania
Chief Justice M. T. Phelps, Phoenix, Arizona
Mr. Henning W. Prentis, Jr., Lancaster, Pennsylvania
Col. Willard F. Rockwell, Pittsburgh, Pennsylvania
Mr. Hubbard S. Russell, Maricopa, California
Lieut. General George E. Stratemeyer, Winter Park, Florida
Mr. Ernest G. Swigert, Portland, Oregon
Mrs. Garvin E. Tankersley, Bethesda, Maryland
Dr. Charles C. Tansill, Washington, D.C.
Mr. E. McL. Tittmann, New York, New York
General Albert Wedemeyer, Boyds, Maryland
Hon. Burton K. Wheeler, Butte, Montana
General Robert E. Wood, Chicago, Illinois
Dean Clarence Manion—Legal Counsel, South Bend, Indiana
Brig. Gen. Bonner Fellers—Study Coordinator, Washington, D.C.

This committee published a thirty-two-page pamphlet entitled *Foreign Aid and You.* 280,000 copies were distributed to government officials, members of Congress, all daily newspapers, periodicals, commentators, columnists, trade associations, and key individuals.

## *Foreign Aid and You*

### I

### *Our Foreign Aid*

We Americans have always had an historic policy of service to mankind. It is part of our heritage and our religion. For a century and a half and to all parts of the world, we have sent funds, supplies, missionaries, doctors, teachers and technicians to lend a help-ing hand to those in need.

Reflecting this humanitarian spirit, our government has ex-tended aid when and where the need arose. As early as 1794 the Congress voted relief for the victims of the Haitian Massacre. In 1812 relief was voted for earthquake victims in Venezuela. In 1921 to 1923, despite a hostile Kremlin, the Congress authorized relief for Russian famine sufferers. According to Russian leaders of that time this disaster aid, directed by Mr. Herbert Hoover, saved 20 million lives. Although relations with Japan were strained in 1923, the Congress authorized generous relief for victims of Japan's worst earthquake.

Person to person aid, together with governmental disaster relief, lifted American world prestige to unprecedented heights.

After World War II, however, our government's attitude toward aid abroad changed drastically. Its foreign aid is now continuous and has been expanded until it has become global, with heavy com-mitments made for years ahead.

To rehabilitate the war-torn countries in Europe our govern-ment launched the Marshall Plan. This was superseded by the present mutual security program which extends foreign aid to more than 70 countries. In the process of this expansion, the North At-lantic Treaty Organization (NATO) was created to strengthen Western Europe against the Red threat from the East.

Current fiscal appropriations for foreign aid are authorized un-der the Mutual Security Act, Public Law 853, 85th Congress. As part of foreign aid Public Law 480, 83rd Congress authorizes dis-posal of agricultural surplus commodities.

Foreign aid is divided into two major classifications: military assistance and economic aid.

Military assistance includes: military hardware, military train-ing, offshore procurement, (military material bought in foreign countries) , weapons development in Allied countries.

Economic aid includes: grants in aid (cash or commodities) , Point IV (technical assistance), contributions to the United Na-tions, surplus agricultural products, development loans, President's special assistance and contingency fund.

This varied and complex foreign aid program has now become an instrument of foreign policy. As such it should have one pur-pose only—to "provide for the common defense," and "promote the general welfare" of the United States. When foreign aid impedes our welfare, the Congress has no lawful power to appropriate.

In 1948 some 450 people were employed to administer and distribute foreign economic aid. Ten years and $41 billion later this staff has grown to 12,000 directing 2,000 projects. In addition, some 9,000 persons are engaged in the military assistance program which has totaled $23 billion. As of December 31, 1958, there was a total of $6.6 billion in unexpended foreign aid funds.

## II

### Foreign Aid and Defense

Proponents of foreign aid argue that it offers the best means of avoiding war. They remind us that since NATO came into being the Soviets have not taken one square foot of Western Europe.

Whether or not the Soviets, with their 175 regular divisions and the world's largest air force, intended to occupy Western Europe is not known. Obviously Western Europe's 21 NATO division defense, with insufficient air support, is not an effective war deterrent. If the Soviets ever entertained invasion plans, one weapon alone has deterred them: the U.S. Strategic Air Command (SAC).

Meanwhile Western Europe, more prosperous than before World War II, is not carrying its proportionate share of the NATO defense effort. But we are carrying far more than our share. We have stationed 5 American divisions and some tactical air units in Europe. These forces spend and require substantial sums for their support and maintenance. This is not foreign aid money but it supplements foreign aid in that it places more American dollars at the disposal of foreign governments.

Despite our huge defense contribution, European NATO strength in comparison to that of the Soviets is almost negligible.

The population of prosperous European NATO countries is 50% greater than ours. But our eager assumption of a heavy defense role in Western Europe has caused our allies somewhat to disregard the Red threat and to rearm reluctantly. To stimulate them into creating more military might for their own defense we should advise them that it is not our policy permanently to garrison Europe. There should be a systematic withdrawal of American troops, particularly in the lower echelons, as fast as these can be replaced by European NATO members.

To bolster morale after Sputnik I, President Eisenhower promised nuclear Intermediate Range Ballistic Missiles (IRBM) to our NATO Allies. The plan was to establish a line of 36 IRBM squadrons from England through Southeast Europe and on into Turkey. More than a year later only four IRBM squadrons had been accepted. These are being based in Britain. Administration leaders had placed great faith in Europe's use of the IRBM as a war deterrent. This cool Allied reception of the IRBM, Britain excepted, is considered by some military experts as the greatest failure in our post-war defense planning.

There is a good reason for this reluctance. In an all-out nuclear war the Kremlin forces, unless prevented by SAC, have the capability of destroying Western Europe in a matter of minutes. The European defense against Red bombers and missiles is inadequate. We cannot afford to provide Europe with even a reasonable defense. Accordingly, this understandable fear of Red nuclear incineration may in the event of war force our European NATO Allies into neutrality. If that happens, we may be denied the use of many of our overseas bases and the United States and Canada would be left to face the Soviets, while the remainder of NATO is neutral.

A number of the Central European, South Asian and Far Pacific countries have received in all more than $10 billion in military assistance. Yet some of these recipients are hostile to the United States. So it is possible that some of our own weapons might one day be turned against us. This has happened before.

Limited military information makes it difficult for the American people to know our true defense position. It would appear that: the Red Air Force challenges SAC; we have yet to gain missile ascendancy; we have undertaken to defend the free world; our forces, deployed globally, are over-extended; our own continental defense against bombers and missiles is inadequate.

So far as the survival of the American people is concerned, military assistance to European and Asiatic countries is not essential. Authoritative studies show convincingly that the Western Hemisphere can be defended and made self-sufficient both in peace and in war.

In the past 12 years we have spent about $23 billion for foreign military assistance. In addition, our overseas military men are spending more than $3 billion annually. Suppose dozens of our cities are wiped out in an all-out nuclear war. What excuse can our political leaders who survive offer for such a tragedy, if we continue to arm other nations while neglecting adequately to defend our own people?

### III

### *Impact of Foreign Aid on Political Systems*

One of the main benefits claimed for foreign aid is that it helps prevent the growth of communism. Actually, it has tended to promote philosophies akin to communism.

The Marshall Plan greatly assisted Britain's recovery from war's devastation. But the fact that Britain instituted and carried out her industrial nationalization program at the very time that our foreign aid funds were being received, is more than mere coincidence. The $7 billion foreign aid which we have contributed to Britain's economic program, directly or indirectly, has helped to nationalize the Bank of England, and the gas, electric, railway, canals and coal mining enterprises of the United Kingdom. Our dollars also have assisted Britain to adopt socialized medicine. Thus, Britain has taken a long stride toward total socialism. Through too much foreign aid, too long continued, we have done Britain, our ally, a great disservice.

But this is not all. In a like manner our aid has helped to strengthen the nationalization processes in Norway, Austria, France, Italy, Turkey, Pakistan, India, Indonesia, and even in Communist Poland and Yugoslavia.

Nationalization of industry and state capitalism have been fostered in countries receiving our funds. Our dollars and credits have gone mostly to foreign governments and provided the means to start state enterprises or to take over privately owned businesses. In many cases as a condition upon which we granted foreign aid, we have encouraged the recipient governments to move into industrial operations with programs similar to the Soviet Seven-Year Plan. In so doing, our foreign aid is helping to establish the very system of state slavery we set out to combat.

American-financed nationalization does more than merely put a foreign government in business. It serves to destroy the free enterprise of the recipient country. Nationalization both here and abroad reduces the tax base and therefore raises taxes for others. Government business is subsidized by our continuing foreign aid; most free enterprises do not enjoy such subsidy. For the free enterprises which survive our aid, there is always the threat of expropriation.

By assisting recipient countries to nationalize their industries, foreign aid contributes materially to the creation of governmental systems and institutions hostile to those which have been derived from our Declaration of Independence and our Constitution.

The argument is advanced that by raising living standards foreign aid prevents the spread of communism. It is a mistaken idea, however, that communism breeds on poverty. There is no proof that a high standard of living is the enemy of communism.

All of the Eastern European countries, except Czechoslovakia, have always been relatively poor. Czechoslovakia, however, has long been among the most prosperous countries of Europe. Yet, Czechoslovakia through political intrigue went communist. In Central and Western European countries communism has thrived in the prosperous industrial areas. In the relatively poor countries the population has usually resisted communist influence.

For instance, communists are strongest in Italy and France. In Italy the communists are stronger in the prosperous northern industrial areas, while in Southern Italy, where the people are poorer, the conservatives have built a stronghold. In France the communists are stronger in the prosperous cities; they are weaker in the poorer rural areas.

In Ireland, among the least wealthy countries of Western Europe, the communists have made little headway.

In India, which has received substantial aid, between 1952 and 1957 the communists increased their vote from 4,000,000 to 12,000,000. Today the Communist Party is the second largest in the Indian Parliament.

Many Americans will be astonished to learn that strong encouragement for foreign aid originally came from Joseph Stalin. His *Marxism and the National Colonial Question,* pages 115-116 reads in part:

"It is essential that the advanced countries should render aid—real and prolonged aid—to the backward nationalities in their cultural and economic development. Otherwise, it will be impossible to bring about the peaceful co-existence of the various nations and peoples—within a single economic system that is so essential for the final triumph of Socialism."

Through foreign aid the United States is following Stalin's spending prescription for the establishment of "a single economic system that is so essential for the final triumph of Socialism." From the start the Kremlin has been determined to make capitalism pay for its own funeral.

## IV

### Foreign Aid and Free World Economy

In a recent speech Mr. William McChesney Martin, Chairman of the Federal Reserve Board, said:

"One distressing experience (during a recent trip abroad) was to find among intelligent and perceptive men in those countries a growing distrust over the future of the American dollar."

At home, this growing loss of confidence in the dollar is evidenced by the current flight of gold from U.S. ownership. Foreign governments and banks with dollar credits in the U.S. can demand and receive payment in gold. But our government will NOT redeem in gold dollar credits owned by U.S. citizens.

Foreign governments, partially with the aid of credits made available to them through our foreign aid, have been salting away American gold, or piling up dollar balances in our American banks. In addition, individual foreigners, again with the help of our foreign aid, have become heavy investors in American securities. It is estimated that there are about a billion in market value of United States securities held abroad. This could all be converted into foreign Central Bank demands on our gold stock.

At the beginning of 1958 our gold reserve amounted to $22.9 billion. During 1958 alone, $2.26 billion in gold has been taken from us by foreign countries. Should this loss of confidence in the dollar continue, the gold outflow could collapse our currency.

Since 1950 dollar deposits in this country by foreign governmental agencies have increased from $3.9 billion to $8.7 billion. In addition, foreign individuals and foreign banks now have dollar deposits in our banks of $5.8 billion. This total of $14.5 billion in foreign holdings is convertible into gold upon demand of the holders. In other words, 70 per cent of our gold reserve is subject to foreign demand.

There is no evidence in 1959 that this flight of gold has ceased.

Our gold stock reduction menaces our economy. Today the U.S. gold ratio to our money has actually declined to a figure lower than that during the depth of the 1933 depression!

The Federal budget of the United States has been balanced only five times in the last 27 years. The Federal debt is now $283 billion. This crushing American debt, borne by only 6 per cent of the world's population, is greater than the combined national debts of all other countries in the world. More than a fourth of our Federal debt has resulted from budget deficits caused by our foreign aid programs. Annual interest on the aid portion of our debt is about $2 billion. This interest, together with foreign aid appropriations totals some $7 billion annually. Thus our past and present foreign aid programs are consuming the equivalent of 20 per cent of our personal income tax collections.

It has been reported that a major portion of foreign aid money is spent within the United States and thereby strengthens our economy. Doubtless government contracts for foreign aid materials have brought profits to U.S. corporations and may have influenced them and their workers to support foreign aid. However, when the manufacturer's product is given away, rather than strengthening our economy, it siphons off our wealth. Money spent for goods and services to be used as foreign aid creates consumer buying power but not consumer goods for Americans. Hence such foreign aid is by its very nature inflationary.

It is alleged that foreign aid is responsible for the employment of 600,000 American workmen. This claim ignores the fact that American workmen are already suffering from unemployment resulting from foreign aid grants to competitive industries abroad. Moreover, the International Cooperation Administration (ICA) purchases frequently discriminate against American production. For example, in 1957, our ICA textile expenditure was $96.3 million, of which only $7.2 million was spent for American textile products. Today we have nearly five million unemployed; Foreign Aid has been a contributing factor.

Administration propaganda seeks to minimize the impact of our foreign aid burden by emphasizing that it is a mere one per cent of our gross national product. What this propaganda does not tell is that foreign aid facilitates the flight of gold from U.S. control and consumes the equivalent of 20% of our personal income tax.

The Administration is eager to keep foreign aid and all foreign policy strictly on a bi-partisan basis in the Congress. In the last three Presidential campaigns, candidates of both major parties carefully avoided making foreign aid an issue. As a consequence, taxpayers in our Republic have never had an opportunity to express themselves on foreign aid at the polls.

Unfortunately, our acknowledged Federal debt is only a fraction of our real debt. It has been reliably estimated that our true Federal debt obligations amount to about $838 billion. This figure is reached by totaling existing legislative commitments of $105 billion, Social Security obligations of $350 billion and a Federal Reserve contingent liability of $100 billion, together with the Federal Treasury debt of $283 billion.

In addition to the $838 billion Federal debt obligations, our private individual debt is $238.5 billion. Our net private corporate debt is $236.1 billion. The state and public local debt is $50.9 billion.

The inflationary result of these enormous debt burdens, coupled with confiscatory income taxes, is fast undermining our economy.

To illustrate: Because of taxes and inflation, in 1957 it took an income of: $4,806 to match in purchasing power a 1939 income of $2,000; $13,004 to match a 1939 income of $5,000; $30,971 to match a 1939 income of $10,000; $333,377 to match a 1939 income of $50,000.

If things go during the next 18 years like they went during the past 18—and the spenders seem to be determined to have it that way—the dollar will be worth less (in 1975) than 25¢ and it will take an income of: $10,538 to match a 1939 income of $2,000; $33,240 to match a 1939 income of $5,000; $92,141 to match a 1939 income of $10,000; $835,393 to match a 1939 income of $50,000.

As a result of this dollar devaluation and the increased velocity of money circulation, in the past 20 years the value of fixed incomes, of all bank accounts, insurance policies, government, state and municipal bonds, and all other indebtedness has been cut in half. Thus the losses already inflicted on the American people are enormous. The same processes continue—and the end is not in sight.

The impact of our foreign aid on the economy of nearly all of the recipient countries is likewise inflationary and damaging. Many times foreign aid has financed new producing and manufacturing facilities without coordinating secondary industries and markets. This has resulted in dislocation and the need for further gifts. With the exception of Germany, every country receiving our foreign aid in the past 10 years has found that its currency is softer than before the aid was given.

The initial aid which the United States extended to countries devastated by World War II unquestionably accelerated their recovery. However, it is utterly impossible for the American taxpayer to transfuse the economy of the free world, with a new money blood stream, except temporarily. The recipient country begins to live on the transfusion; its economy becomes geared to an income which it cannot, by itself, sustain.

The time has arrived when free world countries must help themselves. They must establish sound, enduring economies of their own lest they perish, the victim of predatory socialistic forces. For us to continue foreign aid is a disservice to the recipients. The longer this aid is extended, the longer will be their delay in establishing self-sufficiency.

## V

### Foreign Aid Administration

The field supervision of 2,000 economic aid projects scattered about the globe is a prodigious undertaking. It involves the allocation of large quantities of grant aid (money); it involves engineering and technical assistance. Qualified specialists to manage and operate so many foreign projects of widely varying nature are impossible to obtain.

On the planning and policy level in the ICA and the Department of State, the practical experience of the personnel has not qualified them to manage what is actually the largest engineering, supplying and banking operation in the world. Men who would be able to handle such jobs enjoy good positions in private enterprise and are unwilling to serve under the direction of Federal bureaucrats.

In the past decade the agency administering economic aid has had its name changed several times, quite possibly in the hope that the American people would forget its past record. During that time, the economic aid agency has had eight directors. No director has held office for more than 2½ years and one served only a few months.

This rapid turnover results in the directors becoming captives of what is now recognized as a self-perpetuating bureaucracy. It operates on the principle that no matter how wastefully money is spent, if enough is spent it will do some good. This lack of competent personnel has resulted in innumerable instances of waste running into many billions of dollars.

A few among numerous will illustrate:

A total of $3 billion foreign aid funds has been granted to foreign powers to help reduce their national debts and to balance their budgets. To extend this aid, we ironically had to borrow the money!

There are instances of U.S. Government checks having been turned over to foreign officials for budget support with no record of how the money was spent.

Foreign aid has given more than $2 billion to governments that are hostile to the United States. This includes the Soviet Union, Yugoslavia, and Poland.

To build an American exhibit in Moscow to be completed in July 1959, $3.2 million foreign aid has been authorized.

Last year India received $325 million in foreign aid. A substantial part of this aid was given to support India's second five year plan. Our dollar credits enabled the Indian government to purchase equipment with limited Indian commitments to buy American goods.

Point IV was originally established to export American "know-how" to the underdeveloped countries. Instead, Point IV has become inextricably involved with industrial development, lush engineering contracts and surveys that have no relationship to the original purpose.

From an official report on foreign aid to oil rich Iran, the "United States aid and technical assistance programs in Iran which, between 1951 and 1956, totaled a quarter billion dollars, were administered in a loose, slipshod and unbusinesslike manner . . . it is now impossible—with any accuracy—to tell what became of these funds."

The official in charge of Iran foreign aid was later promoted and is now head of foreign aid in Korea where our spending obligations are greater.

In 1953 our government made $745 million, almost ¾ of a billion dollars, available for the support of the French and their allies in the prosecution of the Indo-China War. Our arrangements with the French for the control and accounting for this money were cumbersome and loose. Only a part of the $745 million had been spent when the French surrendered. Because of poor accounting and auditing the United States does not know how all of the $745 million was spent. After many months of attempted audit and negotiation the United States was able to recover only $95 million.

Our financial support of the British military aircraft program in the fiscal years 1953-54-55 was approximately $450 million. The planes being financed were unduly delayed in development. By the time full production was achieved, the planes were obsolescent. The *London Financial Times* wrote in December 1954, that our offshore financing of these British aircraft was "in fact just a rather clumsy method of making a grant of cash." Actually part of this cash served to make possible a British government subsidization of its commercial jet transports in competition with United States manufacturers.

A *New York Times* dispatch from Karachi, Pakistan, dated February 18, 1959, discloses that corruption and inflation are rampant; that "of the $839 million received by Pakistan in foreign aid, of which $703 million came from the United States, only $186 million according to an official admission was utilized on "constructive works."

The Development Loan Fund is a new foreign aid device for extending development assistance to foreign countries. It will make what amounts to second mortgage loans and accept soft local currencies in payment for loans in dollars. The Development Loan Fund also lends money to assist American business in the establishment of overseas factories.

The ICA will provide insurance coverage on private overseas investments against certain exchange losses and expropriation and other risks. Thus, American taxpayers' dollars subsidize overseas factories, the products of which compete with those of our American workmen.

The Fairless Committee, which was appointed by the President in 1957 to evaluate the foreign aid program, adversely criticized the concept of the Development Loan Fund and soft currency loans.

No comprehensive and independent audit of foreign aid expenditures seems ever to have been instituted.

The Congress votes foreign aid appropriations; the Executive Branch of the government handles the apportionment and disbursement of funds. Once funds are in the hands of our Executive Branch it appears that the Congress exercises almost no control over management, expenditures and projects.

The Congress has a responsibility to its tax paying constituents. It should assert control over expenditures of foreign aid appropriations. It should make its appropriations more specific. It should further limit the power of the Executive to effect the transfer of foreign aid funds. Too much flexibility amounts to writing a blank check.

The Congress should create a bi-partisan Congressional Committee or Hoover-type Commission with sufficient funds to conduct a thorough investigation of foreign aid. This should include a check on the programing and expenditures for foreign aid projects and should continue until all foreign aid is terminated.

## VI

### Moral and Psychological Aspects of Foreign Aid

A large part of foreign aid support in the United States stems from some of our religious leaders. Good Samaritans that they are, they associate foreign aid with the religious obligation of individuals to help others. It is a moral act for a person to make a voluntary contribution of money or effort to help another person. By extending aid religious leaders seek to kindle an inner light in those to whom help is given.

This is, of course, in accordance with the Christian Concept that reform of societies is a revolutionary process which starts by a change of heart from within the individual. However, this Christian teaching is the direct opposite of the Marxist Theory, which our governmental concept of foreign aid parallels.

Marx held that societies are changed from without and that individuals change, not from within, but rather in accordance with their external environment through things material.

Frederick Engels, Marx' collaborator, wrote: "The ultimate causes of all social changes and political revolutions are to be sought not in the heads of men, not in their better insight into eternal truth and justice, but in the changes in the methods of production and exchange; they are to be sought not in the philosophy, but in the economics of a particular epoch."

Our foreign aid program, curiously for a Christian people, follows the Marxist teaching. Foreign aid is expressed in terms of money, production, and materialism. The money for foreign aid is not a gift from our people to the foreign peoples. Foreign Aid is money extracted from the American people by confiscatory income taxes and then bestowed by our governmental bureaucrats upon a foreign government to do with it as it pleases.

Missionaries serving in countries receiving foreign aid report grave concern about the adverse effect of our aid among the people with whom they work. One is compelled to conclude that our religious leaders endorse governmental foreign aid only because its materialistic motivation has not yet been disclosed to them.

Americans are crusaders. It is our American trait to endeavor to create others in our own image. Whether or not other peoples want to reflect our image fails to deaden our zeal. Through foreign aid we have attempted to superimpose our modern, highly industrialized, fast moving system upon underdeveloped countries with less complex living standards, slower tempo and different cultures. It has taken us 175 years to reach our present standard of living. Foreign aid seeks to lift underdeveloped countries to a parity with us in a decade or two. It is most unrealistic.

Foreign aid reflects a patronizing attitude toward foreign peoples. It is a sly attempt to buy their allegiance, which is presumed to be for sale.

In the recipient countries, our foreign aid program results in confusion, misunderstanding and sometimes chaos. After nearly 15 years of foreign aid we are probably the most disliked nation in the world!

There is also a human principle which strongly influences the reaction of recipients to our foreign aid program. If one country is made a recipient, how can aid to others be denied? If one recipient is granted more than others, all recipients then clamor for more. The war devastated Philippines, our trusted wartime ally, is now understandably in turmoil for the reason that others less deserving are higher on our foreign aid totem pole.

Unless foreign aid is soon terminated, our country faces economic peril. This peril is inevitable because neither this nor any other Congress will reduce or restrain spending at home so long as it votes colossal foreign handouts.

Our Congressmen know that, so long as they dissipate billions of dollars overseas, to be re-elected they must also continue expensive domestic benefits. Foreign aid is a street without end—unless the street is barricaded. If long continued, it will result in an ever expanding bureaucracy of careerists dedicated to passing out American taxpayers' dollars all over the globe.

The fate of our foreign aid program is a matter which the American people must decide now. No matter how much we spend, it is clear that we cannot buy world leadership and good will. If we are to lead, we can lead only by example. We cannot force our image upon others. We must resume our progress and pursuit of liberty under the Constitution. Then and only then will others respect us.

## VII

*From the foregoing, the following facts are inescapable:*

1. That our government intends that foreign aid shall be continuous and global.

2. That the threat of communist aggression rules out our continuing to dispense lavish foreign aid when our own economy is threatened and our defenses are inadequate.

3. That in a number of recipient countries our foreign aid helps to strengthen political systems hostile to our own.

4. That our foreign aid speeds rather than retards the growth of communism; it inflates our economy; it is partially responsible for the alarming flight of gold from our control; it is destroying our foreign markets and increasing unemployment among American workers.

5. That by the very nature of the foreign aid we extend it must be inefficient and wasteful.

6. That our governmental foreign aid program is unsound in principle.

## VIII

*To remedy these conditions we recommend the following:*

1. That our traditional generous private charity and governmental grants to relieve disaster be continued; that we encourage the expansion of our private missionary efforts.

2. That in countries which we are morally obligated to defend and which are directly threatened with Red aggression, military assistance—for the time being—should be continued but on a realistic basis.

3. That foreign aid which directly or indirectly promotes Governments that are hostile to our Constitutional concepts of government be terminated immediately.

4. That so long as governmental foreign aid is continued the recipient should pay a part of the cost of the proposed project; that our aid should terminate when the conditions on which that request is based have been remedied; that private technical, scientific and educational assistance be extended only to friendly peoples who seek our aid on a cash or loan basis.

5. That until foreign aid is terminated, the Congress take steps properly to exercise close supervision and control over the manner in which all foreign aids funds are being spent; that all future economic aid, plus what can be salvaged from unexpended foreign aid funds, be diverted to and handled by the Export-Import Bank.

6. That the $3.9 billion requested by the President for the fiscal year 1960 be reduced $2.0 billion, and that each year thereafter foreign aid be substantially reduced until terminated within three years.

---

In a show-down fight for survival the will to win is a prerequisite to a victory. When an advantageous opportunity is neglected, then the will to win is either absent or quiescent. In any event, those intent upon the complete communization of America by way of the welfare state can be counted upon to press forward with more confidence and vigor when meeting with no resistance.

American management is presently passing up a golden opportunity to turn the tables on the left-wingers, who for many years have preached class hatred in an effort to drive a wedge between employees and management.

This opportunity is available in the form of a leaflet-petition put out by the Citizens Foreign Aid Committee. Besides presenting evidence before Congressional committees and preparing and mailing pamphlets exposing the fallacy and the fraud of the foreign aid program, the Citizens Foreign Aid Committee has gone one step further. They have provided a simple and effective tool whereby the people back home may speak up and be heard by the members of Congress. The leaflet-petition, reproduced below, eliminates the necessity of composing and writing a letter, but yet when signed by an individual, conveys the desired message to the Congressman receiving the leaflet-petition.

## *Just a Minute, Mr. Congressman, before YOU vote our money and our jobs away . . .*

Within the next few weeks Congress must decide whether to continue the foreign aid program. The White House Crowd and the bureaucrats on the payroll of the State Department want it continued indefinitely.

They say it is good for us: they say that it prevents war, that it helps business and that it stops the spread of communism.

We say that it is bad for us: it cannot prevent war, it hurts business and it has completely failed to stop the spread of communism.

Mr. Congressman, YOU must side either with the bureaucrats or with the people back home who do all the work, who pay all the taxes and who cast the votes.

It may help if we give you just ONE specific example to show the fallacy, the failure and the injustice of the program.

1. The government in Washington, through its confiscatory income tax, seizes about one-third of the earnings of the American people.

2. The government in Washington uses this money to acquire most of the American cotton crop.

3. The government in Washington then sells this cotton to foreigners at several cents per pound less than American manufacturers can buy it back from their own government.

4. The government in Washington then permits foreign mills, paying but a fraction of American wages, to sell their products here at prices below the American cost of production. This unfair competition causes American mills to run short time or to close down.

Mr. Congressman, how does it help American factory employees to be put out of work?

How do these idled factories help American investors?

How does this transfer of jobs and payrolls to foreign lands help the storekeepers of America?

Then on top of all this, you have given the State Department bureaucrats the power to use our tax money to build new factories in "under-developed" lands to compete with us even further.

Read for yourself in the words of Nathaniel Rafler, a bureaucrat on the payroll of the State Department's International Cooperation Administration, how this bit of doublecross works:

"Confirming my comments of this morning, I wish to reiterate the International Cooperation Administration is prepared to render many forms of assistance to any one or more of your members who may be interested in establishing textile plants in Indonesia.

"International Cooperation Administration would be prepared to make loans from its New Development Fund. We would also be prepared to insure such investments against the political risks of expropriation, inconvertibility of currency, and war damage.

"Furthermore, we would furnish technical assistance by financing on-the-job training in Indonesia, or training here in America for Indonesians, in technical and managerial skill.

"We also might be able to finance the installation of public facilities such as power, transportation, etc., if not otherwise available."

For Heaven's sake, Mr. Congressman, did we send YOU to Washington to vote our jobs and our money away in this absurd attempt to reform and uplift the human race all over the world?

How can it stop other countries from going communist if Congress continues to vote America into bankruptcy, self-destruction and bureaucratic enslavement?

Since the end of the war, 72 billion tax dollars have been given away in all parts of the globe by an army of bureaucrats now numbering over 12,000.

From foreign-owned factories built with our gift dollars now comes a flood of manufactured articles that displace our goods, not only abroad, but here at home. For the first time since 1865 England sells us more than she buys from us. Day by day this displacement of our goods threatens American jobs and payrolls with contraction or extinction in the following industries, besides textiles:

| | |
|---|---|
| Iron and steel mill products | Copper |
| Pulp and paper products | Lumber and lumber manufacturers |
| Fertilizer | Machinery and equipment |
| Cement and other non-metallic minerals | Motor Vehicles |
| Non-ferrous metals and products | Engines and parts |
| | Freight cars |

To our fellow Americans: If you are opposed to the senseless transfer of American jobs and payrolls to foreign lands, then sign the following petition and mail a copy to your Congressman as well as a copy to each of your two Senators.

## PETITION

Dear Mr.———————: I believe the first duty of the American government is to protect American citizens.   I expect you to protect me by opposing the foreign aid program.

    Name————————————
    Address—————————————

In less than 2 months time, and without the expenditure of a single penny in advertising, requests for over 105,000 copies of the leaflet-petition have been received from 26 states.

This, however, is but a drop in the bucket compared to what it might be, if American management would only open its eyes and seize this chance to drive home the basic fact that employees, stockholders, and management are all in the same boat. Not only does this leaflet-petition enable factory employees and stockholders to register individual protests against the exportation of American jobs and payrolls, but more important than that, it exposes the lie of class hatred which is the principal weapon of the left-wing labor bosses, the communists, and the unprincipled politicians. No one is too dense to see that if a boat goes down, all aboard go down too. Even further, it is readily apparent to the local merchants that the transfer of payrolls to foreign lands cannot help them.

Here is a chance for American management to break off its retreating, defensive, rear-guard action and, armed with the truth, to assume an offensive against communism. But has American management seized this opportunity to permit employees, stockholders, and other local citizens to protest against the one-world ideas of the State Department bureaucrats?

Well, here is the present score for the textile industry, which perhaps is the most seriously affected of all, since, the arrogant bureaucrats in the State Department have even indicated that in their plans for creating one big shiny nice new world the textile industry in America is expendable.

The leading weekly trade publication, *America's Textile Reporter,* mailed 14,000 copies of the leaflet-petition and in an editorial urged industry-wide participation; but to date only twenty-one cotton mills have given their employees and stockholders a chance to join in the protest.

A check on these mills shows almost unanimous response and eager participation by the employees. It staggers the imagination to ponder the impact that a nationwide avalanche of these individually signed petitions would have upon Congress. The tool is available, but a desire to use it is needed. Is there to be no fight against self-destruction on the part of American management? What is the answer?

The sickening answer seems to be that the self-destruction of America will never be averted by today's crop of businessmen, unless there is a sudden and definite reversal in their thinking and in their acting.

---

There is nothing new about Foreign Aid—except possibly the name, and means of dispensing billions of dollars.

Following on the heels of World War I, when we were badly bitten by the save-the-world bug, still uncounted and now forgotten millions were poured out over the earth's surface, often with an abandon and a wanton waste that sometimes reached quickly-hushed scandal proportions.

History is only repeating itself. One phase of this is revealed in the following item (based on a report of a correspondent of the Scripps-Howard newspapers sent to the scene) as printed in the *National Program Letter* of Harding College for February, 1960:

## Report on Foreign Aid

Most Americans have read in recent years the reports of gross extravagance and waste in some of the foreign aid programs. There have been dramatic, even sensational exposures. A most recent shocking report was contained in the series of articles from Viet Nam by reporter Albert M. Colegrove, published in Scripps-Howard newspapers from coast to coast. Colegrove went to South Asia to investigate reports on waste and graft which he had received from authentic sources.

Writing from Saigon, he began his newspaper series with this statement: "The American aid program in Viet Nam is an outrageous scandal." Actually it is no more a scandal in Viet Nam than it is in some other nations. But, Mr. Colegrove's report on foreign aid spending in this tiny nation ought to dramatize in the minds of all citizens the unnecessary waste of our hard-earned money, and the need to put a clamp on our Federal government's spending.

Here are a few items from the report of Albert Colegrove in Viet Nam:

An American adviser, going through the books of Radio Viet Nam, the official government radio station (set up with U.S. money) found a mysterious entry for 14 radio towers costing $28,-500 for which U.S. aid officials had paid. That was almost three years ago; no one has yet laid eyes on those towers. But—when the American persisted in making inquiries of the Vietnamese, he was called on the carpet (by U.S. State Department officials) and bawled out for stirring up trouble.

The U.S. Government has arranged to provide a powerful complicated 50,000 watt short-wave radio transmitter system costing over $100,000 (in addition to one already built with U.S. dollars) so they can beam propaganda at Communist North Viet Nam. But, after almost five years of American aid the Saigon water system remains so inadequate that the poorer people line up for blocks at 7 A.M. to fill their buckets with water that trickles from a handful of public pumps.

"Is there a predictable happy ending (to all this waste and stupid expenditures); can South Viet Nam be helped out of its lopsided financial dilemma?" Mr. Colegrove asks, and then replies: "American press agents talk happily of a new basket-making center and write of 'gradual but steady progress toward economic independence.' But President Diem himself, talking with me, was not so cheery. He said, 'You people should not demand miracles, expecting Viet Nam to be solvent within three or four years.' Then he added significantly: 'Many experts think undeveloped areas like South Viet Nam will need help for 25 years.'

"An American businessman, a former government worker, here almost five years, said bluntly: 'We spend and spend, and our government experts haven't proposed a single new answer to the problem. All they can come up with is determination to maintain the status quo. We'll never solve the economic problem this way.

Meantime these people are living off our handouts and are quite satisfied to do so.' "

And, another item on the radio station built with American funds: The director of Radio Viet Nam was one Maj. Doan Van Cuu, a veterinarian whose specialty was the intestinal disorders of elephants. The three "chief technicians" were non-engineers whose qualifications were that they had friends or relatives at the presidential palace. Major Cuu was the director—he isn't now. A horde of police, acting on information received about Cuu's unique bookkeeping (which never had been open to American inspection) swooped down one day—a trifle late. Major Cuu had just burned his books in the alley. Some $446,000 of the money entrusted to him remains to be accounted for today.

---

In 1957 the late Eugene W. Castle, founder and first president of Castle Films and a vigorous and outspoken opponent of Foreign Aid, wrote his book, *The Great Giveaway* (published by Henry Regnery Company, Chicago) which is today probably the definitive work on the subject.

It is from this book that the following quotations are taken.

## *The Great Giveaway*

### EUGENE W. CASTLE

There are eight specific reasons why the foreign-aid program, as presently carried on, is a potential threat to our own self-interest. Let us consider these eight dangers.

1. The aid program has grown up haphazardly without coordinated relationship to any long-range national foreign policy. In reality, foreign aid has been a crash program, improvised step by step to meet existing or fancied emergencies. Admittedly at times, there has been justification for some sort of aid policy as a temporary expedient. However, there has been no justification for its perpetuation as a continuing and permanent national policy. Inevitably, a point is reached where a policy, helpful perhaps in the teeth of an emergency, becomes hurtful as a permanent American commitment. That point appears now to have been reached in foreign aid.

2. Persistence of the United States in its foreign-aid program

has become a distinct deterrent to the working out of a rational foreign policy since every move is first predicated upon the giving of money. Moreover, it is an infirmity of foreign aid that it gives to most Americans the delusion that the answer has already been found to our foreign-policy dilemma. As long as our chief policy-makers believe that they can obtain peace by the seemingly easy method of subsidization of other nations, they will not fully avail themselves of the opportunities and benefits which are often secured through conventional diplomacy. They live ever expectantly in a world of short-cuts and political detours.

In today's setting, the task of evolving a workable American foreign policy is beset with major difficulties. It requires the highest and most courageous type of statesmanship. But we are not exhibiting such statesmanship when we attempt to buy our way out of difficult international situations. All too often we find ourselves postponing important decisions to a less propitious time. A foreign policy of continuous handouts to insatiable "allies" and "neutralists" merely delays and makes more difficult the ultimate day of reckoning. It does not escape it.

3. Our false sense of security is frequently bolstered by the self-deceiving pronouncements of the United States Information Agency. This $140-million-a-year cave of winds, politically created and maintained, has harmed instead of helped the thinking of millions of foreigners who were once our friends; but it has been a veritable master at the art of mind-conditioning the American people at home. Under the guise of selling America to foreigners, this agency has propagandized itself to Americans in a manner never before attempted in the entire peacetime history of our country.

One of the chief promotions of the USIA has been a false idea of the efficacy of foreign aid. Large numbers of Americans have gone along with the successive foreign-aid programs because they have been reassured by government-paid propagandists that there is no other course open except that of dispersing our resources abroad. That the foreign-aid program does not remove the basic causes of future wars—that it merely softens up the nation for the ultimate day of reckoning—is a fact which is invariably missing from the cheery USIA handouts or the Voice of America incantations.

4. Although the aid program prides itself upon the services it

has rendered to foreigners, the program, after its first crisis beginnings, all too often has not aided the foreigner but has actually harmed him. This is true because foreign aid has all the inescapable weaknesses of a hothouse operation. It saps the will to self-help by offering the foreigner easy exits from his political and economic dilemmas. It supplies artificial props and supports to the foreigner's economy which keep it in a perpetual state of false expectation and dislocation.

A convincing case can sometimes be made for emergency assistance to spark the recovery of a neighbor nation from disaster. But it is difficult to defend an emergency intervention which lasts for more than ten years. Instead of aiding many of these countries, such subsidization immobilizes them. The initiatives and the risks which would bring sound and balanced recovery remain untried when Uncle Sam is standing by, checkbook in hand, anxious and ready to wipe out the red ink. The United States, through its mistaken aid policies, has probably retarded the return of many free nations to normalcy by several years. In some parts of the world we have prolonged economic dislocation instead of removing it.

One Representative informed Congress that on a trip to Europe last year he asked point blank the head of a central European country: "Do you expect at any time in the near future to see the light of freedom?" The ruler stroked his chin and said: "Well, sir, not as long as you in the United States keep bankrolling us."

Another case in point is friendly Turkey where, in our anxiety to assist a brave nation, we have encouraged, with our aid dollars, ambitious undertakings which could not possibly be sustained by the normal Turkish economy. Though such a policy may sometimes be justified in war, in time of peace (uneasy peace) it can prove harmful instead of helpful.

Once the majority of the fifty-five aided countries realize that they can no longer depend upon American subsidization, they will themselves take serious steps to bring their economies into adjustment within the limits of their own resources. When every country can stand on its own two feet it will like us the better for it. Nations, like people, are proud, and want financial as well as political independence.

5. But the real peril of protracted foreign aid is to the United States itself. The aid programs involve us directly and often dangerously in explosive situations throughout the world. Even if we

had the most careful Washington supervision and safeguards, we would be constantly being drawn into the enmities and the internal disorders of foreign countries. Frequently we are swept beyond the boundaries of our true national interest into areas of the world where we should never have become involved.

It is not isolationism to point out that America cannot range recklessly throughout the globe, trouble-shooting for distressed nations, without assuming enormous and unnecessary risks, and possibly in several countries at the same time. By accepting the role of global almoners, in the opinion of many foreigners, friend and foe, we have become a nation of international busy-bodies, rushing from trouble-spot to trouble-spot with our remedy of dollars. We expose ourselves needlessly to all the world's shocks and alarums.

With all its resources, has America the wealth or the wisdom to play such an Olympian role?

True, there are certain areas in the world where America cannot escape the responsibility of rendering assistance to underdeveloped nations—particularly those in our own hemisphere—in a prudent and practical manner, honestly administered. This can largely be accomplished through the encouragement of freer trade, privately financed, to relieve the burden of government largess with its ever present bureaucratic pitfalls.

The peril of peacetime foreign aid is that it tends to draw us continually into fields, situations and activities beyond the proper scope and jurisdiction of our Federal government, even within our own country. We have been drawn into the tangled affairs of Egypt, of North Africa, of Afghanistan, of Iran and of Burma, to mention but a few. We have frequently become partisans in the internal affairs and programs of these countries. By doing these things we increase the ever-lurking danger of possible involvement in foreign wars. It is difficult to see how the United States can play the part of Atlas in this fevered world without further involvement in constantly recurring foreign conflicts. Foreign-aid projects in peacetime obviously increase the chances of exposure to these conditions.

6. The price we pay for such global commitments results in a corresponding weakening of our own home security. While we thinly spread our strength throughout the world, our home front develops dangerous gaps in its defenses. We simply do not have

money enough to underwrite the world and still assure security to New York, Minneapolis or Los Angeles. Our resources will not stretch that far.

Today America is playing games with Civil Defense. While we build airbases in Spain and Morocco, we haven't sufficient funds available at home to build protection for ourselves in our congested cities to safeguard us from the danger of atomic warfare. So far, few, if any, strategic plants have been relocated underground despite the swift approach of the age of intercontinental missiles. Though we live in an age of atomic power, we still are too poor to reconvert our sea and air transportation, except upon a painfully slow experimental basis. We have cut back our orders for B-52s largely because we haven't the money to produce them; and yet we do find the money to finance questionable sociological experiments in the remote and unrewarding areas of the world.

While we giddily distribute our national patrimony, Soviet Russia keeps her substance at home, or releases it to other nations in barter, or in exchange for tightly secured commercial paper. She gives away nothing, not even to Red China, her principal satellite. If world conflict comes, Russia's strength will not be spread out perilously over four continents; it will be concentrated in the homeland.

Communist Russia has learned the elementary military truth of the deadly danger of diffusion; aid-obsessed America has not.

7. Great though our resources may be, the American taxpayer cannot afford the ever-mounting cost of the foreign-aid program. For more than two decades, the United States has lived in a deficit economy. During these years, our national debt has towered up from $19,487,002,444 in 1932 to $274,374,222,802 today. Overhanging every man, woman, child and babe-in-arms in America is a built-in per capita national indebtedness of $1,660.56. In addition, the American carries a burdensome state and local indebtedness. In only three of the twenty-four years since 1932 has the United States Treasury succeeded in making any reduction in this colossal debt structure, and the reduction in each of these years was slight.

Ordinary foresight would suggest that a nation in debt to such an extent has no bounties to give away. Yet it is soberly proposed that we continue pouring out our billions in a give-away program which our chief policy-makers would project ten years ahead. Such a program simply does not make sense. Even a moderate down-turn in our national economic well-being could precipitate an over-night situation of acute distress to most Americans. And it must be remembered that tens of millions of us who can least afford it would be the most severely hurt. The time to lighten the load of such a ruinous program is right now, before our nation has been permanently harmed.

8. Even if we could afford the various aid programs, our experience has shown us, with bitter examples, that we do not possess the trained administrative personnel to plan and carry through such a program effectively. The history of foreign aid has been littered with the wreckage and rubble of incompetent and wasteful administration. The task of shoring up sick economies or planning vast development projects is a task for the highest order of engineering brains. But we have assigned such tasks largely to civil service routineers and irresponsible political headline-hunters.

All human experience shows that government is hopelessly unfitted to conduct large-scale economic operations of this nature. Private initiative, which has the driving necessity of showing a profit and which cannot unload its mistakes upon the taxpayer, does the job infinitely better. Our foreign-aid program has paid lip-service to private investment, but in practice it supplants the private investor. It interposes the sterile hand of the state between human wants and demands, and the private initiative which can supply them. The political promoter and the global headline-hunter replace the economist and the technician.

If no other fault inhered in the foreign-aid program, it would fail at the level of administration. The capable brains who might possibly make it work are not at the service of the aid agencies.

It is a tragic fact that the American people, regardless of political affiliation, have no voice in the decision to spend billions in taxpayers' dollars for foreign aid. No American citizen has ever been afforded the opportunity to express his opinion and desire at the ballot box on this most vital matter. We must therefore depend solely upon those members of the Congress of both political parties who will reject the continuance and enlargement of a program that the Congress itself had previously ordered liquidated.

Today, we are the sole remaining internationalists in the world. All other nations have become isolationists in their own self-interest.

For any government to continue to borrow money in order to

give it away is an act of incredible folly. And to do this until the debt incurred in the name of global goodness approaches sixty billion (1957) dollars is simply inviting financial ruin.

Foreign aid is motivated by a lofty ideal. In a war, or after-war reconstruction period, it may have a temporary place in our nation's foreign policy. But when it becomes a substitute for foreign policy—when it is allowed to overshadow the normal processes of American diplomacy—it becomes an evil and not a good.

\*        \*        \*

Do you want to push back the Sahara Desert?

You probably have never thought about it. Yet you are financing just such a project in Libya with the dollars you pay in taxes for foreign aid, under a program for which Congress voted $4 billion in June, 1956.

Is it essential to American freedom that the desert be turned back in Libya? So say the global-minded spenders in Washington. They have made this project part of the Mutual Security program. It is one of thousands of devices they have evolved over the past ten years in their effort to keep America free—and to scatter $60 billion of the taxpayers' dollars to the four winds of the world.

The cost of this project is confidential. Not even Congress has been told. Compared with the billions spent and being spent, however, it is but a tiny fraction of the whole.

It is one of many undertakings designed to keep your tax dollars busy abroad for years to come. So long as Sahara encroaches and so long as the present planning of Washington bureaucracy continues, you will be called on every year to pay taxes to finance this and similar schemes. . . .

Perhaps you would be interested in learning of bigger and more costly ways of spending your tax dollars. If so, Washington's bureaucracy can oblige; there are many such enterprises. One is a $100 million plan for developing the Mekong River Basin.

Perhaps you are not familiar with the Mekong River. It is a 2,600-mile stream that rises in Tibet and empties into the China Sea. Our spenders think it offers a promising location for an Asian TVA. Congress willing, they plan to develop it.

Mekong would be a top-flight spending project. Other fine opportunities are open through our foreign-aid program. One involves the lovely Litani River, whose development would be most helpful to Lebanon. Your money is a partner there in training engineers to be employed by the project authority. Lebanese funds are in with yours.

Another foreign-aid project is a TVA for the Jordan River, no longer the peaceful stream of Biblical days but now one of the most hotly contested waterways in the world. Still another project is public power for Pakistan—a multiple earth dam, fostered and financed in part by the giveaway experts of the International Co-operation Administration.

\* \* \*

Here are some other foreign-aid items:

We gave $7 billion to Britain that helped bring that country the plight of the former Socialist Labor government.

We poured more than $6 billion into France.

We gave billions to rebuild war-torn West Germany in the most lavish manner conceivable.

We gave more than $1 billion to the shaky government of Indo-China before that country capitulated to the Reds.

We gave the government of Norway $300 million, which they promptly applied to the reduction of their internal debt.

We gave Denmark $100 million, which they used the same way.

In the name of foreign aid we are paying for free airplane excursions for thousands of Arabs visiting their religious shrine at Mecca.

We are paying all living expenses and tuition costs for the sons of hundreds of wealthy Persians attending American universities.

In Portugal our hand-outs have paid for a fifteen-mile, six-lane highway, connecting Lisbon with the gambling resort of Estoril.

We have imported traffic cops from South America to teach them to become better traffic cops.

We have shipped stage comedies to France, opera singers to Italy, and drama groups to Germany.

We have built an Italian village nobody wanted to live in and an Iranian road that leads to nowhere.

In the Netherlands we paid for a unique project—"social psychology and human relations practice"—for the purpose of studying the behavior of the Dutch. They were found to behave very well, indeed!

In twenty-four countries we have financed formidable competition for American iron and steel plants. More than seven hundred million American dollars have been expended by the Government to build iron and steel plants abroad. Of that total, $245,716,000, according to the Department of Commerce, was in the form of outright grants and "direct repayment is not required." The remainder was in the form of easy loans.

The World Bank, of which the United States is the chief moneyed member, contributed $165,290,000 additional in long-term loans, bringing the total to $866 million.

One of our pet projects is a $20 million nuclear center for Asia to bring atoms-for-peace to that area. A team of American engineers and field men of ICA have been working on it. The center probably will be located in the Philippines, though it appears to have generated little enthusiasm among the natives it would be designed to serve.

## Postscript, 1959

Since *The Great Giveaway* was first published in March, 1957, there have been no basic changes in the foreign aid story, only more and more of the same things—more waste, more extravagance, more corruption, more employees added to our free-spending bureaucracy.

Here are but a few examples of how our American dollars have been scattered throughout the world during the past two years:

Last November a fourteen-story, super-deluxe hotel was opened in West Berlin. The hotel was built with "counterpart" funds originating from foreign aid. Cost to the American taxpayers— $6,400,000. Marshall Plan funds are being used to build other deluxe hotels in India and elsewhere.

We continue to pour hundreds of millions into the Philippines and Korea without even attempting to stop corruption within the governments of those countries.

We continue to pour hundreds of millions into Yugoslavia and Poland despite the fact that we know that the dictators who rule these Communist countries would turn against us in time of war.

We continue to pour hundreds of millions into Nehru's India. Our last gift, made at Christmas time, was accepted with the terse official comment: "Not enough."

India has received $325 million in grants and loans from us during the past fiscal year, yet she is not one step closer to us nor one step farther from Soviet Russia than when the giving began.

We gave millions of dollars to Iraq, after the Communist revolution there had succeeded and we had sent American Marines to Lebanon to protect it from Iraq.

Later, after Lebanon had proclaimed its "neutrality," we gave the new government of Lebanon millions of dollars to assist its recovery from last summer's civil war.

In Southeast Asia our foreign aid builds libraries; the Communists stack these American libraries with Marxist books. The United States builds factories; the Kremlin dispatches union organizers and troublemakers to turn the workers against "Western Imperialism." The United States builds hospitals in remote areas; the Kremlin sends native nurses to inject the patients with Communist ideology.

Last year, when Congress responded to the pleas and pressures from President Eisenhower and voted excessive billions for Mutual Security, it assumed that these vast sums would be used exclusively to safeguard the United States from world Communism.

Congress and 175 million Americans were unaware of the fact that the funds demanded to defend the country against world Communism would be utilized, in part, to promote "cultural exchange" with the Soviet Union.

Now, with the approval of the President, $3,200,000 of Mutual Security funds have been "transferred" to finance the building of an American exhibit in Sokolniki Park in Moscow, scheduled to open July 4, 1959. After the exhibition has ended its six-weeks run, the Russians will get the building from Uncle Sam for much less than its construction cost.

Several years ago the President asked Congress for a $100 million a year "blank" check for a period of ten years for the purpose of making long term "loans" to underdeveloped countries. The Congress properly and promptly rejected this request.

Now, under the name of the Development Loan Fund the White House is insisting that it must have not $100 million but approximately $700 million per year for years to come and for the same long-term global bribery idea that Congress once rejected.

*    *    *

Under the label of foreign aid the American taxpayers, who have never known military defeat, have been compelled by our ruling politicians to pay more treasure into the coffers of foreign powers than all of the vanquished people in history have been required to pay their conquerors.

Through a national referendum on foreign aid let the people themselves decide whether or not they want to continue the spending of our money and our resources to promote socialistic schemes and maintain Communistic regimes in foreign countries. Let the people decide whether they want to put an end to foreign aid which spells victory for our enemies and will, in the end, wreck our national economy. Only a national referendum will stop this growing menace and take the global giveaway away from the politicians. This would be a real victory for our solvency and a major blow to our enemies who now are sure they will ruin us with our stupendous foreign aid.

To accomplish this, an immediate nation-wide crusade, led, and vigorously maintained by millions of patriotic and unselfish Americans is urgently needed. Only such an effort can restore our integrity, sanity, and solvency before it is too late. And it is much later than we think.

---

Dr. Elgin Groseclose, a native of Oklahoma and currently the head of a firm of financial analysts and consultants in Washington, has an acquaintance with the under-developed areas of the Middle East that extends over a period of thirty-nine years. During World War II he served as Treasurer General of Iran, by appointment of the Iranian Parliament. On March 31, 1960, Dr. Groseclose appeared as a witness before the Senate Committee on Foreign Relations in connection with the Foreign Aid Program. Excerpts from his testimony follow.

## Foreign Aid and Economic Progress

### ELGIN GROSECLOSE, PH.D.

"Give us the idea that made America great," a young Iranian exclaimed to me, perplexed by the Point Four Program.

What is the political idea that made America great? It is a set of principles found largely though not entirely in the Bill of Rights. It means such things as equal justice for all; trial by jury; freedom from arrest and seizure; due process of law; right of free assembly; freedom of the press, of speech, and of worship; the writ of habeas corpus; right to speedy and public trial, to be confronted with witnesses, and to have counsel; defense against harsh penalties and unusual punishments. These are some of the political ideas that in action give tranquillity to the state, encouragement to honest industry, and the accumulation of wealth. These are the lamp which should be set upon the headland as a beacon for the peoples of the newly formed sovereignties of Asia and Africa, groping for a way to peace and security, hungry for the crust of an idea upon which to feed their infant institutions.

In many of the countries of the East, the establishment of a system of simple justice—a properly administered court of appeal—would do more to allay political unrest and the spread of subversion than billions in foreign aid.

But for our foreign aid officials to proclaim such ideas is officially frowned upon, as an interference in the political affairs of other peoples.

At the same time, however, the program interferes violently in the economic affairs of these peoples, confusing traditional patterns of livelihood and creating insoluble problems of economic adjustment, so that more and more money has to be poured in to save, if possible, disastrous ventures.

What are some of the economic ideas upon which American progress rests? I will give one by way of illustration—the idea of prompt and just reward for effort. Foreign visitors from underdeveloped lands are shown our great industrial machines, but seldom is their attention directed to the little brass plates affixed to them, or what they signify. I refer to the patent notices. The patent notice is an advertisement to the world that society and government defend the right of an inventor to the proper fruit of his ingenuity. The patent system is relatively new in history—dating from the English Statute of Monopolies in 1623 but owing its present general influence to the philosophy of the Constitution of the U.S. The ideological origin of the concept, however, is ancient in the Judeo-Christian tradition. It may be found in a law given to the Jewish people by Moses—"The wages of him that is hired shall not abide with thee all night until the morning." (Leviticus XIX, 13.) Upon this principle rests our whole system of private enterprise, and one reason for the backwardness of many countries of the East is the ignorance of this beneficent law. Thus, the slavery that persists in parts of Africa and the Middle East in this twentieth century, the Anti-Slavery Society reports, is fed by the practice of hiring innocent free Negroes and bringing them into practical bondage through neglect to pay their hire.

From my professional experience of thirty-five years, I will testify that the root of economic progress is a moral idea—or a set of ideas —and the principal defect of the Foreign Aid Program is that it substitutes for an informing idea a conglomerate of materialistic techniques which are being transplanted to a foreign soil without the generative force that brought them into being. Instead of Johnny Appleseed as its prototype, planting abroad the living ideas of progress, it is more in the nature of a banana peddler, whose passing is marked by a scattering of mouldering and dangerous peelings. Here is the source of the perplexities—the ineptitudes, the failures, the maladministration, the corruption—which the Congress and the administrative agencies are struggling to correct. I have no charges to level against the Foreign Aid personnel, many of whom I know, and whose idealism and integrity I respect, but the system and the philosophy with which they have to work degrades their efforts and brings them frustration, if not temptation.

I was in Iran when the Foreign Aid Program, under pressure from Congress, was suddenly jacked up from a million-dollar technical assistance program to a fifty million dollar dollar-aid program. I was with the Deputy Director and saw the look of astonishment when the cable was read: "We can't spend a third that amount without graft and corruption," he exclaimed. And we know now how true were his words in the sorry tale of a quarter billion dollars wasted, revealed by the subsequent Congressional investigation of the Iranian program.

The defect of the Foreign Aid Program is that it tries to do with dollars what only ideas can accomplish.

We hear a great deal of what is called the revolution of rising expectancy; the universal hunger and demand for a better life. My anxiety over the Foreign Aid Program is that it promotes the very unrest it seeks to allay. This revolution of rising expectancy —natural and deep-seated—is under American influence being perverted into a pursuit of materialism. Through our Foreign Aid Program, the U.S. is holding up to the world, as the good life, a rising standard of material well-being, rather than a rising standard of political and personal morality, upon which only a good life can be built. . . .

The Foreign Aid Program represents, however, the first mass effort to condition whole societies, the policies of governments, and the affections and loyalties of peoples, by the administration of "environmental conditioning," through the mechanism of grants, loans, and other forms of material assistance.

A formal statement of the theory is found in the study prepared in 1957 for your Committee by the Center for International Studies of the Massachusetts Institute of Technology. Entitled "The Objectives of United States Economic Assistance Programs," this reports states:

"The proposition is that a comprehensive and sustained program of American economic assistance aimed at helping the free underdeveloped countries to create the conditions for self-sustaining economic growth can, in the short run, materially reduce the danger of conflict triggered by aggressive minor powers, and can, in say 2 to 3 decades, result in an overwhelming preponderance of societies with a successful record of solving their problems without recourse to coercion or violence.

"The proposition presumes that a feasible and properly designed program of American economic assistance could within two decades catalyze self-sustaining economic growth in most of the underdeveloped free world."

The study concludes: "An effectively designed program of aid for economic development is the best instrument available to the United States for encouraging the growth of politically mature, democratic societies."

The theory of foreign aid, here stated, poses a fundamental contradiction. The results are declared to be "politically mature, democratic societies." We do not know what the authors of the Study intended by the phrase, but we may assume it to mean a society in which all the members participated in political decisions, and in which they acted as mature citizens, that is, responsibly and without the caprice or sudden passion condoned in children. It would be a society, we may gather, that would not be carried away by whim, sudden passion, or private interest.

Since, however, societies are but aggregations of individuals, it is not possible to conceive of a politically mature, democratic society in which the vast majority of individuals were not politically mature in their behavior and democratic in their attitudes and convictions. This raises the question as to how any group of individuals can be changed in their personal attributes by a change in their material condition. Will a rise in the standard of living make a person less avaricious, say, or less subject to prejudice, hatred, jealousy, ambition, or other passions which have been the destruction of societies as well as individuals? If the proposition has any merit, then it could be argued that citizens should be classified according to their tax brackets, on the corollary that the higher the person's income, the less subject he would be to the passions of humankind, the more politically mature and democratic he would become, and hence the more desirable as a citizen.

Christian teaching, it may be remarked, has generally stood for the view that fundamental changes come from within, that no matter how much one whitewashes a sepulchre, it still contains dead men's bones. It is indeed a paradox, that with so many direct sayings on the subject from the Founder of Christianity, so many churchmen persist in the conviction that societies can be reformed, the world made peaceful, and universal freedom and justice assured by the mechanism of appropriating money and spending it for dams, cement mills, railways, seed wheat and new ploughs to increase the material abundance and raise the standard of wants.

Much of the public confusion over the Foreign Aid Program, and much of the misdirection and extravagance in the administration of the program, are traceable to the attempt to operate in contradiction to observed experience and in defiance of the lessons of history.

Thus, a prime objective of the program is to allay, in the recipient countries, the unrest and dissatisfactions which the Communist Party may exploit for internal revolution or which lead to foreign adventures that upset the international peace. But the program dismisses as inconsequential the causes of unrest that have kept the race in turmoil since history first was written, from the abduction of Helen to the ambitions of an Egyptian colonel. It has no balm to allay the fevers arising from territorial claims and the dynastic claims of princes, from boundary disputes, religious differences, racial jealousies, insults to nation or to national heroes, the ambitions of military commanders, and visions of national destiny. Of the causes of internal unrest that lead to rebellions and the overthrow of governments—such things as a sense of injustice over taxation and governmental impositions, official laxness and corruption, venal courts, police brutality, uncertain paydays, inflation of the money, impressments and conscriptions, expropriations and condemnations, official caprice, official impotence, and feeble leadership—the foreign aid program has nothing to say.

For over a hundred years Egypt has been the recipient of European capital and technical assistance in the development of the Nile Valley, and today exhibits modern railway systems, hydroelectric works, water impoundage and distribution systems, textile mills, banks and exchanges, and all the associated paraphernalia of modern economic civilization. But it cannot be demonstrated that in consequence Egypt has achieved a "politically mature, democratic society"; nor is there any evidence to suggest that the present political orientation of Egypt would be different had the capital and technical assistance been received from the United States. Indeed, it is hypocrisy to suggest that American capital and technical assistance are going to do better in Asia than European capital and technical assistance because the American variety is not "tainted" with a colonial motive.

The captivation of theorists and of large elements of the electorate with the possibilities of foreign aid is due in part to the apparent success of the European Recovery Program. Here is a case of assuming *post hoc, ergo proter hoc*. If it be admitted that American intervention in European affairs beginning in 1948 produced a stiffening of resistance to Communism, it has not been shown, nor can it be shown, that this was due to American economic assistance more than to the psychological effect of American concern and moral support. On the contrary, the great centers of Communist strength in Europe remained just where they were before Marshall Plan aid began, and in the very areas in which American aid was most liberally administered, that is to say, in the industrial districts. Communist strength in Italy, contrary to the "economic well-being" thesis, has been greater in prosperous northern Italy than in impoverished southern Italy, and foreign aid officials discovered, to their consternation, that Communist Party enrollment was frequently greater in the factories providing the highest wage rates, the most liberal employee benefits, the most congenial working conditions.

The paradox of the Foreign Aid Program, in the area in which it proposes to operate with authority, namely, the economic sphere, is that the effect of pouring in funds and technical assistance to build up the economic structures of various foreign countries has most generally been only that of introducing confusion and instability into the economies. The reason for this is implicit in the theory of foreign aid. The theory premises a homogeneity of culture which is not proven by observation. It assumes that what is good for the United States of America is good for everybody, from the British Isles to the islands of Micronesia. If steel mills, say, are significant in the American economy, they should be good also for the Indonesian. American agricultural techniques should be of interest to the melon growers of Iran and the yam farmers of Africa. This view overlooks the fact that American techniques are themselves in a state of flux, and that what was considered the last word in a science only a decade ago is now antiquated. We may cite the agricultural practices of the nineteen twenties, that of deep plowing for one, that nearly ruined vast areas of the Great Plains by erosion and wind blowing of precious top soil. Margaret Mead, the anthropologist, has pointed out that even so simple an innovation as an iron plow may have catastrophic consequences for agricultural communities in India. It throws the carpenter out of work and upsets age-old community patterns. It requires heavier draft animals which in turn need more fodder than may be available. The wooden plough is light and can be carried from plot to plot, and as a farmer may have several widely scattered plots or strips, the iron plough makes necessary a general rearrangement and consolidations of holdings.

The result is that unless the United States government is prepared to take over the management of the economy bodily, and reconstruct it from top to bottom—a task for which it commands neither the wealth nor the political fiat necessary to accomplish—it had better leave reform for the people themselves to achieve through ways with which they are familiar and which are fitted to their traditions.

In Turkey, under the stimulus of the American aid program, a large tractor import program was instituted in an effort to modernize farming. As the tractors were supplied to the Turkish government out of foreign aid funds, and by the government to the farmers on easy purchase terms, the momentary result was a glow of prosperity. But a tractor farm economy requires a completely different environment in which to operate from the ox and wooden plow economy it supplanted. If the tractors were to be kept fueled with gasoline and in repair, the farmers had to produce a surplus for the market. This required in turn roads by which to move the crops to market. Involved also was the development of foreign markets. This meant competition with other exporting countries— notably the United States. The result is that after twelve years of foreign aid, Turkey is no nearer a self-sufficient economy than ever. Turkey, which in 1945 had an export surplus of $33 million and in 1946 of $74 million, has had trade deficits ever since, ranging to as high as $193 million in 1952, $184 million in 1955, and $88 million in 1959.

In 1950 the government of Afghanistan, actuated by the economic development theories of the foreign aid program, and aided by an Export-Import Bank loan, embarked on an ambitious scheme of water control and land reclamation in the Helmand Valley. This became eventually one of the largest American financed and constructed developments in Asia. The project, while it has its defenders, has not proven a success, partly because of lack of trained administrators, partly because of engineering defects, but largely, it appears, because it failed to take into account the reluctance of the tribes to leave their traditional nomadic life for the sedentary life of tillage. The failure of this attempt at environmental conditioning has not only put grave strains on the Afghan economy but has threatened the political stability of the country and thrown it in the orbit of Soviet Russia. This is the opinion of qualified observers, and the following from the report in the *New York Times Magazine* (March 18, 1956) by Peggy and Pierre Streit who visited the country in early 1956 is illustrative:

"The Helmand Valley Project, which was to have been a boon to Afghanistan, has today placed a dangerous strain both on the Afghan economy and on the nation's morale. Some Western observers in Kabul reason that recent Afghan-Russian trade agreements and the Afghan acceptance of a $100,000,000 Soviet credit represent a partial attempt to mitigate this plight. If this is so, the United States may have unwittingly and indirectly contributed to driving Afghanistan into Russian arms."

A further contradiction in the foreign aid program is the paradox of a government attached to the principles and system of private enterprise officially encouraging the development of statism and monopoly abroad. The United States is in fact doing concretely what Soviet Russia has been doing only through propaganda: it is pouring out vast sums to promote totalitarian and communistic economic and political systems. It fosters five-year plans, seven-year plans, state planning boards, imitation TVA's; it has put governments into the electric power business, into cement manufacture, into slaughter and meat processing, textile manufacture, tanning, sugar refining, milk processing, and other commercial undertakings.

A paradoxical effect of the Foreign Aid Program, not understood by theoretical economists, is the inflationary effect of foreign aid. According to theory, foreign aid funds should be deflationary in effect in the recipient countries, since they increase the supply of goods available within the economy without increase of the money supply (since the goods are provided as U.S. gifts). This theoretical result does not follow in practice. The reasons are simple. The effect is somewhat like that upon a high school boy's allowance from the gift of an automobile. The young man has more possessions but less money, for even though the automobile may save him carfare, he becomes involved in the expense of gasoline, tires and repairs, not to say a whole scale of expenditure which the status of an owner of an automobile seems to impose. Foreign aid funds are usually given under conditions of counterpart contributions by the recipient government. Thus, if the United States donates a steel mill, the local government has to pay for its erection and operation. Often a whole web of new expenditure is involved, for such items as roads and housing facilities, the development of ore supplies, the construction of railways to handle the ore, communication facilities, and all the various items of so-called "social overhead." Stimulated by this activity, prices begin to rise, beginning with wages in the environment of the undertaking, followed by the prices of things which the workers buy. Finally, the government, to finance its share of the development, increases its borrowings, which add to the inflationary pressure, and finally resorts to the printing press.

This discussion would not be complete without giving recognition to the vocal demand of a large element of the electorate for some national expression of the moral conscience. The question to be considered is whether there is an alternative to the foreign aid program as such an expression. The viewpoint expressed here is not that the moral conscience should be ignored, or that it should be denied expression; the view here taken is that the Federal Government is not the proper instrument for the expression of the charitable and benevolent impulses of the citizens. This is a government of delegated powers, and the attempt to use it as a charitable agency abroad is not only unconstitutional, but is self-defeating of such purpose.

The greatest contribution this country can offer to the rest of the world is not the material products of the American livelihood system, but the American idea. By the American idea is meant the complex of ideas imbedded in American political, economic, social and moral practice, that are the ultimate dynamic of American culture.

What is the American idea? Some think it is a Cadillac complex and chrome plated plumbing, the right to throw bottles at the umpire, and to be noisy in foreign lands. It may be these things, and worse, but it is also a group of ideas drawn from the parent cultures of Europe and the Middle East—ideas which, developed, matured, or simply re-furbished, are the proper coin with which "to pay back to the countries of the world some of the things we in the past have gained from other countries." Here are some of them, drawn from Judeo-Christian Scriptures, that have made possible the economic strength and industrial power of this country: dignity of labor; right of the workman to his hire; equal justice before the law; personal responsibility; confidence that for every problem there is an answer, for every need a response; a just weight and a just balance; a respect for exact truth.

If these components of the American idea are understood, then the task is simplified: the American idea becomes one of a community of ideas having a common purpose in the illuminated moral conscience of mankind. It will diffuse of its own accord, as irresistibly as a fragrance on a breeze—from the activities of American overseas commerce and communications; from overseas missionary and philanthropic enterprise; from the arts of the motion picture, radio and written word; and most importantly, from a foreign policy of confidence and courage and respect for the idea.

# XII

# Foreign Trade and You

TWENTY-SEVEN YEARS AGO, Garet Garrett, one of the greatest journalists and editors of a past generation when editorial eyes seemed more adept in penetrating the sham of social, economic and political humbuggery than is the case today, wrote an article, "The Economic Drive Against America." (*Saturday Evening Post,* April 15, 1933.) He summed up the tragic story in these words:

> For more than a year this country has been the object of a worldwide economic drive, producing or tending to produce the following effects, namely:
>
> To intensify and prolong the American phase of universal depression;
>
> To increase unemployment here and to arrest it in foreign countries; . . .
>
> To annul our tariff laws and at the same time to override the laws whereby we meant further to protect American labor by limiting immigration from countries having a low standard of living;
>
> To stimulate unnaturally the sale of foreign merchandise in the American market and at the same time to hinder the sale of American merchandise in foreign markets;
>
> To unbalance the economic position of this country by bringing the weight of more than half the world's selling to bear upon it, while at the same time diverting from it the support of more than half the world's buying;

To create in this country hoards of gold, impounded to the credit of foreign countries, the first effect of which was the same as if Americans themselves were hoarding the gold, as they have been exhorted not to do, and the second effect of which might be much worse because the foreigner owners, having hoarded it here and earmarked it, could take it out of the country whenever it pleased them to do so;

And, lastly, to propagate in this country a motive for war-debt cancellation as the price of economic peace.

That was twenty-seven years ago! That story has not yet ended. Under different names, with different slogans, and strangely enough, now with motive power generated here in the U.S., the drive against the United States goes on. The invasion of the American market by cheap, foreign-produced goods is reaching alarming proportions.

Deciding to look into the current situation to find facts, and not to engage in fancies, the *New York Daily News* published a series of articles, from which we quote the following.

## Low-cost Imports Imperil Us

### JOHN LEWIS AND ECKERT GOODMAN

The torrent of low-priced foreign products pouring into the U.S. has already resulted in the destruction of long-established industries and is threatening, here and abroad, to create unemployment, depression and even starvation in some areas.

Last year, imports reached an alltime high of nearly $15½ billion. At the same time, our exports remained at slightly over $16 billion.

The balance of less than $1 billion was not nearly enough to pay for U.S. economic and military aid abroad, totaling more than $3 billion, and make up for the $2 billion spent by American tourists in foreign countries.

Thus we can be said to have lost, as a nation, over $4 billion on our last year's international transactions.

As a result of this trend, which has become more marked yearly, our Fort Knox gold reserve has dwindled from a high of $24½ billion 10 years ago to less than $19½ billion today, as foreign nations and banks demanded gold for dollars owed them.

And according to Dr. Franz Pick, an international monetary authority, about $18 billion of our remaining gold is "mortgaged" either to foreign investors or foreign governments, which can with-draw the bullion at what amounts to a moment's notice.

Meanwhile, the Russians, with the equivalent of $10 billion worth of gold safely stashed away, and producing more than $600 million worth of new gold a year, are reported to be planning an eventual international financial revolution, in which the ruble will replace the dollar as a standard of world currency.

So far, the greatest impact of foreign imports has been felt by relatively small U.S. industries in which technical know-how and skilled labor are not essential assets.

But today, not even our giant billion-dollar corporations are wholly safe from the economic challenge abroad. About 140 differ-ent industries—ranging from adhesives, agricultural implements and aluminum ware to wood products, woolen blankets and zinc—are already feeling "the pinch," as a result of underselling by for-eign competitors.

To learn at first hand the effects that imports and exports are having on our nation and our way of life, a team of *News* reporters spent several weeks questioning heads of industry, labor, sales man-agement and government throughout the country.

Here are some of the facts they uncovered:

Twelve years ago, we imported less than 1,500 foreign automo-biles, during a twelve-month period in which our car exports reached an all-time high of nearly 261,000.

Last year, imports soared to a record-breaking peak of 668,000 cars, while our exports dropped to a post-World War II low of less than 117,000.

While U.S. truck exports have remained at a more or less con-stant level of between 180,000 and 190,000 a year for the past 15 years, imported trucks have risen from an insignificant 15 in 1946 to nearly 22,000 last year.

Meanwhile, Japan's automobile industry, riding the crest of an unprecedented boom, expects to turn out a record 300,000 cars this year, with thousands of them ear-marked for sale to their best overseas customers—American citizens. And Russian cars reported to sell for less than $1,500 have already been announced for dis-tribution in the U.S.

Last year, Japanese electric companies sold American customers nearly 4,000,000 radios, mostly of the portable transistor type, com-pared with only 641,000 sets two years ago. These imported radios now represent nearly half of all the sets with four or more transistors sold in the U.S.

Sales of Japanese-made transistors to the American radio-manufacturing industry have risen from some 10,000 in 1958 to nearly 2,000,000 last year, and half a dozen major U.S. radio makers are now selling (under their own brand names) pocket model radios made wholly in Japan.

In the past 10 years, the number of Japanese-made sewing machines imported into the U.S. has risen from less than 65,000 to well over a million. An additional 100,000 machines are imported from Italy, Germany and England.

Today, Singer is the only remaining major manufacturer of sewing machines in America. The White Co., for 80 years our second biggest maker, threw in the towel three years ago and now distributes, on a worldwide basis, Japanese-made models.

In the textile-apparel industry, which employs about 2,000,000 American workers, the economic situation is especially acute. During the last three months of 1959, imported cotton in the form of bolts of cloth, shirts, blouses and other items of everyday wear rose at a colossal rate—setting an all-time record of a billion square yards.

Last year, one out of every seven sport shirts sold in the U.S. was made in a foreign country.

---

Following on the heels of the charges made by Garet Garrett came the Reciprocal Trade Agreements, proclaimed as a temporary emergency measure. They are still in force twenty-six years later. What does it all mean to you and you and you?

On this point we quote from an address by Robert T. Stevens, President, J. P. Stevens and Co., Inc., before the Annual Meeting of the Montana Society of Engineers, April 26, 1958.

## An Economic Danger

### ROBERT T. STEVENS

An enormous number of well-intentioned and fine people really believe that these so-called Reciprocal Trade Agreements are actually "reciprocal." Nothing could be further from the truth. This legislation was enacted originally in 1934 as an "emergency" measure to aid the country during depression times and was frankly called "an emergency measure for emergency conditions." It has been renewed 10 times for varying periods and the emergency never ends, in spite of the fact that since Pearl Harbor, in 1941, our country has experienced greater economic growth than ever known by any nation since time began. Instead of being an "emergency" measure, today its friends now call it an "anti-recession" measure. They move with the times and always have an opportunistic reason for renewal.

This "emergency" measure has kept growing like a blight; wider, more complex and more dangerous, at the expense of many American workers and many American businesses. While textiles and other soft goods were hit hard at first, today, the whirlwind of cheap imports is affecting many kinds of goods and machinery. Our people divide sharply on this subject and the Congress itself breaks up into large blocs of those who are for and those who are against, or those who lean toward or those who lean against. Many of our people have tranquillized their own convictions by repeating a little sing-song that deserves some comment. The sing-song goes something like this: "Free Trade means no conflict between nations and that means no wars and that in the end means that our sons will not go forth to battle." Who among us has the courage to take issue with such sentimental reasoning? It is a strong America that will deter war, not an America with holes in its military and economic armor.

The shocking fact is that many American markets and American jobs are just as easy for foreigners to take as stealing a baby's candy. Let's consider these salient points—

1. Wages paid to workers abroad, making all kinds of goods that we buy, range from 35¢ or 40¢ an hour down to about 8¢ per hour. By comparison I'm sure it is unnecessary for me to cite the hourly rates of the average worker in the U.S.

2. In 1934 when the tariff cutting spree began, the average tariff levels protecting our industries were 46.7%—now they are 11.7%. The so-called protection is three-quarters gone! And there will be more of the same if the act is renewed as proposed.

This has been mercilessly destructive to the basic foundations of American jobs. You, as engineers, know full well that no amount of technological improvement in processing can compensate for those wage differentials, in the light of what you know about present day equipment here and abroad. As a matter of fact, many foreign countries have very modern, new equipment that was partly paid for by you and by me, as American taxpayers. How can we as a nation give money, know-how and lowered tariffs to our friends abroad and not have trouble at home. We can't eat our cake and have it too!

Now what about the "reciprocity' in our Trade Agreements? Well, in the first place, as these successive trade agreements were made with various countries, all the benefits were passed around to all the other trade agreement countries. As you know, this is called the "most favored nation" clause. It is not surprising that the country with the lowest wages and the required skills gets the business. Obviously, again, because our wages are five to ten times greater than those of other countries we didn't get the business, we got the "bizness."

The whole thing reduces itself to very understandable elements if we take a look at the facts and forget the much touted slogans. For most items, wages are the deciding factor in measuring what country will make which product, depending upon where the necessary skills and materials can be made available. For example, England controlled the wool goods export market for centuries. In recent years the Italians, with lower wages and excellent skills, have chased the British woolen goods off many trade routes. And now the Japanese are invading the wool goods export market in a big way. Japanese goods made of wool are seriously affecting the already stricken woolen manufacturing industry of the U.S. This is bad for the wool growing industry in which Montana is so vitally interested, as well as being bad for the American worker.

With our generous showering of goods, services and money upon so many lands, in addition to having cut our average tariff rates by three quarters and with foreign wages so far below ours, what did our foreign friends do? How did they reciprocate? The facts show that the 89 trading nations, other than the U.S. have developed no less than 36 different, ingenious practices, restrictive to international trade and investment.

The problem is the same whether it be in Rhode Island, Ohio, Georgia, or Montana. Only the names of the products involved are different. The blight is on a vast variety of items: textiles, machinery, machine and hand tools, chemicals, metals, cameras, appliances, and countless others. The great State of Montana is probably first in the nation in zinc, third in copper, and fifth in lead production in the United States. As you know, the price structure is not only disheartening but is ruinous to many American mining companies. It is tough on many Montanans who depend so greatly upon these metals for their livelihood. We get the same end result whenever low cost imports shut down plants and mines and people are put out of jobs.

Probably one of the least understood phases of the market place, and certainly the phase misunderstood by most of the proponents of free trade, is the psychological effect of the sale of a small quantity of really cheap and unrestricted imported goods on the basic price level of the rest of the domestic supply. The result is dramatic, immediate and destructive. The price of all the rest of the goods, no matter how high the wages, rent, heat, light, taxes and other items of cost that went into them, will grind inexorably downward with the sureness of the pull of gravity.

Unrestricted imports encourage the disintegration of price levels based upon American costs. There may be a temporary advantage to consumers but, if uncontrolled, it will wreak havoc on employment in America. The result is decreased purchasing power, hardship, relief and a lower standard of living. American jobs must be preserved for American workers.

What advantage is there to the American worker and his family if we permit the further liberalization of these foreign trade laws? The gains that have been made in the fields of minimum wages, overtime pay, social security, industrial safety, health and welfare could be seriously affected. Any manufacturer can now escape American labor legislation and most American taxes simply by locating his plant abroad. The laws governing interstate commerce should not discriminate against goods produced in the United States.

Why should two identical garments, one manufactured in the United States and the other manufactured in Japan run into different rules at our state borders? If, as is true, we have legislated costs on the U.S. product, is it fair or reasonable that foreign goods should move in interstate commerce entirely exempt from the rules that apply to American manufacturers?

In my judgment, the American people are too fair minded to approve this type of unfair competition if they understood it. The point is that our laws should take into account the high costs of American manufacture when evaluating the entry of foreign goods into our country. Tariffs, quotas, or a combination of both are necessary if we are to preserve our American standard of living. And let us not forget that American industry has twice been the "arsenal of democracy" in world wars. Is it wise, in the nuclear age, to decimate, under the halo of reciprocal trade, industries which were essential to allied victories in World War I and II?

It is fantastic to many American businessmen to speak of this idea of international trade as "reciprocity." Almost alone, we have done all the giving and yielding and losing. It was all the American Government's idea in the first place, 24 years ago, and we sold it all over the world. The act took the tariff control out of the hands of Congress and gave it to the Executive Branch. The control of American international trade should go back into the hands of Congress, where it belongs.

---

In another address Mr. Stevens rightly contended that the displacement of American workers by imported manufactured products amounts to the "export of American jobs."

## The Export of Jobs

### ROBERT T. STEVENS

If we are to maintain reasonable textile employment and increase the standard of living of the American textile worker, the problem of imported textiles, whether made of cotton, wool or synthetics, will have to be dealt with on a worldwide scale. Failure to do so will inevitably result in the displacement of countless workers and the exporting of American textile jobs. . . .

Even though American textile workers have been hard pressed by the rising tide of imports, they are not the only American workers who are adversely affected by the shift in our foreign trade. . . .

Jobs must be thought of in terms of products. Let us look at a few products for export, and compare them with imports. In the recent past, imports of new passenger automobiles into the United States quadrupled from 108,000 in 1956 to 434,000 cars in 1958. For the first time in American automotive history 1958 imports exceeded exports. If the present trend continues throughout 1959, somewhere near 600,000 foreign cars may be landed here, and it is expected that we will export only about 20% of that number. Are we exporting American jobs? . . .

New steel plants in Europe and Asia, some built with American financial assistance, are threatening our steel workers' jobs in a more permanent fashion than the strike could ever do. These are the facts. In 1957, the United States exported 5.2 million tons of steel mill products and imported 1.1 million tons. This ratio—of almost 5 to 1 in favor of steel mill exports—dropped to less than 2 to 1 in 1958, when exports fell to 2.7 million tons and imports reached a high of 1.7 million tons. So far this year, steel imports are running double United States exports. This pattern is without historical precedent. I might add that a most reliable source has informed me that total imports for 1959 will be about 5 million tons of steel—up from 1.1 million tons two years ago. Are we exporting American jobs? . . .

The list of American products adversely affected by indiscriminate imports grows almost daily. The transistor radio industry of Japan offers a good example. Exports this year from Japan will be more than doubled over 1958 and no less than 60% of the four million transistor sets to be shipped abroad by the Japanese are expected to land in the United States, Japan's next biggest customer will receive only 10%, or about one-sixth as many as will be crowded into our markets. Are we exporting American jobs? . . .

From 1947 through 1958 imports of woolen and worsted fabrics increased by 64.4%. During this same eleven-year period, domestic production of woolen and worsted apparel fabrics declined by 42%. Does it make sense to import still more woolens and worsted? And what about the latest threat—imports of men's clothing from the Far East? Are we going to export the clothing worker's job too?

----

Another significant approach to the Trade Agreements Act is made by Leland I. Doan, President, The Dow Chemical Company, in an address before the Economic Club of Detroit, February 24, 1958. An excerpt follows.

## Foreign Trade in Our Changing World

### LELAND I. DOAN

Any discussion of foreign trade sooner or later gets around to focus on the Trade Agreements Act. This one is no exception. I might note parenthetically that, however often you may hear it, the word "reciprocal" is not in the title. Reciprocity, or mutuality, however, is in the Act in theory and we wish there were some of it in fact.

It is again being proposed . . . that the Trade Agreements Act once more be extended and that the President be given considerable latitude in adjusting our tariffs. The practical effect will be a broad reduction of present tariffs with one or two minor escape clause raises.

For some reason which rather escapes me, this particular Act seems to have become a sort of sacred cow with the proponents of lower tariffs. One is given the impression that if the Act is not extended our whole foreign trade situation will be thrown into a state of chaos. Actually, failure to extend it would in no way nullify any existing agreements. It would simply mean that until some other legislation were passed our present agreements and tariff schedules would remain in status quo. Hence, I cannot quite buy the atmosphere of urgency which so often surrounds the requests for its extension. . . .

Anyway, its supporters contend that it has assisted our export industries. Perhaps it has, but let us look at a few facts.

In 1929, before the onset of the depression, total United States exports accounted for five per cent of our gross national product. In 1956, after 24 years of trade agreements, non-military exports accounted for only 4.2 per cent of GNP. Somehow this does not strike me as stimulation.

I expect there are many here in Detroit who believe the trade agreements program has benefited the automobile industry. Again, in 1929 our exports of motor vehicles totaled more than 544,000 units. This was 10.1 per cent of U.S. production. In 1956 exports of motor vehicles accounted for only 368,000 units, or 5.8 per cent of our total production.

All in all I cannot convince myself that the Trade Agreements Act has been very effective in expanding our foreign markets. Even so, we are repeatedly told that we must reduce our tariffs and buy more so foreign countries will have the dollars to buy more from us.

This is the trade-for-trade's sake fallacy rearing its head. Our own Department of Commerce last October presented to the House Ways and Means Committee a paper titled, "The Role of Foreign Trade in the United States Economy." The gist of this paper was to the effect that, for the nation as a whole, the fundamental role of exports is that of paying for needed imports.

It acknowledged the importance of the immediate monetary earnings of those engaged in export, but then concluded, and I quote: ". . . but what exports contribute to the economic welfare of the whole nation is an efficient means of obtaining goods which are either not available here or are producible domestically only at total higher costs, in terms of human capital and natural resources than those of the exports exchanged for them."

If we can accept the validity of these economics—and I, for one, certainly can—then when we talk about importing more so we can export more, we are getting the cart before the horse and encouraging an artificial sort of exchange which, while it may profit the traders, constitutes no real economic gain.

But suppose we take the altruistic approach which is often a part of this argument—that foreign countries need more of our goods but lack the means to buy them. We say, "These poor people want our products but can't buy them. We must find some way for them to get the dollars."

I don't doubt this situation exists in some spots because I even know a few Americans who don't have the dollars to buy everything they want.

The records of the Department of Commerce quite clearly show that in recent years our foreign customers, in total, have had sufficient dollar balances to finance their trade with us. In the four year period from 1953 through 1956, other countries increased their holdings of gold and dollar assets by $7 billion. Even during the years 1955 and 1956, when foreign purchases of our goods were at very high levels, the annual surplus of foreign dollars receipts over expenditures was $1.5 billion. While some of this increase may be in dollars we gave them, still the stubborn fact remains they preferred to retain our dollars rather than trading them for our products.

Thus, in the round, the dollar shortage seems to be more imagined than real. But what of individual countries? We must recognize that whereas, with the exception of a few quotas on agricultural products, tariffs have been our only means of attempting to equalize our labor costs with those of others, most countries of the world make use of a multiplicity of restrictive practices. Some of these have the effect of creating a sort of artificial dollar shortage.

Others take an even more direct means of making the importation of American goods difficult, or even prohibitive.

For example, 62 countries require import licenses, 46 countries require export licenses, 33 countries require exchange licenses, 23 countries utilize multiple exchange rates, 16 countries have preferential exchange systems, 13 countries require advance deposits on imports—and so on and on.

Our imports from Brazil are second only to those from Canada, principally coffee and cocoa, which are on our free list. Yet since 1948 our share of the Brazilian market has receded from a little over 50 per cent to less than 25 per cent. Our exports to Brazil have in the meantime been falling for she has used the dollars earned for purchasing in Europe.

Brazil has multiple exchange rates ranging from 18.36 cruzieros to more than 308 cruzieros to the dollar. Further, the government levies a tax of ten per cent on all foreign exchange and an additional surcharge of 25 cruzieros per dollar on exchange used for importing wheat, coal and publications.

Similar discouragements to trade can be found at every turn. Britain allows only token imports of many American products. For example, the annual U.S. quota for motorcycles is only 50 units. Greece has import duties on canned goods as high as 200 and 300 per cent of CIF value. Indonesia has import surtaxes, according to category, ranging up to 175 per cent. To import a $2,500 American automobile into Chile the buyer must pay a duty of 200 per cent—$5,000—and make an advance deposit with the government of $15,-000. Thus the car costs him $7,500 and he has to tie up twice that amount while waiting for it.

And we complain about the price of automobiles here!

Considering all these things, plus the fact that we have reduced our tariffs on the average by 75 per cent since the end of the '20's, I do not see how the United States can be accused of impeding world trade or that further broad reductions under trade agreements would accomplish the stimulation that seems to be desired. I do see inherent hazards to our own economy.

Let me make it clear at this point that I do not advocate tariff schedules that will protect inefficiencies in American production, nor do I advocate duties that will prevent foreign goods from competing in the American market.

I do advocate schedules that will equalize production costs so

American producers will have a more even break in the competition. And I have no reticence about my conviction.

The free trade theory is based on the premise that the most efficient producer should supply the commodity. But there is a vast difference between true efficiency and cost of production in terms of U.S. dollars.

You cannot tell me that low wage scales are a mark of efficiency. Nor can you tell me that governmental subsidization of exports represents efficiency. Quite the opposite. One of the reasons for the foreign worker's lower wage scale, and lower standard of living, is that he is less productive. This may not be his personal fault. He may actually work harder but with inferior tools. But any way you slice it he is less productive and therefore less efficient.

The hooker is that while he may, let us say, be 50 per cent less productive his wage may be only 25 per cent of the American worker's. Simple arithmetic then reveals that while the product is less efficiently produced it has none-the-less been produced at half the cost of the American product in terms of U.S. dollars.

If, then, we do not equalize this imbalance by means of an appropriate import duty we are tending to drive the efficient American producer out of business while we encourage the less efficient foreign producer.

This contradicts the very essence of the free trade goal and I cannot for the life of me see where it makes economic sense.

In our own country we have the Fair Labor Standards Act. Among other things it denies the sale in interstate commerce of the goods of employers who pay substandard wages or provide substandard working conditions. Is it conceivably fair that we allow to foreign employers access to markets that we deny to our own nationals? The proponents of lower tariffs are, in effect, suggesting that we do just that—that while we have outlawed the sweatshop in America it is perfectly moral and businesslike to buy from the sweatshop of Europe or Asia or South America.

This leads me to note that comparative costs of production are not entirely a matter of technology, productivity and labor-management bargaining.

Since 1934 we have had the Fair Labor Standards Act, the Social Security Act, the Wagner Act, and the Walsh-Healy Act.

All of these have added to our costs of production and our

productive machine has further borne a constantly rising tax burden.

I am not criticizing or complaining about these things. I am saying that they are economic facts of life which must be recognized as influencing our competitive position in relation to other countries. We have placed certain burdens upon ourselves because we felt it to be in the public interest. Is it unfair to ask that we be protected against those who do not bear similar burdens?

---

Lest these words seem to smack of what "modern liberals" might call an outburst of the voices of "modern reactionists" let us turn back the pages of history to February 23, 1937, when that stalwart Senator from Michigan, Arthur H. Vandenberg, brilliantly analyzed the results to that date and meaning of the Reciprocal Trade Treaties which, lest we forget, are with us yet.

## Giving Away America

### A. H. VANDENBERG

As for agriculture, which was supposed to be the chief beneficiary of this new arrangement through providing foreigners with greater power to buy our farm commodities, it is the chief victim of the plan. While nonagricultural exports have substantially increased, though not in line with imports, agriculture's exports were practically static in 1935 and actually decreased $38,000,000 in 1936. It is no wonder that most farm organizations view the situation critically.

I am unable to believe that this is healthy for America, or that this adverse trend can continue indefinitely without jeopardy. I fear that the present American trade agreement school of thought encourages this jeopardy, and that the present trade agreement formula—in the hands of earnest internationalists—multiplies it. I repeat that I do not believe that this is a time for general tariff reductions without regard to the difference in costs of production at home and abroad.

Indeed, Mr. President, we need new industries to help take up our employment. Inadequate tariffs and hostile trade agreements make the creation and nourishment of new industries difficult if not impossible. This is a particularly serious matter in respect to agriculture, where science is constantly striving to find new industrial uses for farm commodities, a process which probably is the most hopeful of all permanent and realistic farm relief formulae.

But just when American science and ingenuity find a way to make starch out of the sweet potato, the State Department makes a trade agreement with the Netherlands which opens the domestic market to foreign starch. When American science and ingenuity find a way to make paper out of slash pine in the South, the State Department makes a trade agreement with Canada which discourages this brave domestic effort. When American science and ingenuity develop a new process for making cotton rugs with hemp backs, the State Department makes a trade agreement with Belgium which all but renders the domestic effort null and void. I am unable to believe, Mr. President, that this is the way to build America.

This brings me to the third general proposition which I wish briefly to discuss. The record likewise fails to prove that the trade agreements are accomplishing their intended purpose, if that purpose was to bring us full measure of compensation for the domestic privileges which we give to foreign nations. The record proves, on the contrary, that export trade often grows as well, and often better, without trade agreements than with them. I discuss the former proposition first.

The trade agreements are stimulating imports, Mr. President, faster than they are stimulating exports. The able Senator from Florida (Mr. Pepper), who now occupies the chair, himself knows, through the experience of the winter-vegetable growers in his own State of Florida, that there is a hazard to agriculture in these imports. He is one of those who have joined in an effort to see to it that, if there are to be further trade agreements, we shall not be traded out of our boots in this aspect.

The trade agreements, as I have said, are stimulating imports faster than they are stimulating exports. This disparity will disclose itself upon examination of the figures on comparative trade with any treaty country. I quote from *The Trend of United States Foreign Trade,* an official publication of the Department of Commerce. These figures compare the first 11 months of 1936 with the first 11 months of 1935 in respect to six countries with which trade agreements were operative all or most of last year.

Listen, Senators. The able Senator from Mississippi undertook to demonstrate with metaphor rather than mathematics the great advantage that we have gained from these agreements. Let us look at the last record for six of these major-agreement countries. Our exports to Belgium—that is, what we sent to them—fell off 1 per cent, while our imports from Belgium—that is, what we bought in competition with our domestic production—increased 46 per cent. I do not know what trade agreements had to do with that, but I do know that Belgium is a trade-agreement country; and it may be a coincidence or it may be the law of cause and effect, but whichever it is, there is the record; and the amazing thing is that it is about like the record with respect to all the trade-agreement countries.

Our exports to Canada—that is, the advantage we are supposed to get out of this so-called bargaining—went up 17 per cent; but our imports from Canada, which measure Canada's advantage, went up 30 per cent.

Our exports to Cuba went up 11 per cent but our imports from Cuba went up 19 per cent.

Our exports to the Netherlands went up 7 per cent but our imports from the Netherlands went up 22 per cent.

Our exports to Sweden went up 9 per cent but our imports from Sweden went up 21 per cent.

In every instance, with the single exception of Brazil, our import increase with trade-agreement countries was greater than our export increase, and in every such instance the import increase was heavily greater than our 17-per cent average increased imports in trade with all the countries of the world. Undoubtedly our so-called bargains were not the only influence upon this balance against us; but it certainly looks very decidedly as though we were getting the worst of the so-called bargains. In the case of Cuba, for example, the boasted stimulation in the first full treaty year showed our imports from Cuba to be up $67,000,000 while our exports to Cuba were up only $28,500,000. In other words, for every $1 of increased exports we have accepted $2.35 of increased imports, and this is typical of what is happening all along the line.

How many times we can repeat that sort of an economic victory and still be solvent, Mr. President, is beyond my comprehension.

Nor is this all the picture. These disparities, running heavily against us, count only the direct loss and gain. There is yet another loss, namely, the loss from the generalization of these American rate reductions to some 50 other nations which under the "most-favored-nation" formula, get all the American benefits which we grant in each individual contract without contracting any direct equivalent concessions in return. This loss is so far-flung and indefinable that it is impossible to estimate its influence upon our vanishing balance of trade; but we have some interesting collateral evidence in at least one instance.

Again I beg the Senate to listen. During the first 11 months of 1936 our exports to England were up 2 per cent over the corresponding period of 1935; but our imports from England were up 24 per cent, or just 12 times as much as the trade benefit flowing into the United States. In the face of such an exhibit, it is not surprising to hear the editors of the famous London *Economist* say:

"It is fully possible . . . that Great Britain has already gained more from the concessions made by the United States in her treaties with other countries than could be obtained in a direct Anglo-American treaty."

Mr. President, I am driven by all these exhibits to the irresistible conclusion that we are not "getting our money's worth" out of the Hull program; but that on the contrary, we are once more "giving away America."

---

Through the channels of foreign aid and foreign trade we are giving away America, and as we give away America we put our freedom on the international auction block.

I frankly and sincerely believe in the theory of free trade. I would openly espouse the cause of free trade if we could start all over again with the currency of all countries freely redeemable in gold, with all tariff barriers removed, and without the imposition of internal artificial handicaps.

Is there anything free about American industry, labor or agriculture today? If not, how can we talk of free trade in the world until we regain freedom in America?

How can trade be free when I am compelled, as a factory president, to turn over a portion of my employees' wages to a government that gives the money away to build brand new foreign-owned factories in the low-wage areas of the world, with assurance that their products can be shipped freely into this country? The tax bite here is so confiscatory that we have not been able to replace older machines with new, while in these new giveaway factories the machinery is the best and the latest that can be had.

How free is it when another portion of the tax money seized from our employees is used to acquire the American cotton crop for resale abroad at some 25 per cent less than we can repurchase our own property from our own government?

How free does this make the cotton farmers when their natural home market is threatened with extinction and they are made the wards of the government, dependent upon handouts of money seized from others?

Twenty-three years ago Senator Vandenberg proclaimed on the floor of the Senate that we are giving America away. What would he say today after twenty-three years more of chipping away at freedom? Isn't it time to call a halt to this mounting national tragedy?

# XIII

## Education — Foundations — Government — Churches

Just as one doesn't have to be an expert mechanic to know when there is something wrong with his car, one doesn't have to be a professional educator to know that something is terribly wrong in our educational system. In both cases, one can tell by performance. "By their fruits, ye shall know them," and as Augustin G. Rudd, in his magnificent book, *Bending the Twig*, says: "The pitiful fruits of the New Education now are apparent—including elementary school children who cannot read, high school graduates who cannot spell, maturing upper-class pupils who cannot perform simple operations of arithmetic. Parents now recognize that something evil has happened to their schools."

For generations American education had its roots deeply imbedded in the religious, social, economic, and political philosophy and faith of our Founding Fathers.

Early in the 19th century (1839) Horace Mann, in a Fourth of July oration in Boston, gave this educational message to the country:

> The great experiment of the capacity of man for self-government is to be tried anew, which wherever it has been tried—in Greece, in Rome, in Italy—has failed through an incapacity in the people to enjoy

liberty without abusing it. If in all governments, wisdom and good-ness in a ruler are indispensable to the dignity and happiness of the subjects, then in a government like our own—where all are rulers—all must be wise and good or we must suffer the alternative of debase-ment and misery.

It is not enough that a bare majority should be intelligent and upright. We need general intelligence and integrity as we need our daily bread. By the vote of a few wicked men, or even of one wicked man, honorable men may be hailed from office, and miscreants ele-vated to their places; useful offices abolished and sinecures created; the public wealth which has supported industry, squandered upon mercenaries. . . . If votes come from ignorance and crime, the fire and brimstone that were rained upon Sodom and Gomorrah would be more tolerable.

Select schools for select children should be discarded. Instead of the old order of nobility, a new order should be created—an order of teachers, wise, benevolent, filled with Christian enthusiasm and re-warded and honored by all.

"Christian enthusiasm" permeated the thinking of Horace Mann whose influence in education can hardly be measured. "Christian enthusiasm" permeated his concept of education:

I hold it to be one of the laws of God that the talents of man can be developed in the best way and can produce the most beneficial results only when they act in full consonance with all the precepts and the principles of religion. The pursuit of knowledge or science is the pursuit of truth.

Moral education is a primal necessity of social existence.

National virtue is as much a product of wise institutions as is na-tional wealth.

However loftily the intellect of man may have been gifted, however skillfully it may have been trained, if it be not guided by a sense of justice, a love of mankind, and a devotion to duty, its possessor is only a more splendid as he is a more dangerous barbarian.

Educate your children. Educate them in the great eternal principles of justice and right which underlie the entire length of human exist-ence.

Then came William Holmes McGuffey, about whom I quote the very significant book, *A Layman's Guide to Educational Theory*, by Charles W. Coulter and Richard S. Rimanoczy (D. Van Nos-trand Company, Inc., New York) :

Nineteenth Century American education was primarily based on book learning, and McGuffey was the most important person in the preparation of those books.

The only work that has outsold McGuffey is the Holy Bible.

McGuffey's Readers were more than readers: while learning to read, the beginning student was absorbing doses of the vitamins of moral law and principles of behavior.

This has lately been criticized as a form of indoctrination, and we suspect that is precisely what McGuffey's Readers had in mind.

They were more than aids in the proper use of the English language, more than instruments used to develop an appreciation of poetry.

The books were compilations of excerpts from the writings of great statesmen and politicians, well known moralists and outstanding religionists of the previous century.

They reflected the great schisms, political, religious, and moral issues of the period.

They emphasized the identity of the moral and natural law, defined the Christian fundamentals from which sprang the social virtues of truthfulness, temperance, modesty, kindness, and tolerance.

They assumed the Fatherhood of God, the brotherhood of man, the wickedness of war, crime, and inhumanity, and above all, they buttressed the concept of the sacredness of property and bulwarked the position of the middle class in society.

The educational theories of Mann and McGuffey were the dominant theories of 19th Century American education.

But then came the revolution; and under the leadership of philosopher John Dewey, the "Frontier Thinkers" began to take over. This story, in part, is told dramatically in the following excerpts from a series of radio talks by the noted commentator, author, and editor John T. Flynn.

## They War on Our Schools

### JOHN T. FLYNN

I charge that a number of influential educators, teamed up with socialist propagandists and politicians, have for twenty years been trying to use the public schools to shape the minds of children in support of socialist theories.

In nineteen thirty-two, Dr. George S. Counts, a professor of Education in Teachers College of Columbia University, wrote that we live in an age of revolution, that we are witnessing the rise of a civilization built on science and technology and that in our era, we are shifting from the discussion of human liberty to considerations that "have to do with the production, distribution and consumption of wealth." Then he wrote that "capitalism no longer works," and says the society of the future is to be a "planned, coordinated and socialized economy."

He says this must be done through the schools. Then he says boldly that "teachers should reach for power and then make the most of their conquest," and that "to the extent to which they are permitted to fashion the curriculum and procedures of the school they will influence the social ideals and behavior of the coming generation."

But Counts did not stop there. He and a group of teachers got a grant of three hundred thousand dollars from the Carnegie Foundation to study the teaching of the social sciences in the schools. When finished it filled seventeen volumes. The last volume contained the conclusions. Here is one of them: "The age of individualism is closing and a new age of collectivism is emerging." And then it proposed that the teachers go to work upon the minds of their pupils to prepare them for the new collectivist society.

The men behind this plan were not nobodies. A number of eminent educators agreed to the report. It cost three hundred thousand dollars, paid for by the Carnegie Foundation. It was published under the auspices of the American Historical Association. What did they mean? Don't take my word for it. Harold Laski, the socialist leader of the British Labor Party, wrote of it: "Stripped of its carefully neutral phrases the report is an educational plan for a socialist America." That was twenty years ago.

These professors could not openly preach socialism in the schools. They never used the word Socialism. They called it the Planned Economy. They focused the attention of students in the public schools—particularly the high schools—on the things wrong in America.

As the cure for all these overstated ills, the student can be told that we would be freer and happier and more prosperous if we planned our society. Doesn't that sound reasonable? Of course the government would make the plans. And all that would be necessary would be for the federal government to take over a few great central instruments of service and production—the railroads and other forms of transportation, the production of electrical power, the production of just a few basic materials such as coal and steel and oil, and, of course, credit—that is, banks, insurance companies and so on—that's all. Of course the government would not take the rest;

it would merely make plans for the rest of industry and business—and could enforce these plans by deciding what business could use the railroads or could get power, oil, coal, iron and steel and, of course, credit. This is a precise blueprint for British Fabian Socialism—Creeping Socialism, as I call it. But the name "Socialism" never appears.

The next operation in this conspiracy has been to insert this socialist poison into the textbooks. It is not necessary to infiltrate all textbooks, merely those on history, government and economics. And as these three subjects are now in many schools lumped together in a single volume, the job is that much easier.

Dr. Harold Rugg, of Teachers College, Columbia, outlined the methods. He said: "The schools must be used to create a new social order." The first step, he said, must be to develop a new outlook upon life and education among teachers. We must impregnate the young mind with the dramatic wonder of change. We must undermine the child's belief in the greatness of our history and institutions. We must make them realize that the United States has been a failure and that this is because we are a planless society and must turn to national planning by the national government.

Rugg began by providing textbooks. He wrote fourteen of them and fourteen student work books together with fourteen teacher guides. After this, school books on this pattern poured from the presses. The Rugg books alone have sold over five million copies. In 1940, Dr. Ralph Robey made an examination of six hundred social science textbooks in high schools. He declared: "A substantial portion of the social science textbooks now used in high schools tend to criticize our form of government, and hold in derision or contempt the system of private enterprise."

But here is a priceless exhibit, which shows how this drive is something promoted on the highest levels. The Association of Secondary School Principals and the National Council of Social Studies, a department of the National Education Association, have sponsored a series of study guides—in pamphlet form—to supplement texts in high schools. It is called "Problems in American Life." One of the pamphlets in this series is called "The Role of Government in a System of Free Enterprise."

The authors are Oscar Lange and Abbe Lerner. Is it not interesting that this instruction pamphlet for American business should be written by a Pole who had not been long in this country? Oscar Lange is a Pole who was enjoying a grant from the Rockefeller Foundation as a professor in Chicago University. Lange became a naturalized citizen. But as soon as Stalin's armies seized Poland, Lange quickly abandoned his citizenship here and hurried over to Poland and sometime later became the foreign minister of the Soviet puppet government of Poland. Later he came here as its representative in the United Nations. Was there nobody in America to write a book of instruction about American business but this communist refugee?

Our people are deeply devoted to the principle of free speech. I hope they never lose that. Now it is this fact which the radical schoolmen trade on. If they are spotted and denounced they promptly appeal to the historic tolerance of our people. They deny they are communists or socialists. And they appeal to the teacher's right of academic freedom.

Now first, there is no such thing as academic freedom; the teacher has freedom—period. He has the same freedom that you and I have, to adopt his own philosophy and speak his mind. But when the teacher enters the classroom, he must remember it is not a soapbox. It is not a hall he has hired. It is the property of the community.

In every community the people hate intolerance. But there are always a few who are professional champions of free speech. But being abysmally ignorant of the nature of the drive to use our schools to overthrow our American system, they rush to the defense of any teacher or school official who is caught using the public school to promote socialism. The radical schoolmen make a powerful use of the ignorance of these blind champions. Now let me give you an example of this.

I have called your attention to a recently published series of articles which denounced those Americans who have dared to question these plans to use the schools for radical propaganda. These articles called attention to the case of Pasadena, California, where a new superintendent of education got into such hot water that he was forced to quit. He has been pictured as a martyr. Pasadena engaged Dr. Willard E. Goslin, as Superintendent of Schools in 1948. After being safely installed, Goslin began to introduce what is known as Progressive Education.

Pasadena parents began to see and hear of curious and revolutionary arrangements. Children were not to be taught much of anything—neither reading nor writing, spelling, grammar, arithmetic or history. They were to just more or less pick these up while they fiddled around in their own way in classrooms. Learning was to be incidental. Goslin supported all this.

The parents learned that every conceivable force or institution other than the schools would be kept away from the pupils. The church, the Boy or Girl Scouts and similar organizations and, as far as possible, the family, were to be prevented from reaching the child's mind.

Then Dr. Goslin brought from Minneapolis, Dr. Robert Gilchrist as his assistant superintendent. He was a director of the American Education Fellowship. Its announced purpose was "to channel the energies of educators toward the reconstruction of the economic system; and the establishment of a genuine world order, in which national sovereignty is subject to world authority, an order in which world citizenship assumes at least an equal status with national citizenship."

The people of Pasadena became alarmed. They had wished to improve their system of public education. But they had never dreamed they were to support a system of schools the central purpose of which was to prepare their children for the socialist society of the future, as Dr. Counts put it, or which was "to become rightful agencies of social change" as Dr. Theodore Brameld, who visited Pasadena, assured them. Pasadena was their town. The children in the schools were their children. The bills for all this were being paid by them. They didn't like the fare Dr. Goslin was serving. They held a school election and by a vote of two to one they disapproved an increase in the tax rate for Goslin's projects. Goslin attempted to pressure them into yielding and they asked for his resignation.

The plan is not to teach Communism and not to teach Socialism. It is to sneak over on the minds of children and parents, a little at a time, first a small fragment and then a larger slice of the socialist objectives:—government ownership of the railroads, the crimes of business, the greed of business men, the sufferings of labor, government ownership of power, socialized medicine, the great role of government debt in regulating the economy, government management of everything—banks, insurance—handouts for everyone.

Now, what can we do about it? Well, the first thing is to remember not to play into the hands of this gang by making charges you cannot prove.

Second, do not charge that the school in your town is teaching Communism. You will never be able to prove it. They do not teach Communism. Do not make reckless charges about the school having communist teachers. There are very few communist teachers. And where there are, it is difficult, almost impossible, to prove it. Don't make loose charges. Remember that the vast majority of teachers in your school are neither communists nor socialists. Many are quite as deceived by this movement as you may be. Teachers do not like to hear their profession maligned or their schools traduced. Remember that if anything of this nature is going on in the school in your town, it is done cautiously, craftily and by only a few people.

Remember that the work is done chiefly in that department of the school which deals with the social sciences. Remember also that the poison is to be found, if it is there, chiefly in the books and courses on history, economics and government.

If you feel there is something amiss in your school, do not act precipitately. Do not shout Communism or Socialism. Seek the advice in your community of thoughtful and soberminded men and women. Go first to your school authorities and present your complaint without publicity. You can appeal to the public when you are satisfied that the school authorities will not act.

—Printed with permission from America's Future, Inc.

---

In the past several years, E. Merrill Root, Professor of English at Wheaton College, has written two provocative books: *Collectivism on the Campus* and *Brainwashing in the High Schools*, the latter being the result of his analysis of eleven of the most widely used United States history textbooks revealing overwhelming evidence of hostility to traditional American principles.

What an appalling contrast to the history books written before the turn of the twentieth century when historians were inclined to write history, not the current polyglot jargon of left-wing social studies.

On February 22, 1960, Professor Root made an address before the Texas Society Sons of the American Revolution in Houston. He points up some of these facts with dramatic effect.

## The Quicksands of the Mind

### E. MERRILL ROOT

What are the quicksands of the mind? What are their dangers, where do they lie, and how may we avoid them? How do they threaten to engulf the Republic that we love, and how may we and the Republic return to the granite on which alone we may stand and endure?

We must first realize the true threat and peril to our way of life, to our Constitutional Republic, to the United States of America. Too many Americans see the chief threat in the wrong place. Under the shadow of Sputnik and the hydrogen bomb, too many people see our peril only in the material threat and the military danger. They see our danger in the gimmicks and gadgets of mechanical war—in the tanks that roll, in the bombs that fall, in the missiles that zoom. And that is a danger. And therefore we must be prepared against all and any international skullduggery and mayhem. Our defenses must be strong; our power of retaliatory attack must be sure.

But having said that, and having affirmed the need of military preparedness, I must hasten to say, with all the high seriousness at my command, that this is not our greatest danger. Any military man will tell you that weapons are important—but that morale is even more important. The will to fight—that is what makes good soldiers. Faith, hope, and love—the consecration to a cause—the morale of high motivation—the clear mind, the fervent spirit, the resolute will—these are our greatest assets. And at what do our enemies aim? They seek to subvert our faith, our hope, and our love; our patriotism; our love of America; our belief in the Constitutional Republic. Their chief attack is by the infiltration of our culture and the subversion of our souls. They would capture our minds by brainwashing; they would hypnotize our wills by brainwashing.

One brilliant professor, infecting his students with his own cynical criticism of free enterprise, his own sentimental affection for collectivism, can do more to destroy us than the blitzkrieg of a panzer division. One persuasive textbook, pouring scorn over our patriotism, ridiculing private initiative and ballyhooing government subsidies and control, dispensing sugar for collectivism and acid for free enterprise, may confuse the minds of youth and paralyze the wills of youth and so render us impotent to man the bulwarks of freedom. Such books confuse us intellectually and they soften us spiritually.

Teachers and books that gnaw at capitalism with weasel teeth; that discredit patriotism as an evil called "100% Americanism" and that equate it with the Ku Klux Klan; that belittle our Founding Fathers and reduce our Constitution to a class document and "a rich man's plot" against the rest of us; that split America into a civil war between the "privileged" and the "underprivileged"; that sneer at the Spanish-American War as mere American "imperialism"; that see the expansion of railroads and industries and oil wells as "exploitation" by predatory "Robber Barons" and "Napoleons of Finance"; that make Henry Wallace's "Progressives" the only true Americans; that stress the seamy side of American life— slums, strikes, plutocrats, bloated Senators, etc.—as the only reality —all these present America exactly as the Communists want us to see it. And, by so doing, they destroy our faith, our hope, and our love; they confuse our minds and hypnotize our wills; they subvert our morale; they soften us up for the easy kill.

Therefore we must realize that our greatest danger today is not outward military attack but inward cultural subversion. The true hot war today is the cold war. The mortal peril today is brainwashing. The great war today, as Major William E. Mayer, the army's chief expert on psychological warfare has publicly said, is the war of ideas and ideals. He says that this "will render mechanical weapons, if not obsolete, at least needless, since we are engaged in a war basically of ideas." Therefore our real war today is not a battle of bullets, but of brains; not of missiles, but of minds; not of space, but of spirit; not of weapons, but of wills. If our enemies take the City of Mansoul, they will not have to worry about capturing the city of man's body.

That means that the real battlefield today is not some remote no-man's-land half way around the world, where the tanks roll and the guns roar and the bombs fall, but in the every-man's-land of our magazines, our television, our pulpits, our plays and our books and pictures and music, and (beyond all else) in our classrooms and our textbooks. It will not matter in the end whether the young people in our schools and colleges are brainwashed into surrender by witting agents of the Communists or by the witless dupes and tools who call themselves "liberals" in the ironic modern sense of that perverted term. Our survival as the United States of America demands that they shall not be brainwashed at all! Our greatest problem is not the false demand for "academic freedom" to call the latest fashionable perversion "truth," but the realism that finds the truth which alone can make us free.

Thus our greatest danger is not atomic fission, but academic fission; not radioactive fall-out, but scholastic fall down. Our greatest danger lies not in the threat of the hydrogen bomb over our cities, but in the nuclear destruction of our minds by our perverted culture. If the collectivists capture the minds of youth, why should the Communists bother to roll the tanks or to drop the bombs? They are already here. If teachers indoctrinate young people with the belief that free enterprise is piracy, that property is theft, that the government should be our orderly policeman from the cradle to the grave, why should the Communists bother to loose the divisions to launch the missiles? They are already here. If our young people are conditioned to believe that private initiative should do nothing and government coercion should do all, why should the Communists bother to start a shooting war? They have won the war without firing a shot. They are already in the saddle and ride America.

And the terrible irony is that it is not the outright Communists who fight and win the ideological battle. It is not even the avowed Socialists. It is the gentle Fabians, the suave "liberals," the dupes and sentimentalists, who are cynical about free enterprise and sentimental about collectivism. They are the quicksands of the mind into which we may sink.

What sense does it make to give our young men guns to defend America, when students' minds are being brainwashed till they are ready to welcome "the Russian occupation of the United States"?

I think I know the answer when I read the too many of our textbooks in history, and see how they mock and degrade patriotism, and how they sentimentalize collectivism and even Communism, and how they make America seem a sort of cosmic slum. Does that not explain, too, the 20 or more Americans—including Robert Maynard Hutchins—who recently were featured in England as they told the world what was wrong with America, but never what is right with America?

Recently, in the city of Indianapolis, Indiana, the *Indianapolis Star* reported a survey and questionnaire undertaken by a class of high school seniors. These students went out and interviewed 100 people at random. The question they asked was: "What is capitalism?" Now if our schools during the last two decades had been on their intellectual toes, surely 100 people in the conservative state of Indiana would have been able to give intelligent answers as to what capitalism is. But did the people interviewed give intelligent answers? Out of 100 people questioned only 6 gave intelligent answers. Only 6 out of 100! And the people questioned were all high school graduates, most of them were middleclass people, many of them had industries or businesses which they owned. Yet listen to their answers. Four teachers answered: "I don't know." Two citizens said: "That [capitalism!] is something like communism." A store owner said: "Capitalism is only for big business." Another teacher said: "It's a way of life just as communism is a way of life." Another teacher said, after long and profound cogitation, "Money." A machine-shop foreman said: "It is a system in which the big money men have control." A businessman said: "Capitalism is money, that is, only the wealthiest people run the business." A grocer said: capitalism is "The evil behind the large businesses that are trying to drive smaller businesses off the market." A worker said: "Capitalism is big business and big money." A drugstore owner said: "I don't believe in it; it's the money man in control." A restaurant owner said: "It has something to do with capital or big business." A grocery manager said that it is "A gouging to see who can make the most money." Now all of these people ought to have understood the system under which we live, and to which we owe our high standard of living. All of them should have known the simple facts of life, as Carroll Reynolds, director of the Indianapolis Economic Education Department, knows and says it: "Ownership of a share of stock, of an insurance policy, of a time deposit in a bank, makes anyone a capitalist." But here are these teachers, owners of stores, managers of stores, prosperous workers, all goofing. They do not know. They think capitalism is bad. They are against it—while they live by it! Where have our teachers and our textbooks been, what use would it be to have more education if it is to be education like this? And why should the Communists bother to loose the tanks or drop the bombs? They already control the minds of a normal group of people in Indianapolis, 94 to 6! What good will it do to give our young men guns and tell them to fight the communists, when they don't know what capitalism is and what the Republic is for which they fight?

We spend a great deal of breath saying that we must subsidize, build up, increase our education—but what good would all that do if our education has left us as ignorant as these people in Indianapolis? We are told we need more and more "classrooms"; should we not first ask: *"What goes on in those classrooms?"*

I think I know one reason why, in our classrooms, we are not told what capitalism is. It is because we have textbooks that deliberately tell us what it is not. I am thinking of one textbook which I review in *Brainwashing in the High Schools*. It says, in the index, "Business: see also Panic." Business, see also panic! Doesn't that help to explain why people in a city like Indianapolis don't understand what capitalism is? Or in another of the texts I review, the suffering and catastrophe of the First World War is supposed to have been all right not because we had to defeat Germany abroad, but because, at home: "our country was transformed suddenly from the scene of thousands of independent competing businesses into one great workshop under government direction." Do you see what they do and how they do it? They gnaw at capitalism with weasel words; they praise collectivism with sly insinuation. It is good, even at the cost of a terrible war, if "thousands of independent competing businesses" are "transformed into one great workshop under government direction." Do you see why the man in the street, if he has been to high school, doesn't know what capitalism is—and is against it? Why should the Communists come? They are already here!

Or take another example of how education spreads the quicksands of the mind. A favorite indoor sport of "liberal" professors is debunking the Founding Fathers, and especially the great George Washington whom we honor tonight. The *Chicago Tribune,* on November 20th, 1958, had a news story about a Professor Richard W. Van Alstyne of the University of California. The good professor had just written an article for a Canadian university. In this, says the *Tribune,* he called the American Revolution a "myth," and he said "that the pledge to the flag is recited by the simple-minded as proof of their loyalty." He further said that "the American Revolution produced platitudinous words such as freedom, liberty, and independence." He also claimed that "men such as Washington sought to overcome personal failure and disappointments and win fame through the revolution." Do you see what the smart alecs of education try to do, and how they try to do it? They undermine patriotism: to recite the pledge to the flag is to be "simple-minded." Words for which our forefathers died—"freedom, liberty, independence"—words for which you and I would die today—are "platitudinous." The very center and foundation of our Republic, George Washington, merely "sought to overcome personal failure" and "to win fame" by fighting the revolution! Such words are a quicksand under our faith, our hope, and our love; such words are a quicksand to engulf America. They are a part of that sick pseudosophistication, that smart-alec cynicism, that historical negativism and spiritual nihilism, which are destroying the intellect of America. Why should we give our young men guns and tell them to go out and fight communism, while at home we tell them they are "simple-minded" to pledge loyalty to the flag and that George Washington was just a sort of Charles van Doren, a sick soul in search of an escape from failure and a flight to fame?

When the *avant garde* professors—who are not Communists at all, but only smart-alec "liberals"—so subvert our faith, our hope, and our love, by debunking our revolution and throwing acid over the Founding Fathers, why should the Communists start a shooting war? They are winning without a shot.

Or take examples of quicksands in our textbooks. I assume that many of you have read already my *Brainwashing in the High Schools;* if you have not, it is too long a story to tell you here. . . .

I will merely say that if my knowledge of American history and America were founded on those books, you could say of me, as Major William E. Mayer says of the prisoners in Korea who collaborated, that I would prove that "it is tragically clear that the American educational system, fine as it is, is failing miserably in getting across the absolute fundamentals of survival in a tense and troubled international society. This failure needs to be publicized."

In these eleven textbooks, not one made clear that the real Russian Revolution set up a Constitutional Republic, which was then overthrown, not by the Russian people, but by a minute minority using first fraud and then force. Not one text favors Congressional investigations of communism. Every text refers to all attempts to counter infiltration and subversion as "a Red scare," "hysteria," or as what one of them ungraciously calls the fright of "old ladies of both sexes." None of them makes clear, or names, or warns against, the traitors in the Ware Cell, or Harry Dexter White, or Alger Hiss. Not one of them, when, as they often do, they refer to authors like the late Louis Adamic, mentions his long and unsavory communist background. They all fail miserably in giving us the facts of life about the rise of communism, the danger of communism, the subversion of communism, the treachery of our own communist agents in high places. They leave the student in a mid-Victorian hush-hush about the political facts of life. Thus they let students sink into a quicksand of the mind, and if our students sink into the quicksands of the mind, America will sink into the quicksands of the mind. And so sinking, we shall perish from the earth. The Communists don't have to roll the tanks, or loose the bombs, or hurl the missiles: they merely have to drug our minds and hypnotize our wills. That is what they plan to do; that is what they are successfully doing.

What do we need? To turn from the quicksands and to find the granite. What is granite? It is truth, it is reality, it is things as they are in the mind of God. The relativists, the skeptics, the negativists, the nihilists, have destroyed much of our sense of reality: we must regain it. As they say in the Chris Colt song, "There is a right, there is a wrong." In philosophy, in ethics, in aesthetics, we must return to absolutes. And in politics we must return to absolutes. We are not a democracy, we are a Republic; we are not a welfare state, we are a government that should uphold free enterprise; we don't want the state to be our orderly policeman from the cradle to the grave, we want freedom, and individual initiative, and what Emerson called "the infinitude of the private man." And in religion we must return to the granite of reality. We need to say, and to act on, the foundation of our Republic: God.

---

"It is difficult for the public to understand," says Mr. Rene A. Wormser, a distinguished New York attorney who was counsel to the Reece Committee which made an investigation of the powerful tax-exempt foundations, "that some of the great foundations which have done so much for us in some fields have acted tragically against the public interest in others, but the facts are these for the unprejudiced to recognize."

Ida Darden, a brave and dedicated lady of Fort Worth, Texas, who publishes a small monthly paper called *The Southern Con-*

*servative,* not only understands Mr. Wormser's point but has tried to do something about it. In her January, 1956, issue she wrote the following open letter to Henry Ford II.


# Two Open Letters

### IDA DARDEN AND A. G. HEINSOHN, JR.

On February 24, 1953, the Congress of the United States appropriated $300,000 to be used by the Congressional Committee on un-American Activities in investigating Communist infiltration of the American government.

The next day, on February 25, 1953, you made pikers out of the Congress by appropriating $15,000,000 to be used, as it turned out, in attempts to prevent any investigation of Communist infiltration of the American government.

The Foundation you set up was called the Fund for the Republic but it is only now that the people of this country are coming to realize that the Republic in whose behalf the Fund is being expended is the Soviet, and not the American Republic.

As one who, from the very first, editorially exposed the objectives of the Fund for the Republic, I naturally am extremely gratified that the American people are finally becoming conscious of the danger to our country which this project poses.

Under the administration of this Fund by Robert M. Hutchins, the nation's champion addle-brained egghead, and one of the staunchest defenders of the rights of Communists in the United States, its activities have inspired nation-wide suspicion of you and the Ford organization.

This loss of confidence in the principal Ford executive must inevitably bring shame and reproach to the honorable name of your grandfather who accumulated the money you so heedlessly give away without reservation, restrictions or restraint.

Lately you seem to have become alarmed over this sweeping resentment against you as attested by the increased activity of your press agents, enormous gifts to non-political units and your own public statement disclaiming any knowledge of, or responsibility for, the objectives or disbursements of the gigantic Fund for the Republic.

Informed Americans, however, are going to be slow to buy your assertion that you willingly turned over $15,000,000 for purposes of which you were ignorant and to be expended by persons of whose subversive record you had no knowledge. Responsible business executives, Mr. Ford, are simply not that careless with money.

Even though it is generally conceded that the genius of the founders of American industry is seldom reproduced in their progeny, it will be difficult for the American people to ascribe such monumental stupidity as this to one of Henry Ford's descendants.

The only alternative, therefore, is the widespread conclusion that you knew what you were doing when you did it and that you now wish to stem the flood-tide of criticism and buy back favorable public opinion by an enormous donation to schools and hospitals.

The gift to the hospitals is a worthy gesture but the majority of the educational institutions who were the recipients of your generosity will merely supplement the propaganda of the Fund for the Republic by continuing to brain-wash American youth.

So you will have to come up with a better plan if you hope to minimize the damage that Hutchins has done to your reputation and to the American economy and which he will continue to do until his money runs out.

Otherwise, the good name of the Fords cannot be retrieved nor their former record for probity in dealing with the public, re-established.

There are scores of honorable and irreproachable organizations in this country whose objectives are the exact opposite of those to which the Fund for the Republic is committed and they offer, in my humble opinion, the solution to the unhappy dilemma into which your ill-advised bequests have plunged you.

Since I have not the slightest connection with any one of these organizations, I claim complete exoneration from the charge of any personal interest in the proposal which I shall make.

To name just a very few such organizations: The Committee for Constitutional Government; Daughters of the American Revolution; Defenders of the American Constitution; Americanism Committee of the American Legion; Sons of the American Revolution; Campaign for the 48 States; For America; We, The People; Congress of Freedom; Foundation for Economic Education; National Economic Council; Federation for Constitutional Government; National Pro America; Organization for Repeal of the Sixteenth Amendment; Minute Women of the United States; Western Tax

Council; Church League of America; American Progress Foundation and scores of other great organizations, groups and publications who are working as earnestly for the preservation of the American form of government as the Fund for the Republic is striving to destroy it.

If you really wish to prove your sincerity and refute once and for all time growing accusations that Ford money is being utilized to subsidize movements for the overthrow of the American form of government, I earnestly plead that you be equally generous with the foregoing and similar organizations to whose good name no such taint attaches.

Your total gifts to the Fund for the Republic and the hospitals and universities are reported at $515,000,000 but it is a matter of general knowledge that you still have an even greater amount stashed away in your sock and your piggy bank.

And so, in all good conscience, I beg you to select an amount somewhere in between the $15,000,000 which you gave to the Fund for the Republic and the $500,000,000 you donated to hospitals and colleges and divide it equally between the above-mentioned and similar groups which will thus enable them to broaden and extend their Americanism programs to an extent that they will be in position to largely offset the subversive activities of the Fund for the Republic.

This generous and patriotic gesture on your part will generate within you a feeling of pride and self-respect which you cannot possibly experience so long as fellow travellers, Communist Fronters and others of questionable loyalty are the sole recipients of your endowments.

The shifting of your sympathy and influence to the cause of Americanism and the contribution of your resources and treasure to incorruptible Americans who are immune to the blandishments of Communist propagandists and whose collaboration with foreign conspirators could not be bought at any price, will lift you to new and exalted heights of self-approbation from which you will be forever barred so long as only subversives and suspected traitors grace your Foundation payrolls.

All this I ask in behalf of the memory of the first Henry Ford whose brains, energy and initiative provided you with your chief claim to distinction and whose unchallenged loyalty to his country reflected only honor and glory on a name which is now being dragged in the mire by Hutchins and his stable of Soviet stooges.

Of course Mrs. Darden received no reply, nor did I receive a reply to the following short letter I wrote Mr. Ford after her letter.

January 16, 1956

Mr. Henry Ford II
President, Ford Motor Company
Dearborn, Michigan

DEAR MR. FORD:
There are some of us who still believe in American self-reliance, trust in God and in human progress via evolution according to the laws of nature. We take a dim view of rapid human uplift à la Karl Marx, Paul Hoffman or Robert M. Hutchins.

None of us have inherited wealth such as yours, but some of us from our own earnings have set up modest Foundations, funds from which go to groups seeking to preserve American self-reliance and trust in God.

I believe Mrs. Ida M. Darden lays it on the line, Mr. Ford, in her editorial which is enclosed. Why don't you join us and recommend to the directors of the Ford Foundation that they consider making contributions to the patriotic organizations mentioned by Mrs. Darden?

Sincerely yours,
A. G. HEINSOHN, JR.
President, Cherokee Textile Mills

These letters are mentioned to bring out into the open one of the mysteries of our times. Here are the descendants of the early builders of America setting up tax-free foundations whose income is channeled into the hands of the left-wing organizations favoring socialism by way of a bigger and better welfare state.

How their ancestors, who started as poor boys in a country of free men, must be turning in their graves.

To get into this record a concise summary of this shameful blot on the history of America, the Dan Smoot *Report* of June 15, 1959, is reprinted.

## Foundations

DAN SMOOT

On April 28, 1950, Clinton E. Jencks, President of Amalgamated Bayard District Union, Local 890, International Union of Mine Mill and Smelter Workers, in the State of New Mexico, filed an affidavit (as required by the Taft-Hartley labor law), swearing that he was not a member of the communist party.

Using FBI evidence to prove that Jencks was a member of the communist party when he filed that affidavit, the Department of Justice prosecuted Jencks for perjury—saying that he lied when swearing that he was not a communist.

The federal district court in New Mexico convicted Jencks, and the Circuit Court of Appeals upheld the conviction.

At his trial, Jencks was given full opportunity to face all of his accusers in open court. No information supplied by unnamed informants was used against him. He was permitted to examine every piece of evidence used to prove that he had lied under oath.

Nonetheless, the United States Supreme Court, on June 3, 1957, reversed the lower courts—on the ground that Jencks should have been permitted to see all confidential FBI reports on communist meetings which Jencks was accused of attending. The Supreme Court ordered a new trial for Jencks. But in order to try Jencks again, in compliance with the Supreme Court's decision, the Department of Justice would have to reveal to Jencks and his lawyers virtually everything the FBI knows about communist activity in the State of New Mexico, the center of our nation's secret research on atomic energy.

Hence, the Department of Justice decided not to try Jencks again.

This man, once convicted of perjury for denying that he was a communist, went free. What happens to a man with a record like that?

These are strange times.

On May 13, 1959, officials of the University of California confirmed that Clinton E. Jencks has been granted a graduate fellowship to study economics at the University, in preparation for a master's degree. Mr. Jencks plans to be a teacher!

The University disclaimed all responsibility, saying that it had not granted the fellowship. The grant to Jencks was make by the

Woodrow Wilson Fellowship Foundation of Princeton, New Jersey, which is a subsidiary of the Ford Foundation.

Mr. Hans Rosenhaup, national director of the Woodrow Wilson Fellowship Foundation, said that a University of California professor had originally suggested Jencks for a fellowship. Mr. Rosenhaup would not tell who the professor is.

Mr. Rosenhaup said that Jencks has "made his peace with society," that he has "strong idealistic convictions with the courage to back them up," that he has a "strong motivation toward teaching," and that he "wants to start a new life."

The group which actually examined Clinton E. Jencks and found him to be such an idealistic and courageous fellow with a strong yen to teach American youth, was a five-member "regional selection" committee for the Woodrow Wilson Fellowship Foundation. The Chairman was Travis Bogart, English professor at the University of California.

Professor Bogart characterized Jencks as "absolute top quality . . . first class . . . a man who could teach."

Bogart said his committee knew of Jencks' "dramatic background" but did not go into the question of whether Jencks is now a communist.

This Ford Foundation grant to Clinton Jencks, made with disregard of American public opinion, is just one of a long series of such incidents.

The great tax-exempt foundations of America have become the most powerful of the sinister forces in our society. With almost unlimited funds for underwriting every movement that is destructive of basic American principles, and to fight every person or organization trying to support Americanism, the billion dollar foundations (Rockefeller, Ford, Guggenheim, Sloan, Rosenwald, and so on) have bought for themselves such prestige that the public generally reacts with indignation against anyone who criticizes the foundations.

For example, the Ford Foundation established the Fund for the Republic with a 15 million dollar grant in 1952—at a time when public awareness of the communist danger was seeping into the thinking of enough Americans to create, for the first time, a powerful anti-communist movement in this country. It soon became apparent to all well-informed persons that the Ford Fund for the Republic, under the direction of notorious anti-anti-communists, was set up for the primary purpose of discrediting anti-communism in America.

By late 1955, the Fund's activities (publicly granting awards to fifth-amendment communists and supporting practically every major pro-communist cause) had become so blatant that public indignation was rising significantly. Just at the right time the Ford Foundation announced a gift of 500 million dollars to the colleges of America.

Newspapers—also beholden in many ways to the big foundations —which will not publish news about the foundations' anti-American activities, give banner headlines to the lavish benefactions for purposes universally believed to be good.

Where will you find a college administration that will not defend the Ford Foundation against all critics—if the college has just received, or is in line to receive, a million-dollar gift from the foundation?

How far must you search to find college professors or school teachers who will not defend the Foundation which gives 25 million dollars at one time, to raise the salaries of professors and teachers?

Where will you find a plain John Doe citizen who is not favorably impressed that the hospitals and colleges in his community have received a multi-million dollar gift from a big foundation?

Every significant movement to destroy the American way of life has been financed in whole or in part by foundations, which are not only entrenched in public opinion as great benefactors of our society, but which are actually so powerful that they can't even be investigated by the Congress of the United States.

On August 1, 1951, Congressman E. E. Cox (Democrat, Georgia) introduced a resolution in the House asking for a committee to conduct a thorough investigation of tax-exempt foundations.

Congressman Cox said that some of the great foundations, "had operated in the field of social reform and international relations (and) many have brought down on themsleves harsh and just condemnation."

He named the Rockefeller Foundation, "whose funds have been used to finance individuals and organizations whose business it has been to get communism into the private and public schools of the country, to talk down America and to play up Russia."

He cited the Guggenheim foundation, whose money, "was used to spread radicalism throughout the country to an extent not excelled by any other foundation."

He listed the Carnegie Corporation, the Rosenwald Fund, and other foundations, saying:

"There are disquieting evidences that at least a few of the foundations have permitted themselves to be infiltrated by men and women who are disloyal to our American way of life. They should be investigated and exposed to the pitiless light of publicity, and appropriate legislation should be framed to correct the present situation."

Congressman Cox's resolution, proposing an investigation of foundations, died in Committee.

On March 10, 1952, Cox introduced the same resolution again. Because he had mentioned foundation support for Langston Hughes, a Negro communist, Congressman Cox was accused of racial prejudice. Because he had criticized the Rosenwald Fund for making grants to known communists, he was called anti-semitic. But the Cox resolution was adopted in 1952; and the Cox committee to investigate tax-exempt foundations was set up.

Congressman Cox died before the end of the year; and the final report of his committee (filed January 1, 1953) was a pathetic whitewash of the whole subject.

A republican controlled Congress (the 83rd) came into existence in January, 1953.

On April 23, 1953, Congressman Carroll Reece (Republican, Tennessee) introduced a resolution proposing a committee to carry on the "unfinished business" of the late Cox Committee. The new committee to investigate tax-exempt foundations (popularly known as the Reece Committee) was approved by Congress on July 27, 1953. It went out of existence on January 3, 1955, having proven, mainly, that the mammoth tax-exempt foundations have such power in the White House, in Congress, and in the press that they are quite beyond the reach of a mere committee of the Congress of the United States.

---

Rene A. Wormser, after serving as counsel to the Reece Committee, wrote a book on the subject with which he had become so well acquainted: *Foundations: Their Power and Influence*. One chapter from this book must be included in the record.

## Foundations and Radicalism in Education

### RENE A. WORMSER

### The Control of Education by Foundations

A very powerful complex of foundations and allied organizations has developed over the years to exercise a high degree of control over education. Part of this complex, and ultimately responsible for it, are the Rockefeller and Carnegie groups of foundations. The largest of the foundation giants, The Ford Foundations, is a late comer. It has now joined in the complex and its impact is tremendous; but the operations of the Carnegie and Rockefeller groups start way back.

There is little question that the initial efforts of the Carnegie and Rockefeller foundations in the field of education produced substantial and salutary results. Certainly the standards of our institutions of higher learning were materially improved as a result of the early work of these foundations. Yet the Reece Committee questioned whether their actions were wholly commendable. The reason for this doubt was that coercive methods were used.

Dr. Ernest Victor Hollis, now Chief of College Administration in the United States Office of Education, once explained the background of this coercive approach as follows:

". . . Unfavorable public estimate of the elder Rockefeller and Andrew Carnegie, made it inexpedient in 1905 for their newly created philanthropic foundations to attempt any direct reforms in higher education."

The method used, therefore, he said, was one of indirection—"indirectly through general and non-controversial purposes." "For instance," said Dr. Hollis, "there is little connection between giving a pension to a college professor or giving a sum to the general endowment of his college, and reforming entrance requirements, the financial practices, and the scholastic standards of his institution." Yet one was tied to the other. It was a case of conform, or no grant! When to conform meant bathing in a stream of millions, college and university administrators and their faculties were inclined to conform.

About this type of coercion the Committee report said:

"We question, however, whether foundations should have the

power even to do good in the coercive manner which was employed. We cannot repeat too often that power in itself is dangerous. What may have been used for a benign purpose could in the future be used for the promotion of purposes against the interests of the people. It does not write off this danger to say that good men ran the foundations. It is power which is dangerous—power uncontrolled by public responsibility."

Merely to recognize the satisfactory results of benign coercion, to point to the highly desirable academic reforms for which this coercion was responsible, is not enough. Such a mistake was made by those who lauded the internal reforms of fascism in Italy and ignored the cost in freedom and liberty. Power is in itself dangerous. When we make it possible for financial power to exercise substantial control over education, we endanger our welfare. Perhaps the risk is worth taking in order to preserve freedom of action to foundations. But we should be conscious of the risk, and alert to what transpires. The Walsh Committee had heard witnesses testify to the fact that colleges had abandoned their religious affiliations in or before 1915 to conform to requirements established by foundations! Today, school policymakers anticipate the idiosyncrasies and preferences of foundation officials in a manner similarly producing conformity.

Consider what the Ford Foundation could do with its billions of capital. It could use this monumental fund to promote whatever educational theories a Dr. Hutchins of the moment were to persuade the trustees to support. Nor need it be difficult for such promotion to succeed. The country is full of colleges and universities starving for endowment. The number of miserably paid academicians is legion. Professors have to eat; and universities have to pay their janitors. While it is possible that the majority of academicians and administrators would resist, their aggregate voices would not be as powerful as those of a minority of academicians subsidized in the publication of their writings, and a minority of administrators whose institutions flowered financially. How difficult to resist if pressure for change in educational concepts were accompanied by a persuasive flow of hundreds of millions, or even billions!

There is much evidence that, to a substantial degree, foundations have become the directors of education in the United States. To what extent this has been brought about by conditions attached to financial support since the early activities of the Carnegie and Rockefeller foundations, it is difficult to assess. We do know that their first efforts to reform the colleges were only a beginning.

Accrediting organizations and other instruments in the form of civic, professional, and school associations were created or supported to implement the reform plans of these two foundation groups. The American Council on Education became their major executive agency. Other clearing-house organizations, operating variously in higher, secondary, and primary education, and later in the field of "adult education," received heavy support. Among them were The National Education Association and associated groups, The Progressive Education Association, The John Dewey Society, The National Council on Parent Education, and the American Youth Commission.

While the results of the first phase of foundation operations in education were entirely beneficial, that cannot be said of later stages. Together with an enormous amount of benefit, the foundations were responsible, as well, for much that has had a decidedly deleterious effect upon our society.

Research and experimental stations were established at selected universities, notably Columbia, Stanford, and Chicago. Here some of the worst mischief in recent education was born. In these Rockefeller-and-Carnegie-established vineyards worked many of the principal characters in the story of the suborning of American education. Here foundations nurtured some of the most ardent academic advocates of upsetting the American system and supplanting it with a Socialist state.

## The Birth of Educational Radicalism

Whatever its earlier origins or manifestations, there is little doubt that the radical movement in education was accelerated by an organized Socialist movement in the United States. In 1905 The Intercollegiate Socialist Society was created under the direction of Jack London, Upton Sinclair, and others for the active promotion of socialism. It established branches in many major colleges and universities, where leaders were developed who were to have considerable future influence; among them were Bruce Bliven, Freda Kirchwey, (Senator) Paul Douglas, Kenneth Macgowan, Isador Lubin, Evans Clark, and John Temple Graves, Jr.  Robert Morss

Lovett, a man with a total of 56 Communist-front affiliations, became the first president of the Society. Stuart Chase, selected by The Social Science Research Council to write the showpiece on the achievements of social scientists, was an early writer for this organization. This Society was no transient organization. It still exists and operates today as a tax-exempt foundation, having changed its name some years ago to The League for Industrial Democracy.

The movement generated or accelerated by the League was likened to the Fabian Socialist movement in England by Mr. Aaron Sargent, one of the witnesses before the Reece Committee. Mr. Sargent is a lawyer who has had considerable experience in special investigations and research in education and subversion. He had been a consultant to the Senate Internal Security Committee in 1952 and represented patriotic organizations in numerous public hearings concerned with educational and other tax-exempt activities. At the Reece hearings, Mr. Sargent cited *Fabianism in Great Britain,* a book by Sister Margaret Patricia McCarran, daughter of the late Senator McCarran, in which she described the gradual extension of influence of the Fabian idea. Mr. Sargent called the Socialist movement in America, that propelled by The Intercollegiate Socialist Society, an offspring of the Fabian movement.

The American movement seized upon some of the teachings of John Dewey, who, as Mr. Sargent put it,

> expounded a principle which has become destructive of traditions and has created the difficulties and the confusion, much of it, that we find today. Professor Dewey denied that there was any such thing as absolute truth, that everything was relative, everything was doubtful, that there were no basic values and nothing which was specifically true.

Mr. Sargent added that, with this philosophy,

> . . . you automatically wipe the slate clean, you throw historical experience and background to the wind and you begin all over again, which is just exactly what the Marxians want someone to do.

This rejection of tradition carried with it an undermining of the doctrine of inalienable rights and the theory of natural law which underlie our system of government. It has become intrinsic in the "liberal" philosophy which assumed the Dewey point of view that, while there may be fundamental rights which are sacred, they are subject to constant review. In any event, proceeds this approach, some are not as sacred as others, whether or not they may be listed together in the Declaration of Independence and the original Constitution or its amendments. Certainly these "liberals" believe that the right to private property is only a second-class right, or maybe third-class.

Mr. Sargent very persuasively told the story of the growth of the radical movement in education. The Dewey philosophy took hold just about the time John D. Rockefeller established his first foundation, The General Education Board, in 1902. The era was one of reform agitation, and there is no doubt that much reform was needed in various directions. But the moderate and sensible reformers of the era were very often overwhelmed, and to some extent seduced, by a small army of Socialists, crypto-Socialists, and collectivists who took advantage of the necessary reform movement to propel their own radical philosophies and theories of government. These found grist for their mills in the teachings of John Dewey. As Mr. Sargent said, they took advantage "of the existing discontent to make considerable inroads in academic fields."

The National Education Association became enamored early of the Dewey philosophy. It was at Columbia University, however, the institution in which Professor Dewey taught so long, that perhaps the greatest strides were made in applying this philosophy to teaching. In 1916 the Department of Educational Research was established in Teachers College (part of Columbia University). This department was responsible for the creation of The Lincoln School in 1917, which, to use the words of a Teachers College pamphlet, "kindled the fire which helped to spread progressive education."

The same pamphlet noted that John D. Rockefeller, through The International Education Board, donated $100,000 to establish an International Institute at Teachers College. It noted as well that a Dr. George S. Counts had been made associate Director of the Institute, and Dr. Counts became one of the leading radicals in education.

The growing radicalism which was beginning rapidly to permeate academic circles was no grass-roots movement. Mr. Sargent cited a statement by Professor Ludwig Von Mises that socialism does not spring from the masses but is instigated by intellectuals "that form themselves into a clique and bore from within and operate that way. . . . It is not a people's movement at all. It is a capitalization on the people's emotions and sympathies toward a point these people wish to reach."

### Carnegie Finances a Socialist Charter for Education

"Mr. Sargent gave convincing evidence that efforts to use the schools to bring us to a new order, collectivist in nature, followed a plan and that this plan was supported by foundation money. He cited the *Conclusions and Recommendations* of the Commission on Social Studies of The American Historical Association. The American Historical Association is the professional association of historians and as such one of the organizations participating in The Social Science Research Council. The work of its Commission was financed by The Carnegie Corporation to the extent of $340,-000. The *Conclusions* was the last section of the Commission's final report, produced in 1934. It had an enormous and lasting impact upon education in our country.

The *Conclusions* heralds the decline of capitalism in the United States. It does not oppose the movement for radical change. It accepts it as inevitable:

> Cumulative evidence supports the conclusion, that, in the United States as in other countries, the age of individualism and laissez faire in economy and government is closing and that a *new age of collectivism* is emerging. (Emphasis supplied.)

But that is not all. It continues:

> As to the specific form which this "collectivism," this integration and interdependence, is taking and will take in the future, the evidence at hand is by no means clear or unequivocal. It may involve the limiting or supplanting of private property by public property or it may entail the preservation of private property, extended and distributed among the masses. Most likely, it will issue from a process of experimentation and will represent a composite of historic doctrines and social conceptions yet to appear. Almost certainly it will involve a larger measure of compulsory as well as voluntary cooperation of citizens in the conduct of the complex national economy, a corresponding enlargement of the functions of government, and an increasing state intervention in fundamental branches of economy previously left to the individual discretion and initiative—a state intervention that in some instances may be direct and mandatory and in others indirect and facilitative. In any event the Commission is convinced *by its interpretation of available empirical data* that the actually integrating economy of the present

day is the forerunner of a consciously integrated society in which individual economic actions and individual property rights will be altered and abridged. (Emphasis supplied.)

\* \* \*

The emerging age is particularly an age of transition. It is marked by numerous and severe tensions arising out of the conflict between the actual trend toward integrated economy and society, on the one side, and the traditional practices, dispositions, ideas and institutional arrangements inherited from the *passing age of individualism,* on the other. In all the recommendations that follow, the transitional character of the present epoch is recognized. (Emphasis supplied.)

\* \* \*

Underlying and illustrative of these tensions are privation in the midst of plenty, violations of fiduciary trust, gross inequalities in income and wealth, widespread racketeering and banditry, wasteful use of natural resources, unbalanced distribution and organization of labor and leisure, the harnessing of science to individualism in business enterprise, the artificiality of political boundaries and divisions, the subjection of public welfare to the egoism of private interests, the maladjustment of production and consumption, persistent tendencies toward economic instability, disproportionate growth of debt and property claims in relation to production, deliberate destruction of goods and withdrawal of efficiency from production, accelerating tempo of panics, crises, and depressions attended by ever-wider destruction of capital and demoralization of labor, struggles among nations for markets and raw materials leading to international conflicts and wars.

The report of the Commission proceeds to say that we must make an "adjustment" between "social thought, social practice, and economic realities" or "sink back" into a *primitive* form of life. This adjustment must be made, apparently, in some collectivist manner, for the report, continuing, says that there are many varied theories to use, "involving wide differences in modes of *distributing* wealth, income and cultural opportunities." I have italicized the verb "distributing," which forcefully disclosed the collectivist, planned economy objectives of the authors of the report.

But no inferences regarding their intention are needed. They were utterly frank in their recommendations. Teachers must "free the school from the domination of special interests and convert it into a truly enlightened force in society." And the "board of education" must have as its objective *"to support a school program conceived in terms of the general welfare and adjusted to the needs of an epoch marked by transition to some form of socialized econ-*

*omy."* The Commission then discusses "the lines along which attacks can and will be made on the problem of applying its conclusions with respect to instruction in the social sciences." And the "pay-off":

> As often repeated, the first step is to awaken and consolidate leadership around the philosophy and purpose of education herein expounded . . .

This was a call to the teachers in America to condition our children to an acceptance of a new order in process of transition. As to the nature of this intended order, there can be no doubt. Professor Harold J. Laski, philosopher of British socialism, said of the Commission's report:

> AT BOTTOM, AND STRIPPED OF ITS CAREFULLY NEUTRAL PHRASES, THE REPORT IS AN EDUCATIONAL PROGRAM FOR A SOCIALIST AMERICA.

Mr. Sargent's comment upon the report, produced by Carnegie Corporation money, is highly significant:

> What these gentlemen propose to do is set forth in their chapter at the end talking about next steps. It says that it is first to awaken and consolidate leadership around the philosophy and purpose of education expounded in the report. That *The American Historical Association* in cooperation with the *National Council on the Social Studies* has arranged to take over the magazine, *The Outlook,* as a social science journal for teachers. That writers of textbooks are to be expected to revamp and rewrite their old works in accordance with this frame of reference. That makers of programs in social sciences in cities and towns may be expected to evaluate the findings. That it is not too much to expect in the near future a decided shift in emphasis from mechanics and methodology to the content and function of courses in the social studies. That is the gist of it. This report became the basis for a definite slanting in the curriculum by selecting certain historical facts and by no longer presenting others. . . .

Did The Carnegie Corporation denounce or renounce this call for a socialization of America? Indeed no. Its 1933-1934 Annual Report said this:

> . . . Both the educational world and the public at large owe a debt of gratitude both to the Association for having sponsored this important and timely study in a field of peculiar difficulty, and to the distinguished men and women who served upon the Commission.

This reaction of The Carnegie Corporation is most astounding. In his statement to the Reece Committee, Mr. Charles Dollard, the president of this foundation, contended that the *Conclusions* and *Recommendations* of the Commission on the Social Sciences do "not advocate socialism." He said that what the authors were accepting was "not socialism. It was the New Deal." He attributes their attitude to widespread disillusionment concerning our economic system, prevalent during the years of depression. He makes the further apology that once the funds had been granted, the Foundation did not have "the power to censor or rewrite the works produced under its grants." He takes the position that "works will be supported by corporation (foundation) grants containing views that differ from those held by trustees and officers."

Mr. Dollard does not explain the commendatory remarks of the Carnegie foundation after the publication of the last volume of the Commission's report. Nor does he convincingly absolve the foundation from responsibility for the Commission's work. The grant was not one for scientific research, but one essentially for the development of new principles in education. As such, it supported the formulation of a philosophical value system, based on a priori assumptions of goals of education and desirable forms of government and social organization. Such a system might well be supported by reference to facts in the manner in which Aristotle's *Rhetorik* advises the use of facts for the end of persuasion. But the basing of principles on a priori value concepts is meta-scientific. The work of the Commission was not a scientific search but an effort to persuade America in favor of a new ideal in public life and in education. The support of this project was essentially political.

Mr. Dollard's emphatic denial of the partisan-Socialistic character of the *Conclusions* and *Recommendations* of the Commission could mislead only those who had not read the work itself. He may attempt to identify the concepts of society contained in it as "New Deal," and it is true that some of the Socialist convictions disseminated by the document were shared by the fathers of the New Deal. But the overlapping of the Socialist ideas of the Commission with the New Deal did not absolve the financial supporters of responsibility for this political undertaking. It is clearly desirable that foundations abstain from tampering with scientific research once a grant has been made to an unpolitical scientific organization. When, however, foundation money is offered for a program of a politico-social nature, responsibility for its impact on society cannot be dodged by a semantic manipulation of terms such as "socialism" and "New Deal" or any other political deal.

There was consistency in the position of Mr. Dollard in defending the Commission's work, in supporting the selection of Stuart Chase and of Dr. Myrdal, and in supporting *The Encyclopedia of the Social Sciences* after its bias became well known. It seems fair to conclude that this consistency had at its base a sympathy for the political objectives which these activities furthered.

One may wonder how it came about that foundations such as Carnegie and Rockefeller, controlled by trustees whose membership was overwhelmingly conservative, could lend themselves to the radical movement in education. One answer I have already given: they left decisions far too often to subordinate employees and to intermediary organizations. Another is that they were totally unaware of the pitfalls in the projects which they financed. Foundation apologists explain it differently. They say that these foundations made grants to respectable organizations and for respectable purposes; having done so, they were obliged to keep their hands off; therefore, they cannot be held accountable for what was produced.

This justification of foundation trustees cannot be accepted by reasonable persons. As I have pointed out, there is an obligation to make sure that objectivity would accompany the operation of a proposed grant. What is equally important—*there is an obligation to examine the product and, if it is found to lack objectivity, to take means to protect the public against its effects.*

The trustees of The Carnegie Corporation were acting in a field in which they had only limited competence when they authorized the heavy grant which produced the report of the *Commission on Social Studies.* Granting, for the sake of argument, that they had the right, nevertheless, to take what risks to society were involved, their failure to repudiate the result was a dereliction of duty. Upon learning that this product was "an educational program for a Socialist America," they might have offset whatever negligence or incompetence was connected with the creation of the project, by organizing another project, with at least equal financing, to be made by a group of eminent educators who believed that our governmental and economic system was worthy of preservation and that the schools should not be used as political propaganda machines.

## The Radical Educators

The report of the Reece Committee referred to numbers of the educational elite who supported and followed the plan laid down by the Carnegie-financed Commission on Social Studies. They were all, in various ways, connected with the educational complex supported by the millions of the Rockefeller, Carnegie, and other foundations.

Among the favorites of this foundation-supported radical movement in education was Professor George S. Counts, a leader in the project to use the schools to reform our political and social order. A pamphlet entitled "A Call to the Teachers of the Nation," published by The Progressive Education Association, a tax-exempt organization largely supported by major foundations, was prepared by a committee of which Dr. Counts was Chairman. It included this "call":

> The progressive minded teachers of the country must unite in a powerful organization militantly devoted to the building of a better social order, in the defence of its members against the ignorance of the masses and the malevolence of the privileged. Such an organization would have to be equipped with the material resources, the talent, the legal talent, and the trained intelligence to wage successful war in the press, the courts, and the legislative chambers of the nation. To serve the teaching profession in this way should be one of the major purposes of the Progressive Education Association.

In one of his many radical books, *Dare the School Build a New Social Order* (John Day Company, 1943), Professor Counts said:

> That the teachers should deliberately reach for power and then make the most of their conquest is my firm conviction. To the extent that they are permitted to fashion the curriculum and the procedures of the school they will definitely and positively influence the social attitudes, ideals and behavior of the coming generation.

He continued, that a "major concern" of teachers should be "opposing and checking the forces of social conservatism and reaction."

Another professor of education named in the Committee's Report is Professor Theodore Brameld of New York University, who minced no words in an article in *Science and Society:*

> The thesis of this article is simply that liberal educators who look toward collectivism as a way out of our economic, political and cul-

tural morass must give more serious consideration than they have thus far to the methodology of Marx. . . .

Professor Brameld, along with Dr. Gunnar Myrdal, was among those "experts" cited by the Supreme Court in the *Brown v. Board of Education* segregation decision. These are strange authorities for the Supreme Court to rely upon. That many men such as these (politicians in educators' clothing) have achieved such prominence may be laid closely at the door of foundation support.

Another of these "educators" gives us an idea of how close they come to totalitarianism. In an article in *The Progressive Education Magazine,* Professor Norman Woelfel wrote:

> It might be necessary paradoxically for us to control our press as the Russian press is controlled and as the Nazi press is controlled.

Professor Woelfel felt strongly that the elite in the social sciences should reform the world. His *Moulders of the American Mind* was dedicated to

> the teachers of America, active sharers in the building of attitudes, may they collectively choose a destiny which honors only productive labor and promotes the ascendency of the common man over the forces that make possible an economy of plenty.

And, like so many of his kind, he is against tradition and against codes of morality. He wrote:

> The younger generation is on its own and the last thing that would interest modern youth is the salvaging of the Christian tradition. The environmental controls which technologists have achieved, and the operations by means of which workers earn their livelihood, need no aid or sanction from God nor any blessing from the church.

> \* \* \*

> In the minds of the men who think experimentally, America is conceived as having a destiny which bursts the all too obvious limitations of Christian religious sanctions and of capitalist profit economy.

Elsewhere he wrote:

> The call now is for the utmost capitalization of the discontent manifest among teachers for the benefit of revolutionary social goals. This means that all available energies of radically inclined leaders within the profession should be directed toward the building of a united radical front. Warm collectivistic sentiment and intelligent vision, propagated in clever and undisturbing manner by a few individual leaders no longer suits the occasion.

The educators of whom we speak were leaders in their field, prominent in the counsels of that most powerful organization of teachers, The National Education Association, which advertised itself as "THE ONLY ORGANIZATION THAT REPRESENTS OR HAS THE POSSIBILITY OF REPRESENTING THE GREAT BODY OF TEACHERS IN THE UNITED STATES."

## The Progressive Education Association

Quotations already given from publications of the Progressive Education Association will indicate its character. Had it been devoted entirely to improving educational methods, it might have served a worthy purpose in education. Its leaders, however, were devoted not only to new methods of teaching (many of these methods, found to be entirely impractical, have since been abandoned) but also to following the thesis of the Commission on Social Studies that educators must use the schools to indoctrinate youth into an acceptance of collectivism. Its periodical, *The Social Frontier*, of October, 1934, stated in an editorial, that it "accepts the analysis of the current epoch—outlined—in *Conclusions* and *Recommendations*, Report on the Social Studies of the Commission of the American Historical Association."

Its sinews of war were supplied by foundations. Up to 1943, says the Reece Committee report, foundations had contributed $4,257,-800 to this Association. What the aggregate figure is to date, I do not know. During its long and intense career, the Progressive Education Association, which later changed its name to the American Education Fellowship, created an unenviable record of leftist propaganda. Its publications, called at various times *The Social Frontier, Frontiers of Democracy,* and *Progressive Education,* contain a long record of attempts to suborn our educational system to an acceptance of radicalism.

Typical is the issue of December 15, 1942, in which Professor Harold Rugg, of Teachers College, Columbia University, contributed a "call to arms." He announced the Battle for Consent. The "consent" was the consent of the people to change. His theory was simple. Education must be used to condition the people to accept social change. The social change was to be that, of course, espoused by Professor Rugg, involving a war against some of our most precious institutions.

## The Collectivist Textbooks

There were plenty of teachers ready to follow the lead of the American Historical Association's Commission on Social Studies, and their efforts extended into all aspects of education. New textbooks were required to take the place of the standard and objective works used in the schools. These new books could be used to indoctrinate the students, to give them the pathological view of their country upon which sentiment for collectivism could be built. The writer of a conservative or classic textbook has difficulty getting the funds to enable him to produce his work. At best he must rely on an advance from a publisher, and it is rarely that even a slim one might be forthcoming. In contrast, a foundation-supported textbook writer, as a rule, can apply a substantial part of his time, or all of it, to his writing. Moreover, the very fact of foundation support (or the support of an intermediary distributing organization) for his project, and the consequent inference of approval, will create a favorable climate of opinion for the acceptance of his work by schools. At least before the recent Congressional investigations, radical writers found it a simple matter to get foundation bounty. Under the influence of cliques in the world of teaching, the schools in the United States were flooded with books which disparaged the free-enterprise system and American traditions.

The notorious Rugg textbooks were of this class. They were prepared by Professor Harold Rugg, who began, in the Lincoln Experimental School, financed by Rockefeller foundations, to issue pamphlets which grew into this series of textbooks. Five million copies of the books were poured into American schools up to 1940—how many since, I do not know. They were finally banned from the schools in the State of California after a panel of competent men appointed by the San Francisco Board of Education unanimously held them reprehensible. One of the reasons given by this panel was that these books promoted the thesis that "it is one of the functions of the schools, indeed it appears at the time to be the chief function, to plan the future of society. From this view we emphatically dissent." The panel's report continued:

Moreover, the books contain a constant emphasis on our national defects. Certainly we should think it a great mistake to picture our nation as perfect or flawless either in its past or in its present, but it is our conviction that these books give a decidedly distorted impression through overstressing weaknesses and injustices. They therefore tend to weaken the student's love for his country, respect for its past and confidence in its future.

Mr. McKinnon, one of the panel, added that these books denied moral law; that Professor Rugg was trying to achieve "a social reconstruction through education"; and that they promoted change as apparently desirable in itself, and "experiment" in government, education, economics, and family life as of paramount importance. "Throughout the books," he said, "runs an antireligious bias."

Let us take a closer look at Professor Rugg. In his book *Great Technology,* Rugg, who had visited China the previous year on a mission to prepare a "social reconstruction and education" project for that country, said:

> Can independent ways of living be carried on any longer on an irresponsible competitive basis? Must not central public control be imposed on the warring, self-aggrandizing captains of industry? Can this control be set up with the *consent of a large minority of the people* quickly enough to forestall the imposition of dictatorship either by business leaders or by an outraged proletarian agriculture bloc, which seems imminent?

He asked these questions not about China but about the United States!

Millions of textbooks written by this man were used, at one time, in our country. In his *Great Technology,* his *Social Chaos and the Public Mind,* and other works, he advocated social change. Following the *Recommendations* of the Carnegie-financed Commission on the Social Studies, he suggested that such change required the indoctrination of our youth through the schools. He recommended that social science be the "core of school curriculum" to bring about a climate of opinion favorable to his philosophy. Through the efforts of this and other followers of the *Recommendations,* and through the operation of the patronage network of Teachers College of Columbia University, the educational philosophy which Professor Rugg espoused soon pervaded the American school system. This philosophy involves:

> implementing an expectancy of change; picturing the America of today as a failure; disparaging the American Constitution and the motives of the Founders of the Republic; and presenting a "New Social Order."

Professor Rugg characteristically advocated production for use, not for profit (that old Socialist slogan) ; reconstruction of the national economic system to provide for central controls, to guarantee a stable and a high minimum living for all; division of the social income, so as to guarantee at least a ten times 1929 minimum for all; measuring wages by some yardstick of purchasing power, reeducation of the "parasitic" middleman in our economy and his reassignment to productive work; recognition that educators are a group "vastly superior to that of a priesthood or of any other selected social class." "Our task," he said, was "to create swiftly a compact body of minority opinion for the scientific reconstruction of our social order. This body of opinion must be made articulate and be brought to bear insistently upon the dictators of legislative and executive action. The alternative to this extension of democracy is revolution."

In 1941 Professor Rugg denied vehemently that he was a Socialist or that he had ever been one. However, in 1936 he had been a member of a committee of 500 supporting the Socialist candidacy of Norman Thomas. He was a director of The League for Industrial Democracy in 1934-1935. But no collateral evidence of his political position is necessary to disclose his Socialistic point of view. He has stated it himself in his numerous writings. His employment of the Socialist plank "production for use, not for profit" is quite enough to identify him.

A group of "liberal" educators defended the Rugg textbooks. Prominent among these was Professor Robert S. Lynd, a former permanent secretary of The Social Science Research Council, himself an advocate of change toward socialism. Professor Rugg was also defended by a number of members of the Committee on Textbooks of the American Committee for Democracy and Intellectual Freedom.

The money for Professor Rugg's six textbooks came indirectly from Rockefeller foundation grants to the Lincoln School and Teachers College. While foundations approached in 1922 had refused direct support of the pamphlets, Professor Rugg reports that preliminary estimates set the amount of money required at a sum far beyond that which the Lincoln School or Teachers College could be asked to supply. They did, however, support the project in other and altogether indispensable ways. In fact, if they had not given it an institutional connection and a home, no such un-

dertaking could have been started. Even their financial contribution, however, was considerable. It consisted of the writer's
salary as educational psychologist in the school (1920-1929) and
as professor of education in the college, the salary of his secretary
(1920-1930), and an allowance for a part-time assistant during
several years.

Mr. Aaron Sargent also testified in detail regarding the *Building
America* textbook series, which the Reece Committee report characterized as another "attempt by radical educators financed by
foundations to suborn the schools." It was The General Education Board, a Rockefeller foundation, which provided over $50,000
for the production of these books, taken over and intensively promoted by The National Education Association.

The State of California barred these books also from its schools,
after a legislative committee, the Dilworth Committee, investigated
and concluded in its report that they were subtle attempts to play
up Marxism and to destroy our traditions.

Mr. Sargent pointed out that there had been a "blackout" in
history teaching in California for about twelve years; during this
time no history textbooks were provided by the Department of
Education, which was operating under the radical-devised scheme
of "social studies." After an investigation, history books were again
furnished, as the law required. In the meantime, the *Building
America* books largely took their place, giving children distorted
facts and consciously directed misinformation regarding our history and our society.

The report of the Dilworth Committee, as a result of which the
California Legislature refused any appropriation for the purchase
of *Building America* textbooks, concluded that these books do "not
present a true historical background of American history and progress, and that the cartoons and pictures appearing in said books
belittle American statesmen, who have been upheld as heroes of
American tradition and have been idealized by the American people; yet on the other hand the 'Building America' series glam-
orizes Russian statesmen and (is) replete with pictures which do
great credit to these leaders of Russian thought." The report goes
on to say that the "books contain purposely distorted references
favoring Communism, and life in Soviet Russia, in preference to
the life led by Americans."

In this regard, the Committee felt that pictures representing conditions of starvation among American families hardly presented a true picture of family life in America. When children in the 7th and 8th grades, the Committee said, compare such pictures with the illustrations of Russian family life, they will conclude that family life in Russia is "equal or even preferable to that in the United States." It was found that the "books paint present economic and social conditions in America in unfavorable light and have the opportunity to propagandize class warfare and class distinction." It was concluded, further, that the texts present a materialistic picture of government and economy in America and in the world rather than the idealism of the American way of life. Specific criticism was made of the reference books listed in the *Building America* pamphlets as guides to additional information. These recommended books were found to be highly biased and likely to indoctrinate pupils in a manner contrary to the best traditions of America.

The editors and authors of the *Building America* series were careful enough to present both sides of various problems and questions. This was done, however, in most instances, in a manner strongly indicating editorial bias in favor of Socialist measures and ideas, a preference emphasized by the editors who selected the illustrations. The pictures were likely to impress children even more than the text itself and were selected clearly to arouse doubts about American institutions and American historical figures.

The pamphlet about Russia contains numerous propaganda pictures from Soviet information sources. The "objectivity" of the authors may be illustrated by their statement: "The Russians like our system of government no better than we like theirs." This implies that there is much to be said on both sides. It also assumes an absurdity—that the suppressed Russians, unable to speak their minds, favor the system which has been imposed on them.

The Bolshevik revolution and regime are presented as a blessing to the Russian people. In the description of the long road which led to communism, there is not one word of fact or criticism regarding the murderous Red terror of 1917 and 1918, or the treachery of communism in destroying the hopes of Russia's democratic revolutionaries. Conditions in Russia are presented wholly in terms of Soviet apology. There is a chapter on making the State safe for socialism, including this: "Probably no other nation ever made such rapid strides in extending educational opportunities for the people." The depicted image of social progress contains no word of reference to the obliteration of freedom, to the concentration camps, to the purges and to the worldwide, Moscow-directed subversive activities.

Pictures of everyday Soviet life present scenes in a church, in art galleries, in concert halls, and at a meeting of a Soviet "trade union"—the whole gamut of Red propaganda of the period. "As more consumer goods were produced and the scheme for buying and selling improved," it said, the wants of consumers were more satisfied. There is no mention, however, of the actual tragic dearth of consumer goods, even before the German attack; there is nowhere a picture of the privation of the Russian people under communism.

Nor is this all. Fearful lest statements by outsiders might disillusion the child readers of these books about Russia, the authors are careful to prepare a defense. "*Some* writers mention *some* use of force by the government to attain its ends." (I have emphasized the double use of "some.") Yes, *some* writers mention a denial of the right to strike or protest; secret police; the absolute power of one man over the lives of the people; and the lack of any civil liberties in the American sense of the word—but the authors imply that there is another sense, a Soviet sense of civil liberties. The Russians, say the authors, have more self-government than they ever had before; *the new Russians* call their dictatorship the "democracy" of the working classes; there is no more discrimination against certain races and creeds; etc. etc. etc. The authors have the effrontery to say that "rights that mean so much to Americans —freedom of assembly and the press—are little missed in Russia . . . to them (the Russians) the new leadership is better than the old." They indicate also that, though it does not appeal to Americans, the Russian system is here to stay.

The Dilworth report said of the book on China: "This book is peculiarly useful to the Communists as a medium to further disseminate the current party line concerning conditions in China." The pamphlet on civil liberties contains pictures of Sacco and Vanzetti, of the Scopes trial, of Browder, of the Scottsboro Negroes, of strike riots being subdued. The whole collection, in spite of its pretended objectivity, is loaded with "liberal" propaganda. It is a reminder of the "Aesopian" language used by Communists in their communication system.

It is difficult to believe that The Rockefeller Foundation and the National Education Association could have supported these textbooks. But the fact is that Rockefeller financed them and the NEA promoted them very widely. They were still in use in some parts of the country at the time of the Reece Committee investigation.

Another foundation-supported piece of "education" literature is a pamphlet entitled "The American Way of Business." It was one of a series prepared by the National Association of Secondary School Principals and the National Council for Social Studies, both branches of the National Education Association, under a grant from the Rockefeller General Education Board, to provide teachers with source material on some social problems. Who wrote it? Oscar Lange and Abba P. Lerner. Mr. Lange will be remembered as the professor at the University of Chicago, when Dr. Hutchins was its president, who later renounced his American citizenship to accept appointment as the ambassador to the United Nations from Communist Poland. Mr. Lerner has been a collectivist for a long time.

This book gives our children such ideas as these:

Public enterprise must become a major constituent of our economy, if we are really going to have economic prosperity.

*     *     *

It is necessary to have public ownership of banking and credit (investment banks and insurance companies).

*     *     *

. . . it is necessary to have public ownership of monopolistic key industries.

*     *     *

It is necessary to have public ownership of basic natural resources (mines, oil fields, timber, coal, etc.) .

*     *     *

. . . in order to insure that the public corporations act in accordance with the competitive "rules of the game," a special economic court (enjoying the same independence as the courts of justice) might be established . . . and that the economic court be given the power to repeal any rules of Congress, of legislatures, or of the municipal councils . . .

These texts, financed by The Rockefeller Foundation and distributed by the National Education Association, must have influenced the thinking of hundreds of thousands of defenseless young

Americans. They may well have contributed to the recent philosophy of reckless public spending and overgrowth of government.

These books I have mentioned are but a few examples of what has happened to teaching materials in our schools and colleges. Professor E. Merrill Root gives a quick survey of this development in his *Collectivism on the Campus,* in which he includes a chapter entitled, "The State Liberals: Their Textbooks." The rise of communism he says, has produced a strange result among the textbook writers. Conservatism is not even given house room. Communism is disliked, but the only alternative offered is "some such appeasement as welfarism or Fabian socialism." He quotes Professor David McCord Wright of McGill University:

> What sometimes happens, for instance, in economics courses, is that the Marxian indictment is presented, followed by some sort of "social-democratic" or heavily interventionist answer, and that the capitalist case never gets heard at all.

The vast majority of textbooks now used in colleges and schools on subjects in which a political slant could be given are heavily slanted to the left. This was demonstrated by Professor A. H. Hobbs of the University of Pennsylvania, whose work in disclosing some of the vices and foibles of modern sociology earned for him martyrdom in his career. In his analysis of a great number of sociology textbooks in his book *The Claims of Sociology: A Critique of Textbooks,* he found (p. 157):

> Inclusion of a chapter on social change is an integral part of the system of sociology textbooks. Such chapters . . . are designed to leave students with favorable final impressions about the subject. After depressing the student with portrayals of the amount of unemployment, poverty, crime, vice and slums; after shocking him with descriptions of the insidious war propaganda and the horrors of war; after creating in him qualms about the amount of social disorganization and raising him to rebellion against the "dead hand of the past" upon society, the author of contemporary texts must assuage him. Mitigation of the depressive effects of horrendous description of social evils is attained in a chapter which is "constructive," "optimistic," "positive," and "looking-beyond-social-defects-of-the-present-toward-a-bright-future-which-we-can-make-for-ourselves" in outlook.

In seventy out of eighty-three texts, Dr. Hobbs found sections devoted to social change. "There is agreement that traditions, conventions, and social inertia are the principal obstacles to social progress. . . . Authors in sociology texts increasingly emphasize economic security as a fundamental social value and the principal goal toward which social change should be focused." Twenty-seven textbook authors call for the use of the social sciences in a program of social planning. As used in these texts, the term "planning" or "social engineering" involves control of social processes by long-range subjection of society to guidance by social scientists.

Dr. Hobbs formulates the attitudes of the majority of the sociology textbooks currently in use with these words:

> Educational practices and principles which involve discipline or drill, and the teaching of traditional beliefs about the government, the family, or the economic system are inefficient and harmful. These should be replaced by including educational programs which will train students to think for themselves and to behave only in accordance with self-derived principles of "rationality." Independent thinking will emancipate student personalities from the stultifying effects of traditional beliefs and enable them to adjust to existing social situations and to promote social change.
>
> Democracy is highly desirable but the present form of government is not democratic, principally because business interests exert too much control over it . . . Increased government control over business and industry is the most important step toward attainment of the political ends, but such controls constitute only one phase of broader social planning.
>
> Maldistribution of wealth and income and unemployment are the outstanding characteristics of our social system.

It is no wonder that some of our citizens, facing the political character of so much of what purports to be sociological teaching, have difficulty distinguishing among the terms "sociology," "the social sciences," and "socialism."

## Reference Works

To both teacher and student, reference works are important instruments in the educational process. We have already seen that the all-important *Encyclopedia of the Social Sciences,* created under foundation financing, was heavily slanted toward radicalism. Let us look at another reference work, *The Encyclopedia Americana.*

Financed by The Rockefeller Foundation, both Columbia University and Cornell University established courses described as an

"Intensive Study of Contemporary Russian Civilization." It was chiefly to the staffs of these projects that the editors of *The Encyclopedia Americana* turned to write its section on Soviet Russia. A *dramatis personae* of this venture included such deeply biased workers as these:

> Sir Bernard Pares (who opposed American help to Greece and Turkey and supported the claim of Soviet Russia to Constantinople);
>
> Corliss Lamont (whose record of procommunism needs no elaboration);
>
> Harriet L. Moore (named by Louis Budenz as a member of the Communist Party);
>
> Vladimir D. Kazakevich (one of the editors of *Science and Society*, a Marxist quarterly; a frequent contributor to *Soviet Russia*, a pro-Communist publication. Mr. Kazakevich left the United States in 1949 after exposure as a Soviet agent)

and others of very doubtful objectivity.

When the work was completed, Cornell University was so pleased with it that, with the permission of the *Encyclopedia*, it converted the Russian section into a textbook, *USSR*, which was used at Cornell until 1954. In the meantime, many other colleges and universities had adopted it, including Columbia, Rutgers, Swarthmore, Chicago, Pennsylvania, Michigan, Southern California, Washington, and Yale.

At least 15 out of 20 contributors were, according to Professor Warren S. Walsh of Syracuse University, "pro-Soviet in varying degrees." About one third of the material in *USSR* was prepared by Mr. Kazakevich. That he could have been selected for this work was truly amazing. Professor E. Merrill Root, in his *Collectivism on the Campus* quotes these words from Mr. Kazakevich, appearing on February 27, 1940, *Russky Golos:*

> The crocodiles of imperialism will continue to swallow everything they get. For the neutral countries today the English crocodile is more dangerous than the German one. In order to prevent the lawlessness of this crocodile, you've got to drive a pole into the back of its neck.

Professor Root continues, "Perhaps this chaste language seemed scholarly to the scholars of Cornell, for they invited Kazakevich to lecture on the campus during the summer. His lectures became a part of *The Encyclopedia Americana* (as he was an "expert in a special field") and of *USSR.*

Professor Roman Smal-Stocki of Marquette University has said of *USSR* that it is justly a "fellow-traveling guide to the Soviet Union."

It may, of course, be true that The Rockefeller Foundation bears no direct responsibility for what was produced. Perhaps the projects which it financed were wholly desirable. Perhaps it was entirely the fault of Columbia and Cornell Universities that a strange collection of radicals and pro-Communists were included on the staffs of the Russian projects, and the fault of Cornell that it did not recognize or become concerned over the biased nature of the book which it published. But the fact remains that it all came about through Rockefeller financing. If this is in the nature of that "risk taking" which many foundation executives maintain is the duty of the modern foundation, something is badly wrong, somewhere.

I ask again: is it not the duty of a foundation which takes such risks to examine the results and to repudiate them if they have been unfortunate? As far as I know, The Rockefeller Foundation has done nothing to inform the public that it is not in sympathy with what its financing produced in this instance or in any other. Here, indeed, is a strange situation. Foundations consider themselves entitled to take credit for the outcome of a grant, the results of which are socially approved. On the other hand, when the grant has failed, or if its product meets with disapprobation, or is seriously questionable, then responsibility is shifted to the recipient of the grant. This is an odd interpretation of the "venture capital" concept. "We are entitled to take political 'risks' with the tax-exempt money we administer," say foundation managers. "If the project turns out safely, it is to our credit; if the risk turns out to have been too great, or if the result is an unhappy one, that is not our fault and we have no responsibility either to inform the public of the error or to take any steps to correct the injury done."

## The Citizens Education Project

The Citizens Education Project was created at Teachers College of Columbia University under financing, far exceeding one million dollars, provided by The Carnegie Corporation. "That the *Project* was carried on with considerable bias to the left is unquestionable." There arises, then, the question of responsibility. The Committee report stated that it was unable, without further inquiry, to determine whether this was the fault or the intention of either the Project managers or of the Carnegie foundation. It continued its comment, however, as follows:

> We do, however, see responsibility lodged with *The Carnegie Corporation*. It may not have had the duty to supervise the project or to direct it in transit—this may even have been unwise. But, as the project represented a substantial investment of public money and its impact on society could be very heavy, it seems clearly to have been the duty of *Carnegie* to examine what had been done and to repudiate it if it was against the public interest. This, as far as we know, *Carnegie* did not do.

What was the objective of this Project? To educate for better citizenship. How was this to be accomplished? One of its chief products was a card-index file. The cards summarized books, articles, films, etc., being arranged topically so that teachers could use the files in teaching citizenship. The files were sold to schools at nominal cost. In essence, this was "canned" material for teachers. The teacher did not have to read a book; he or she could just look in the card file and read a quick digest prepared by the Project. There is some doubt that this method of teaching through canned media is desirable. Granting that it might be, the greatest objectivity would have to be used in preparing the digests and comments on the cards, as well as in the selection of items to be included. As the Committee put it:

> . . . even those who believe in "canned" education cannot defend the slant with which this card system was devised, unless they believe that education should not be unbiased but should be directed toward selected political ends, and radical ones at that.

The Committee report gave several, out of many, examples of the radical slant. Books were included which could not be reasonably defended as proper for recommendation to school children—books by Communists and pro-Communists. Radical books were given approbation; conservative books were given the doubtful treatment. Let me give one illustration. *The Road to Serfdom,* by Frederick A. Hayek, a valuable commentary on the fallacies of socialism, is called "strongly opinionated." In contrast, the *Building America* textbooks, to which I have earlier referred, are described as "Factual, Ideals, and Concepts of Democracy."

Many conservative books of importance were not even listed. But *A Mask for Privilege* by Carey McWilliams was described as

"Historical, Descriptive." (Mr. McWilliams's record of Communist-front associations consume four pages of the Reece Committee report; 337 *et seq.*) *Rich Land, Poor Land* by Stuart Chase (whose collectivist position has been described earlier) was called "Descriptive, Factual, Illustrative." *Building for Peace at Home and Abroad* by Maxwell Stewart (whose Communist-front association consume about five pages of the Reece Committee report: P. 375 *et seq.*) was labeled "Factual, Dramatic." And Howard Fast's *The American* was called "Historical, Bibliographical." (Mr. Fast's Communist associations occupy four pages of the Committee report. He has since renounced the Party.)

## Several Sloan Foundation Projects

The Sloan Foundation, created in 1934, has had its regrettable moments. Its intention seems to have been to specialize in economic education and to seek truth through sound scholarship. But it supported the heavily left-slanted Chicago Round Table Broadcasts to the tune of $35,000 and the Public Affairs Pamphlets with $72,000. It supported a motion-picture-making program at New York University which concentrated on presenting the darkest image of the backward hinterlands of the South, possibly to arouse compassion but more likely for propaganda purposes. It deserves credit for having supported the sound economic teaching program of Harding College. Whether it merits credit for having contributed $19,000 to the Lincoln School at Columbia University is questionable.

The Public Affairs Committee was directed by Maxwell Stewart, a one-time editor of the Communist English-language newspaper, *Moscow News*. Several witnesses have called Mr. Stewart a Communist, but we do not know what his party allegiances were during his more than a decade of management of the Public Affairs pamphlets. They had a circulation of millions of copies among high-school and college students, among libraries, adult education groups, and government employees. Among the members of the board of directors of this publishing organization were such well-known "liberals" as Lyman Bryson, Luther Gulick, and Ordway Tead.

We find these names also: Frederick Vanderbilt Field, Mark Starr, and Harry W. Laidler, all of whom may be classed as extreme leftists. The presence of these names on the roster of any organization should have indicated to the Sloan trustees what the publishing venture was all about. Among the authors of the pamphlets we find Louis Adamic, James G. Patton, Maxwell Stewart, and E. C. Lindeman. Stewart wrote by far the largest number of the approximately one hundred pamphlets. The style of these books is reminiscent of the *Building America* textbooks. They show a pretense of objectivity, but in giving both sides of an issue they leave no doubt that they believe the left side is sound.

If my information is correct that The Sloan Foundation reorganized its management and deposed those who were responsible for its leftist orientation, there is ground for rejoicing and for hope that other foundations, whose trustees have lacked alertness in the past, may follow suit.

---

But the tragic story of what is happening to American education doesn't end with the foundations. The Federal government has had to get into the act; and through the yeoman efforts of our "frontier thinkers" and welfare-state-minded bureaucracies and members of Congress the question of Federal Aid to Education has become one of the hottest of the day. Mr. C. R. Petticrew, Vice President of the College Life Insurance Company of America, shows that Federal Aid is pure sham.

## The Sham of Federal Aid to Education

### C. R. PETTIGREW

The arguments for federal aid to education are few but persuasive. They appeal to the best that is in us—to our traditional spirit of fair play and help to the underdog; to our willingness to share our substance with those less fortunate; to our faith in education as a solution for most problems in human relationships.

The current crisis in our schools, brought about by the fabulous spurt in the birth rate since World War II, has reinvigorated the proponents of federal intervention and perhaps presented them with their best opportunity to date to secure such legislation. Consideration of the suggested programs leads to the conclusions that the goal sought cannot be reached, the need pictured is exaggerated, and the prescription proposed will kill the patient.

Advocates of this federal aid have stated that the White House

Conference on Education, held in Washington in December, 1955 " . . . concluded that federal aid is necessary and embodied an appropriate recommendation in its report to the President." The record, however, is clear that this Conference officially found that:

> No state represented has a demonstrated financial incapacity to build the schools it will need during the next five years.

What is the present national picture regarding classrooms? This same Conference on Education estimated the nation's public schools' need over the next five years at 375,000 classrooms. An estimated 67,000 will be built in 1957. At this current rate, 335,000 rooms, or 88 per cent of the total estimated need, would be built in five years. But in addition the rate of construction has been increasing from 60,000 in 1955 to 62,000 in 1956, and to the 1957 figure of 67,000. In four more years, without any federal aid, the rate may well increase enough to take up all the slack, even if the 375,000 were not an exaggeration.

As to the problem of catching up, from the fall of 1954 to the fall of 1955, enrollment increases raised classroom needs by 36,000 additional rooms. The nation built 60,000. The following year enrollment increase called for 36,000 to 40,000 additional rooms; 62,000 were built. Department of Commerce figures put the gain in public school construction from 1952 to 1956 at 61 per cent. In that same interval, all other public construction increased only 17 per cent.

Indiana is not the largest nor the smallest of states, not the richest nor the poorest. There the local communities and the state government have developed five ways to finance public schools:

a. Issue of bonds (up to 2 per cent of assessed valuation).

b. Use of a Cumulative Building Fund at the state level.

c. Use of private holding companies (selling bonds up to 10 per cent of assessed valuation).

d. Use of Common School Fund Commission.

e. Use of the State Veterans' Memorial School Construction Act.

In order that a community may be eligible for the use of the State Veterans' Memorial School Construction Act, it must be bonded up to 90 per cent of its bonding power and it must have levied a school tax of fifty cents per $100 of assessed valuation for at least three years.

By these methods, Indiana has brought its school building construction up 131 per cent from 1954 to 1956. (Enrollment went up only 10 per cent during the same period.) Indiana's needs, between now and 1960, have been established as 1100 new classrooms a year for increased enrollment, and 500 classrooms a year to correct overcrowding.

What have Indiana's citizens done about it? For the year ending June 30, 1956, they built 1,800 classrooms and remodeled over 150 additional. For the year ending June 30, 1957, they are building 2,100. For the year ending June 30, 1958, they will build 2,400.

What is the picture in some of the other states?

a. Over the past five years Alabama enrollments went up some 23,000, but in 1955 alone more than 1,000 new classrooms were completed.

b. Most spectacular is South Carolina. While the five-year increase in enrollment is only 7,493, the classrooms completed in 1955 number 2,200.

c. In Oklahoma, where proponents of federal aid to education say 500 new classrooms are needed, the state and local communities have raised the money for, and are planning to build, 1200 new classrooms.

d. Figures of the Louisiana Public Affairs Research Council show that 61 of the 67 parishes and cities in that state have sufficient bonding capacity to raise all the school construction funds they need, with half a billion to spare.

Let it be emphasized that all this has been done without federal aid to education. Many believe that if all other states would take similarly decisive steps toward self-help, there would be little demand for federal aid to education.

Roger A. Freeman, who was appointed to serve on two presidential commissions to study the fiscal capacities of the states to meet their school needs, made this statement about the current Federal Aid to Schools issue which is being brought up in the 85th Congress:

> What we are faced with is not a Federal School Construction Aid program, but the first and fateful step in the nationalization of the public schools!
>
> It would be naive to assume that the federal government would spend several billion dollars a year for any purpose, and have nothing to say on how the money was to be spent. . . . Sooner or later they would suggest—with the big stick of non-compliance behind it—that

schools conform to their ideas of how they should be organized and administered. This is what has happened to all other major federal grants-in-aid programs as the amounts increased. History teaches that political power inevitably follows the power over the purse.

Advocates of federal aid to education frequently refer to the Smith-Hughes Act, support to vocational education, support given land-grant colleges, and to the federal aid being given now for the construction of schools in certain affected areas, saying "It is a matter of record that in all of these instances, the federal government has scrupulously avoided interfering in matters of educational policy."

What are the facts?

In 1916 Congress passed the Smith-Hughes Act providing financial aid for local vocational educational systems, claiming that the measure would not bring federal controls.

Today federal regulations fill a 108-page book: *Administration of Vocational Education.*

One sentence on page 4 tells the real story. It reads:

Each state is required to submit a plan which must meet with the approval of the Federal Office of Education.

In the field of vocational education, the performance of the federal government perfectly sustains the contention that no major program of federal aid has been continued without controls. Each state, as a prerequisite to receive federal funds, executes a plan-book-agreement with the United States Office of Education. Under this are regulated every phase of the program—teacher training requirements, curriculum, length and frequency of class periods, physical facilities that must be made available, etc. So pervasive are the controls that many school districts refuse the funds, which are insignificant anyway, to escape the domination.

George E. Myers, Professor of Vocational Education at the University of Michigan, deploring the controls that accompany federal funds, in an article in the *Harvard Educational Review,* for May 1938, had this to say:

Many state directors of vocational education are coming to be looked upon as agents of the United States Office of Education rather than as employees of their state boards. . . .

The late Congressman John Lesinski (Democrat, Michigan) strongly believed in federal aid to education. In 1950, however, when he was Chairman of the House Education and Labor Committee, he prevailed upon the committee to kill the federal aid proposals of that year, saying "It is impossible to draft a general federal aid to education bill which will not contain a great degree of federal control over local school systems. I am convinced, after the hard study we have put to the question, that no acceptable bill preventing federal domination of local schools can be drawn."

The ultimate dilemma to which federal control would lead has perhaps nowhere been stated more simply, or with more clarity, than in an address by John Foster Dulles before the American Political Science Association in 1949:

> Would not our youth for the first time in our history be subjected to the risk of indoctrination by whoever might at a single time come into power at a single place?

—Reprinted with permission from *Christian Economics,* August 1, 1957.

---

Much of the demand for Federal Aid to Education is a façade behind which lurks the overpowering desire to control education. So says Thurman Sensing of the Southern States Industrial Council.

## Federal Control of Education

### THURMAN SENSING

The $1.8 billion federal aid to education bill approved by the Senate February 4th defies both American principles and good common sense.

In the first place, the provision for payment of teachers *salaries* means federal control over instruction in the classrooms of 50 states. This is aping the Russian system of centralized direction of national education, a system that should be abhorrent to patriotic Americans. It is foolish for anyone to deny that this would be the result, for it is an ancient truth that whoever pays the piper calls the tune.

Even if it could be demonstrated that federal aid to education would not mean the beginning of the end for local control of schools, the aid bill still would be 100 per cent wrong. It would be wrong because it is neither needed nor logical. The so-called "shortage" of classrooms is a "liberal" myth. Few communities operate schools on a double shift. Those communities that have a double shift in some grades are only making effective use of their classroom space. For school buildings, which cost millions of dollars, to be used only a few hours a day is a waste of the taxpayers' money that is absurd, if not downright intolerable.

Moreover, there has been considerable juggling of figures on this fictional classroom "shortage" and repeated under-estimation of what the states can and will do in the way of school construction.

In 1955, for example, the California Teachers Association testified that federal aid was a necessity because school construction needs over the next five years would approximate $1 billion. The group said the state couldn't meet that need. Well, between 1955 and 1960 the State of California devoted $2.1 billion to school construction! The federal-aiders have been made to look mighty silly in that state.

In a few areas there are shortages of school room space. In the crowded Harlem district of New York City, for instance, school facilities are in short supply as migrants push into the city from Puerto Rico and the South. But why should the people of 50 states be taxed to build new schools in Harlem?

In South Carolina, for example, all the proceeds of a 3 per cent sales tax have been devoted to school construction since 1951. Like many other Southern states, the Palmetto State has fine school buildings and no need or desire for federal aid. North Carolina is another state that has invested heavily in public schools for years. To tax these and similarly situated states to support school construction in a handful of metropolitan districts lacking in self-reliance would be nothing less than robbery. States that neither want to give nor wish to take federal aid money deserve consideration from national lawmakers.

And why shouldn't New York State or any other state that has a classroom problem assume its own burdens? Traditionally, public education has been a local and state responsibility. There's not a word in the Constitution that says the federal government has any responsibility or right to interfere in this area of American life. Furthermore, there's no merit in a state like New York sending its money to Washington and then seeking its return. It would be far more just, reasonable and practical for every state, large or small, to depend on its own assets and own initiative in the building up of a school system.

But, of course, the federal aid for education movement is the result of constant propagandizing by "liberals" who aren't interested in classrooms but in control over schooling. They see federal aid to education as the entering wedge for a socialist society. Thus every effort should be made by informed Americans to arouse their fellow-countrymen to the dangers in the federal aid to education bill.

---

Dr. V. Raymond Edman, President of Wheaton College, states his reason for turning thumbs down on federal scholarships.

## No Federal Scholarships, Thank You

### DR. V. RAYMOND EDMAN

The advocates for Federal aid to education are vocal and well organized. We are familiar with their arguments for immediate aid to the colleges and universities, lest we be overwhelmed by the rising tide of enrollments, or die because of rising costs that may prove to be beyond our means.

We here at Wheaton, along with some others, perhaps a minority, do not favor panaceas such as Federal scholarships and grants-in-aid. Our persuasion is based upon principles fundamental in the American way of education.

We do not believe that basically education is a responsibility of the Federal Government. We do not hold that Article 1, Section 8, Paragraph 1 of the Constitution which grants to the Congress "the power to lay and collect taxes . . . and provide for the common defense and general welfare of the United States" includes education. That responsibility was left very wisely to the individual states and the local districts thereof.

It should be the motivation of the children to secure an education. If they lack the inner urge to prepare themselves thoroughly for life, no amount of outward advantages and encouragement can help them.

Therefore, we believe that Federal scholarships, good as they may seem on the outside, can be a real handicap to the highest interests of the American people.

It is our strong persuasion that this original responsibility for education should be kept at the local level. There is no substitute for the endeavor of free men to provide education for the children of their own community. There is no doubt that bureaucracy can build bulging budgets but not school buildings and public spirit for education.

Colleges like Wheaton are Christian because they have been founded by godly men and women in the fear of God for the purpose of educating their young people. This education includes not only the organized fields of human learning, but even more important, the Christian theistic view of the world, of man, and of man's culture in the light of Biblical and natural revelation.

Christian colleges are independent of government control or subsidy, and are dependent upon Almighty God and His people for their maintenance and enlargement. Thus they are free to teach the truth as they find it in the Bible and in the world around us. Christian schools are free from the imposition of politicians and the blusterings of bureaucrats.

They are free to be themselves, and they propose to perpetuate that freedom for American youth.

Free men are free because they are responsible to a faithful Creator and to their fellow human beings. They are free because the open Bible is a lamp of liberty. They are free because life, liberty and the good life are rights given by the Creator. They are free because government is by the consent of the governed in the fear of God.

To perpetuate this freedom the Christian colleges of mid-twentieth century America must be strengthened, and by all means kept free of government control or subsidy.

---

Addressing the National Convention of School Administrators at Atlantic City (1959), Dr. W. W. Hill, Jr., Director, Division of Educational Research and Services of the College Life Insurance Company, calls attention to the menace and waste of Federal Aid.

## Federal Support for Education Is Unnecessary

### DR. W. W. HILL, JR.

For almost 100 years it has been argued that the Federal Government would have to assume some responsibility for public education to divert some sort of disaster. In 1870, for example,

Congress even considered a bill which would have established a national school system with the President appointing the superintendents.

Congress was assured then and just about every year, month and day since that something had to be done for education. Yet, since 1890, when public education began to expand in this country, public school expenditures have increased 65 times although enrollments are yet to triple. Per capita spending has risen from $10 to more than $90 and the percentage of national income going into public education has more than tripled.

Federal support is not needed and it is not a satisfactory substitute for state and local responsibility in education. The national government now is engaged in almost all projects known to man. Although some of the programs cost billions each year, none are adequately financed in the opinion of those who execute them or in the opinion of those receiving direct benefits.

State and local governments have consistently given more sympathetic consideration to education than to any other function of government and have furnished us with a system of education superior to any other known to civilization. Federal support might very well cause a deterioration in financial support as school boards and legislators prepare budgets with Federal aid in mind. This would be a serious mistake. Tax reductions are needed, but they are needed at the Federal level.

The fiscal position of the Federal Government is deplorable, worse than that of any state, and it seems to be growing worse. Assuming more of the responsibilities being discharged by the states and communities can only make matters worse.

Federal aid means that we discriminate against the citizens in New York, New Jersey and Connecticut in favor of the citizens of Mississippi, Arkansas and Kentucky. It would ignore existing spending patterns, tax burdens as well as cultural, economic and social priorities of communities and states. For reasons which have nothing to do with education, the states that would lose the most are the ones making the most noise about Federal support.

Equalization of school costs might be more important if we could equate expenditures and achievement. Success has never blessed the serious efforts to do this. Economic conditions, building costs, pupil-teacher ratios, state of school organization, environment and attitudes toward education make such an equation unlikely.

Federal support, while discriminating against about half the population, would mean shifting some portion of the school cost burden from sales and property taxes to the net income tax. This may seem desirable to those who scream about high property tax rates while immune to the loss of amounts several times larger through witholding procedures.

The Federal budget generally is out of balance in good years and bad. Any Federal funds would have to come from borrowings and it somehow seems absurd to use loan funds for routine, every-day, operating expenses.

No one really expects Federal aid without the controls. Such controls would lead to Federal standards, more uniformity, more conformity, more centralization and eventual loss of local control by school officials and patrons.

Those who have unlimited faith in the wisdom and purse of the national government need only to examine the farm program. If there ever was a colossal failure, it is the Federal farm program. While wasting billions, farmers are bound in a straight-jacket and told how much wheat and tobacco they can produce. If they plant more than their allotment they can lose their tractors, combines and even their farms.

We tolerate the loss of freedom in agriculture, would we not also tolerate the loss of our schools?

Vocational education aid and aid to Federally-impacted areas are highly regarded by some people. But after 40 years of Federal vocational aid, we find that vocational education is the weakest part of our school system. In only a few years through aid to im-pacted areas, the Office of Education has wasted $60 million or more on elaborate buildings, gymnasiums and for the purposes not authorized by Congress.

Since the states that would benefit from Federal funds are not demanding assistance, and since local governments are doing a better job in education than the national government is doing in the administration of its untold number of services, and since the national government cannot afford the services now rendered, it would be unwise to have it attempt the impossible—an equitable Federal school program without dangerous controls.

Much of the deception, witting or unwitting, in the cry for more and more schoolrooms is bared in this lucid editorial by Raymond Moley, based in part on the study made by Roger Freeman and his book, *School Needs in the Decade Ahead.*

# Unnecessary School Aid

### RAYMOND MOLEY

Congress began its big bite into the 1961 surplus when the Senate passed a $1.8 billion, two-year bill for school construction and teachers' salaries. The House will omit teachers' salaries and probably pass a smaller school-construction bill. The President's modest request is for help to needy districts to service their school bonds.

Not one of the 51 senators who voted in such haste could have believed that their pass-the-buck bill could become law. And I doubt that any of them could have believed the rumble-jumble of figures with which they embellished their arguments.

Calamitous reports of our decaying schools moved President Truman to order a "school facilities survey" in 1951. This booby trap he left with his successor. The report was replete with exaggeration, wild guesses, and downright inventions. It was based upon a questionnaire to state school authorities which invited them to answer their wants, not needs—figures etched by itching fingers.

Imagine President Eisenhower's embarrassment when he was induced to say in a message in 1955 that there was need for 300,000 classrooms and two months later his Secretary of Health, Education, and Welfare admitted that there had been an enormous exaggeration in his figures.

Then the U.S. Office of Education started its own annual estimate of classroom shortages. These were: For 1956, 159,000; for 1957, 142,300; for 1958, 141,900; for 1959, 132,400. Since every state official has his own way of estimating a shortage, such figures reflect only a state of mind. They show, however, a declining "shortage" estimate.

Without Federal aid, states and districts have executed abundant building programs. The classrooms "in use"—a more reliable figure than "needs" reported by the Truman survey—seven years ago numbered 983,000. The 1959 survey of the Office of Education indicated 1,279,000, an increase of 30 per cent. The pupil enrollment meanwhile increased only 20 per cent.

A representative of the Office of Education estimated last December that 610,000 classrooms were needed to be built between 1960 and 1970. That estimate of 61,000 classrooms a year is almost exactly what Roger Freeman estimated in his 1958 book, *School Needs in the Decade Ahead,* which brought upon his head screams of dissent from the NEA and other Federal-aid exponents.

But over the past five years the states and districts have been building 66,740 classrooms annually. Thus there can be no justification at all for saying that states and districts cannot close whatever gap there may be. For school districts can and will continue to build, if Federal aid is not introduced. That aid would be a most effective tranquilizer. This effect of Federal aid has been shown in many other fields.

According to an admission exacted from Secretary Flemming, education officials who answered telegraphic inquiries identified only 270 out of 35,000 school districts which have exhausted their legal bonding capacity. This handful of districts are "borrowed up" and cannot get help from the states. It is a primary responsibility of the states to see that they are helped. The proposal of the President is to help servicing of bonded indebtedness in cases of need.

Another very important fact should be considered. The crest of the wave of new school enrollment is behind us, since the war babies are now leaving school. The Bureau of the Census says that the average annual increase in school-age population (5-17 years) from 1955 to 1960 was 1,494,000, but will drop to 1,145,000 in the coming five years. And from 1965 to 1970 the number of new enrollments will shrink to 644,000.

The schools are not being starved under the states and districts. Over the past twenty years, enrollments grew 43 per cent; school expenditures, 563 per cent (from $2.3 billion to $15.5 billion).

To be sure, many improvements are needed in educational standards and efficiency in using the plants we have and are building. Financial neglect is not the heart of the problem.

> —Reprinted with permission from *Newsweek,* February 29, 1960.

---

At this point, we might well be reminded of the sharp comment by Professor Root: "We are told we need more and more class-

rooms; should we not first ask: 'What goes on in those classrooms?' "
A generation ago, George Bernard Shaw published a book called
*The Intelligent Woman's Guide to Socialism and Capitalism.* In
1957, Russell Kirk, one of the most brilliant minds in the conservative camp, countered with a book called *The Intelligent Woman's
Guide to Conservatism.* One of the most brilliant chapters in this
book is the one quoted here.

## Conservatives and Education

### RUSSELL KIRK

For the reflecting conservative, the purpose of education is clear.
That purpose is to develop the mental and moral faculties of the
individual person, for the person's own sake. Now this process of
cultivating the mind and conscience of young people (here I speak
of education in the sense of "schooling," though it is quite true that
self-education ought to continue most of any man's or woman's
life) has certain lesser purposes and incidental benefits. One of
these lesser aims is to instruct young people in the beliefs and cus-
toms which make possible a decent civil social order. Another of
these lesser aims is the inculcation of certain skills and aptitudes
which will help young people as they come to man's estate. Yet
another is the development of habits of sociability—teaching boys
and girls how to take a normal part in society. And there are more
purposes and benefits.

Yet the conservative does not forget that the essential aim, and
the chief benefit, of formal education is to make people intelligent
and good. Schools cannot, wholly by themselves, make people intelligent and good; natural inclinations or disinclinations, the family, and the community have a great deal to do with whether young
people are wise or foolish, good or bad. But schools can help in
the process. And if schools neglect this primary function in favor of
vague schemes for "group play" or "personality unfolding" or
"learning by doing" or "adjustment to the group" or "acquiring
approved social attitudes," then they have become bad schools.

The conservative always thinks first of the individual human
person. What is bad for individuals cannot be good for society. And
if most individual men and women are reasonably good and reasonably intelligent, the society in which they live cannot be a very bad

one. Therefore—especially in this time which Ortega y Gasset calls "the mass-age," this time in which standardization and various forms of collectivism threaten the whole concept of true individual personality—the conservative never ceases to emphasize that the school exists primarily to help improve the understanding and the moral worth of private persons. The school is not merely a custodial institution, to keep young people in a tolerable captivity while their parents are busy elsewhere. It is not merely a place where young people are taught how to make money in years to come. It is not merely a means for indoctrinating young people in certain approved social attitudes. No, it is something much more important: it is an institution for imparting a sound intellectual and moral discipline to the rising generation. The conservative is not afraid of the abused word "discipline." Without discipline, men and women must spend their lives either in mischief or in idleness. The best form of discipline is self-discipline; and self-discipline, mental and ethical, is what the schools try to impart to students.

But to the modern radical who is faithful to his own first principles, formal education is something quite different from what the conservative thinks education should be. To the radical—communist, or fascist, or socialist, or any sort of radical ideologue—the school is an instrument of power. It is a means for indoctrinating the young with what the radical believes to be the concept of the good society. The school, in the radical's opinion, exists to serve "society," not primarily to serve the individual human person. And the scholar, in the radical's opinion, ought not to waste his time searching for Truth: instead, he ought to be preaching approved social doctrines to the young, or in advancing the class struggle, or in planning for a better world. The radical thinks of the school as a means for improving, or at least changing, society in the mass. To the modern radical, the very idea of encouraging the development of private talents merely for the sake of private character is annoying. He thinks of the school as a means of advancing toward some form of collectivism. He cannot see the trees for the forest. The private person, and the private person's reason, are very little to him; the amorphous masses are everything.

Now of course there are persons of radical political views among us today who do not embrace the radical theory of education that I have suggested above. But these are inconsistent radicals, just as there are inconsistent conservatives. If the only real object of life is the material betterment of the masses, presumably to be accomplished through the establishment of equality of condition, then there is no point in encouraging development of strong private opinions and strong individual minds. What collectivism requires is not strong personalities and a high degree of private culture, but rather unquestioning conformity to the secular dogmas of collectivism. The more consistent and forthright radical educators, like Professor Theodore Brameld, confess this truth and urge us to convert the schools into propaganda-devices for teaching the doctrines that "everybody belongs to everybody else" and that one person is as good as another, or maybe a little better. Quite candidly, they call themselves Social Reconstructionists—educators who would employ the schools to build a new collectivistic society. They intend to break down all the old beliefs and loyalties, through the process of educating the young, and to supplant these old beliefs and loyalties with artificially cultivated attachment to collectivistic doctrines. Some of them would teach "the religion of democracy," to replace the religious convictions in which nearly all schools had their origins. They do not want reverent or inquiring minds; they desire only submissive and uniform minds.

When such theories as these are baldly presented to the American public, that public promptly rejects them. But what the American public has not yet rejected is something more subtle, less candid, and—in the long run—perhaps as dangerous: the educational notions of the late John Dewey. Sound sense and fallacy are blended in Dewey's theories, but the fallacies have become almost official educational dogma in our country, while the sound sense either has been forgotten or has lost its significance because of altered social circumstances. Dewey desired the state schools to become a means for making the American population homogeneous. Hostile toward traditional religion (though sometimes giving it lip-service of sorts), he hoped that a thoroughgoing and aggressive secularism in the schools would take the place of the religious concepts which have been the foundation of American morals and politics. Hostile toward the works of the higher imagination, he proposed to substitute "group endeavor" and "learning by doing" for the literary studies and intellectual disciplines which had given American education its established character.

Dewey's theories and influence cannot be examined in detail here; they have been intelligently criticized in recent years by Canon Bernard Iddings Bell, Professor Arthur Bestor, Mr. Mortimer Smith, Mr. Albert Lynd, Dr. Gordon Keith Chalmers, and others. What I am trying to do is to suggest that attitude toward formal education which the intelligent conservative ought to take. The intelligent conservative combines a disposition to preserve with an ability to reform. And our schools need reform most pressingly. Despite all the talk about "education for democracy," they seem to be educating for mass-submission; dreary secular indoctrination is substituted for the inquiring mind. The Republic cannot long survive if its citizens are incapable of apprehending general ideas, or even of reading and writing; and the failure of our schools—and, to a considerable extent, of our universities and colleges—has brought us to just that pass. Many college graduates today cannot write a simple letter as well as a sixth-grade student would have written it fifty years ago.

So the conservative believes that we ought to say less about "group dynamics" and "social reconstruction" in our schools, and do more to restore the old and indispensable disciplines of reading, writing, mathematics, the sciences, imaginative literature, and history. He thinks that we need to bring back definite "subject-matter" courses and abolish vague catch-alls like "social studies" (taught as a single amorphous course) and "communications." He thinks that our colleges and universities could profit greatly by a return to humane learning—to the real humanities, those disciplines designed to teach ethical understanding and develop the higher imagination; they ought to redeem themselves from an excessive vocationalism, from a mistaken eagerness to attract students which gives everyone a degree but no one an education, and from a false specialization. Alfred North Whitehead remarked once that the ancient philosopher aspired to teach wisdom, but that the modern professor aspires only to teach facts. Isolated facts, the conservative thinks, do not constitute an education; and vague sentiments and "approved social attitudes" have still less to do with the true educational process. For what the Republic requires is a citizenry endowed with a knowledge of the wisdom of our ancestors, and a respect for that wisdom; a citizenry endowed with the ability to form opinions and make judgments. And what the truly human person requires is a grasp of those genuine disciplines of the mind which make it possible for him to become, in the full sense, a reasoning being. An "education" system which does less than this is not educational at all, but only a propaganda-apparatus in the service of the state.

With the medieval schoolmen, the conservative is of the opinion that we moderns are dwarfs standing upon the shoulders of giants —able to see further than our intellectual ancestors only because we are supported by the great bulk and strength of their achievement. If we spurn the wisdom of our ancestors, we tumble down into the ditch of ignorance. Lacking the old disciplines which inculcated ethical principles and encouraged the ordered imagination, any people sink into a cultural decline; and they are liable to become the victims of any clever clique of unprincipled manipulators.

Yet, despite all thses faults in twentieth-century American education, the conservative knows that our system possesses still some considerable merits. Conspicuous among those virtues is the diversity and competition surviving among our educational institutions. We have not merely state schools, but a large number of private and church-supported schools; and the conservative approves this healthy variety. Disciples of Dewey like Dr. James Conant urge us to sweep away private and parochial establishments and force the whole population into a common mode of schooling, completely secularized and intended to "teach democracy." The conservative sets his face against such arrogant proposals. On the contrary, he thinks we are fortunate in escaping the deadening influence of uniformity in the educational process. He is glad that we have not merely state universities, but old endowed private universities of high reputation, hundreds of private and church-sponsored colleges, opportunity for experiment, freedom of choice among professors and students. If a nation desires intellectual vitality and originality, it will encourage this variety; if it is resigned to stagnation and secular conformity, however, a nation will embrace the uniformity-designs of Dewey and Conant.

Centralization of any sort is suspect to the conservative; and centralization of the educational establishment is one of the most dangerous forms of centralization. It is with marked hostility, then, that the conservative looks upon proposals for federal subsidies to the public schools. The man who pays the fiddler calls the tune, the conservative knows; and besides, education is more vigorous when it is supported by local endeavor. The only very valuable piece of information to come out of the White House Conference on Education, in 1955, was the conclusion that no state in the Union is unable to bear its own educational responsibilities. Private citizens, local communities, and the several states, the conservative knows, are the best judges of their own educational needs and interests. When he is approached with proposals for consolidation and unification, he shrewdly suspects that somewhere in the dim background of these proposals is someone's Grand Design for employing the schools as a tool for turning society inside out. And the conservative has no intention of turning society inside out. He thinks that to abuse the schools for such a purpose would be to corrupt education. The natural function of formal education is conservative, in the best sense of that word: that is, formal education conserves the best of what has been thought and written and discovered in the past, and by a regular discipline teaches us to guide ourselves by the light of the wisdom of our ancestors.

A Scottish friend of mine writes me of the confused notions that curse our age: "People seem to accept premises that have been rejected by the wise through all the ages, and there is a horrible ominous throbbing in the air like the sound of countless trotters on the cliffhead at Gadara." All the good places and people, he continues, are being sacrificed "not to a candid malevolence but to unbearably specious cant." Unbearably specious cant characterizes much of what passes for education among us nowadays. One of the works of conservative reform most urgently needed is a return to right reason, a restoration of honorable disciplines in education. And the first step in this reform must be a recognition of the enduring principle that education is intended for the elevation of the mind and conscience of the individual human person. It is not intended to be a toy for radical doctrinaires to play with, nor yet to be a great sham affording profit and prestige to what Mr. David Riesman calls "the patronage network of Teachers' College, Columbia University." The conservative respects the works of the mind; the radical, in our age, seems to be smugly content with cant and slogan.

---

Just as the radical "frontier thinkers" took education by storm, theological "frontier thinkers" will be found in the pulpit and the seminary and among the members of the hierarchy of the various denominations who preach a social gospel that leads from God to the State. The state of the religious faith of the individual is lost in the haste to reform society by law. It is, therefore, highly fitting to close this chapter with another essay by Dr. Russell Kirk.

## Conservatives and Religious Faith

### RUSSELL KIRK

Not all religious people are conservatives; and not all conservatives are religious people. Christianity prescribes no especial form of politics. There have been famous radicals who were devout Christians—though most radicals have been nothing of the sort. All the same, there could be no conservatism without a religious foundation, and it is conservative people, by and large, who defend religion in our time.

Lord Hailsham, a talented English conservative of this century, in his little book *The Case for Conservatism*, remarks, "There is nothing I despise more than a politician who seeks to sell his politics by preaching religion, unless it be a preacher who tries to sell his sermons by talking politics." Yet he goes on to say that conservatism and religion cannot be kept in separate compartments, and that the true conservative at heart is a religious man. The social influence of Christianity has been nobly conservative, and a similarly conservative influence has been exerted by Buddhism, Mohammedanism, Judaism, and the other higher religions.

In America, a sense of religious consecration has been joined to our political institutions from the beginning. Almost all the signers of the Declaration of Independence and the delegates to the Constitutional Convention were religious men. Solemn presidential proclamations, since the beginning of the Republic, have invoked the might and mercy of God. Most of our leading conservative statesmen and writers were men profoundly religious— George Washington, an Episcopalian; John Adams, a Unitarian; James Madison, an Episcopalian; John Randolph, an Episcopalian; John C. Calhoun, a Unitarian; Orestes Brownson, a Catholic; Nathaniel Hawthorne, a Congregationalist; Abraham Lincoln, a devout though independent theist; and many more. "We know and we feel inwardly that religion is the basis of civil society, and the source of all good and all comfort," Edmund Burke wrote.

Now a conservative is a person who sees human society as an

immortal contract between God and man, and between the generations that are dead, and the generation that is living now, and the generations which are yet to be born. It is possible to conceive of such a contract, and to feel a debt toward our ancestors and obligations toward our posterity, only if we are filled with a sense of eternal wisdom and power. We deal charitably and justly by our fellow men and women only because we believe that a divine will commands us to do so, and to love one another. The religious conservative is convinced that we have duties toward society, and that a just government is ruled by moral law, since we participate in our humble way in the divine nature and the divine love. The conservative believes that the fear of God is the beginning of wisdom.

The conservative desires to conserve human nature—that is, to keep men and women truly human, in God's image. The dread radical ideologies of our century, Communism and Nazism and their allies, endeavor to stamp out religion root and branch because they know that religion is always a barrier to collectivism and tyranny. A religious person has strength and faith; and radical collectivism detests private strength and faith. Throughout Europe and Asia, the real resistance to collectivism has come from men and women who believe that there is a greater authority than the collectivistic state, and that authority is God.

A society which denies religious truth lacks faith, charity, justice and any sanction for its acts. Today, more perhaps than ever before, Americans understand the close connection between religious conviction and just government, so that they have amended their oath of allegiance to read, "one nation, under God." There is a divine power higher than any political power. When a nation ignores the divine authority, it soon commits the excesses of fanatic nationalism, intoxicated with its own unchecked power, which have made the twentieth century terrible.

Any religion is always in danger of corruption; and in our time, various people have endeavored to persuade us that the Christian religion endorses some sort of sentimental collectivism, a "religion of humanity," in which the Christian idea of equality in God's sight is converted into a dreary social and economic equality enforced by the state. But an examination of the Christian creeds and the Christian tradition will not sustain such an interpretation of Christian teaching. What Christianity offers is personal redemption, not some system of economic revolution. The human person is the great concern of Christian faith—as a person, not as part of a vague "People," or "The Masses," or "The Under-privileged." And when Christians preach charity, they mean the voluntary giving of those who have to those who have not; they do not mean compulsion by the state to take away from some in order to benefit others. "Statists that labor to contrive a commonwealth without poverty," old Sir Thomas Browne says, "take away the object of our charity; not understanding only the commonwealth of a Christian, but forgetting the prophecy of Christ." The Christian religion does indeed enjoin us to do unto others as we would have others do unto us; it does not enjoin us to employ political power to compel others to surrender their property.

Any great religion is assailed by heresies. In the year of the Communist Manifesto, Orestes Brownson declared that Communism is a heresy from Christianity; and he is echoed today by Arnold Toynbee and Eric Voegelin. Communism perverts the charity and love of Christianity into a fierce leveling doctrine that men must be made equal upon earth; at the same time, it denounces real equality, which is equality in the ultimate judgment of God. And other ideologies which would convert Christianity into an instrument for oppressing one class for the benefit of another are heresies.

Another distortion of Christianity is the radical doctrine that "the voice of the people is the voice of God." This, Lord Percy of Newcastle writes, is "the heresy of democracy"—that is, the disastrous error of supposing that God is simply whatever the majority of people think at any given time. The conservative knows that popular judgment commits blunder after blunder; it is anything but divine; while an immutable Justice which we perceive only imperfectly and dimly, and try to imitate in our human laws, is the real source of truth in politics.

A third perversion of Christianity is the heresy that this earthly society of ours can be made perfect, by world planners and civil servants and enactments. The Christian knows that perfection, either in human beings or in society, never will be attained upon earth, but can be found only in a higher realm. This delusion of the possibility of earthly perfection lies behind most socialistic and totalitarian schemes. A professed Christian cannot be a professed Utopian. Our fallen nature, in the eyes of the sincere Christian, will not be redeemed until the end of all things; therefore we are foolish if we expect that political and economic revolution will bring perfect justice and happiness. Men and women are creatures of mingled good and evil; in the best of us, some evil is present; and therefore political constitutions, just laws and social conventions are employed to restrain our evil impulses. Human beings without just and prudent government are delivered up to anarchy, for the brute lies just under the skin of civilization.

To presume to establish a synthetic paradise upon earth, predicated upon a fallaciously optimistic notion of human nature, will expose us to the peril of a reign of unreason. Vague schemes of world government ordinarily are afflicted by this folly. There never has been a perfect age or a perfect society, and there never will be, the religious conservative knows. All the political contrivances of mankind have been tried before, and none of them have worked to perfect satisfaction.

This is not to say that the religious conservative believes that all ages are the same, or that all evils are necessary evils. One age may be much worse than another; one society may be relatively just, and another relatively unjust; men may improve somewhat under a prudent and humane domination, and may deteriorate vastly in an insensate time. But the pseudo-gospel of Progress as the inevitable and beneficent wave of the future—a doctrine now shattered by the catastrophes of this century—never deluded the religious conservative. He does not despise the past simply because it is old, or assume that the present is delightful simply because it is ours. He judges every age and every institution in the light of certain principles of justice and order, which we have learnt in part through revelation and in part through the long and painful experience of the human race.

The religious thinker who criticizes our present society is not bound to maintain that one time is all white and another time is all black; he can pick and choose. If we pick and choose discreetly, we may hope to improve our own society considerably, though we never will succeed in making our society perfect. Human history is an account of men and women running as fast as they can, like Alice and the Red Queen, in order to stay where they are. Sometimes we grow lazy, and then society sinks into a terrible decline. We are never going to be able to run fast enough to arrive at Utopia. And we should hate Utopia if ever we got there, for it would be infinitely boring. What really makes men and women love life is the battle itself, the struggle to bring order out of disorder, to strive for right against evil. If ever that struggle should come to an end, we should expire of boredom. It is not in our nature to rest content, like the angels, in an eternal change-lessness. In one sense, the religious conservative is a Utopian, but in one sense only: he believes that the possibility of near-perfection does indeed exist, but it exists only within individual human persons; and when that state is attained individually, we call it sanctity.

Nor ought we to be discontented with this imperfect world of ours. G. K. Chesterton, in his "Ballad of the White Horse," tells of how King Alfred (a high-minded conservative some centuries before the word "conservative" was thought of) had a vision of the Virgin Mary; and when he asked her what of the future, Mary told him this:

> I tell you naught for your comfort,
>   Yea, naught for your desire,
> Save that the sky grows darker yet
>   And the sea rises higher.
>
> Night shall be thrice night over you,
>   And heaven an iron cope.
> Do you have joy without a cause,
>   Yea, faith without a hope?

Now these words made Alfred glad, for all their seeming grim-ness. For Alfred, as a Christian leader, knew that we are put here upon earth to struggle for the right, to contend against evil, and to defend the legacy of human nature and civilization. This is the conservative task in all ages; and, as Jefferson wrote, the tree of liberty must be watered from time to time with the blood of martyrs.

# XIV

# Sparks of Resistance

OUR COUNTRY was born in revolt against tyranny—a revolt sparked by individual colonial clergymen who preached the theology of freedom, sparked by the resistance of daring men such as those who staged the Boston Tea Party, and sparked by courageous politicians such as Patrick Henry who, not knowing what others would do, spoke for himself alone: "Give me liberty, or give me death."

But our liberty today is in dire jeopardy on many counts, not the least of which is the fast and loose way in which the Supreme Court has been playing with the Constitution, chipping away at the intent of its authors.

In the latter part of 1957 the *Indianapolis Star* published a series of seven editorials which, according to publisher Eugene C. Pulliam, "were written after long and careful study of recent court decisions and of the historical relationships between the Supreme Court, Congress and the Presidency . . . in order to focus wider public attention on the most critical constitutional issues of our times." We quote from several of this series.

## The Runaway Court—I

Something has gone wrong at the roots of America's government. The three-way balance of constitutional authority is tipping crazily. Alarmed lawmakers have introduced a dozen serious proposals in Congress to shackle the United States Supreme Court within the limits of the Constitution. The President strongly, though inadvertently, has expressed dissatisfaction with his appointees to the court. Governors, bar associations, respected attorneys, even lower courts, have shown open dismay at the way the Supreme Court is going. Every forum of free opinion has added its criticism on one count or another.

There has never been another such clamor against the high court, which depends as surely as do executive or legislative branches upon the consent of the governed for its authority. The court has been the hub of turmoil many times before, most recently as a result of President Franklin D. Roosevelt's court packing scheme, but always before it has had more friends than traducers in the places where public opinion begins. Today the tide of influence is setting against the court, no matter where the minor cross currents stirred by its separate decisions run.

The court is engaged in a race which, if persisted in, can be won only by destroying the governmental system we revere. It is competing against time to enforce new doctrines before nebulous public resentment becomes hardened public resistance. It has on its side the die-hard popular belief, which is false as a china nest egg, that the law is what the court says it is. In a constitutional crisis such as the court is precipitating, vague generalities cannot continue to win acceptance. The public is already stirring to awareness that the court is not an originator, but an instrument of the law.

In the struggle that is shaping up, intelligent decisions can be supported only out of full understanding of the issues. The *Star* intends to present a series of editorials, of which this is the first, dealing with the causes, the proof and the impact of the court's defection, and with possible defenses against it. At the outset it should be recalled what the court's position is in our government. No other operation of the Federal system is so thoroughly misunderstood.

One article and one amendment to the Constitution relate directly to the Supreme Court. Another article defines the "supreme law of the land" without mentioning the court at all.

Article III provides: "The judicial power of the United States shall be vested in one Supreme Court, and in such inferior courts as the Congress may, from time to time, ordain and establish. . . ." Notice that this judicial power is not regarded by the Constitution as indivisible. It does not say that the power is vested in "one Supreme Court, to be administered by it through such inferior courts." It says the power belongs to the Supreme Court *and* the inferior courts.

This was not a slip of the pen. The men who wrote the Constitution did not intend the Supreme Court to be, in fact, supreme. They made this undeniably clear when, in the same Article III (Section 2), they decreed that "the Supreme Court shall have appellate jurisdiction, both as to law and to fact, *with such exception, and under such regulations* as the Congress shall make." Nothing could be clearer. Congress is given the sole right to divide the judicial power between the Supreme Court and the lower courts.

All other references in the Constitution to judicial power set up limitations; none grants broader authority. The 11th Amendment forbids the Federal judiciary to act in cases brought against one state by a citizen of another state. There are numerous provisions detailing what the courts *may not* do. They may not, for example, deny trial by jury in criminal prosecutions.

In Article VI the Constitution comes directly to grips with the question, what is the supreme law of the land? It says: "This Constitution, and the laws of the United States which shall be made in pursuance thereof, and all treaties made, or which shall be made, under the authority of the United States, shall be the supreme law of the land." No mention at all is made of the Supreme Court. The law is what the Constitution says it is and what Congress acting within constitutional limits says it is.

No Federal court has any legal authority whatsoever to rule out or alter a law passed by Congress unless the law violates the Constitution. No Federal court has any authority or right to change the Constitution by so much as one word, either by "interpretation" or subterfuge. To do so is as illegal as armed robbery, and deserves no more respect.

We are, all of us, as morally bound to resist usurpation of power by the Supreme Court, or any other court, as we are to resist any other violation of the law.

## The Runaway Court—II

The easiest place to destroy the Constitution is in the United States Supreme Court. Fortunately, America has had few occasions to recall this elementary truth, yet today there is great need to remember it. A long roll call of recent Supreme Court opinions threatens to drastically alter the shape of American government. Our vulnerability through the court needs the understanding of every thoughtful citizen if it is to be overcome.

The Achilles heel of our constitutional republic was not created by the Constitution itself. The first of this series of editorials demonstrated that the court's original grant of power was not at all what it is now generally conceived to be. Except for a picayunish list of matters over which it has original jurisdiction under the Constitution, the court is entirely dependent upon the will of Congress for the breadth of its authority over appeals from lower courts.

None of the court's recent lawmaking opinions, which will be discussed specifically in later editorials, falls within the area of the court's original jurisdiction. The cases went before the court, not because they had to go there, but because Congress had not exercised its right to prohibit them from going there. Had it done so, the decisions of the lower Federal courts would now be what is so glibly and erroneously called "the law of the land." Most of the lower court decisions were the exact opposite of the later Supreme Court rulings.

The irony of it is that the dominant position of the Supreme Court over national life has been established by the kind of stratified tradition at which majority members of the present court aim their sharpest jibes. Chief Justice John Marshall, during his 34 years on the Supreme Court bench beginning in 1801, inaugurated the idea that the Supreme Court is the last word on what is and is not constitutional. Marshall's innovation was accepted not because the Constitution required it, but because it provided a seemingly reasonable guide for judicial action.

The potential danger of the Marshall doctrine was foreseen early in the nation's history by some famous patriots. Thomas

Jefferson, worried over the fate of the Constitution he helped shape, said: "It is a very dangerous doctrine to consider the judges the ultimate arbiters of all constitutional questions. . . . The Constitution has erected no such tribunal."

For many dormant years Jefferson's warning seemed to be an extremist view. With few notable exceptions, the same body of tradition which supported its expanded power constrained the Supreme Court to honor the Constitution. Until our own time the court as a general rule exercised its extraconstitutional authority in support of the Constitution. But then came what Ralph H. Gabriel in his thoughtful book, *The Course of American Democratic Thought,* calls "legal realism."

"The realists," wrote Gabriel, "looked upon written constitutions and the positive laws that issued from the legislatures as instruments of social engineering."

The public is more familiar with this philosophy when it is expressed in another way. The Constitution, say the "realists," is a document which must be constantly revised in keeping with the times. This argument has enough of a ring of logic to it to be popular. But the "realists" are reformers in a hurry. They close their eyes to the process of amendment provided in the Constitution. They prefer to make the Constitution what they think it should be by judicial "interpretation." They, above all others, argue that the law is what the court says it is, because if they can make that claim stick, the sociological and political future of the nation is at the mercy of the majority of "legal realists" who now occupy the Supreme Court bench.

There is ample evidence that the present Supreme Court has twisted the Constitution and the law into weird shapes to further the individual social philosophies of some justices. The danger foreseen by Jefferson as a result of Supreme Court assumption of a power not delegated to it has materialized in a socio-political philosophy which holds that the Constitution is an instrument to be used by the court, and not the court an instrument to serve the Constitution.

For the future of their nation, Americans must insist that it is the Constitution which is supreme over the court, not the court over the Constitution.

## The Runaway Court—III

The United States Supreme Court under Chief Justice Earl Warren is engaged in amending the 10th Article of the Bill of Rights. On the books this article still says, "The powers not delegated to the United States by the Constitution, nor prohibited by it to the states, are reserved to the states, respectively, or to the people." Whether it is the intention of the Warren court to stop at judicial amendment, or eventually to repeal the provision entirely without bothering with constitutional process, remains to be seen.

A score of opinions by the court in the last two years support the conclusion that repeal by ossification is the final goal. Having adopted the peculiar philosophy that the Supreme Court is somehow divinely chosen to keep the Constitution in tune with the times even at the cost of ignoring it, the court has managed to make law—which is not a judicial prerogative—in direct opposition to the 10th Amendment.

Examples in proof of the court's duplicity are so outstanding they cry for the attention of every citizen who might be concerned for the welfare of his government as he has known it, or as he might want his children to know it. For these are decisions which strike at the heart of an American's right to a voice in his community affairs on a community level.

*Pennsylvania v. Steve Nelson* was such a decision. Nelson is an admitted Communist leader who was tried and convicted in Pennsylvania courts under a Pennsylvania anti-sedition law. Despite the provision of Article IV, Section 2, of the Constitution, which recognizes a state's right to prosecute for treason, the Supreme Court threw the case out. Why? Because, it said, the Federal government had pre-empted the sedition field by passing the Smith Act. As a result the anti-sedition laws of 42 states and of Alaska and Hawaii were made unenforceable.

*Schware v. Board of Bar Examiners of New Mexico* and *Konigsberg v. State Bar of California* provided two decisions of a kind. In both cases the United States Supreme Court overruled state supreme courts and state bar examiners. It said in effect that the states cannot be permitted to determine that Communist or Com-

munist-front activities reflect on the moral character of an appli-
cant for a license to practice as an attorney. It might as well have
said that no state can require good moral character of the men
who, upon being admitted to practice in state courts, become in
fact officers of those same state courts. There is nothing in the
Constitution to justify this invasion of rights which historically
have belonged to the states.

In *Slochower v. Board of Education of New York* the Supreme
Court reversed three state courts and nullified an entirely reasonable state law which provided for the discharge of subversive teachers, or those who refused to discuss subversive connections. The
Supreme Court itself subsequently admitted it was in error about
the facts of the case, but nevertheless refused to alter its erroneous
opinion.

In *Sweezy v. New Hampshire* the Supreme Court ruled that the
highest law-enforcement officer of the state, the attorney general,
did not even have the right to question a college professor about
subversive activities. Where the Nelson case led off by denying the
right to states to prosecute for attempts to overthrow the government—and that means state governments as well as Federal—the
Sweezy case followed up by prohibiting the states from even investigating treason!

As if to prove that the Sweezy opinion was not an accidental
result of something the justices ate, it was reinforced by a companion opinion in *Raley, Stern and Brown v. Ohio*. Here the
Warren court held that the state had no right at all to punish
for contemptuous refusal to answer a state legislature's questions
about subversion.

Of course all of these Supreme Court opinions were of considerable comfort to Marxist communism, which by Supreme Court
decision is a conspiracy for the treasonable overthrow of the American government. But above and beyond the issue of communism,
the opinions themselves subverted the Constitution by substitut-
ing the personal philosophies of the majority justices for the rule
of law which has withstood all challenges for almost 200 years.

The danger of communism is grave enough, but it may be that
a graver danger yet exists in a court which attempts to use one
phrase in the Constitution to amend the rest of it, and ends by
concluding that there is no Constitution at all except what the
court writes.

## The Runaway Court—IV

What kind of government does the United States Supreme Court think should rule over Americans?

A decade ago the question would have been meaningless. Today its answer is of vital import because the court is re-shaping the form of our government with a speed which, unless checked, will leave little that is recognizable for another generation. Bolstered by the glib falsehood that the law is what the court says it is, alibied by the materialist assumption that the precise principles of the Constitution exist only through judicial interpretation, the Warren court already has decreed changes so stunning that a normal person's first reaction must be, "I'm imagining things."

The court's attack has not been on state's rights, alone. Federal administrative authority came under Supreme Court fire in one of the most amazing rulings ever handed down. In the case of John Stewart Service, the court held that the Secretary of State could not discharge his own employe for security reasons because another group of the secretary's employes, comprising his Loyalty Review Board, had previously failed to recommend discharge. The ruling was made in the face of an act of Congress empowering the secretary to fire any employe within his sole discretion without regard to hearings or other administrative procedure.

Federal law enforcement procedure was temporarily disrupted by the famous ruling ordering Federal Bureau of Investigation files thrown open to criminal defendants, specifically a suspected Communist, Clinton E. Jencks. As a result of the decision President Eisenhower privately expressed something less than pleasure with at least one of his own appointees to the Supreme Court. At the urging of the U.S. Justice Department, Congress hastened to undo some of the damage with a law which partly nullified the court's opinion.

But for an all-inclusive demonstration of illegal judicial lawmaking founded upon error and ending in a blatant attempt to put into the Constitution something which is not there, the Watkins case has few equals. The court ruled in this case that the House Committee on Un-American Activities had no right to require John T. Watkins to answer questions about his former associates in the Communist party. The reason, said the court, was that the committee had not told Watkins what specific law his testimony might help it write.

The law the court virtually created, which can nowhere be found in either Constitution or Federal statutes, is that congressional committees cannot conduct investigations *unless they know in advance what legislation the investigations will show to be necessary!* As a practical matter, the opinion put an almost immediate halt to effective congressional investigation of communism in the United States. But just as the decision on FBI files was immediately seized upon by drug peddlers and other common criminals to gain freedom, so the Watkins decisions will apply to virtually all fields of congressional investigation.

The Watkins decision, which reads as much like a piece of political oratory against "Red baiters" as it does like a Supreme Court opinion, was notable for its factual errors as well as its weird conclusions. The opinion, for example, recommended that congressional committees adopt the tactics of Canadian Royal Commissions of Inquiry because of their "success in fulfilling their fact-finding missions without resort to coercive tactics." The fact is that Royal Commissions may arrest witnesses, hold them incommunicado for many days, conduct questioning in secret, punish witnesses for failure to answer any question and do not recognize any immunity such as the Fifth Amendment provides. A congressional committee can do none of these things.

Another almost childish error of fact is the court's statement that congressional investigations such as those of the Committee on Un-American Activities were of a "new kind" which had developed "in the decade following World War II." The fact is that congressional investigations into Communist subversion were in full swing in 1919, and the Committee on Un-American Activities itself was founded in 1938.

Neither the court-made law in *Watkins* nor factual error in arriving at it strikes as dangerously at the American heritage as the clear attempt in the same opinion to amend the Constitution by unconstitutional means. The opinion, written by Chief Justice Warren, says, ". . . nor can the First Amendment's freedoms of speech, press, religion, or political belief or association be abridged." The First Amendment *does guarantee* freedom of *speech, press, religion* and *assembly*. But what are these supposed freedoms of "political belief" and "association" which Warren has added? Is freedom of political belief the right to assassinate a government? Is freedom of association the right to associate in a criminal conspiracy? One can only guess what the Supreme Court would hold, once this court-made amendment has solidified into accepted law.

The kind of government the court appears to want is a government by jurists acting without restraint by written statute. It is not the kind of government under which America can survive in freedom.

## The Runaway Court—V

Too much of the law of our land is being rewritten today by sociological authors with one eye on some personal ideology and the other on book publication royalties. They hold no governmental office, elective or appointive. They are under no oath to support the Constitution. Yet the justices of the United States Supreme Court have shown a disturbing tendency to regard their opinions above both Constitution and legislative law.

Justice William O. Douglas, writing the court's opinion upholding constitutionality of compulsory unionism in railroad operations, said: "One would have to be blind to history to assert that trade unionism did not enhance and strengthen the right to work. See Webb, *History of Trade Unionism;* Gregory, *Labor and the Law*." One of the books he cited as an "authority" *was written in the 1890s.*

Chief Justice Earl Warren, in the historic school desegregation cases, wrote: "Whatever may have been the extent of psychological knowledge at the time of Plessy v. Ferguson, this (new) finding is amply supported by modern authority." In reversing the 58-year-old Supreme Court doctrine in favor of separate but equal school facilities, as it had been enunciated in the Plessy case, Warren went on to cite six supposed authorities, then added, "And see generally Myrdal, *An American Dilemma*."

To keep the record straight, we repeat what we have shown so many times, that we bitterly oppose public school segregation. But we would be false to our principles if we did not recognize that the reliance of the Supreme Court on sociology instead of law makes a mockery of law. The Swedish sociologist, Gunnar Myrdal, in the very same book which is given all-inclusive acceptance by Warren's opinion, writes that the Constitution of the United States is "impractical and unsuited to modern conditions," and that its adoption was "nearly a plot against the common people."

Sociology, while still an infant science and subject to all the errors of infancy, nevertheless is entitled to thoughtful consideration *when laws are made.* If the Constitution is to be amended, the advice of social scientists should be given as much weight as the people think wise. But the place for sociology is in the *making of laws,* not in their judicial administration. Sociologists should be heard when an amendment to the Constitution is considered by Congress and the states, not when someone proposes an illegal amendment through the back door of court decision.

The court is in fact exceeding its own powers under the Constitution when it attempts to say that a law which meant one thing yesterday must mean another today because "times have changed." The processes of legislative action and constitutional amendment were specifically designed to meet changing times. The Supreme Court is not assigned any part in these processes. The court has no right to pass upon the *wisdom* of any law. It has the right, and this only by consent of Congress, to pass upon a law's *constitutionality.*

The Constitution in its highest sense is a set of moral principles laid down for the guidance of this nation. It has for several years been under indirect attack by political and juridical pragmatists who profess to believe that it can be kept alive only by being changed from day to day in keeping with the will of "the majority" or the findings of sociology. Essentially, they propose a government of expedience administered by the judiciary. The eventual outcome of their program could be nothing but a kind of disorderly society in which no one knew, from hour to hour, what the law might be.

Unfortunately, the Supreme Court has gone a long way toward adopting the theory that the Constitution has no validity except what the court and its "authorities" permit it to have. It has sought to give the writings of obscure authors greater power in the lawmaking process than Congress has. It relies more upon sociologists than upon lawyers for its references.

If "justice under the law" is to remain the American creed, this trend must be halted.

## The Runaway Court—VI

The United States Supreme Court needs curbing. It has leaped the boundaries of constitutionality, replaced rule by law with rule by the court, usurped or shriveled the rightful functions of legislative and executive departments and attempted to make of the states mere puppets to sociology. The justices have refused respect to their own predecessors and ignored the competence of better men in the lower courts. Action to offset this assault upon the balance of American government is imperative.

Remedies that have been suggested range all the way down from the extreme of impeachment. More moderate are measures introduced in Congress, where the final responsibility is placed by the Constitution.

The heart of the problem is how to *preserve* the Supreme Court, not how to punish it or humble it. The goal that must be sought was expressed by Chief Justice John Marshall many years ago. He wrote: "The Constitution is either a superior, paramount law, unchangeable by ordinary means—or it is on the level with ordinary legislative acts, it is alterable when the Legislature shall please to alter it. If the former part of the alternative be true, then a legislative act contrary to the Constitution is not the law. If the latter part be true, then written constitutions are absurd attempts on the part of the people to limit a power (of government) in its own nature illimitable." Substitute "court decrees" for "legislative acts" and "the court" for "the Legislature," and Marshall's doctrine is still valid.

It is not the Supreme Court as an institution which is at fault today. It is the philosophy of the justices who control it at this moment of history. On the theory that the law is "what the court says it is," the justices are setting precedents right and left denying the validity of the Constitution as "the supreme law" which means what it says. Precedent when it is unchallenged becomes habit for future generations. The people through Congress must find a way unmistakably to repudiate the philosophy of the present justices, to re-state their faith in government by law. Otherwise they will surrender the future to government by whim—the doctrinaire whim of any combination of five members of the court.

Americans need to declare their adherence to the Constitution and written law with such force that the justices of this court, and those who follow them, can make no mistake about the country's temper. A constitutional declaration that our courts must adhere only to the law, and not to the Supreme Court when the Supreme Court violates the law, would provide the shock the Warren court so badly needs. It should be the first order of business in Congress.

---

It is not in the American tradition to take injustice supinely nor to refuse to face problems courageously and beat them down. The men who wrote the Declaration of Independence and the Constitution and the men and women who crossed and settled a continent were not made of such weak stuff. Our courage has been diluted, our resistance weakened, and many heads brainwashed, but the voice of resistance can still be heard. Witness the following.

## Servitude Without Pay

### GEORGE PECK

In February of 1948, Miss Vivien Kellems, a manufacturer of Westport, Conn., made the startling announcement that she would defy the Federal Government by refusing to deduct and pay the Withholding Tax from the pay envelopes of her employees.

In making this announcement Miss Kellems stated that the Withholding Tax law was "illegal, immoral and unconstitutional." She asked the Government to prosecute her and thus bring a test case before the courts. She held the firm conviction that the Withholding Tax commandeered every employer into involuntary servitude, assumed that every American worker was unfit to administer his own affairs, that it sowed seeds of dissension between employer and employee and concealed the hold that the politicians and bureaucrats had acquired on every pay envelope.

Well, the Federal Government refused this redoubtable lady's challenge. It knew full well that no fair United States court would ever rule that any American should be forced to act as an unpaid tax collector. In May, it sent four Internal Revenue agents to her factory to demand payment of the taxes she had refused to withhold. These agents knew that these taxes had been promptly paid by all of her employees, but they claimed the full amount as a 100 per cent penalty for her failure to deduct. Upon Miss Kellem's refusal to pay this penalty, the agents, *carrying no court order,* went to her bank and intimidated its officers into surrendering out of her account the full amount of $1,685.40.

Miss Kellems continued NOT to deduct from her employees, and in August 1949, the agents returned demanding $6,100 as a penalty, again despite the fact that every dollar of income tax had been paid promptly directly to the Federal Government by her employees. Again Miss Kellems refused to pay the penalty, whereupon they seized the $6,100 from her bank account.

Miss Kellems demanded a refund which was refused. She filed a claim with the Federal District Court in New Haven in January, 1950, and in February, 1951, finally secured a trial. The Court ordered a refund of the $1,685.40 and $6,100, which had been seized illegally from her bank account. But the matter of the constitutionality of the Withholding Tax was not tested. It still in 1960, remains untested.

The one way to get rid of of this unconstitutional Withholding Tax is to get rid of its parent, the personal income tax. This can be accomplished by getting behind the 23rd Amendment, originated and sponsored by our associate, Willis E. Stone. This Amendment in its Section 4 says: "Congress shall not levy taxes on personal incomes, inheritances, and/or gifts."

And now another voice has been added against serving the Government without pay. We quote a letter written by A. G. Heinsohn, Jr., President, Cherokee Textile Mills, Sevierville, Tenn.; and Chairman, Tennessee Independents, on March 25, 1960, to Congressmen Carroll Reece and Howard Baker. The letter shouts for itself, requiring no comment from us. It reads:

"Since I pay taxes in two districts this is a joint letter.

"On a tract of cut-over land I employ two mountaineers.

"On January 2, 1960, I sent my check for $206.00 to the Internal Revenue Service to cover Social Security taxes on the wages paid them. It was deposited five days later.

"Now the Internal Revenue Service threatens to fine me. Not for failing to pay the tax. No, they are going to fine me because they don't like the WAY I paid it.

"To please them it seems that I must carry my records around and when the Social Security tax on wages paid these mountaineers exceeds $100.00, I must search out an 'authorized' bank and make some kind of a deposit.

"Now, gentlemen, where did you ever get the power to make me an errand boy for bureaucrats whose salaries I already pay? What will these bureaucrats do when we dopey tax-paying slaves perform all the work?

"Shall I turn communist and seek Supreme Court sanctuary?

"Why are you in Congress?

"To vote us deeper into bureaucratic enslavement or to protect our liberty and our property as you swore on the Bible to do?

"Since you voted me into this involuntary servitude, you get me out. Tell that bureaucrat to jump in the lake. I don't work without compensation."

## Repeal Income Taxes

### WILLIS E. STONE

The State of Nevada is the third State to adopt a Resolution for the "Proposed 23rd Amendment," and provides a promise of relief from the agony of "Income Tax Day."

This amendment will curb the "tax, spend and elect" philosophy which seems to have dominated the political scene for so many years. There have been many who feel there is no hope of ever controlling the appetite of the tax collector, yet the action taken first by Wyoming, then by Texas, and now by Nevada, indicates there is every chance in the world of solving the problems of unlimited federal taxing and spending.

The "Proposed 23rd Amendment" is a simple declaration of basic policy, as it does not add to, nor subtract from, the original terms of the Constitution. It is designed to give the Constitution new force and effect. It provides that:

"Sec. 1. The Government of the United States shall not engage in any business, professional, commercial, financial or industrial enterprise except as specified in the Constitution.

"Sec. 4. Congress shall not levy taxes on personal incomes, inheritances, and/or gifts."

The "Proposed 23rd Amendment" is generally seriously considered whenever it is energetically brought before the Legislature of a State because the States also are having tax troubles these days.

The pre-emption of State taxing powers, and the steady encroach-
ment of federal agencies on State jurisdiction is felt keenly by
the administrators of State governments.

Those who gloomily forecast that nothing can be done to control our rush into national socialism should review the facts.

Within the past few months working organizations to promote
public understanding of the "Proposed 23rd Amendment" have
been developing in 37 States. In some of these the amendment
has been put before the Legislature for study and action.

In Wyoming a Resolution for the amendment was adopted by
a voice vote in the Democratic House and approved without dissent in the Republican Senate, and signed by a Democratic Governor because he wanted to go on record in favor of it.

In Texas, where not a single Republican is to be found in the
State Legislature, the "Proposed 23rd Amendment" was approved
by the House on a vote of 80 to 55 and was approved the following
day by the Senate on a voice vote.

In Nevada thirteen (9 Republicans and 4 Democrats) of the 17
members of the State Senate jointly initiated the Resolution. It
quickly passed the Senate and on March 11, 1960, was approved
by the Democratic House by a 31 to 10 vote.

Here is powerful evidence that people get results when they go
to work to get action on the "Proposed 23rd Amendment" designed to solve our tax-and-spend problems of government.

Every citizen, every community, city, county and state will prosper under the terms of the amendment—and so will the federal
government. This is true because the amendment will reestablish
a rule of just and equal law. It will cause the federal government
to sell vast enterprises back to the American people from whom
they were taken. These enterprises will be put back on local, state
and federal tax rolls. By getting rid of these bureaucratic enterprises—more than 700 of them—the costs of the federal government
will be cut more than in half, which will be more than enough to
offset the revenue lost through repeal of the 16th (income tax)
amendment.

States will again have sovereignty over the areas within their
boundaries, and the conflicts between state and federal governments will vanish.

It is people, however—just we people—who will profit most.
Again we will get a full day's pay for a day's work—without taxes

being withheld. It will mean better than a 20 per cent increase in take-home pay for the American people without changing the rate of pay by a single penny.

This is the reward available by reestablishing the power of the Constitution through the "Proposed 23rd Amendment." It is worth the effort to make this question of economic freedom the main issue this year of 1960.

## Letters of Protest

One day there appeared in our local evening paper an insulting editorial taking the cotton mills of America to task for complaining about the unfair Japanese competition which the government in Washington was forcing upon them. I wrote a letter of protest, which they refused to publish. I then ran it as a paid advertisement in our morning paper.

Editor, *Knoxville News-Sentinel*
Knoxville, Tennessee

DEAR SIR:

Your "Dogs In The Manger" editorial of August 12th, has just been called to my attention. I would appreciate your publishing this reply, provided it is given in full. Otherwise do not print any part of it.

You say that citizens in the cotton textile business should not be protected by the Federal Government from an uncontrolled flow of low-cost cotton fabrics and garments made in Japan. We who do seek this protection you compare with dogs.

Well, let's see.

Suppose the Federal Government used tax money seized from the *Knoxville News-Sentinel* and from its employees to purchase American newsprint. Suppose the Federal Government resold that newsprint to Japanese newspaper publishers at 30% less than American newspapers could buy it. Suppose Japanese newspaper publishers, paying one tenth the wages paid by the *Knoxville News-Sentinel,* could publish a paper in Knoxville and could offer advertising space at considerably under the *Knoxville News-Sentinel's* cost.

Would the *Knoxville News-Sentinel* (Scripps-Howard Chain) welcome such competition?

The *Knoxville News-Sentinel* says:—"We have got to help support Japan in the present circumstances, in one way or another." Does this really mean that the *Knoxville News-Sentinel* is willing to act as a sacrificial goat in the starry-eyed process of throwing American wealth away abroad or does the *Knoxville News-Sentinel* only favor such sacrifices when made by other American citizens?

Perhaps the *Knoxville News-Sentinel* can explain how the transfer of textile payroll money and garment payroll money to Japan will help our local merchants. Perhaps the *Knoxville News-Sentinel* can explain to the textile and garment factory employees in this area the great benefits of being put out of work by the Japs. Perhaps the *Knoxville News-Sentinel* can explain to the citizens whose savings built our local mills and factories how noble it would be for them to hand their business over to the Japs.

Strange, isn't it, that a few of us are stubborn enough to still believe in America; old fashioned enough to believe that the government's first responsibility is to protect American jobs, American payrolls and American property. So, in the opinion of the *Knoxville News-Sentinel* this makes us dogs, does it?

Very truly yours,

A. G. HEINSOHN, JR.

Cherokee Textile Mills, Sevierville, Tennessee

To further protest the absurd government policy toward Japanese textiles, the following letter was written to Senator Gore:

The Honorable Albert Gore
Senate Office Building
Washington, D.C.

### ARROGANT MASTERS IN CONGRESS

DEAR SIR:

On June 24, 1956, a petition signed by 442 employees of this mill asked you to protect them against possible loss of their jobs due to the importation of low-cost textiles from Japan.

The Congressional Record of June 28, 1956, shows that you voted AGAINST Tennessee workers and FOR the Japanese on a motion to limit these imports. The motion failed to carry in the Senate by a

45 to 43 vote because you and your fellow turncoat, Estes Kefauver, sold us down the river.

Now, Senator, would you be kind as to explain to us simple country folks back home just exactly how it helps Tennessee factory employees to be put out of work by the Japanese?

Explain to the 220 decent American citizens who invested their savings in this plant and thus created jobs for some 500 Tennessee workers, just how it benefits them to hand their business over to the Japanese.

Explain to the merchants of Tennessee how the transfer of factory payrolls to Japan will help them.

Explain to the cotton growers of Tennessee how much better it is for them to exchange their trust in God, their freedom, their right of jury trial and their legitimate markets for bureaucratic masters and handouts of money picked from the pockets of other citizens by the tax collector.

Tell us, if your labor-boss patrons will permit it, are you in Congress to protect the freedom, the jobs and the property of Tennessee citizens, or are you so big for your britches that you now seek to regulate the world at the expense of your tax-paying slaves in Tennessee?

The time for pussy-footing is past. Plain talk is in order and since you seek re-election this fall, let us know now just where we stand so that we may decide whether to keep on voting for an arrogant master or start looking for a real American to represent us in the Senate.

Sincerely yours,
A. G. HEINSOHN, JR.

John R. Donaldson, a farmer friend of mine, got a taste of U.S. Department of Agriculture tyranny and wrote a letter to the U.S. Attorney in the Northern District of Ohio.

I sent copies of this letter to my representatives in Congress and asked them, "Is this America or Russia?," and further called their attention to the fact that "unless the Members of Congress who really believe in their oath of office are patriotic enough to remove the nose ring of today's unprincipled political parties, how can the self-destruction of America be averted?" Here is John Donaldson's letter.

April 3, 1959

To: U.S. Attorney
United States District Court
Northern District of Ohio
Western Division

Regarding: United States of America vs John R. Donaldson
          Civil No. 8029
          Appeal No. 13,763

I herewith denounce this judgment against me as being a gross violation of all American constitutional and Anglo-Saxon concepts of the term "due process of law."

I was denied the right to a trial before a jury even though this right is guaranteed by the 7th Article of the Bill of Rights and is also guaranteed by the Federal Rules of Civil Procedure enacted by Congress for the conduct of the courts.

I was prejudged guilty of overplanting wheat before entering the court and was given no opportunity by the court to prove the falseness of such claim even though I was fully able to do so.

Further, the United States Department of Agriculture and the Department of Justice offered not one iota of proof of any kind to support the claim against me.

This case simply brings to a focus what has been going on, with a few notable exceptions, for the past 5 years in wheat penalty cases in the federal courts; wherein the farmers have been accorded the same consideration that a Jew would have received in the courts of Nazi Germany.

In this prostitution of American Justice the federal courts have assumed the same shameful role as that enacted by Pontius Pilate in the tragic drama of Calvary. Fundamental human rights have been sacrificed to socialistic or communistic expediency.

I extend this denunciation to include the Department of Justice, which has cared not one whit for justice, but has been concerned only with exacting by any expedient method the "pound of flesh" from the farmer.

Above all I extend this to include the communistic monster, the U.S. Department of Agriculture, which has subjugated the American farmer into serfdom and is eating out the substance of the American people.

JOHN DONALDSON

"Eating out the substance!" Sounds as if John has been reading the Declaration of Independence. More people should.

Some sparks of resistance will not be hard to find in this open letter to Mr. John J. McCloy.

### Easy, Now, Mr. McCloy

### OPEN LETTER

Mr. John J. McCloy, Chairman
The Chase Manhattan Bank
Pine Street
New York, New York

DEAR SIR:

This statement of yours made last December 15 (1959) before the Investment Bankers Association of New York is deserving of further scrutiny:

"There is no question about the internal strength of our economy—it is stronger than ever."

It is with some trepidation that the undersigned operator of a couple of pint-sized cotton mills questions the head of a huge New York Bank. But, after all, size does not determine truth. And the bigger they were the louder they voiced their false pronouncements back in 1929.

No one in his right mind wants to live through another depression. But if a force greater than man did create this universe, and if in so doing, did impose certain natural laws beyond the control of puny man, and if these natural laws have been arrogantly violated over a period of years, it is quite possible that a painful hangover period awaits. In fact, the more positive the claims to immunity, the more likely is the day of reckoning. Because when man boasts the power to control the laws of nature, he is in effect denying the existence of God.

How can America be "stronger than ever," when after 28 years of Roosevelt-Truman-Eisenhower new deal, fair deal, modern Republican chicanery:

*First:* We find our freedom vanishing.

To be sure we can still write letters like this, we can still attend the church of our choice and we can still speak out against the un-constitutional concentration of power in Washington.

But can we:

(a) Keep what we earn?
(b) Farm as we wish?
(c) Work as we choose?
(d) Dispose of our property freely?
(e) Possess gold?

Isn't the loss of economic freedom the forerunner of the bayonet and the firing squad, with subsequent loss of all freedom? Isn't that the warning Woodrow Wilson voiced in these words:

> The history of liberty is a history of the limitation of governmental power, not the increase of it. When we resist therefore the concentration of power, we are resisting the processes of death, because a concentration of power is what always precedes the destruction of human liberty.

*Second:* We find our dollar dishonest.

An honest dollar is one that can be redeemed in gold. Human history shows that when government removes this safeguard to fiscal honesty, insolvency follows. In 1943 our national debt was 19½ billion dollars. Today it is more than 290 billion dollars. If "internal strength" is built by ruining the purchasing power of the dollar through deficit spending and dishonest monetization of the debt, then all the lessons of the past, learned the hard way, are indeed meaningless.

*Third:* We find our government infiltrated.

The communist conspiracy to conquer the world was but a gleam in Lenin's eye in 1918. But before he died in 1924 he prescribed along these lines:

> First we will take Eastern Europe. Next the masses of Asia. Then we shall encircle that last bastion of capitalism the United States of America. We shall not have to attack: it will fall like overripe fruit into our hands.

Roosevelt's ill-fated recognition of Stalin's regime in 1933, his tragic acceptance of Russia as a needless ally a few days before the end of World War II; the treacherous scheming of Alger Hiss in the forming of the United Nations; the unbelievable red-carpet appeasement of Khrushchev in America recently—all of these acts have played directly into the hands of the communists so that today there are some 700 million non-Russian, non-communists living as slaves behind the Iron Curtain. In America the communist infiltration of our government is so effective that, despite documentary evidence from the FBI and from Congressional Committees, their expulsion from positions of trust and power seems virtually impossible.

No, Mr. McCloy, surely a nation that has abandoned moral and spiritual values by exchanging personal responsibility and trust in God for false political promises of something-for-nothing is not "stronger than ever."

Isn't this the time to pray humbly for divine guidance; to seek a way to throw off the atheistic-socialistic-communistic yoke imposed upon us by the faithless, unprincipled politicians in control of both parties?

Sincerely yours,
A. G. HEINSOHN, JR.
P. O. Box 152, Sevierville, Tennessee

---

Mr. Roger M. Blough, Chairman, United States Steel Corporation, challenges some "free-wheeling assumptions" that have been loosed by the liberal clique, in his forthright and factual testimony before the Subcommittee on Anti-trust and Monopoly of the Senate Committee on the Judiciary.

## The Great Monopoly Myth

### ROGER M. BLOUGH

In these hearings, we are prepared to present the whole financial story of United States Steel, as it stands today after seventeen years of inflation—the facts about our costs, our prices and our profits. But in my statement here this morning, I am impelled to discuss a couple of other free-wheeling assumptions that have been standing unchallenged in the record, and that seem to me to be considerably cluttering up the landscape of proper understanding.

One of the most persistent of these unfounded assumptions is that a big corporation, like United States Steel, has no real competition; that it thus enjoys "monopoly power" or "concentration of power" which enables it to boost its prices to what have been described here, I believe, as "unendurable levels"; and that in this way it reaps fabulous profits, the public interest to the contrary notwithstanding.

But that is the assumption. What are the facts? Does United States Steel really possess that kind of power? Does it actually get these fabulous profits? Let's look at the record:

When United States Steel was created fifty-six years ago, it was the biggest corporation America had ever seen up to that time. It produced twice as much steel as all of its competitors put together.

Now self-preservation, of course, is one of the most basic of all instincts. So if United States Steel did possess, in those days, the "monopoly power" frequently attributed to it, then presumably it would have expanded its production at the expense of its competitors; or certainly—at the very least—it would have held its own ground against them. In which event, we would expect to find that United States Steel today still produces no less than 66 per cent of the total domestic output, as it did back in 1902.

The fact is, however, it does not. Today it produces less than 30 per cent of the steel that is made in America; and where once it turned out twice as much as all of its competitors put together, its competitors now turn out more than twice as much as it does.

It is true that U.S. Steel has grown during this period and that, last year, it produced about three times as much steel as it did in 1902; but its competitors have grown far more lustily. They produced fifteen times as much steel as they did in 1902!

Yes, over the years, United States Steel's share of total domestic production has declined continuously, right down to the present day, while its competitors have taken an ever-increasing share of the market away from it. For every ton of steel-making capacity that we have added during these years, our competitors have added almost three tons to their capacity; and this year—for the first time —our share of the total capacity of the industry dropped to 29.7 per cent.

These are the facts, Mr. Chairman. Here on the record itself is the most conclusive possible evidence of the vigorous competition that exists within the steel industry. To persist in the discredited assumption that there is an absence of competition in steel, is to renounce reality and to cling to delusion. And to argue that concentration in this industry is on the rise, is merely to say that concentration among the smaller companies is increasing at the expense of United States Steel. This, then, is a new concept of concentration—a kind of concentration in reverse!

Let us not forget, moreover, that vigorous and successful as U.S. Steel's competitors have been, they are by no means the only competition which we must meet in selling steel. With American wage rates three times as high as those which are paid to steelworkers abroad, we face increasing competition from foreign imports; and in certain product lines, this competition has cut heavily into our market.

Beyond that, too, is the intense competition that steel faces from other industries producing a host of products that can be used as substitutes for steel. Thus aluminum is striving mightily to replace steel in the automotive market, in the building industry, and in containers. Plastics are contending against steel in the manufacture of pipe, and for hundreds of other uses. Detroit has been experimenting with the use of fiber-glass for automobile bodies. The steel we produce for the manufacture of tin cans competes against glass, paper and other substances. In the construction field, steel must vie with prestressed concrete, wood, masonry, slate, asbestos and other materials too numerous to mention. And always it must compete against other metals such as copper, bronze, lead, magnesium and so on.

So let no one suppose that the customers of any steel company are unresourceful in protecting their own interests. They will buy their needs from the company best able to compete for their patronage in terms of price, quality, service, dependability and availability. And in the end, they alone will decide—as the American customer always does—which companies shall grow, which shall wither, which shall survive and which shall die. Theirs is the power to regulate and to control.

---

The following letter to the *Knoxville News-Sentinel* was not only published, but given top priority on the editorial page.

News-Sentinel Forum, Knoxville, Tennessee, November 26, 1958

CALLS GORE AND KEFAUVER "SOCIALISTS" AND WANTS INCOME TAX ABOLISHED

EDITOR, THE NEWS-SENTINEL:

This is in reply to your splendid thought-provoking editorials of November 2 (This One's Over-Used) and of November 20 (Apathy—The Unforgiveable Sin) .

As you say, it is true that the Executive, the Congress and the Supreme Court (Democrats and Republicans alike) are guilty of leading America into bureaucratic enslavement and bankruptcy, but would this be possible if we people back home did not condone it?

For example, if the editors of the Knoxville News-Sentinel are opposed to Socialism, then why do they urge the voters of Tennessee to keep sending Estes Kefauver and Albert Gore to the United States Senate?

The voting record of both of these men is open betrayal of states' rights and individual freedom. The record shows their zealous support of laws leading to bureaucratic enslavement. In fact, so outstanding has been their performance along these lines that they are given top endorsement by Walter Reuther's COPE, the political tool through which Reuther is gaining control of the Congress and of the nation.

If our Chambers of Commerce are so opposed to the Socialist-Communist trend in Washington, then why have they so roundly excoriated the National Chamber for branding the Tennessee Valley Authority as socialistic?

Do we citizens in this area not object to the loss of our freedom as long as we think we are getting something for nothing from Washington? Isn't loss of freedom an exorbitant price to pay for a cutrate electric bill? Wouldn't it be better to pay the legitimate rate for electricity and free ourselves from the Communist income tax?

Surely we must know that a Washington handout is but partial return of money previously seized from us through the income tax, which was devised by Karl Marx and prescribed by him in the Communist Manifesto for the self-destruction of America.

We must know that it is our money being redistributed in exchange for votes. We must know that political promises of something for nothing in contradiction of the laws of nature are the very essence of insecurity. We must know that true security exists when free men under God can enjoy the fruits of their own labor and be protected in the possession thereof.

The domination of Congress by Walter Reuther is about complete and from neither party comes a clear-cut denunciation of Socialistic big government in Washington. Neither party has the character to place truth and principle above political fraud.

We liberty-loving conservatives, who have been denied a real voting choice at the polls because there is little or no difference today between the Democrats and Republicans in Washington, must find a way to make our voices heard if the self-destruction of America is to be averted.

Instead of demanding bigger and better handouts from Washington, would it not be more appropriate to demand that the men we send to Congress concentrate instead on such patriotic objectives as those expressed by the Daughters of the American Revolution? These are:

1. Congress should curb the Supreme Court's unconstitutional and illegal activities and force it to stick to judicial activities as laid down in the Constitution.

2. We should abolish the income tax and those 731 illegal corporations which are (illegally) draining the Federal Treasury of $28½ billion per annum.

3. We should abolish so-called foreign aid "which is a definite Communist plan for destroying countries founded on the free enterprise system."

4. We should repeal the GATT (free trade) agreements, which are destroying many American industries and factories for the benefit of a few industrial behemoths.

5. We should withdraw recognition of Russia and all its satellites. (The D.A.R. pointed out that Russia has violated 50 of its 52 agreements with the United States.)

6. We should get the United States out of the United Nations and the United Nations out of the United States.

7. We should defluoridize all government and municipal water systems that have had sodium fluorides dumped in them at the prodding of selfish or subversive interests.

8. We should stop the move toward socialized medicine.

9. We should have Congress investigate (and forbid) the use of mental health bills to commit to state asylums persons guilty of political activities against the cliques in power.

10. We should uphold the integrity of the races God put on this earth, and oppose miscegenation.

11. We should condemn the political, economic, socialistic and one-world activities of the National Council of Churches.

12. We should oppose the haphazard and confusing proposal to "merge" the three major armed services "under one uniform."

A. G. HEINSOHN, JR.

Box 152, Sevierville

---

Strong and logical resistance to our march toward socialism is voiced by Harold B. Wess, now professor in the School of Business Administration, The American University, Washington, D.C.

## We Can't Have Freedom Without Capitalism

### HAROLD B. WESS

President Eisenhower, in a news conference, July 17, 1957, had this to say about his "many long discussions about our respective doctrines" with Soviet Marshal Zhukov: "I was very hard put to it when he insisted that their system appealed to the idealistic, and we completely to the materialistic, and I had a very tough time trying to defend our position. . . ."

Later in the conference, in answer to a question by one of the newspapermen, the President added: ". . . they ask these people to believe that their greatest satisfaction in life is in sacrificing for the state."

President Eisenhower is not alone in this confusion. Millions of Americans—including statesmen, politicians, college professors, teachers and students—have a blurred image of our society.

Since the meeting with General Eisenhower, Zhukov has been fired—despite his great contribution to "the state." He is lucky to be alive, and since under communism he cannot own anything, he is entirely at the mercy of the state.

This "state" which Zhukov described as "idealistic" makes it impossible for him to find work in some private industry because there is no private industry. In our country a general who retires can seek and does often find employment in private industry. He can and does go into business for himself. He can and usually does own a home and a car. He quite often has savings with which he can do what he pleases.

On the basis of Zhukov's own experience, then, which doctrine is the more "idealistic"?

What we need is an economic psychiatrist who will dig out, from the sewage of our subconscious minds, all the ugly things that the enemies of capitalism have implanted there. We will then stop apologizing for the word "capitalism." The fact that we have to resort to such phrases as "modern capitalism," "controlled capitalism," "enlightened capitalism," "people's capitalism," is evidence enough that we somehow think that "capitalism" is a naughty word. Talking about "modern capitalism" is like talking about "modern humanity." It is a device used by the enemies of capitalism and by its weak-kneed apologists. Of course capitalism is modern. It is modern because it is a system which is dynamic, flexible, and free to develop and evolve.

Socialism and communism—like all forms of dictatorship—are frozen societies. The Nazis believed that they had achieved a society which would last a thousand years. The Communists believe the same. They believe that they have a system which is the ultimate in perfection and which will last forever. None of these systems tolerates any authentic change. Since change is the only constant in life, these systems must ultimately collapse or wither.

Capitalism, on the other hand, is a way of life which has in it the inherent ingredients of growth and change. Capitalism adjusts to changing times and changing conditions. Because of its fundamental principles capitalism makes possible peaceful revolutions like the change in the pattern of income distribution.

What, basically, is capitalism? Shorn of economic jargon, capitalism is a social order in which the individual has the inherent right to own property and capital and the right to pass it on to his children and others. It is a social and economic system where the individual is free to own property, free to work for himself or others, free not to work for the Government, free to choose his employer, his job or his vocation.

John Locke in the 17th century said that there are three primary natural rights, "life, liberty and property." So long as the individual's livelihood is entirely dependent on the state, be it socialist dictatorship or Communist, he is automatically denied these natural rights of "life, liberty and property." That is the reason why only under capitalism can a man be free and be master of his own life.

When a government becomes the sole owner of all property and tools of production the political bureaucracy will use every means to continue to enjoy its ownership.

In addition to this total power, the Communist dictatorship also uses ideology, indoctrination and propaganda in order to enslave the people and make sure that nothing will happen to deprive them of their ownership.

The crucial point about capitalism is that with ownership in the hands of individuals, rather than in the hands of government, such government tyranny is impossible. There is no greater power than that of a government which owns and controls everything. Once a government bureaucracy holds complete ownership it will exert power and propaganda in order to continue to enjoy its ownership.

We miss the whole point of the freedom inherent in capitalism when we emphasize the high productivity and high standard of living of our system as evidence of its superiority to other systems. High productivity and superior standards of living are the result of our freedom! Our success as a capitalist society is the fruit of the incentives of a free people. The Communists promise to outproduce us. They also hold out a promise to their people of a better standard of living in the never-never land of the future. Even if they succeed, and I doubt it, their people will still be the pawns of the state, the slaves they are now.

These are the facts President Eisenhower should have pointed out to Zhukov. That is why capitalism is truly idealistic and communism crass materialism. A slave state may be able to build a pyramid or a sputnik in a comparatively short time as measured by history, but in the long run it must decay from the lack of the individual's urge to create and to express himself.

There are many kinds of social and economic societies in the world today, and it must be evident to any unprejudiced mind that the most advanced societies, in terms of the freedom of the individual, are predominantly capitalist. I say "predominantly capitalist" because most of the capitalistic societies have allowed a socialist component to be introduced into the economic system. Unfortunately the United States, too, has fallen prey to this trend. Nevertheless, the societies where capitalism outweighs the socialistic components have greater freedom, virility and growth, and a higher standard of living than their more collectivized competitors.

In this connection, let us remember that excessive taxation is a form of socialism. What the individual earns through his own efforts is being taken away from him by the Government, thus further strengthening the centralized bureaucracy. It also means that the individual is less and less able to invest his savings in stocks, bonds, real estate and other savings media, so that he becomes more and more dependent on the Government. The time can come when the Government might take away even the last remnant of his savings, as Soviet Russia has done from time to time by forcing its people to turn over their money in exchange for new, devaluated currency. This could very easily happen in our country when the Government debt becomes too high.

We tend to delude ourselves into the belief that total socialism which is really communism, will not come to us. But so prominent a socialist as Norman Thomas is quoted in the Congressional Record (April 17, 1958, p. A3080), as follows: "The United States is making greater strides toward socialism under Eisenhower than even under Roosevelt, particularly in the fields of Federal spending and welfare legislation."

A question arises as to why neither party has been willing or able to check this trend. Obviously it is due to the pressure from the entrenched bureaucracies already in power, the desire to secure votes through reckless spending of taxpayer's money, and the failure to appreciate fully our drift toward socialism.

In a mixed economy such as ours—part socialist but predominantly capitalist—the socialist part lives off the fat supplied by the capitalist segment. The process of this erosion is gradual and almost imperceptible. We are therefore unaware of the gradual shift—from a predominantly capitalist to a predominantly socialist society. If this process is not halted there will be no fat to live off and we shall find ourselves with a powerful, centralized socialist bureaucracy in complete control.

In a capitalist society the individual has the inherent right to own capital and property, and to pass it on to others; he is free to work for himself or others, free to choose his job or vocation, free not to work for the Government; he is assured of his personal freedom, he is assured of his God-given power of self-determination and he is protected from arbitrary control by a centralized bureaucracy. Let us keep our vision clear, for: "Where there is no vision, the people perish." (Proverbs 29:18).

—Reprinted with permission from Human Events,<br>November 10, 1958.

# XV

# Rays of Hope

THERE ARE TRULY encouraging rays of hope in the seemingly hopeless shape of things to come. Many of these hopeful rays have permeated the preceding chapters. The more basic and significant rays of hope must, and now will be brought into sharp and burning focus.

We have come to this tragic point in the course of human events not merely because of stupidity in not honestly and carefully pre-assessing the probable results of a course of action entered upon. It is an indisputable historical fact that things seldom, if ever, work *out* as they are feverishly worked *up* by the unprincipled or unwitting leaders of thought in action in every realm of human affairs.

This is only part of the answer. We have to dig deeper. It is evident that fundamentally the responsibility must fall on leaders who have turned education into evil propaganda: education that has become brainwashing, mental conditioning to accept new standards in which our culture is being watered down, as can be clearly seen in art, literature, and music; in which economic principles and historical tradition are perverted to meet the purposes of the collaborators in collectivism; and in which our moral and spiritual heritage is being junked, too often, sad to say, by those whose lives are supposedly dedicated to its preservation and furtherance. Take, for example, Dr. Brock Chisholm, formerly Director General of the World Health Organization (an agency of the United Nations) and more recently President of the World Federation for Mental Health, and Vice President of the World Association of World Federalists, who calls for "the reinterpretation and eventually eradication of the concept of right and wrong which has been the basis of child training. . . ."

Just as education, in broad outline, has put us in the hole, education will have to get us out, and there are rays of hope that this will come to pass, primarily through an understanding of and compliance with Natural Law, or God's Law, on which all human action must be based.

Toward this end great strides are being made.

No problem will ever be solved or progress made until that problem is faced up to, recognized, and then intelligently tackled.

On this score one of the most encouraging signs of the times is the fact that businessmen are facing up to the need of more economic education for businessmen. An outstanding example is found in the address of Mr. L. R. Boulware, Vice President of the General Electric Company, before the U.S. Chamber of Commerce, Washington, D.C., January 27, 1960.

## The Urgency of More Economic Education

### L. R. BOULWARE

I have one consuming fear about the new or increased interest in politics by us businessmen.

It is that a lot of enthusiastic political activity will suddenly take place before the acquisition of the economic knowledge needed to give such activity the proper direction and effectiveness—needed, in fact, to keep the activity from doing immense harm instead of any good.

Politics is the cart. Economics is the horse.

The danger is not just that we may get the cart before the horse but that we will find ourselves with an entirely horseless cart—a cart we will unwittingly help roll back down the hill which we have struggled up during our prior history.

*I believe the elimination or sharp reduction of economic ignorance is the most pressing problem of our country and the world.*

I believe it is the most pressing problem of business. If business had no political problems in connection with government, we businessmen and the rest of the public would still need to eliminate or sharply reduce economic ignorance—in our own mutual interest—in order for the business process to be permitted to function up to anything like its usefulness to consumers, workers, savers, suppliers, neighbors, tax collectors, and the rest of the public—as well as to us professional managers of business.

I believe we businessmen and other intelligent and dedicated citizens of this country can accomplish any research and communication or teaching job that is judged important enough to warrant our best effort.

But how to alert and convince these thought leaders of the relative importance of the job to be done is the problem.

Yet it seems so obvious that—if economic ignorance had not been, and were not now, so widespread in Europe, Asia, Africa, South America and North America, including the United States—we would not have such recurring problems, of such anxiety and long-continuing expense in lives and treasure, as those presented by Hitler, Stalin, and the lesser dictator-destroyers closer home.

If it were not for this ignorance, the newly free peoples in Asia and Africa would not be expecting magic simply from having their own government. I am for people being free, of course, but what I am afraid is too surely going to happen is that too many of them are going to lose their freedom almost before they have it—simply by embracing ideas they are wrongly assured will protect and enhance their freedom and well-being.

If we U.S. citizens were not in general so economically ignorant and thus politically gullible in such marked degree—or even if this were not so often true of our paid professionals and voluntary leaders in economics such as public servants, editors, teachers, clergy, union officials, people in the professions, and us businessmen—it would not now appear to the more nervous of us that most all the candidates of both parties are convinced it is "good politics" not only to compete for the favor and support of top union officials but also to be prepared openly and publicly to be materially guided in office by these union officials who are pushing the country in what we businessmen think is so much the wrong direction economically by promoting deficit spending, inflation, resistance to technological progress, privileged legal and illegal violence, substitution of debilitating central government planning for the incentives, rewards and progress of the free market, and other damaging invasions of personal liberty and well-being.

Our real trouble—the basic reason bad things can be made to look good to most of us citizens—is that we do not understand this unprecedented freedom and well-being we enjoy. We do not know how it was achieved, how we can preserve and enhance it, how we can impede and damage it by the very measures we are wrongly told will improve it. We do not know how the level of living is raised here—or even in a socialist country.

Yet to the individual voter—regardless of the qualifications of any particular voter—is decentralized the basic economic decision-making power as to the increasingly numerous, complex and important public issues of our times. To the same citizen—as a consumer, worker, saver and taxpayer—is decentralized most every one of the basic economic decisions of daily living. These decisions obviously determine the opportunities and rewards—the usefulness to all concerned—of the country's business enterprises with which most all of us here are connected directly or indirectly.

Is the average voter—the average consumer, worker, saver—competent to make such decisions? Has he had as much help in his decision-making equipment as we businessmen—who are at the crossroads of economics and politics—should have been able to give him and trying to give him?

As to what would be required for the country to be served as well by economics—as it is by technology—let's look at the varying degree of technological knowledge that was found to be required at varying levels to make the automobile industry function in the notably satisfying way it has.

The top laboratory level concerned itself with the fundamental departures and with inquiry into the laws of nature. Thence came the electric self-starter, the anti-knock gasoline, the high compression engine, the instantly drying lacquer to replace 25 coats of slow drying paint that wasn't then any good.

At the next level, that of the car manufacturer, the engineers designed the car and the annual changes to wed the available knowledge, including improvements, with changing public taste.

At the dealer level, the technical knowledge required was that required for demonstrating and servicing the car.

At the consumer level, of course, the technical knowledge required was the least—but still impressive. The driver had to be taught what buttons to press, how to steer and brake, how to treat the accelerator with respect, that water would not work instead of gasoline, and that he shouldn't try to drive with the brakes on.

Most all the 70 million U.S. cars, trucks and busses are out every day in the hands of that number of licensed drivers from the 80 million available. Yet relatively few fatal or even very damaging mistakes are made in a whole year. And any relatively minor mistake that comes to the attention of the police is recorded on the back of the driver's license.

I want to emphasize that driver's license. It is a certificate of basic competency to use frightening power. It's continued possession is proof of practically mistakeless care in the use of that power —else the license would have been taken away.

Think of what is proclaimed by that license—adequate knowledge of the law, sober dexterity in handling lethal power, alertness to traffic signals and the actions of others. The driver's original teacher—and the driver's examiner—couldn't have been impractical dreamers; they both had to have been intensely practical people. The traffic cops keep the driver's actions toeing the mark of practicality—or away goes money first and then the license.

The automobile—deadly weapon that it is—is still no such powerful instrument for good or evil as is the vote of the citizen on economic matters at the ballot box or the market place.

In any event we must wind up with helping a safe majority of citizens at the final level to know and keep in mind the economic facts of life that correspond to the automobile facts about pushing the right buttons, steering and braking intelligently, not trying to use water for gas, not trying to get anywhere with the brakes on, and not ganging up to take the other fellow's car away from him by force rather than by a fair and acceptable payment willingly taken by a free seller-owner.

Experience in all other fields of knowledge acquisition—and beginning experience in revived teaching of the basic economics and morals of our freedom and well-being—give every evidence that citizens at the average voter and worker level can and will listen and learn in this field—if presented with controversial questions obviously affecting them and if given basic, sound, credence-worthy guidance in making the decisions that fall within their ability. Then—as in going to a reliable garage for repairs—the citizens can go to a reliable representative or leader for the solution or handling of economic matters beyond their ability or knowledge.

Let's look at just a few questions of the type I believe they can learn to answer right and thus be proofed against being fooled by demagogs into taking action contrary to their interests:

1. Do you inescapably live a something-for-something life on this earth? Or is something-for-nothing actually available to you through business, or government, or unions, or theft, or magic?

Does government spend somebody else's money on you? Or does it spend your own on you—after sizable deductions for your money's "expensive political nights out on the town" while it was on its round trip to Washington, or the state capital, or the city hall?

Do you believe that any government can "give" its people more than (or even so much as) it first takes from its people? What happens when you and your neighbors demand your Congressman bring back from Washington more than you and your neighbors send down there? In order to appear to do as you demand, does or does not your Congressman have to vote for 437 other projects in like proportion—one each for the districts of the Congressmen whose votes are necessary for the haul you want? Do you or don't you pay for theirs while they are paying for yours?

2. Can we all live better by each doing less and less for other people while expecting them to do more and more for us?

3. But if something-for-nothing were available—which it isn't—could you live with yourself while being morally the kind of human being who would want something-for-nothing?

4. When you finally have something you think government must do, is your money then spent most usefully and economically by the smallest and nearest government unit or by the largest government unit farthest away?

5. Are your wages—and wage increases—at the expense of owners or of consumers? Can any employer or government or union or thievery or magic protect your job for long against a lower-cost producer here or abroad? Should everyone's pay be the same—with no one drawing more or less than you do? Is a general increase in the rate of pay inflationary if it is more than 2%—regardless of

what the profit or the productivity increase of the particular business may be? Does the labor content of the average income dollar in this country amount to more or less than 70¢?

6. Are so-called "taxes on business" really taxes on owners or on consumers? Are taxes—which are theoretically "shifted from individuals to business"—actually so shifted? Or, are taxes on business the same kind of business expense as materials, labor, interest, fire, and charity—in the sense they must be collected back promptly from customers or else they will quickly kill jobs and stop or slow down progress?

7. Is the high-bracket graduated personal income tax a worthwhile revenue-producing tax or just an "emotional" or "good politics" tax that makes it appear "the many" unsuccessful are being benefitted by penalties on "the few" successful? Does it really penalize the few high income people or penalize in the end the many consumers? Have the lawmakers always found they have to provide other off-setting incentives for the all-important contributions to the common good made by the most productive investors and the most productive managerial, professional, and artistic citizens?

8. Is it cheaper and more productive for you to support your unemployed fellow citizen in idleness or in an artificially created job where he does what people don't want done and, in the process, wastes materials, distorts markets, raises direct and indirect taxes, and misdirects investment from more productive purposes?

9. Is a government deficit a way of avoiding taxes or is it still a tax that will show up as the brutal tax of inflation included in consumer prices? Should you recognize it as not a part of the price business is getting for "the goods" but as the price of certain government activities which the politicians didn't dare collect from people directly and visibly? For instance, can you name the 151 identifiable taxes hidden in the amount you pay for a loaf of bread? Can you name the taxes that make up ⅓ of the price you paid for your last new automobile—only the other ⅔ being for the car?

10. Is inflation an inexcusable fraud on the public? Is it inevitable? Or can and must it be stopped—rather than encouraged or even allowed—if people are to achieve and enjoy optimum economic growth, security and other material and non-material well-being?

11. Can price and other government controls cure inflation without choking the businesses and jobs to death, and is preventing it from getting in the cost end the only way to keep inflation from coming out the price end?

12. Is business a forced gathering of buildings, machinery, inventory and money? Or is business a voluntary gathering of people . . . people seeking to do for each other and dealing only with each other . . . with each willing, on a something-for-something basis, to give an equal value in return for what he wants? Does business thus concern itself primarily with things . . . or with things only through people . . . and then only as a result of people indicating they need or want those particular things and will exchange equal value for them?

Does this mean that "a business" is the many and not the few; that it has no magic resources and nothing to "give away"; that it can furnish these people (its contributor claimants) only with what they have first furnished it; that it cannot, voluntarily or under force, reward any one or more of these individuals or groups with more or less than is coming to them and long survive to supply the desired values, jobs and satisfactions?

Is the profit of a business earned by the owners for the risk and efficient use of capital in pleasing people within an attractive price at which less efficient competitors go broke? Or is profit stolen— stolen from the employee, or the "common" man, or the poor man, or the consumer? Or is profit the poor man's best friend—the best friend of the tax-collector, the job holder and job seeker, the so-called "common" man, and the consumer this year and in the years to come?

Are the owners, who get the profit, the few or the many?

13. Is the free market old-fashioned, out-moded, unworkable and unnecessary? Or it is more workable, desirable and necessary than ever—if people are to live well and be free amid the modern complexity of economic life?

14. Are private initiative, integrity, thrift, risk, competition— and zeal to excel—out-dated virtues no longer needed or even desirable? Or are they needed now more than ever for the individual and common good? Is it still true that the only place where success comes before work is in the dictionary?

The usefulness of business to all concerned—and even more important, the freedom and well-being of all citizens—are in dire peril not so much from foreign enemies as from our lack here at home of the kind of economic understanding, moral insight, and political sophistication that would equip a safe majority of us to give the right answers to such questions as the foregoing.

I sincerely believe it to be the first urgent job of us business managers and other such responsible citizens to start doing our part—and fast—to correct this situation in the way that has been proved so obviously open to us.

———

It is uniquely appropriate to follow Mr. Boulware's statement with the "Master Blueprint" which has been developed by Mr. Fred G. Clark and Mr. Richard Stanton Rimanoczy of the American Economic Foundation, New York City.

## The Master Blueprint

Since the beginning of history Man's political relationships with his government and his economic relationships with his fellowmen have, in principle, remained the same.

In modern times the names have changed, institutions have assumed different forms, interdependence has increased, and the speed of change has been sharply accelerated, but the fundamental problems of human society are as unchangeable as human nature itself.

Millions of people feel incapable of understanding the "great issues" of modern times without realizing that the difficulty arises, not from their supposed ignorance, but from the lack of a simple frame of reference that serves as a "master blueprint" enabling them to identify a given issue, first, as a part of the whole, and second, as a specific problem subject to analysis.

The two following documents constitute such a "master blueprint."

First comes "The Ten Pillars of Economic Wisdom" which deals primarily with the physical movements of things, the role of government, management, capital, and labor, and the significance of money in our economic life.

Second comes "The Natural Laws Governing Man's Economic Progress" which concerns itself with the nature of human nature.

It has been our experience that the person of average intelligence who has mastered these two simple documents finds himself able to analyse the true significance of current events and, what is equally important, able to convincingly communicate this knowledge to other people.

## Ten Pillars of Economic Wisdom

1. Nothing in our material world can come from nowhere nor can it go nowhere; everything in our economic life has a source and a destination.

2. Government is never a source of goods. Everything produced is produced by the people, and everything that government gives the people it must first take from the people.

3. In our modern exchange economy, all payroll and employment come from customers, and the only worthwhile job security is customer security; if there are no customers there can be no payroll and no jobs.

4. Customer security can be achieved by the worker only when the "boss" is allowed by the worker to do the things that win and hold customers. Job security, therefore, is a partnership problem.

5. Money, under a fiscal system without the spending restrictions placed on government by the gold standard, is no measure of the worker's true welfare.

6. Because wages are the principal cost of everything, wage increases (without corresponding increases in production) simply increase the cost of the goods and do not inprove the welfare of the worker.

7. The greatest good for the greatest number means, in its material sense, the greatest goods for the greatest number, which in turn, means the greatest productivity per worker.

8. All production is based on three factors: 1) natural resources, whose form, place, and condition are changed by the expenditure of 2) human energy (both muscular and mental), with the aid of 3) tools.

9. Tools are the only one of these three factors that man can increase, and tools come into being in a free society only when there is a reward for the temporary self-denial that people must practice in order to channel part of their earnings away from purchases that produce immediate comfort and pleasure, and into new tools of production.

10. The productivity of the tools—that is, the efficiency of the

human energy applied in connection with their use—is highest in a competitive society in which the economic decisions are made by millions of progress-seeking individuals, rather than in a state-planned society in which those decisions are made by a handful of all-powerful people, regardless of how well-meaning, unselfish, sincere, and intelligent those people may be.

## The Basic Natural Laws
## Governing Man's Economic Progress

### The Law of Freedom

In order to prosper, every living thing created by God must behave according to its preordained nature.

The nature of Man, God's highest creation, is such that he can reach the peak of his muscular efficiency only when he is free to work towards goals which he has personally chosen.

This law needs no proof; every man knows from his own experience the heights which he can reach when inspired with desire and with pride of individual accomplishment.

That is why no slave society can ever equal the economic performance of a free society.

To prosper, Man must be free.

### The Law of Cooperation

While, to prosper, Man must be free, he cannot prosper alone.

Even in a simple economy, the natural division of labor requires that he work in harmonious cooperation with other men.

In a modern production and exchange economy this truth becomes an imperative because the work of any one man is merely a part of a larger process which can be completed only if every man does his part properly.

This does not mean, however, that Man should not freely choose the particular part he wishes to play: his free will should direct him to tasks which inspire his interest and enthusiasm.

### The Law of Production

Man produces goods and services by changing the form, condition and place of natural resources, turning them into desired and useful things.

To do this he applies his muscular and mental energy aided by tools.

Because Man's energy is inexorably limited by nature, he can multiply his production only by multiplying the efficiency of his tools.

Tools come into being in a free society only when proper payments are made for the use of the savings needed to buy them.

These payments, called profits, are the source of the tools, which are the source of economic progress.

## The Law of Distribution

Since it is obvious that everything produced is always distributed (if necessary even to a junk dealer) the law of distribution deals primarily with the selling price of the goods.

The selling price is naturally arrived at by totaling the amounts of money paid out for production and exchange.

Because every dollar paid out becomes somebody's income, the money needed to buy what is produced becomes automatically available.

Natural distribution (and stable prices) result when all this money is spent on the goods.

If some of the money is not spent prices go down, and if all the money, *plus additional* money, is spent, prices go up.

## The Law of Compensation

This law deals with the share received by each person in payment for his contribution to the total production of the society.

There is no perfectly fair way to divide up production.

The least imperfect way is to permit the supply of, and demand for, different types of contributions to determine the compensation; in other words, maintain a free labor and tool market in which each man sells what he has to offer to the highest bidder.

In this manner, the right man and the right tools are most likely to get to the right places at the right time.

## The Law of Private Property

Legal recognition and protection of Man's natural right and desire to acquire, hold and get paid for the use of private property is one of the essentials of any economy striving to achieve the best possible life.

As a stimulus for hard, sustained, constructive work, the right to private property has no equal.

This desire is deeply rooted in the nature of Man and in the very purpose for which he was placed on this earth.

Private property is a necessary instrument of human dignity and of Man's achievement of the full stature intended for him by his Creator.

### The Law of Inequality

No two men being equal in all respects, the problem of any society striving for prosperity is to recognize and learn to live with this hard fact. Observance of this law requires that free competition be permitted to move each man into the occupation best suited to his talents, and move him upward or downward in the economic scale according to the value placed on his service by his fellow men.

This is called a *fluid society* in which the circumstances of a man's birth have little to do with his opportunities to succeed.

To enforce either artificial equality or artificial inequality is to guarantee inefficiency in the economy.

### The Law of Predictable Money

When an individual or a corporation plans any future course of economic action (be it a personal retirement plan or a billion dollar expansion program) it is highly important that the future value of money be predictable.

Unfortunately, the value of money has always been at the mercy of politicians, and, throughout the ages, government inflation of the money supply has raised havoc with the best laid plans of men and enterprises.

Today, as in most periods of history, all economic decisions involving the future must, if possible, take into account the probability that the value of money will decline.

### The Law of Reasoned Fear

Fear is not cowardice: it is caution, prudence, common sense, and is based on reason.

Any philosophy which creates personal freedom from fear can lead only to disaster.

In modern life two fears are essential to individual freedom and progress.

First is the fear of personal failure; the fear of being unable to serve one's fellow man sufficiently well to attract the economic and monetary rewards necessary to comfort and security.

Second is the fear of too powerful government; fear of government that is able to take away personal liberty.

### The Law of Compromise

In Man's economic life the practice of compromise is called bargaining and is an important factor in any society where individuals are free to make their own economic decisions.

If the people are unable or unwilling to make these compromises, the free market for labor and goods will inevitably be replaced by totalitarian controls of prices and wages.

Free men, therefore, must either bargain with each other or lose their freedom.

In the bargaining process, however, both parties must be free to exercise their natural right of self-determination; for the process to be effective there must not be compulsion or monopoly on either side.

### The Law of Responsible Authority

For Man to do his best in the production and exchange of goods and services, authority must be combined with personal responsibility.

Authority without responsibility breeds arrogance, injustice, favoritism and inefficiency.

Responsibility without authority breeds timidity, reluctance to take necessary risks, and costly delays in making decisions.

Authority combined with responsibility breeds balanced judgment, proper regard for the wisdom of others, justice in making decisions, impartiality in awarding promotions and farsighted prudence in policy planning.

### The Law of Enforceable Contract

When producing and exchanging goods and services, men must frequently base what *they* are going to do on what *other men* have agreed to do.

They must, therefore, be able to enter into agreements having the force of law.

Obviously, enforceable contracts can exist only when government can guarantee equality of rights under the law, and provide equal access to the courts.

In order to be enforceable, a contract must be both legal and voluntary.

It is the duty of government, therefore, to decide what is legal for people to do or not to do, and to outlaw all contracts based on coercion.

---

Any philosophy which tends to disregard Natural Law invites disaster. The penalty of disregard and the reward in compliance are ably discussed by the noted economist, author, and editor, Frank Chodorov.

## The Penalty of Disregarding Natural Law

### FRANK CHODOROV

In the preface of a college economics text book, the author admits that within five years much of what the student may learn from it will be outmoded. Why is this so? Because, according to the modern concept of it, economics is devoid of constants; it deals with the study of how men make a living under prevailing laws, always subject to revision, and according to changing social conditions and institutions. Though the author does not say so, he would have to concede, by his premise, that an economics text book would have to deal with the economics of slavery if that institution were sanctioned by law. Or, for another example, if the practice of granting letters of marque were re-instituted, it would be necessary for a department of economics to include in its curriculum a course in the economics of privateering.

It is because of this approach to economics that our college curricula are loaded down with a hatful of courses: agricultural economics, banking and bonds, real estate economics, retail merchandising, marketing of securities, and so on. Even in the course called "principles of economics" the emphasis is on methodology and institutions rather than on any constant principles. Indeed, a modern economist would not be caught dead with a principle. He rejects, a priori, the possibility of absolutes, and as for "natural law" he puts that down as a myth of the nineteenth century. As a result, after a year of that kind of educational experience the student emerges with a photo-montage of facts and figures which vanish from his memory as soon as he has passed his examination;

he has acquired his "points" toward a degree but no understanding of economics.

It is this atomistic approach, seasoned with relativism, that characterizes the modern school of economics. The classicists, the pioneers in this discipline—Adam Smith, Ricardo, Malthus, Say, Bastiat and their successors down to the latter part of the nineteenth century—approached their task, on the other hand, with the firm conviction that in the nature of things there are laws governing the production and distribution of goods, laws which are self-enforcing, laws which operate regardless of the whims of parliaments, laws which man (in his search for a fuller life) had better learn and comply with or suffer the consequences. In economics, they held, nature has its own ways of applying means to ends, even as it has in the natural sciences; the business of the economist is to apply himself to the study of nature to find out what these laws are, so that man can the better order his economic life. He must concern himself with theory, based on a close study of data, not with the mechanics of business or the vagaries of man-made law.

The classicist would readily admit that natural law is hard to come by, that the reading of nature is beset with great difficulty, that the finite mind of man is poorly equipped for the task, and that constant study of the elusive data must be supplemented with constant experimentation and re-evaluation. The complexity of nature (including the nature of man, which plays a big part in the economic process) makes for errors of judgment. However, when subsequent investigation shows that a presumed law is not a law at all, it is fallacious to throw the baby out with the dirty water; the miscalculation does not prove that there is no natural law. Thus, in the field of physics discoveries during the last half century have upset principles which were once considered immutable, but it would be dangerous to conclude from this fact that there are no immutable laws in physics; that way lies chaos, not only in the understanding of physical theory but also in its application to the building of houses and bridges.

The classical school made many mistakes in their study of economic phenomena and still more mistakes in their conclusions. Subsequent investigation has disproved their "iron law" of wages, their labor theory of value, their theory that population increases faster than the means of subsistence. Much has been learned since these trailblazers began their study. After all, it was only after the appearance of the *Wealth of Nations* in 1776 that serious minds gave thought to the problem of how men living in society make a living; compared with the natural sciences, to which men gave thought thousands of years ago, economics is still in the embryonic stage. That the beginners made mistakes is hardly to be wondered at; the wonder is that they did make discoveries which have stood the test of time.

It was the confusion arising from the errors of these early investigators that gave rise in the latter part of the nineteenth century to the "new" school of economics. Its newness consisted in the rejection of natural law in toto, and in its assumption that man in his infinite wisdom can chart his economic course as he sees fit; there are no absolutes to hamper his whim. Significantly, the idea that economic affairs are purely man-made and man-manipulated arose at a time when agnosticism became fashionable. Underlying the classical approach was the acceptance of an order of things beyond the reach of homo sapiens, controlled by an intelligence he cannot fathom. The laws of nature they equated with the will of God. Therefore, when the "new" economists questioned the existence of God they were logically driven to the denial of natural law. In the business of making a living (which is what economics is all about), the "new" school asserted they could get along without reference to God's laws, if there were any, and they could manage things satisfactorily by expediencies.

The difference between the classical and the modern approach was well illustrated in a debate between two professors. The "conservative" argued that government has no competence in economic affairs, that its interventions must result in an economy of scarcity, and that only in a free market could man attain the plenty toward which he had been striving since the beginning of time. He implied that there were laws of economics over which Congress had no control. In rejoinder, the modern scornfully asserted that he had long given up on magic; by magic he meant natural law. The fact is, as the other debater pointed out in rebuttal, that the modern was a firm believer in magic, the magic of political power; it can do anything. Congress can create plenty, for instance, by merely printing money. It can raise wages and fix interest rates by fiat. It can set rent at any figure it decides upon. All this it can do simply by passing laws and establishing enforcement agencies. And thus Congress disproves natural law.

Does it? A natural law makes itself known by consequences. We know the law of gravitation is at work when we observe that things always fall downward, never upward. When Congress inflates the currency the inevitable consequence is a diminution of purchasing power; this discourages savings, with the result that less capital is available for productive purposes. Inflation thus induces scarcity, not plenty, as the inflationists declare. Or, when Congress presumes to fix rent it discourages investment in building, thus creating a shortage of rental space and increasing the price of what is available. Or, when Congress undertakes to raise wages by fiat a consequent increase in prices discourages consumption, thus inducing going without. And so on. The consequences of political intervention are invariably the same: scarcities.

Why does political intervention in the economy create scarcities? Simply because such intervention runs counter to natural law. It is in the nature of man to expend energy for the purpose of satisfying his desires; that is why he works. The expectation of enjoyment of the fruits of his labor not only sparks his productive machinery but also spurs his imagination. For man is an insatiable consumer; once his animal wants are satisfied he bethinks himself of a multitude of desires; he thinks of entertainment, culture, new worlds to conquer. But, the prerequisite of this expenditure of effort, this stimulus of his imagination, is the certainty of possession and enjoyment. That is, private property.

Contrariwise, if possession and enjoyment is denied him, by an insistant thief or avaricious tax-collector, his inclination is to lose interest in laboring. This characteristic is constant, as evidenced by all we know about the behavior of man, in the past as in the present. For instance, it is an indisputed fact that slave labor is poor labor; that is because the slave, who has no right of property, is not concerned with the quantity or quality of production; it is not his. Now, political intervention, which is always accompanied with taxation and with restrictions on the right of property, invariably discourages productive effort—which is what we mean by creating scarcities. This invariable consequence, even though it may not show up until some time after the interference with the right of property is instituted, proves that there is a natural law operating despite the conceit of political law.

The errors of the classicists arose from insufficient data or inaccurate reading of nature; the confusion of the modern economists arises from the disposition to disregard nature and to rest their case on the magic of variable political power. A modern text book on economics is largely concerned with the laws of intervention and economics is treated as a branch of political science. Only when and if the classical approach is restored, only if economists replace faith in the magic of political law with an assiduous search for the lessons of nature, will economics become a science on which valid predictions can be made. Which is another way to say that economics will come into its own only when we seek understanding of the will of God.

These closing words of Frank Chodorov lead us a step further to the importance of full realization of the "religious dimension of freedom." Therein lies a bright and shining ray of hope. The power of prayer, faith in God, and consequent individual effort under Divine Guidance could bring to pass a spiritual rebirth for both man and nation of far-reaching effect upon the total welfare of mankind. A minister speaks to this point with a clear and prophetic voice.

## What Can a Minister Do to Save Freedom?

### REV. IRVING E. HOWARD

Recently, many citizens, including some in the Department of Agriculture, were distressed by the pitiful fight of Stanley Yankus to control his own farm. Defeated in that fight, he left the land to which his ancestors had fled for freedom and Yankus and family migrated to Australia. The Statue of Liberty still bears the inscription: "I lift my lamp beside the golden door," but freedom is so eroded in America that the door does not appear as golden to refugees from tyranny as it once did.

When the late John Foster Dulles said: "Our institutions of freedom will not survive unless they are constantly replenished by the faith that gave them birth," he underlined the religious dimension of freedom. Faith and freedom are not only intimately bound together, but freedom is indivisible so that loss of freedom in economic affairs is eventually followed by loss of freedom in religion. This ought to be sufficient reason for religious leaders to be alarmed about the shrinking area of human choice in the modern world, and in America in particular. That many are alarmed has been indicated by an increasing number of sermons and books on the subject.

The minister is in a strategic position in this crisis for he is dealing the stuff freedom is made of. Apart from a theistic universe in which man has been "created in the image of God" and called to a high destiny as a "child of God," freedom is meaningless. What sense does it make to be free merely to enjoy sensate pleasure? No one will risk anything to defend that!

The greatest contribution any minister can make to freedom is to strengthen faith in God and in the high destiny of man as a child of God! It ought not to be necessary to suggest that religious leaders should strengthen religion, but when one religious group, the Humanists, adopt as their first article: "Religious humanists regard the universe as self-existing and not created" and when some ministers preach more about the United Nations, race relations and slum clearance than about Jesus Christ, the suggestion is not out of place.

Next to strengthening faith in God, the greatest contribution to freedom a minister can make is to persuade the members of his own flock of the granite-like inflexibility of the moral teachings of his own religion. Minister, priest and rabbi all agree on the Ten Commandments as the core of their moral teachings. Furthermore, this Decalogue is very explicit about the right to private property. Here is an issue upon which the minister should have definite convictions and about which he should be able to do a great deal.

A great deal needs to be done for no moral principle is under more attack than the right to private property. Although Stanley Yankus forced this into the open by his head-on collision, for the most part, the attack on private property in America is covert and gradual. For example, by implication the right to private property is subtly denied by our progressive graduated income tax. When one group in a given society is forced to pay a larger percentage (not merely a larger tax) in order to subsidize other groups in the society, such a system implies that a man with a large income does not have a moral right to whatever part of his income exceeds some arbitrarily fixed limit. Not only does this principle of equalizing wealth deny the moral right to private property, but once the principle is accepted, there is no stopping place until all are reduced to the same level of income. The Ten Commandments forbid one man to covet the wealth of another. What are ministers saying about this legalized covetousness and theft by majority vote?

The right to private property is also denied by a labor union when it demands the right to manage what it does not own. The fact that a worker uses a machine to produce goods does not give him ownership of that machine. If he goes on strike, does he have a moral right to prevent another worker from using the tools or machine to earn for the real owners, the stockholders, a return on the savings they have invested? If the worker remains on the job, does he have a moral right to limit the production of the machine or tools and thus rob the owner of his just return?

If we do not protect the rights of the owners of property, we had better be prepared for a rapid descent down the Communist road. John Adams warned the generation that was fashioning our Constitution: "The moment the idea is admitted into society that property is not as sacred as the laws of God, and that there is not a force of law and public justice to protect it, anarchy and tyranny commence." Whether or not John Adams was right in his judgment, the priest, rabbi and minister are all committed to a religious system which makes the sanctity of private property central in its moral teaching. Events of recent years have indicated that John Adams was right. Wherever private property has been abolished, as in Communist lands, tyranny has followed.

The minister does not have to dabble in politics nor to preach on economics to help stop this decay of freedom in America. He needs only to be convinced of and to convince others of the faith and moral teachings he represents.

----

Contractual commitments have a moral as well as a legal basis. Man's law speaks of the sanctity of contract and property, and the moral law says: "Thou shalt not steal." Yet, the violation of these laws goes on apace.

The welfare state bureaucracy, whether budding or in full bloom, looks upon those who have with envious eyes, and takes what they have to give to others. The welfare state, in simple terms, robs Peter to pay Paul; and Castro, to use him as a current symbol of totalitarianism, steals the property of both native and foreign owners, in his bid for overwhelming power.

William Graham Sumner puts it quite succinctly: "The social and political philosophy which has been spread abroad in the ninteenth century has nourished a doctrine that if a man wants anything which he has not got, it is the fault of somebody else who ought to be found and compelled to give it to him."

Foreign dictators, in fact or name, have become expert—and our own bureaucrats, aided and abetted by many who should know better, are becoming brilliant practitioners—in the art of taking from some and giving to others, whether on the home front, in Foreign Aid, or in regard to capital investments in foreign lands.

But there is a hopeful sign when outstanding business men of the nation meet together for an objective and scholarly discussion of the "Responsibility of Nations in Respect of Contracts with Foreigners and Property of Foreigners."

The Chairman of the Ad Hoc Committee of the National Association of Manufacturers has this to say—and it is something all should hear.

## Ad Hoc Committee Report

1. In the consideration of the responsibility of states respecting contracts with foreigners and the property of foreigners far too much has been said about "nationalization." Nationalization is but one of the several items which concern those who are interested in this subject. It is suggested, therefore, that this committee concern itself with nationalization not as a political philosophy but as a means sometimes employed in violation of a contract with a foreign interest or as a means for the confiscation or expropriation of the property of foreigners. It is frequently fallaciously claimed that nationalization is a legal excuse immunizing the state from responsibility for actions of this character. It is suggested that nationalization as a political philosophy, when practiced outside the United States, is of no interest to this committee unless and until it affects claimed rights of foreigners. Nationalization, when it affects claimed rights of foreigners, becomes a matter of international concern, and if either an American contract or American property is in any way involved it strikes directly at American

interests. Americans then have every right to express their views and urge, if they so believe, that national integrity, good business relations and even the cause of peace will be advanced by a scrupulous regard for contractual commitments and by complete respect for a foreigner's property.

Since we are concerned under such circumstances, we are naturally interested in principles supporting the sanctity of property and the sanctity of contract. We should approach our subject of the responsibility of nations from these two bases.

2. Because of the actions of Iran respecting the Anglo-Iranian Oil Company, of Guatemala respecting the United Fruit Company, of Egypt respecting the Suez Canal Company, and other similar situations revealing national disrespect of contractual commitments and foreign property, organizations and institutions all over the western world as well as many authors, acting independently, are engaging in a reexamination of these matters. At the International Industrial Development Conference held in San Francisco in October of this year (1959) some of the speakers referred to the so-called breakdown of international law. For example, Dr. Hermann J. Abs stated:

> Besides direct open violations of private foreign rights and interests, untold cases of indirect interferences with such rights occur every day. They are apt to make things difficult for foreign enterprises. . . . Such illegal interference with private foreign rights would not have to be taken too seriously if it were seldom practiced and only applied in very special circumstances but unfortunately this is not the case. According to the opinion of certain states and groups of states which still seems to be spreading, the present acknowledged rules of international law are no longer valid. This opinion is already tolerated or even recognized by a number of well-known professors of international law as proving an "evolution," in "international law," including the thesis that expropriations are permissible at any time without compensation. Reference is hereby often made to United Nations resolutions in which similar ideas were expressed.

That brings us to a consideration of what the applicable law is, or should be.

3. It has been said that all law is divided into two divisions: (a) Rules of law which are fundamental principles, eternal truths or constants developed as a result of an objective search for truth and ultimate justice, and (b) Expediencies or devices designed by men to escape the application of principle.

There is much support for this assertion. Let us consider, for example, the so-called rule that "a state has the right to expropriate the property of foreigners provided the expropriation is accompanied by prompt, just and effective compensation." Any lawyer objectively analyzing this statement will find it defective and can prove that it is one of the devices belonging in the second division of law. He would do this by showing that one does not pay compensation for the exercise of a right. He would point out that such a rule was one probably resulting from diplomatic negotiation where each of the parties was seeking justification for its claims. The expropriating state would demand a recognition of its "right" to expropriate and the state of the offended national would demand payment for the property expropriated. In due course the expropriating nation would agree to pay if its "right" were recognized. The claimant state would respond by saying that the payment must be adequate, prompt, effective and just. In due course both faces would be saved by the evolution of the expedient rule above quoted. But isn't it plain that this is just another way of saying that a state which unlawfully seizes the property of a foreigner must pay damages in satisfaction of the improper taking? If a contract is involved, is it not another way of saying that if a state breaches its contract this state must pay damages therefor? Stating the rule in a forthright way such as this would get away from a great deal of the difficulty and confusion engendered by the diplomatic expediency. What we are searching for is not a device to escape application of principle but a statement of principle which everyone can understand—a statement of principle which will lead to improvement of international relations rather than, as in the case of Suez, threaten the peace of the world.

We say this because one device frequently, in fact nearly always, leads to another and then another. History demonstrates that the words "prompt, effective and just compensation" are construed by the offending state as meaning "as little compensation as possible based on the nation's inability to pay and paid if, as and when the offending nation gets around to it." "Prompt" comes to mean "at any time." "Effective" comes to mean a pittance. "Just" comes to mean nothing more than what the offending nation itself deems it is able to pay. It often means "nothing at all." It seems plain that if we are going to have an end to this and restore safety to investment abroad and decency to our international relations, it will be because of the recognition of an old, old principle that when a state has made a contract with a foreigner and that contract is being performed in good faith by the foreigner, the nation must also perform in good faith or in case of violation of its contractual obligations risk the application of sanctions which will be in truth prompt, just and effective, not only in supplying full compensation immediately for the breach but also in causing, where possible, the performance of the contract in question.

4. Much has been said to excuse the inexcusable conduct of nations violating contracts and confiscating property about a state's sovereign rights. There is no subject more confused than this subject of sovereignty. Authors in discussing it frequently fail to define it. The term is immersed in a sort of mysticism. There are many different conceptions of what sovereignty is and by whom it can be exercised. For example, under the old and now obsolete doctrine that "a king can do no wrong," the king possessed exclusive sovereign power. Since he was incapable of evil, even the doing of what people felt in their hearts to be evil was his prerogative and was labelled "a sovereign right." In due course the fallacy of this nonsense produced the exercise by outraged peoples of their power to take matters into their own hands. The all inclusive sovereign power of the king was extracted bit by bit from him by the people and lodged with other governing institutions such as parliaments or retained by the people themselves. Only a small fraction of "sovereignty" was allowed to remain in the sovereign's hands. This type of sovereignty came to be known as "residual sovereignty." It is the sort of monarchical sovereignty that presently exists in Great Britain.

In the United States it is said that sovereign power, as such, resides in the people who delegate certain powers under written constitutions to their governors—the three branches of government: the executive, the legislative and the judicial. Ours is a government of delegated power.

In Islam, there is a fourth type of sovereignty. The classical concept is that God Almighty is the possessor of all sovereign power, including that of legislation. The Imam or king is God's delegate empowered by God to administer the law which comes from God. Under this system a king is obligated to protect the rights of people with whom he contracts.

It is sometimes said that a sovereign—either a government agency of some sort, the king, or a parliament—cannot limit its power by the making of contracts; that "sovereign power" always takes precedence over contractual promises. The superiority of a contract, it is said, would be an "improper" auto-limitation of sovereignty. So again, we see this practice of developing devices to bring about an escape from principle. The making of contracts in truth is an exercise of sovereignty and the performance of one's contractual obligations, whether by an individual or a state, is recognized in principle as the contractor's responsibility which if violated subjects him or it to all applicable sanctions. Auto-limitation, if one wants to call it that, is proper in all particulars. A state which recognizes that has integrity, is a mature state, and enjoys the respect of the international community.

5. We sometimes encounter a theory that one—either a state or an individual—who makes a contract has the legal right either to perform the contract or to break it, provided, in the latter case it or he is willing to take the consequences for the action, these consequences being the application of legal sanctions. This theory is nonsense. Here "legal right" is confused with naked power. Although it was propounded by a great judge, it has long since been cast into the discard. It has been the cause of much trouble and confusion. Probably it was in part responsible for the claim that a state has the "right" to violate its contract provided it responds by paying "compensation" for the exercise of the right. This is the same as saying that evil when bought and paid for becomes good.

6. Nationalization enters into the consideration of this matter only when it is used as an excuse for the violation of contracts or for the confiscation or expropriation of foreign property. This is precisely where, as has been indicated above, the subject should be kept—within the framework of the sanctity of property and contract.

7. Recently in considering ways and means to approach a re-examination of the responsibility of states respecting their contracts, an outline was prepared which is the best thing of its kind that has come to the Chairman's attention. In this outline, a contract between a state and a foreigner is referred to as an economic development agreement. By that term is meant an agreement for a fixed term development of some part or phase of the economy of a state concluded by its government, or a division thereof, with a

foreign private party—a corporation and/or individual—in a position to supply the necessary capital and skill. The question to be answered is how sacred these contracts should be.

8. We should bear in mind that one of our objectives is to make the case for sanctity of contract and property so plain that governments, even and especially our own government, will vigorously support our thesis. The so-called doctrine that the state has a right to nationalize contracts and property, or to abrogate or alter contracts or to expropriate property provided it offers to pay prompt, effective and just compensation is deeply imbedded in world diplomacy. The doctrine is a misstatement of a valid principle which, in its misstated form, has failed miserably. In the claims of the offending state, the state's so-called right takes precedence over its obligation to pay. It can be demonstrated that there has never been a case of prompt, effective or just compensation to say nothing of a case of adequate compensation. This committee has the challenging opportunity to cast a brilliant light upon this failure and to cast a still brighter light upon the principles which will assure an honest and decent exercise of each state's responsibility to those with whom it contracts and to those who enter its borders and make investments there.

9. In seizing this opportunity, it will be important for us to show clearly the position of Economic Development Agreements within the framework of international law, which, in its strictest sense becomes engaged only when the contest is interstatal—when one state takes up the cudgels to protect the rights of its national against another state which, it is claimed, has violated those rights. We must also point out the system of law which should be applied in cases involving claimed violation by a state of contractual rights, whether the cases are between states or between the state and the other contracting party. In my views the applicable law is comprised of the contract itself and the general principles of law recognized by civilized nations unless the parties have mutually agreed otherwise. The International Court of Justice is required by its statute to apply these general principles.

10. It is our obligation and our privilege . . . to search for and urge the use of principles. It is also our obligation and privilege to expose expedient devices and to denounce them. Our task on the contract side has been far advanced by studies already made.

Much more must be done on the property side where the national frequently lacks the protection of contract. . . . Thereafter the building can be commenced. We shall build with principles which men can understand and upon which they can act so that misunderstandings and violations can and, it is hoped, will be resolved with justice.

---

This country has moved far from its moorings, far toward a point of no return—no return from the totalitarian welfare state back to freedom. But that point has not yet been passed. In an address in Dallas, Texas (October 7, 1958), Robert C. Tyson, Chairman, Finance Committee, United States Steel Corporation, states clearly that we are moving toward that point, tells why we have not yet passed it, and "foresees an event which, if it occurred, would mean that we need never reach that point of no return." These excerpts cover the substance of his dramatic presentation.

## Toward a Point of No Return

### ROBERT C. TYSON

The system of economic incentives established in our land is an integral part of individual liberty and neither can exist without the other. That it has worked beyond the dreams of other times and places is witnessed by the historic rise in American living scales. The extent to which we tamper with those motivations is thus worth a minute's meditative consideration by everyone.

The material essence of individual freedom is that no one shall resort to compulsion or intimidation in his dealings with others— that is, no man may take another's property or physically injure or confine him without his consent; and not even government may do these things except to punish those who attempt them. People are only free when their acts are voluntary; and their acts can only be voluntary when the Government's own majestic power of coercion is limited in its exercise to cancelling out coercion, fraud and theft in the dealings of people with each other; and when, above all, that government power is never utilized to implement intergroup despoliation. That is why our Constitution and Bill of Rights bristle with prohibitions on the exercise of government's power. That is why too much government is a potential enemy of freedom and why eternal vigilance is the price of liberty.

Consider now the economic incentives arising in a voluntary society. The system says to each one living under it that he can have for himself whatever he produces, or its equivalent, in voluntary exchanges; but he is permitted no power to take for himself what another has produced except that it be voluntarily bestowed. The maximum incentive that is possible without undermining a similar incentive to others is thereby applied to each individual or family unit. And the corollary is that since no one may despoil another, then no man can escape the need to exert himself productively and so help to meet the inescapable survival requirement of humanity on earth. The system is one of maximum possible incentives and spurs applied to each and every individual living under it. It also is one of maximum possible opportunity for no man can employ coercion to prevent another from entering an occupation similar to his own.

Out of this come automatically what we know as free competitive markets. And imbedded in competitive markets are many of the features that explain the extraordinary rise of the American civilization. Here are some of those features:

Competitive markets, as you know, are our only guarantee of productive efficiency. They are also our only mechanism for the continuous and impersonal dispensing of economic justice. Under competitive markets the seller of anything is free to seek out whoever in the entire land will pay him the most in the light of what must be paid to others for the same thing. Similarly the buyer is free to seek out whoever will sell the lowest price in the light of what others are charging. Whatever the resulting price, it represents the voluntary decision of the interested parties, all of whom have the recourse of refraining from purchase or sale if they deem it unsatisfactory. The fairness of a wage, price, profit or of a loss is never to be determined from its arithmetic magnitude, but only in terms of whether it was achieved in the absence of fraud of coercion from any source—that is, in truly competitive markets.

Competitive markets continuously direct production to yield the maximum consumer satisfaction. I suppose that you have been, as have I, amazed at the great sensitivity and responsiveness of our competitive system to the changing demands of King Customer.

Let some new item please the public, be it television or even hula hoops, and through beckoning profit prospect a new industry is born almost overnight. Let some industry or product lose customer favor and it quietly and impersonally disappears, its manpower and resources being diverted to other more valuable pursuits. Remember the long list of automobiles that exist now only as memories! We know also how swiftly, even frighteningly, our competitive system responds to the alternating inflationary and deflationary influences imposed upon it. Such responsiveness has led many mistakenly to suppose that boom and bust are inherent in the competitive system itself rather than in the abuse it accurately reflects. In our competitive system we have, indeed, a most wondrous invention of mankind. It is stimulator, guider and governor of economic effort, provider of opportunity, dispenser of justice, guardian of efficiency, promoter of progress.

I mention just one more of the many important features of competitive markets because it is a less recognized but nevertheless a happy and gratifying feature. In every human being, I am convinced, there is somewhere some bit of genius or special talent. In totalitarian states it can never by fully released. But through our competitive markets every one can and is both searching for and encouraging it in others and is allowed freely to develop it in himself. Thus we have a precious device for finding, releasing and rewarding all the genius of all the people, and so long as we preserve it I have no fear of limited evil genius rampant elsewhere in this world.

Here then is the secret of the extraordinary rise of the American civilization, and please note that it has all rested on the system of maximum and universal incentives and opportunities inherent in a society that really believes in and actually practices individual freedom.

But what have we done to that system of incentives?

Today's relevant fact—which I doubt anyone seriously disputes—is that we have gone a long way towards undermining it. We have gone far indeed under the driving force of the give-away spiral which inevitably invokes the rob-Peter-pay-Paul nostrum and leads to the process of institutionalized inflation. Perhaps, in this way, we have advanced further than we realize toward the point of no return.

Yet, I personally am certain that we have not passed a point of no return. The American Golden Goose is a tougher bird than most people realize. But I am entitled to a shiver as I attempt to point out how close we may be to a point of no return. I have tried to foresee an event which, if it occurred, would mark the passage of the point; and there is one that comes to mind. That could be the official abandonment in peace time of competitive markets, which would be marked by establishment of comprehensive price and wage controls, rapidly and inevitably followed by allocation and ration controls. This would be the final abandonment of the system under which how much of what was to be produced, by whom, where, when and at what price or wage, was determined by the voluntary and competitive choices of free men. In its place would be substituted the arbitrary decisions of an ever more powerful bureaucracy, motivated by political expediency and self-perpetuation.

I have tried, too, to foresee an event which, if it occurred, would mean that we need never reach that point of no return; and here one also comes to my mind. It is an intangible event, a matter of moral and spiritual attitudes to which I have thus far in these comments deliberately refrained from making an appeal. It is that we shall reawaken our realization of what a precious thing in the history of humanity is individual liberty; of the spiritual and material blessings that flow from its rigorous practice; of the means of obtaining it and maintaining it; of how easily and irrevocably it can be lost; of the spirals that could be spinning us into statism with resolution to halt them. It is, in short, that we shall remember and renew an historic high resolve "that this nation, under God, shall have a new birth of freedom."

# EPILOGUE

## To Carlotta, Gil, Gray, Catherine and Michael

YOUR GRANDFATHER suffers from no illusions. Nor does he for one moment think that it is within his power to solve the centuries-old riddle of human self-destruction.

Perhaps it is a Natural Law that man must rise and sink alternately: rising into the stimulating sunshine of freedom when he places his trust in God and in his own efforts; and sinking into the despair and gloom of enslavement when he abandons his trust in God and exchanges his precious freedom for false political promises of something-for-nothing.

At any rate, this is what has happened in the long course of human history; and from this fact stem two great principles which I want to leave with you as guiding principles in your days ahead.

First, one must be ever aware of the enemies of freedom, and the immeasurable benefits to be derived from freedom.

For one of the finest statements of this principle I turn back seventy years to the words of one of the truly greatest of all great American historians—John Clark Ridpath, who in 1890 completed his *History of the World*. From his conclusion to that book, I quote this section, which could have been written today with equal force and truth.

## *Two Greatest Enemies of Freedom*

### JOHN CLARK RIDPATH, LL.D.

One of the greatest enemies of freedom, and therefore of progress and happiness of our race, is over-organization. Mankind have been organized to death. The social, political, and ecclesiastical forms which have been instituted have become so hard and cold and obdurate that the life, the emotion, the soul within, has been well-nigh extinguished.

Among all the civil, political, and churchly institutions of the world, it would be difficult today to select that one which is not in a large measure conducted in the interest of the beneficiaries. The Organization has become the principal thing, and the Man only a secondary consideration. It must be served and obeyed. He may be despised and neglected. It must be consulted, honored, feared; crowned with flowers, starred and studded with gold. He may be left a starving pauper, homeless, friendless, childless, shivering in mildewed tatters; a scavenger, and a beggar at the doorway of the court.

All this must presently be reversed. Organization is not the principal thing; man himself is better. The institution, the party, the crowd, the government—that does not serve him; does not conduce to his interests, progress, and enlightenment; is not only a piece of superfluous rubbish on the stage of modern civilization, but is a real stumbling block, a positive clog and detriment to the welfare and best hopes of mankind.

Closely allied with this over-wrought organization of society is the pernicious theory of paternalism—that delusive, medieval doctrine, which proposes to effect the social and individual elevation of man by "protecting," and, therefore, subduing him. The theory is that man is a sort of half-infant, half-imbecile, who must be led along and guarded as one would lead and guard a foolish and impertinent child. It is believed and taught that men seek not their own best interests; that they are natural enemies and destroyers of their own peace; that human energy, when liberated and no longer guided by the factitious machinery of society and the state, either slides rapidly backwards into barbarism or rushes forward only to stumble and fall headlong by its own audacity. Therefore, society must be a good master, a garrulous old nurse to her children. She must take care of them; teach them what to do; lead them by the swaddling bands; coax them into feeble and well-regulated activity; feed them on her inspired porridge with the antiquated spoons of her superstition. The state must strengthen her apparatus, improve her machinery. She must put her subjects down; she must keep them down. She must teach them to be tame and tractable; to go at her will; to rise, to halt, to sit, to sleep, to wake at her bidding, to be humble and meek. And all this with the belief that men so subordinated and put down can be, should be, ought to be, great and happy. They are so well cared for, so happily governed!

On the contrary, if history has proved—does prove—any one thing, it is this: Man when least governed is greatest. When his heart, his brain, his limbs, are unbound, he straightaway begins to flourish, to triumph, to be glorious. Then indeed he sends up the green and blossoming trees of his ambition. Then, indeed, he flings out both hands to grasp the skyline and the stars. Then, indeed, he feels no longer a need for the mastery of society; no longer a want for some guardian and intermeddling state to inspire and direct his energies. He grows in freedom. His philanthropy expands; his nature rises to a noble stature; he springs forward to grasp the grand substance, the shadow of which he has seen in dreams. He is happy. He feels himself released from the dominion of an artificial scheme which has been used for long ages for the subjugation of his fathers and himself. What men want, what they need, what they hunger for, what they will one day have the courage to demand and take, is less organic government—not more; a freer manhood and fewer shackles; a more cordial liberty; a lighter fetter of form, and a more spontaneous virtue.

------

Second, it must be remembered that even in the course of human events, no human being can displace God. No human being can force character, principle, morality, ethics or religion into the soul of man. Such a spiritual rebirth must be sought by heeding the words of our Master, "Come unto me all ye that travail and are heavy laden, and I will refresh you."

And my closing comment on this guiding principle refers to an article written some years ago by one of the noblest men and most distinguished surgeons of our era—Dr. Alexis Carrel. The title of his article was "Prayer Is Power," and I give you his concluding paragraph:

Today, as never before, prayer is a binding necessity in the lives of men and nations, the lack of emphasis on the religious sense has brought the world to the edge of destruction. Our deepest source of power and perfection has been left miserably undeveloped. Prayer, the basic exercise of the spirit, must be actively practiced in our private lives. The neglected soul of man must be made strong enough to assert itself once more. For if the power of prayer is again released and used in the lives of common men and women; if the spirit declares its aims clearly and boldly, there is yet hope that our prayers for a better world will be answered.